GUATEMALA GUIDE

GUATEMALA GUIDE

Paul Glassman

PASSPORT PRESS

In Memory of my Best Friend,
Charley Funnell

ISBN 0-930016-08-4

Library of Congress Catalog Card
Number 87-62241

Thanks to Jean Kritz for editorial assistance, to Mike
Shawcross for information, suggestions, and numerous
leads, and to Barbara Houghton for encouragement and
advice. A la vez agradezco a todos los chapines que han
soportado mis preguntas insistentes.

Cover photo: Fiesta in Chichicastenango, courtesy of
Guatemala Tourist Commission.

Published and distributed by:
  Passport Press
  Box 1346
  Champlain, New York 12919-1346
  U.S.A.

Printed in the United States of America

Contents

Introduction

Not too many years ago, I had an image of Guatemala as a sweltering place somewhere in the torrid latitudes. On those rare occasions when the name of the country came up, my mind envisioned workers tending bananas in the hot sun; seedy ramshackle houses in teeming honky-tonk ports; a paradise of exotic tropical foliage and not much else.

Later, I learned that there were mountains in Guatemala, and living among them, so I thought, were pagan Indians who stayed completely apart from the modern world. There were cool climates as well as hot lowlands. An occasional photo in a geography book showed the extraordinary beauty and variety of the land.

Disregarding my preconceptions, I decided to wander down to Guatemala, and to get to know the country firsthand. What I found were Mayan ruins and remote villages with charming inns; volcanoes in constant eruption and a Spanish fortress that once guarded against the incursions of pirates; a city of colonial palaces and baroque churches; Indians wearing exquisite hand-woven clothing for everyday use. Prices were low, and there was hardly a tourist around.

It turned out that at about that time (1967), Guatemala was beginning to experience an increase in tourism that has continued with little interruption. People have been coming to Guatemala for years, but until recently, they came only in small numbers.

It used to be that those who wanted to stay in an Indian village or visit the Mayan ruins would have to crowd into buses for grueling trips over dusty roads, or charter a plane to a remote jungle airstrip. It was impossible to drive to Guatemala. The roads ended somewhere in Mexico. And facilities for visitors were so scarce that only a few people who had heard of the beauty of Lake Atitlán and the charms of colonial Antigua, and were willing to undergo some discomforts, would undertake the journey.

Now the situation is much changed. Paved roads make it possible to get to most places of interest in comfort. Airline service is frequent, and one can drive from Texas to the border of Guatemala in a few days. New hotels, restaurants and resorts have sprung up, and travelers are turning southward as the cost of a European vacation skyrockets. Tourism has become one of Guatemala's major industries.

But while increasing numbers of visitors arrive to experience the remarkable scenery and the unique Indian culture, many parts of Guatemala remain off the beaten track. It's still possible to wander on foot over mountain trails, to visit unspoiled villages just a few hours from Guatemala City, to travel by dugout canoe through jungle wilderness. Despite the overwhelming processes of modernization, much about Guatemala has not changed at all. There is a range of experiences for the traveler that few other countries can match.

This book has been written for the traveler in Guatemala and for people who are thinking about going there. I have included material on Guatemala's history, traditions, arts and economy. But this book is also about places and how to visit them; about the metropolis of Guatemala City and the little towns where people keep pretty much to themselves; about the clothing to take along and the intricacies of driving a shrewd bargain in the markets. In short, this is a practical guide, intended not only to tell you what to see and what it all means, but also to help you to get around and to feel a bit more secure away from home.

Read it all the way through if you wish, or consult the table of contents and the index to find what you need to know. And if there's something missing, or if you want to share with others something that you discover in your travels, please write to me in care of my publisher.

I think you'll find this book useful, and I hope that you enjoy your visit to Guatemala.

1977

After I published the first two editions of this book, Guatemala struggled through its worst period of violence since the Spanish conquest, a cycle of protests against economic and social conditions, open rural revolt, and severe repression. Thousands

2

died or were forced to leave their homes. Travel to Guatemala declined, and the very name of the country took on negative connotations.

And then, after a time, I began to receive letters and overseas calls. People asked for current details about accommodations, and transport, and prices. Was a certain inn still operating? Had a road been paved? Was it once again possible to visit a certain town?

Surprised at the renewal of interest, I gave what information I could. Finally, I decided to go out and see conditions for myself.

So I have been re-tracing my old routes and finding new ones. I have talked to many old friends, and taken notes, and formed and re-formed opinions. I have sat in the Caribbean breeze on the terrace of the Casa Rosada, listened to bird calls in the Petén, and watched the twinkle of lights in villages around Lake Atitlán. And I have come to understand, once again, that people want to visit Guatemala because there is no country like Guatemala.

1987

A Glimpse at the Land

Guatemala, situated at the northern end of the Central American isthmus, borders on Mexico, the Pacific Ocean, the Caribbean Sea, El Salvador, Honduras, and Belize. It covers 132,000 square kilometers (42,000 square miles), an area just larger than that of the state of Ohio. Packed into the country's relatively small area are towering mountains, tropical plains, near-desert river valleys, temperate plateaus, and lowland jungles and swamps.

The backbone of Guatemala is a branch of the Sierra Madre that enters from Mexico and breaks up into a series of smaller ranges spread through the southern half of the country. A chain of volcanoes runs parallel to the Pacific and on into El Salvador, forming the southern rim of the highlands, where most of the population lives. Guatemala means "the land of many trees," and the name of the country was first applied to this area of pine and oak and spruce. Over the years, much of the forest cover has been cleared off and the land planted in corn.

Between the mountains and the Pacific Ocean lies a wide plain broken by rivers rushing down from the highlands. The climate is hot and humid, but the gently rolling land, the ease of transportation, and especially the fertile soil make the Pacific lowlands the richest agricultural area of Guatemala, where most of the sugar cane, cotton and cattle are raised. Bordering this plain on the north is the narrow Pacific slope, where coffee is the chief crop.

To the north and northeast of the highlands, the land drops off more gradually than in the south. In Alta Verapaz, a coffee-growing area to the northeast of Guatemala City, the population density is lower than in the western highlands, and some of the native flora and fauna remain relatively undisturbed. Orchids flourish in the forests, and the quetzal, the rare bird that

4

is the national symbol of Guatemala, can be seen occasionally. Between Guatemala City and the Caribbean is the upper valley of the Motagua River, one of the few arid regions of the country, shielded from rainfall by the Sierra de las Minas. The relatively small Caribbean lowland region is, like the Pacific plain, a hot area with fertile soil. It rains all year along the Caribbean, while most of the country receives rainfall only from May to October.

The Petén, covering the northern third of Guatemala, is a vast, sparsely settled region of swamps, hardwood forest and jungle. Wild boars, jaguars and monkeys roam this remote area where the Maya once erected great cities. Today, roads are being pushed through the Petén, and new land is being opened for farming.

Because of the many climates of the country, almost anything will grow in Guatemala. Plants and trees are nearly endless in their variety. More than a hundred species of orchids are found in the forests. All the tropical fruits—mangoes, papayas, pineapples and many others—grow in the warm areas, and apples and peaches appear at the higher altitudes. Flowers that are rare in other countries grow wild along the roadsides.

But mostly, what is grown in Guatemala is corn—on mountain slopes, in plots hacked out of the jungle, and in the hot coastal lowlands. Corn is seen everywhere, often with vines of black beans climbing the stalks. In terms of its monetary value, the returns on a corn harvest are low. But corn is what most Guatemalans eat—mainly in the form of tortillas—and what their ancestors ate centuries ago.

In the highlands, wheat is raised, though not enough to meet local needs. It's at the lower altitudes that crops for export are grown on a large scale. On the slopes between the highlands and the coastal plains, coffee and citronella are planted. And farther down are the great plantations of sugar, cotton, bananas and rice, and the large cattle ranches. To the north, in the Petén, some of the hardwoods are exploited.

Small deposits of lead, silver, gold and jadeite in Guatemala's mountains have been worked since colonial times, but until recently, minerals have been relatively unimportant. Now, vast reserves of nickel-bearing ore have been found around Lake Izabal, near the Caribbean, and Guatemala is capable of becoming a major exporter of the mineral. And enough petroleum has been discovered to assure self-sufficiency in oil.

5

Some Guatemalan History

PRE-COLUMBIAN GUATEMALA

All over Guatemala are the vestiges of cultures that flourished before the arrival of the Spanish. In the Pacific lowlands are great sculptures of animals and massive stone heads. In the highlands stand the ruins of ceremonial and defensive cities. Spread across the jungles of the Petén are Mayan centers so numerous that they are still being rediscovered.

The older the remains, the more mysterious they are. The highland cities are the least unknown, for in some cases they were still occupied when the Spanish began their conquest. The Maya had a system of hieroglyphic writing, and though most of the characters are still undeciphered, the glyphs, as well as intensive excavations of Mayan ruins, give some idea of their history and way of life. Kaminaljuyú, near Guatemala City, is a puzzle because of the many similarities in its architectural and ceramic styles with those of Teotihuacán, an important center far to the north in central Mexico. Strangest of all are the sculptures around Santa Lucía Cotzumalguapa in the Pacific lowlands, found apart from anything that would give clues as to where the people who made them came from, or what became of them.

Only the hazy outline of the development of these civilizations can be traced. Some time around 2500 B.C., descendants of the peoples who had migrated across the Bering Strait from Asia began to settle in small communities along the shores of rivers and lakes in Mesoamerica. Gradually, they turned from hunting game and collecting wild plants to a more stable way of life based on the cultivation of food crops. The greatest achievement of these early farmers, and the basis of all later development, was the domestication of corn from a wild plant to new species that produced a surplus of food. For only when there were repeated

6

abundant harvests could time and labor be set aside to carve sculptures and build monuments, and to create writing and numerical systems.

The first settlements progressed slowly over a period of more than 2000 years. Pottery, first strictly utilitarian, became more complex. Stone was worked into corn-grinding implements, and later shaped into figures of humans and animals. Simple structures of mud and thatch found religious use, and were set apart on low platforms from ordinary houses. Clay was worked into simple figurines, and later baked to form longer-lasting sculptures. Gradually, these developments in each area took on characteristic styles, and new stylistic influences appeared as trade among the different areas developed.

Of the cultures that arose in what is now Guatemala, it was the Mayan that lasted the longest and left the most traces. The Maya developed at more or less the same time as the Toltec, Olmec and Mixtec in other parts of Mesoamerica. The Maya shared many beliefs and practices with these other peoples, and borrowed some of their achievements. Archaeologists, judging by finds of pottery and other remnants of settled life, place the formative period of Mayan civilization between the years 1000 and 300 B.C., when towns inhabited by people with a common way of life began to appear across an area stretching from southern Mexico into Honduras.

By the early part of the Christian era, many of the Mayan settlements were growing into ceremonial centers. The Early Classic period of Mayan civilization, extending from about 300 to 600 A.D., saw the development of Tikal as one of the major cities in the Americas. The temple pyramids of Tikal, which reached their greatest heights in the eighth century, were the tallest structures in the hemisphere until the development of office buildings in the nineteenth century. The Maya built cities everywhere, in every kind of terrain. If the water supply proved undependable, reservoirs were built. If a hill was in the way, it was leveled.

Most Mayan cities consisted of a main plaza and several lesser plazas, each with temples set atop mounds, or pyramids, and a variety of lesser structures that might include palaces with interconnecting rooms, ball courts, and sweat baths. Set in the paved plazas were stelae—monumental stones—and altars. Mayan nobles were buried with their jewelry and other worldly possessions at the base of most of the temple mounds. Inside the

7

temples, walls were sometimes decorated with paintings, and on the stelae set in the plazas, glyphs recorded dates, names of rulers, births, deaths, and much other information that has yet to be deciphered.

Construction techniques were of the most rudimentary kind. The Maya did not use the wheel in any practical way, so the tons of rubble fill for pyramids and platforms had to be carried on the backs of humans. Structures were faced with limestone blocks joined by mortar. Limestone, available everywhere in the jungles, was easily cut even with the primitive stone tools used by the Maya. When burned, it could be used to make a durable mortar.

What went on in these ceremonial centers is largely a matter of speculation. Given the limited interior space in the buildings, one of the few safe conclusions is that only a small number of people, probably the priests and nobles, resided in them, and that the great mass of commoners, the farmers and the laborers, lived outside the ceremonial precincts. This was the pattern that the Spanish found in the Indian capitals of highland Guatemala. The remains of many small platforms that might have been house foundations give some evidence that the same living pattern might have been followed by the Maya at Tikal. Events in the cities certainly included ceremonial ball games of some sort, which were played all over Mesoamerica, and sacrificial decapitations, evidenced by finds of skulls.

Outside of the city centers, agriculture flourished. The Maya took seemingly dreadful swamps, with their store of water, and reworked them into resources that supported large population centers. Raised fields, laboriously created, were drained and irrigated by man-made canals, which might also have served as transport routes. Corn and possibly cassava and yams were cultivated intensively, to provide a nutritious diet along with ramon nuts and forest fruits.

The Mayan cities did not sit isolated in the jungle. The glyph symbol for the city of Tikal has been found inscribed at Copán, far to the south in what is now Honduras, indicating some contact between the two centers. Raised limestone causeways cut through the jungle, connecting Mayan cities, and cargoes were carried along them on the backs of men, for there is no evidence in the murals of Mayan temples or the scenes painted on pottery that the Maya used pack animals. Trade also followed the rivers of the Petén and the Gulf and Caribbean coasts. Jade was imported from the Guatemalan highlands, and finds of gold figures

8

at Copán indicate that Mayan traders might have ranged as far as Panama. Cacao beans are thought to have been the currency of the Mayan world.

One of the few achievements of the Maya that is understood fairly well by modern archaeologists is their mathematical and calendar system. The Maya employed the concept of zero long before it came into use in the Old World. Their numbering system was based on twenty digits running from zero to nineteen, each represented by a combination of dots and lines.

It often seems that the Maya were obsessed with time, but that impression could result from a hazy understanding of most other aspects of their way of life. As a farming people, they needed a reliable way to measure time, though they refined their system to an accuracy unsurpassed in the ancient world. The Yucatán Maya, for example, figured that the planet Venus passes between the earth and the sun every 584 days. Modern astronomers, using precise instruments, put the figure at 583.92 days.

The Maya had more than one calendar. The basic unit for all of these was the day, which the Yucatán Maya at the time of the Spanish conquest called the *kin*. Twenty numbered kin made up a *uinal*, or month, and eighteen uinals, each with its own name, composed a *tun*, or 360 days. The counting of days continued with the *katun*, equivalent to twenty tuns, and the *baktun*, a period of twenty katúns.

The basic Mayan year, sometimes called the vague year, was made up of 360 days, along with an extra period of five days. A shorter, sacred year, sometimes called the *tzolkin*, consisted of 260 days, each tagged with one of the 260 possible combinations of twenty day names and thirteen day numbers. Any one day would have a name composed of its position in each of the two years (for example, 4 Ahau 2 Cumku), and any such compound name would be repeated only once every 52 solar years.

The Mayan calendar system, and the 52-year cycle, or calendar round, were also used by the other peoples of Mesoamerica, and the tzolkin year is still used for religious purposes by some of the highland peoples of Guatemala today. But the Maya had a third calendar, the long count, which kept track of the number of days elapsed since a date equivalent to 3113 B.C. This date was used in much the same way that we now use the birth of Christ as a starting point for reckoning time. Long-count dates inscribed on stelae give the most reliable information about the development of Mayan cities.

The Maya inscribed other things besides dates, for they had the most advanced system of writing in the Americas. As in Chinese, each symbol represented not a sound, but a word or idea, and was taken from something in nature. Up to now, only numbers, dates, names, places, and glyphs recording significant milestones in the lives of rulers have been interpreted by modern scholars.

After hundreds of years of development, the great Mayan cities of the Petén suddenly went through a period of sharp decline, starting in the ninth century A.D. Nobody knows why, but speculation brings up invasion, revolt, drought, epidemic and exhaustion of the land as possible causes.

But Mayan building and cultural development continued elsewhere until the arrival of the Spanish, and even afterward in the areas outside Spanish control. By the year 1000, the center of Mayan civilization was the Yucatán. There, the Maya came under the influence of the Toltecs of central Mexico, and many of the Toltec gods and culture heroes came into the Mayan pantheon. Toltec motifs found their way into the ceremonial centers, and the greater use of columns and wooden beams gave a new grace and spaciousness to buildings. More is known about the Yucatán Maya than about the Classic Maya of the Petén, for a few Spaniards took note of their customs, and some of their oral history was dictated after they were conquered.

Civil war eventually broke out in the Yucatán, and by the time the Spanish arrived, the ceremonial cities had been abandoned. It took the Spanish twenty years to assert control of the Yucatán, after suffering an initial series of disastrous defeats. And it wasn't until 1697 that the last outpost of the Maya, the city of Tayasal on Lake Petén Itzá in northern Guatemala, fell to the Spanish.

After the Maya migrated northward, other Indian nations flourished in the highlands. The languages they spoke were in most cases related to Mayan, and it's common to refer to them and their present-day descendants as Maya, though in fact they were a blend of the races and cultural currents that preceded them in the region.

The highland nations of Guatemala were almost continuously at war with one another. Unlike the Maya and the people who had inhabited Kaminaljuyú, they built their cities in inaccessible locations surrounded by ravines. From these fortified capitals, they ruled over their own territories and those of subject nations.

In their art and architecture, they copied many of the stylistic elements of the Indian nations of Mexico, but their cities were relatively small, and bare of decoration.

The principal nation of pre-Conquest Guatemala was the Quiché, sometimes called the Maya-Quiché. The name of this people means "many trees," taken perhaps from the forested highlands which they inhabited. They occupied the area running from the present town of Chichicastenango westward past Quezaltenango. Their capital was Cumarcaj, which the Spanish and their Mexican Indian allies called Utatlán.

The Quichés have left one of the few documents to describe Indian history before the Conquest. The Popol Vuh, their sacred book, was set down in the Quiché language using the Latin alphabet a few years after the Conquest. In a form and tone that bring to mind the Christian Bible, it tells of the creation of the world, and of the wanderings of the ancestors of the Quichés from a place called Tulán. There is good evidence that this Tulán was the Toltec Tula, which was shaken by internal struggles just a few years before the Quichés appeared in highland Guatemala around the year 1000. The migrants might have integrated with the natives of the area and adopted their language.

By the time Cumarcaj was founded, about 1200 A.D., the Quichés were a people separate from others in the highlands, making war on them as they extended their dominions. They reduced other tribes to servitude, and when the Spanish arrived, the Quichés were the most powerful of the native nations.

Closely related to the Quichés were the Tzutuhils and Cakchiquels. The Tzutuhils, "flower of nations," lived along the southern shores of Lake Atitlán, and had their capital at Chuitinamit, a hill at the base of the volcano San Pedro. They controlled much of the nearby fertile coastal lowlands. The Cakchiquels originally settled around Chaviar, where Chichicastenango now stands. But when war broke out with the Quichés, they founded a new capital at Iximché, near present-day Tecpán Guatemala. The Cakchiquels also possessed an account of their history, the Annals of the Cakchiquels. In it, mention is made of Tullan, which may be the same Tulán from which the Quichés came.

Among the other pre-Conquest nations of the highlands were the Mams, with their capital at Zaculeu in northwest Guatemala; the Pokomchís, of what is now Verapaz; the Pokomams, who had their capital at the site known today as Mixco Viejo; and a number of

11

lesser tribes. As with the Quiché, Cakchiquel and Tzutuhil nations, their societies were highly stratified. A ruling class of nobles and priests ruled from a ceremonial center, while farmers and laborers grew food and toiled at construction. At different times in the pre-Conquest period, one nation would gain the upper hand in warfare, and subjugate another.

This situation was perfect for the Spaniards. With a minimum of diplomacy, they could use one Indian nation as an ally in a war of conquest against the others, and then turn upon it and destroy its ruling class.

THE CONQUEST

Pedro de Alvarado arrived in the lands of the Quichés toward the end of 1523, at the head of an army of Spanish soldiers and horsemen and Tlaxcalan Indian allies numbering less than a thousand men. Alvarado was supposed to bring the peoples of the area under the rule of the Spanish throne peacefully, if that were possible. But of course it was not, and Alvarado, 34 years old and a veteran of the bloody battles at Tenochtitlán, the Aztec capital, was hardly the man to show diplomacy and tact in dealing with the Indian nations.

The coming of the white men had been prophesied by native priests, as it had been in the Aztec empire. But nothing in the previous experience of the Indians could have prepared them for what was to come. They could not have foreseen that the Spanish would try to subjugate all of them, to use them as slaves and serfs for the benefit of sovereigns across the ocean and for their own enrichment, herd them into new villages, destroy their ruling classes, and impose an alien pantheon of God and saints upon them. It was beyond the farthest stretch of the native imagination that such a holocaust could come to pass. And yet it did.

At almost every battle the Spanish were far outnumbered. But they had experience in fighting in hostile and unknown territory, having subjugated vast areas of Mexico and the Caribbean. They had the dedication of warriors of the cross and soldiers of fortune far from home. The Indians fought not as carriers of a common cultural heritage, but as separate nations. They saw the Spaniards as enemies to be driven off or as potential allies to be used in gaining revenge on other tribes with whom they had long

12

been at war. Ignorance of crossbows, firearms and horses, and of the destruction that awaited them if they lost, brought the defeat of the Indian nations. The outnumbered and sickly Spanish were everywhere invincible.

The invasion route of Alvarado led through the jungle lowlands of southern Mexico, up the mountain pass in the shadow of the volcano Santa María, and toward the Quiché realm. After routing opposition in skirmishes along the way, the Spanish met the main Quiché army near where the city of Quezaltenango now stands, and thoroughly defeated it. During the battle, Tecún Umán, king of the Quichés, was killed by Alvarado himself.

The Quiché lords invited the Spaniards to their capital at Cumarcaj, a fortified city accessible only by a narrow causeway and a steep stairway. Their plan was to cut the causeway and burn the city, with the Spaniards in it. Alvarado suspected the trap, however, had the rulers of Cumarcaj burned alive, and destroyed the town. After subduing the remainder of the Quiché armies, he installed two sons of the vanquished chieftains as his puppet rulers.

During the battles against the Quichés, Alvarado had enlisted the aid of the Cakchiquels. When the campaign was over, Alvarado marched his army to Iximché, the Cakchiquel capital, where Spanish headquarters were established. Emissaries were sent to the Tzutuhils requesting their allegiance to the king and cross, but the messengers were killed. Soon afterward, Alvarado and the Cakchiquels defeated the Tzutuhils in battle on the shores of Lake Atitlán, near where the village of Panajachel now stands.

Alvarado next turned to the coastal lowlands. He made an alliance with the Pipil nation, and carried Spanish control well into what is now El Salvador. By the middle of 1524 he was back in Iximché. Near it was founded Santiago de los Caballeros de Guatemala—now Tecpán—as the first Spanish capital.

The subjugation of the new territories was not yet complete. The Cakchiquels, chafing under Spanish demands for gold, abandoned Iximché and began a guerrilla war against their former allies. For six years the skirmishes continued, but the Cakchiquels found aid nowhere. Their old enemies, the Quichés and the Tzutuhils, were now on the side of the conquerors, and resistance finally collapsed. The Annals of the Cakchiquels tell of how their last king died washing gold for the Spanish.

Meanwhile, Alvarado and his lieutenants, with reinforcements from Mexico, went about subduing the remaining Indian nations, the Mam at Zaculeu, the Pokomam at what is now called Mixco Viejo, and the other smaller groups scattered around the country. The Kekchí, the fiercest Indian nation, was never defeated by Alvarado's armies, but was finally converted to Christianity and the crown by the Dominican friar Bartolomé de las Casas.

Alvarado was apparently a man meant for war and not for governing. He left the administration of Guatemala in the hands of his brother Jorge a number of times, the first in 1527. In that year, the capital was moved after the Cakchiquel revolt to what is now Ciudad Vieja. In Spain, Alvarado defended himself against charges of treason, married into a powerful family, and sailed again for the New World, where his wife promptly died. He sailed to Peru to try to get his hands on some gold, but was bribed by Francisco Pizarro, who had arrived first, into returning to Guatemala. He went to Spain again and married Beatriz de la Cueva, the sister of his first wife, returned to Guatemala, and was finally crushed by a horse during a battle in Mexico in 1541.

Back in Santiago de los Caballeros, Alvarado's grieving widow staged a coup d'etat and had herself appointed captain-general of Guatemala. A series of storms and earthquakes soon shook the city, and finally the volcano Agua let loose the waters that had been dammed up in its crater. The second Santiago de los Caballeros de Guatemala was destroyed, and with it the two-day reign of Beatriz de Alvarado. The survivors migrated to the nearby valley of Panchoy, and there founded the third city of Santiago de los Caballeros, from which colonial Guatemala would be ruled.

COLONIAL GUATEMALA

The Kingdom of Guatemala of colonial times, ruled over by a captain-general, stretched from Chiapas to the border of Panama. In it, the Spaniards sought to erect a miniature Spain. The Spaniards who came to the New World did not see themselves as frontier dwellers doing without the comforts and familiar things of life at home. Towns were laid out according to the traditional Spanish pattern, with public buildings, a church and residential quarters set around a plaza and market. Governors, priests, judges, artists and craftsmen were imported to build and administer the Spanish order.

The capital of the kingdom was the third city of Santiago de los

Caballeros de Guatemala, today's Antigua. It ranked with Mexico City and Lima as one of the great metropolises of the hemisphere. One one side of its main square stood the Palace of the Captains-General, a grand building with a two-story colonnade, representing the authority of the king. Competing with it, both architecturally and symbolically, was the Cathedral, a massive structure with three naves, numerous chapels, and ample gold in its decoration. There were dozens of churches in Santiago, as well as monasteries and cloisters that provided a princely life for the clergy.

At the bottom of the social ladder of the kingdom were, of course, the Indians. At first, they were parceled out as slaves—along with the land they were to work—to the early conquistadores and to the Church orders. A few voices arose to complain about the treatment of the Indians, most notably that of Friar Bartolomé de las Casas, who brought to the Spanish king tales of the massacres and indignities inflicted by the conquistadores upon the native inhabitants. In the New Laws of 1542, Charles V forbade the further enslavement of Indians. In practice, however, forced labor continued through debt servitude, special taxes applied to Indians only, and laws requiring Indians to work without pay for certain periods of the year.

Above the Indians were the blacks, both free and slave, and the mixed bloods, the combinations of Negro and white and Indian. And far above them were the artisans, the bootmakers and artists and silversmiths, who provided the small manufactures and skills needed to create a semblance of European life.

At the very top were the ruling classes, the lords of the Church, the Spanish-born high officials of government, and the Creoles, native-born children of Spaniards. The Church grew to be the real power in Guatemala. With its vast landholdings, it was involved in agriculture, mining and trade, and was exempt from taxes to the crown. It built convents and monasteries all over the kingdom, and its officials lived lives of luxury. Needing designers and decoration for its new buildings, the Church was the principal patron of the arts. Sculpture and painting and architecture flourished in the land as they would never flourish again.

The Church patronized hospitals and founded schools, including the University of San Carlos. But in their quest for power, the religious brotherhoods came into conflict with each other, and sometimes blood was shed. They were subject to criticism for ignoring the conversion of the Indians.

Guatemala exported tobacco, indigo and cochineal for dyes, cacao, cotton and Indian textiles. It developed a substantial cattle industry, and began to grow wheat and other plants imported from Europe. But the Spanish trading system was a burden. In the early years of the colony, goods could be sent only to Spain, and ships left infrequently. To protect its domestic industries, Spain prohibited the manufacture of wine in the colonies, and outlawed the planting of mulberry trees for silkworm cultivation. Pirates preyed on Spanish shipping in the Caribbean, and taxes were heavy. In any case, Guatemala did not have the gold in quantity that the Spanish were interested in, and administration was neglected. Few roads were built, and the countryside stagnated. Holders of land grants did not pay their taxes, and public offices were sold to the highest bidder.

The capital lived an uneasy existence from its founding in 1541. Floods, volcanic eruptions, famine, epidemic and earthquakes ravished Santiago from time to time. But the dead were buried, the rubble cleared, and buildings built and rebuilt as what wealth there was to be had in Guatemala became concentrated in the city.

In 1773, a series of earthquakes destroyed Santiago. In the wreckage of the capital, the conflict between church and civil authority came to a head. The captain-general favored a relocation of the capital to a site that would, it was hoped, be less vulnerable to earthquakes. The archbishop insisted that the capital be rebuilt on its old site. The captain-general removed the civil government to the valley of La Ermita, but the church nobles and religious orders remained in Santiago and started reconstruction, staying even after the king ordered the transfer of the capital. New Guatemala of the Assumption—Guatemala City—was officially founded in 1776, but it wasn't until 1780 that the archbishop gave up his struggle, under direct orders from the Pope. The Church was weakened in the conflict, but it remained a major force well into the period after independence.

INDEPENDENT GUATEMALA

The native-born Creoles of Guatemala had for many years constituted a disaffected class. All important colonial officials were sent directly from Spain, and those born of Spanish blood in Guatemala were limited to buying their way into minor positions of influence. Along with the Creoles, the merchant class was

16

dissatisfied with limitations on trade imposed by the mother country. Among these two groups, some sentiment for independence developed. The Church, of course, was satisfied with the power and wealth that it held under the status quo. And the Indian majority, if any of its number were aware of the political turns of the non-Indian world, could not have thought that independence would make a shred of difference in its condition.

Independence came, after a fashion, on September 15, 1821, when twelve prominent men of Guatemala City signed an Act of Independence of Central America. Soon afterward, Emperor Iturbide sent troops to force Guatemala to join his newly independent Mexican Empire. In 1823, Central American independence was declared again, this time from Mexico as well as from everyone else. A congress decided on a confederation for the region, with some degree of autonomy for the individual states. The first federal president, Manuel José Arce, was overthrown, and the second, Francisco Morazán of Honduras, held out until 1838, when he was deposed after having moved his government from Guatemala City to San Salvador.

Meanwhile, in every state of the federation the Liberals, the original proponents of independence, were struggling, usually on the battlefield, with the Conservatives, the representatives of the Church and the wealthy classes. The early Liberal leader of Guatemala, Mariano Gálvez, oversaw the abolition of the religious orders, the reform of the legal system, and the institution of civil marriage. An epidemic of cholera provoked general dissatisfaction, however, and a ragged army of rebels installed Rafael Carrera as strongman and finally as president.

Carrera, an ignorant and unpolished fellow, managed to govern the country for the Conservatives from the late 1830s until 1865, with a short interregnum. He led his troops time and time again against the Liberals in the other states of Central America, and helped to defeat the American adventurer William Walker, who had managed for a time to take over Nicaragua. He returned many of the Church's privileges, and declared Guatemala's independence from the Central American confederation in 1847, long after the union had ceased to have any real meaning. He also put down the secession of Quezaltenango. It was during Carrera's government that Guatemala agreed to cede control of Belize to Britain, whose merchants had been logging the area for years. Britain never built the road between Guatemala City and Belize called for in an 1859 treaty, and Guatemala has in recent years demanded the

17

return of the territory.

During the rule of Carrera, and of his successor, Vicente Cerna, Guatemala remained a backward country. Transportation was primitive, where it existed at all, and except for the other nations of Central America, which had to take it into account as the most populous and powerful state of the area, nobody outside its borders had much interest in Guatemala. What little trade there was, mainly the export of cochineal and indigo, declined after 1857, when synthetic dyes were developed.

Things changed drastically starting in 1871, when Miguel García Granados led his Liberal forces to victory over the government of Cerna. García Granados held the presidency for only a few months. His successor, Justo Rufino Barrios, began the systematic modernization of Guatemala. Under Barrios, a national bank was established, roads were built, church property was confiscated, and freedom of worship was declared. A national system of schools was set up, and the beginnings were made on a railway system.

But modernization for the commercial elite often worked to the detriment of the Indian majority. Under the Liberals large-scale coffee cultivation was encouraged. The traditional communal system of land tenure was abolished, and lands to which Indians could not prove title were often turned over to coffee planters. To provide workers, the labor laws were amended to allow the owners of *fincas*, large plantations, to advance money to Indians, with the loans to be paid off in labor.

Barrios ruled as a dictator. In 1885, he proclaimed the union of the Central American nations once again, but the neighboring governments didn't want to hear of it. Attempting to impose his regime on Central America by force, he sallied forth with his army, and was killed in the first battle in El Salvador. That was the end of all attempts at Central American political union.

Barrios was succeeded by a number of presidents who followed Liberal development policies. A concession was granted to the International Railways of Central America for the completion of the railroad system that Barrios had started. And large tracts of land in the nearly unpopulated Caribbean lowlands were turned over to an American firm, the United Fruit Company, for the planting of bananas.

In 1898, the government passed into the hands of the dictator Manuel Estrada Cabrera. In 1902, Quezaltenango and the surrounding area in western Guatemala were rocked by an earthquake and the eruption of the Santa María volcano. Later, the Christmas earthquake of 1917 destroyed Guatemala City almost completely. The administration of Estrada was likewise a calamity. The treasury was looted and public officials went unpaid.

Estrada was overthrown in 1920, after he was declared insane at the instigation of the opposition. A string of six presidents ruled Guatemala over the next eleven years, each trying to clean up the mess that Estrada had left behind. Stability returned to the country with the election of Jorge Ubico to the presidency in 1931.

The standard line on Ubico is that he brought order to the country, but ignored many of its basic problems. Ubico, who loved to be photographed in Napoleonic poses and to ride around on motorcycles, imposed new taxes to pay off debts and cover the costs of public works. Programs to improve sanitary and health conditions were instituted, and the debts of the Indians were canceled. As his contribution to the Allies in World War II, Ubico expelled German citizens and confiscated their coffee fincas. He renegotiated the government's contract with United Fruit, granting it exemption from import duties and real estate taxes. Strict honesty was required of government employees, and all political opposition was repressed.

Ubico resigned and fled to Mexico during a student strike in 1944. Three of his trusted army officers took over the government for a few months until they were overthrown by a revolution later in the year. The elections held in 1945 were won by Juan José Arévalo, who had spent many years in exile during the Ubico regime.

GUATEMALA TODAY

Under Arévalo, local government was returned to elected mayors and councils, the press was freed of restrictions, and a social security system was created. Arévalo's successor, Jacobo Arbenz Guzmán, started a program aimed at putting unused land into production, which provoked opposition from the United Fruit Company. Arbenz was overthrown in 1954 by Col. Carlos Castillo Armas, who was actively supported by the United States. After several coups and assassinations of military strongmen, a civilian, Julio César Méndez Montenegro, was elected president in 1966, though the military continued to influence government actions.

In the 1960s, Guatemala went through a period of industrial expansion, following the creation of the Central American Common Market. Companies geared up production on a larger scale for markets throughout the region. The processed food, beverage, shoe, clothing and textile industries grew. Tires, cosmetics, paints, building materials, chemicals, drugs, and many other items that had formerly been imported, began to be produced in Guatemala. Foreign aid helped in the construction of health centers, schools, water-supply systems, market buildings, and new roads.

But with expansion and industrialization came increased social and political tensions. Paternalistic attitudes, developed over centuries of domination of Indian masses by Spanish and then Ladino elites, resisted adaptation to changed circumstances. Independent labor unions, land reform and welfare programs were seen by some powerful factions—and to a large extent still are seen—as threats to the social fabric.

During the term of Méndez Montenegro, the army conducted a campaign against insurgents in the northeast of the country. One of the leaders of that campaign, Carlos Manuel Arana Osorio, became president in 1970. He was succeeded by Gen. Kjell Eugenio Laugerud García in 1974. Gen. Romeo Lucas García took office as president in 1978. Charges of fraud accompanied every election.

Under Lucas, all protest was ruthlessly suppressed. Moderate politicians were regularly assassinated, and their murderers never pursued. Insurrection raged once again, this time mostly in the west of the country. Guerrilla bands attacked army outposts and patrols, the army rounded up suspected rebels and their supporters, and civilians were gunned down, or fled across the border to Mexico and Belize. The chosen successor to Lucas handily came out on top in the 1982 election, but before he could be sworn in, junior officers led by Gen. Efraín Ríos Montt staged a coup and took over the government.

Under Ríos Montt, the anti-guerrilla campaign intensified. In an effort to strangle guerrilla support, Indians were conscripted into civilian defense patrols, and in some cases were concentrated into new settlements under military control. Somewhat of an odd man out among his fellow officers, as a preaching Protestant with social concerns, Ríos was replaced in 1983 by Gen. Humberto Mejía Víctores.

20

In the wake of turmoil in Guatemala and elsewhere in Central America, the economy went into a tailspin. Many of the mechanisms of the Central American Common Market ceased to function, export prices for sugar and coffee stagnated, tourists travelled elsewhere, unemployment soared, and the quetzal, long one of the strongest currencies in Latin America, lost more than half of its value. Bad luck even plagued the most promising development projects. A large nickel-mining project near Lake Izabal was mothballed as the world price of nickel declined, plunging petroleum prices took the gleam off newly developed petroleum reserves in Alta Verapaz, and even the intake tunnels of the huge Chixoy hydroelectric project were found to be leaky.

As the level of violence declined, the military moved toward washing its hands of administering the country. Elections for a constituent assembly were held in 1984, and in 1985, power was turned over to the elected civilian government of Christian Democrat Marco Vinicio Cerezo Arévalo, after the army first declared a self-amnesty and assured itself continuing rural control. The Cerezo administration took office on a progressive platform, but has moved cautiously.

The Guatemalans

RACES AND CULTURES

Most of the eight million Guatemalans are either Indians or Ladinos. After 300 years under Spanish rule, and another 150 years as an independent nation, Guatemala has not blended these two groups into a single culture.

The terms "Ladino" and "Indian" as used in Guatemala have as much to do with the way people live as with their racial heritage. The Indians of Guatemala— *naturales* or *indígenas*, as they prefer to be called—are the descendants of the peoples who lived in the country at the time of the Spanish conquest. Over the centuries, they have altered their clothing styles, their languages, their patterns of settlement and their religious practices. But while changing their ways, they have maintained distinct regional cultures apart from the national life. Most of Guatemala's Indians live in the western highlands, and in Alta Verapaz and Baja Verapaz north of Guatemala City.

Ladinos are Guatemalans who are not Indian—there's no more exact way to define them. Racially, most Ladinos are mestizos, mixtures of Spanish and Indian blood lines. But a Ladino may also be of pure Spanish blood, or part black or oriental. Some Ladinos are pure-blooded descendants of Indians who have given up the Indian way of life.

Ladinos see themselves as Guatemalans rather than as members of a smaller community. They're more mobile than Indians, able to adapt to living in different parts of the country while maintaining their cultural identity. They speak Spanish as their first language, whereas many Indians speak their native dialects and use Spanish—if they can speak it at all—only when dealing with

22

outsiders. Ladinos wear European-style clothing, while Indians often wear the outfits of their native village. Ladinos usually practice orthodox Catholicism, while the religion of Indians is a blend of pre-Conquest traditions and Catholic ideology, though evangelical Protestantism has gained adherents among both ethnic groups. Whereas Indians are usually farmers, laborers, artisans or small-time traders, Ladinos are found in every profession and economic activity.

To outsiders, Ladinos will appear to have much in common with other Latin Americans. Ladinos profess the sanctity of the family, and social life centers on the home. Conflicts between generations are almost unknown. Attitudes about time are relaxed. There is a streak of fatalism ingrained in almost every Ladino: Nobody will protest the blare of religious loudspeakers, no matter how bats he is driven, and, few will dare to question the actions of those in authority. Contradictions between values and practice abound. Profession of Catholicism goes along with infrequent worship. Exaltation of the family is accompanied by common-law marriages and frank acceptance of infidelity.

Many of these characteristics are shared with Indian Guatemalans to a greater or lesser degree, and the differences between the two groups are often unclear. A man may be familiar with the Indian dialect of his native town, but may live in a large city, speak Spanish most of the time, and dress in western clothing. Guatemalans would say that such a man is an *indígena ladinizada*, a "Ladino-ized" Indian. Perhaps the best way to find out if someone is Indian or Ladino is to ask the person.

Relations between Ladinos and Indians have traditionally been those between rulers and ruled. Where the two groups have co-existed in small towns, Ladinos have usually dominated commerce, run the shops, commanded native conscripts. Indians have labored on their own small plots, built the roads, and performed manual labor on coastal plantations. When Indians have sought services or aid from the national government, or collaboration from their Ladino neighbors, it has been as petitioners and subjects, following age-honored social rules and elaborate forms of courtesy.

But rigid tradition has sometimes left no room for resolving conflicts or negotiating grievances. The history of bucolic Guatemala has been punctuated with Indian riots and revolts. As modernization further loosens old bonds, Guatemala faces continued conflict between its two major peoples, or adaptation of

23

its social system.

For most of the history of Guatemala, Indians have been in the majority. The census of 1921 reported that Indians made up 65 percent of the population. By 1981, the figure was down to 42 percent who were culturally identified as Indian.

Only a small part of the change is due to different birth rates or health standards. Much has to do with Guatemala's modernization, and changing patterns of work. With the expansion of lowland agriculture and small-scale industrialization providing jobs in new localities, and improved communication and education, bonds with traditional village culture have been weakened. With a change in language from native dialects to Spanish, a change in clothing and a greater acquaintance with the non-Indian world, many Guatemalans with an Indian heritage have merged into the Ladino population. Racially, however, Indians remain a strong majority.

A few smaller groups complete the mosaic of Guatemala's cultures. Livingston, on the Caribbean coast, is the center of the Carib people. Before the Europeans came to the Americas, the Caribs were a red Indian nation inhabiting parts of northern South America and the island of St. Vincent. The Caribs on St. Vincent rebelled against British rule, and after they were defeated, many migrated to the coast of Central America. There they intermarried with escaped slaves of the British. The mixture created a people who are predominantly American Indian in culture, but are racially mostly of African descent.

Also in the Caribbean lowlands and all along the eastern coast of Central America live a number of English-speaking blacks. Most of those in Guatemala are descendants of laborers brought from the West Indies toward the end of the nineteenth century to build the railroad and work on the banana plantations. Elsewhere in Central America, the English speakers are descendants of slaves brought by the British to work illegal plantations in the Spanish colonies.

Separate from all the other groups in Guatemala are the Lacandón people of the Petén and neighboring parts of Mexico. Never conquered by the Spanish, they speak a dialect that is thought to be closer to Classic Mayan than any of the other Indian languages of Central America. The Lancandones live in scattered encampments, and hunt and fish and cultivate corn. Their matted hair and rough cotton clothing give them a fierce appearance. Only a few Lacandones remain in Guatemala.

INDIAN GUATEMALA

The Spanish who conquered Guatemala were not content to subject the inhabitants to a new master sitting on a throne far across the ocean. As soldiers of the king and cross, they sought to impose a new order on the Indians, to bring them into the fold of the Catholic church, to change every aspect of their way of life. The ruling houses of the Indian nations were destroyed and their written records burned. The populations were forced from the countryside into villages built along the Spanish pattern, with an administrative headquarters, a church and a trading area grouped around a plaza. From these new fortified hamlets, the Indians went out to work their lands, and the lands taken from them by their new masters. They were instructed in the Catholic religion by the friars of the Church orders, who had to battle not only the old pagan ways, but also the more avaricious Spaniards who saw the Indians only as cheap labor to be used for their own enrichment.

The Spaniards forced a cultural revolution upon their new subjects, creating a society that was not a miniature Spain, but which was not the old Indian culture either. In their new villages, Indians adapted to Spanish morality, and covered their bodies with clothing modeled after the trousers, jackets, blouses and skirts of Spanish officers and ladies. These new articles of clothing became standardized within each village, evolving into the native hand-woven garments that one still sees today.

As new customs mixed with old, each town became more set in its ways. The native languages broke down into dialects and accents peculiar to each village, and tribal identification weakened. Indians went out to other towns when they took their goods to market, but they married only within their own villages. Horizons shrank in the towns imposed by the Spaniards, a situation much to the advantage of the conquerors. Revolt was all the less likely when nationalism ended at the village boundary.

The Spanish were less successful in making good Catholics of the Indians. They got the Indians to worship in the churches that they erected in every town, and the cross was adopted rather easily—it had long been a native symbol of the four directions. Franciscans and Dominicans learned Indian languages in order to write manuals of religious instruction. But they could not create a new image of the world in the mind of every Indian. Instead, a gradual fusion of traditional and Catholic religion took place.

The Indian world was populated by gods of all kinds: the rain god, the wind god, gods for the harvest, health, volcanoes, war, thunder and lightning. Their images were kept in shrines in caves, and carried to ceremonial centers at times of celebration, when they were invoked in order to obtain a good harvest or plentiful rains. Individual homes were dedicated to specific gods, and the skulls of ancestors were preserved in stucco and worshiped. Each individual had a *nagual*, an animal co-spirit whose good and ill fortune he shared.

The Spanish forbade the use of the names of the traditional gods, but the Indians obliged by giving the names of saints to their idols. Jesus Christ became not the center of religion, but one of the more important figures in the mix of old and new theology. The old processions of idols came into the Church through *cofradías*, brotherhoods of Indians whose duty it was to care for the image of a saint. On the day of the feast of their saint, they would decorate the image with flowers and candles, and carry it in a procession to the church, accompanied by the music of flutes and drums, and the burst of skyrockets. In the very personal religious world of the Indian, all doctrine was meaningless without the image of a saint.

The opulent monasteries of Santiago de los Caballeros attracted many to the Church orders. But outside the capital, the small, bare churches were often without resident priests. As a result, many of the old customs continued without interference. Traditional prayer men, called *brujos*, *ajkunes* and *chuchkajaues*, were still employed to carry the desires of man to the gods. The prayer men could plant curses or seek to remove them, foretell the future, call for the cure of the sick, ask for the love of a woman or the return of a lost object. They held their ceremonies apart from the Church, in homes or in caves, with incense and candles burning, and with heavy does of liquor.

Though outside authority was present in the Indian towns during the colonial period and after independence, Indians had their own government, both officially and in shadow form. Over the years, a dual religious-civil administration developed, based on the cofradías and the government positions allotted to Indians.

Laymen would become members of the cofradías, and over the years rise to positions of authority. During his year in office, the *alcalde*, head of the brotherhood, would be required to build a shelter for the group's saint, to play host to the other members at ceremonial meals, and to spend large amounts of money for the incense, fireworks and liquor that were part of the cofradía ritual.

The *municipalidad indígena*, the Indian government, operated in parallel with the cofradías. A man would alternate years of service in the cofradía and civil administration, slowly rising in position in each. In his early years of service in the local government, a man's only duty might be to sit for long hours on the porch of the city hall, baton of office in hand, waiting for the mayor to send him on an errand. Later, as a member of the Indian council, he would sit in judgment on whatever matters could be kept out of the hands of Ladino officials. Finally, as a *principal* —an elder who through age and wisdom had come to earn the respect of his people—he would act as a consultant in family matters and community affairs. When it came time to choose replacements for one of the Indian government positions, he and other elders would retire to shrines, where they would ask the gods for advice as to who should succeed. An elder's authority in civil matters would be closely tied to his religious prestige.

Today, the Indians of Guatemala retain much of the pattern of life that developed after the Conquest. Hand-woven clothing is worn in many towns, corn is planted by hand and carefully tended with a hoe, and religious processions accompanied by drums, flutes and fireworks wind their way through narrow streets.

Nevertheless, the Indian way of life is yielding to the Ladino, and at an increasing pace in the last few decades. The Indian villages, once ghettos whose inhabitants stuck to their own values and traditions, are now opening—or reluctantly giving ground as the outside world forces its way in.

Changing patterns of work have lessened Indian isolation. Before the Conquest, some of the highland nations cultivated crops seasonally in the more fertile lowlands. But with the introduction of large-scale coffee cultivation a hundred years ago, mass migrations began. Highland towns were left nearly deserted as whole families moved to the lowlands for months at a time to work on large plantations. Often the labor was debt peonage, as families tried to work off money owed to landowners by their fathers and grandfathers. Conditions improved over the years

27

with the cancellation of Indian debts by President Ubico, and the termination of a subsequent requirement that Indians work for wages for part of the year. But mass migration continues as the only way for many families to earn hard cash to buy those goods they can't make for themselves. Indians working in the lowlands often give up their traditional costumes and their own languages, if only temporarily.

Schools are bringing primary education into many smaller towns, and with it, new cultural values and instruction in Spanish. Those who know Spanish can make their way more easily in the world outside their villages. Where health centers and clinics are available, many Indians rely on western medicine, though Indians still often go first to their *zahorín*, the traditional healer, who with charms, herbs and prayers will try to cure an illness.

Improved transportation has increased contacts with outsiders. Visitors pay well to acquire Indian weaving, but paradoxically, with each such transaction, the weaving loses some of its value within Indian culture, and becomes instead a medium of exchange.

Military service instills national, Ladino values in recruits. It is charged that Indian ways are actively denigrated during training.

Civil unrest, especially in the last few years, has also had an effect. Many have left the villages to which their way of life is so closely tied, and may never return. Some have been resettled in villages where traditional self-sufficiency is no longer possible.

The change in Indian culture is by no means uniform. Some villages cling to their traditional clothing and customs despite contacts with the world outside and continuing disruptions, while others have rushed headlong to adopt new ways.

In some towns of Guatemala, the folk-Catholic rituals are still rigidly observed. But these days, fewer and fewer Indians are willing to devote the time and money that the traditional religious and civil structures require. The Catholic church, with more priests available than ever before, is emphasizing the teaching of the standard forms of worship as an alternative to the mixed practices of the Indians, and evangelical Protestants have gained many converts. The Protestant sects are the exact opposite of traditional folk Catholicism. Instead of the ritual drunkenness practiced in the cofradías, they promote the Bible, sobriety and preaching. Instead of a religion encompassing a single isolated town, they cut across geographical divisions and encourage contact between co-religionists. Foreign missionaries bring not only new religions, but non-traditional aspirations.

Most women still wear *huipiles* —traditional blouses—but the meanings of designs to indicate age and marital status are often lost to today's weavers. In some areas, women make huipiles of material purchased in the market, or use western-style blouses. Many men have given up their native outfits, except sometimes for a sash or sandals or a woolen *ponchito* —a sort of short blanket-skirt—that identify them as Indians.

But despite alien influences and disruptions, in many respects the daily life of Indians remains as it has been for centuries.

Most Indians live in simple adobe houses with the barest of furnishings. The kitchen may consist of nothing more than a few rocks for a wood fire set on a dirt floor in the corner of one room, with no provision for ventilation. Sometimes a *temaxcal*, the traditional steam bath used since pre-Columbian times, is found next to the house. In some parts of the highlands, a roof of tiles is topped with a cross, or a figure of *Tzijolaj*, St. James on horseback, who is thought to be a messenger to the gods.

When going to market, Indian men carry heavy loads in wooden frames on their backs, with additional support from a *mecapal*, a sling placed around the forehead. Women carry smaller burdens in perfectly balanced baskets set on a cloth atop their heads. Often, part of the trip to market is now made by bus. But many traditional trade routes follow mountain trails from one village to another.

The fields of corn that an Indian man cultivates may be a few hours away from his home, high up on mountainsides or the slopes of volcanoes. No matter how great the distance, however, a man will always rise early, often before dawn, and get back home by nightfall. In more traditional towns, each stage in the growing of corn, from seed selection to planting to the harvest, may be accompanied by a ceremony conducted by a native prayer man, who sees that exactly the right procedures are followed to assure the most bountiful crop possible.

Corn and beans and squash are the basic crops of the Indian. Wheat and other grains are grown in the highlands, and vegetables are raised intensively on terraced hillsides in irrigated plots called *tablones*. But these are cash crops. The Indians of Guatemala eat corn tortillas and beans, a few native vegetables, meat on special occasions, and little else, and they produce most of what

29

they eat.

Family roles have changed little. The man of the household works in the fields or at his trade. His wife is in every respect inferior, walking a few paces behind her man, taking his produce to market, and staying home to cook and weave, occasionally pitching in with work in the fields. Indian children are carried on their mothers' backs, and breast fed whenever hungry. Sometimes a cap is pulled down over the eyes of a newborn to protect it from the evil glance of strangers. Boys and girls are kept apart, and at an early age they follow their parents to learn to farm or trade, or to weave and care for the house and their younger brothers and sisters. For Indian children, there is hardly a separate period of childhood. They wear clothes identical to those of their parents, and by the age of six or seven they can be productive members of the family. The strictness of an Indian's upbringing, the limited number of acceptable paths to follow and the set ways of his town serve to develop what seems to outsiders to be passivity or fatalism. But emotion, like everything else in the indigenous way of life, has its proper place.

Traditional marriage customs differ from town to town. Usually, a young man first obtains the consent of the woman he desires, sometimes with the aid of a love charm worked by a prayer man. Parents and town elders consult and fix a price for the bride, for the suitor is taking a valued worker from her family. When all arrangements are complete, the couple may start to live together without further ceremony. If the marriage doesn't work out, the bride's parents return the value of the bread and liquor and whatever else was paid for her. These days, the older customs are followed only in the smaller and more remote towns. A couple may start to live together with a minimum of negotiation and no bride price. And civil marriages and church weddings are becoming more common.

Epitaphs for the Indian way of life have been written many times in this century. But some remote Indian communities have been almost totally unaffected by the forces of modernization. In others, despite lost customs, values and a cultural identity separate from those of Ladinos remain. It is possible that the Indian way of life will gradually merge into the mainstream, as has happened elsewhere in Latin America. Or, it could continue to evolve, even alter in some ways radically, and still contribute to the nation on its own terms. This has been the path of

30

Guatemala's indigenous peoples when challenged in the past. By looking at the way people dress, and speak, and how they express themselves religiously, the visitor to Guatemala today can get some idea of the way Guatemala's native peoples are changing, and come to his own conclusions about their fate.

POPULAR ARTS

The creators and practitioners of much of Guatemala's artistic heritage are anonymous. They are the people who work at their crafts in villages and towns, making clothing and blankets and pottery for daily use, often in their spare time. Though proud of their work, Indian artisans don't constitute a class apart. Though skillful, they usually follow the forms which tradition dictates. But as with many other aspects of the native way of life, the traditional forms are becoming diluted by outside influences.

Weaving and Clothing

The products of Guatemala's weavers are among the best examples of textile arts anywhere. In all parts of the highlands, women spend long hours spinning thread, weaving intricate and brilliantly colored pieces of cloth, and sewing them into garments not for special use, but for everyday wear.

Weaving and the manufacture of clothing were highly developed crafts in Guatemala for centuries before the arrival of the Spaniards. A variety of vegetable fibers was used, but eventually cotton became the standard thread. The common people of Mayan and highland tribes wore only simple dresses and breech clouts. But in the relief sculptures and frescoes of ruined cities, priests and nobles are shown wearing elegant headdresses and overgarments decorated with feathers. Accounts of the conquest of the Yucatan tell of the manufacture and export by the Maya of great quantities of *manta,* the plain white cloth still used to tailor many items of Indian clothing throughout Mexico and Central America.

Wool and silk were introduced to the Americas by the Spanish. In modern times, artificial fibers have found their way into native textiles. Plants, minerals and insects were used to provide the dyes for thread in the pre-Conquest period and for many years afterward. Cochineal, a red insect dye, and indigo, a blue vegetable dye, were major exports. Now imported chemical dyes are used in most native textiles.

Many Indian garments are still made entirely at home, from the spinning of cotton to dyeing to weaving on a backstrap loom. A simple wooden spindle and whorl are used for spinning raw cotton.

To make a traditional backstrap loom, the thread for the warp, or lengthwise strands, is wound around a set of sticks set upright in a wooden board. Two sticks are used to pick up the thread from the frame and stretch it. These become the ends of the loom—one tied to a tree or post, the other attached to the weaver's waist by a piece of rope or a strip of leather. Corn paste is applied to stiffen the strands. After each woof, or crosswise thread, is passed through the loom, it is pounded tight with a wooden batten. A heddle attached to every other warp strand is lifted, locking in the line, and allowing a new woof thread to be passed through the loom. Additional threads may cross only a few lines of the warp. As the weaving progresses, these grow into dancing figures and geometric patterns and whatever motifs are characteristic of each town.

A piece of cloth woven on a backstrap loom is used whole. Joined with other pieces, it may form a pair of trousers or a shirt or a woman's blouse. In addition to the motifs woven into the piece, other designs may be embroidered, often covering the woven patterns almost completely.

The technique of the backstrap loom limits the size of cloth produced. When the Spanish desired large quantities of Indian fabric for the export trade, they introduced the foot loom, which allows continuous weaving of a wider piece of cloth, and eliminates many of the imperfections that are the mark of weaving on the simpler hand loom. While women do almost all the hand weaving in Guatemala, foot looms are operated exclusively by men. The sticks controlling the warp threads are moved by foot pedals. Thread for the warp is fed into the loom by a roller and the completed cloth is gathered onto another roller. The cross strands of the woof are attached to small pieces of wood and passed back and forth by hand. Foot looms are used on a large scale in the towns of Salcajá and Totonicapán to weave material for skirts and blouses. Smaller versions are used to weave long hair ribbons and sashes.

With their primitive methods, Guatemala's weavers produce a wide range of textures and patterns. The standard material from a hand loom is a tightly woven, thick cotton cloth, intended for years of everyday use. But loosely woven fabrics and lacework may be created on the same looms. Sometimes the woven design is seen on both sides of the fabric, so that the garment can be worn inside out. Skirts, huipiles and shirts are often cut from *jaspé* fabric, in which tie-dyed strands of cotton are skillfully arranged so that the undyed parts form patterns and ghost-like figures.

Each town has its characteristic symbols and designs. In a few cases, the origin of the symbols is still known or may be guessed. The two-headed eagle used in Nahualá is believed to have been taken from the emblem of the royal Hapsburg family that ruled Spain during the colonial period, though it might also have been an ancient symbol of the Quiché nation. The bat used on men's jackets in Sololá was the symbol of the last ruling dynasty of the Cakchiquel nation. Lively figures of animals may once have had meaning as representations of *naguales*, animal co-spirits of man. In the past, different symbols were used to indicate a person's marital status, social class and age. But the meanings of most of the symbols have been lost to today's weavers, who use the traditional designs only out of habit.

Indian clothing, as does clothing everywhere, tells much about the wearer. The simplest clothing, bare of embroidery and covered with patches, is worn by the poorer workers who till their fields or migrate to work on coastal plantations. Those who have jobs or small businesses in town usually wear more decorated items. For special occasions, they may keep another set of clothing, woven of the finest thread, *lustrina,* and covered with colorful embroidered and woven figures. The better-off Indians or the clothes-conscious who wish to impress others with their finery will wear such clothing every day. Special versions of a town's outfit are sometimes used for weddings, and for ceremonial occasions by members of a cofradía and their wives.

There is no standard dress for Indian men or women in all of Guatemala. Styles developed in isolated towns, as Spanish ways of dress were adapted to native weaving techniques and the local climate. In the higher and cooler areas, men may wear a *capisayo.* a woolen cloak, or a *saco,* a short, tailored jacket. *Tzutes,* head cloths, may be worn as bandannas, as turbans, twisted around hat brims, or used to wrap valuables and religious objects. They're usually rich in woven and embroidered figures, even when the rest of the outfit is relatively drab. Hats come in all shapes and sizes, and are made of straw, wool, leather or palm leaf. Black stovepipe hats are often used by members of cofradías. Traditional shirts are usually pullovers without collars, but native cloth is now used to make western-style shirts. Loose trousers made from sections of hand-loomed cloth have little tailoring, and are gathered at the waist and secured with a sash; trouser legs are often decorated as elaborately as a woman's huipil. Long *rodilleras,* blanket skirts, are worn in Nahualá and San Antonio Palopó, and shorter versions, called *ponchitos,* are worn around the pants in many highland towns. *Caites,* or sandals, range from a piece of tire tread secured with a few thongs to thick leather-soled models that cover almost the whole foot. Even when they wear western clothing, men may carry a *bolsa* or *morral,* a woolen shoulder bag, which they often knit themselves. The traditional *suyacal*, a rain cape sewn from palm leaves, has now been replaced by the "nylon," a sheet of plastic.

Huipiles, the traditional blouses of Indian women, are usually sewn from two or three sections of hand-loomed cloth. A hole is cut for the head, and the sides are stitched up, leaving armholes. Most huipiles are tucked into the skirt. In Alta Verapaz, the short huipiles, often of lace, hang freely over an inner blouse. In Sololá, huipiles are tailored like traditional men's shirts, and have short sleeves. Many women now wear huipiles of cloth woven on foot looms in the Totonicapán area, or, less frequently, of machine-woven cloth. But as clothing styles change, the huipil is the last part of the town costume to be given up. For visitors, one of the lasting impressions of any Indian village is usually the huipil worn by its women.

Tzutes as used by women are all-purpose cloths for cushioning baskets atop the head, carrying babies, or wrapping goods in the market basket. As with those used by men, they're often superb examples of weaving skills. *Refajos,* or skirts, are made from standard lengths (*cortes*) of material. Most are wrapped around the waist and secured with a sash, but those of Quezaltenango and Alta Verapaz are pleated. Skirt material is woven on foot looms. *Perrajes*, or shawls, may also serve for carrying babies. They're often woven from shiny artificial fibers. An extra huipil may be used instead of a shawl in cold weather. *Fajas,* or sashes, come in a variety of widths and patterns.

Indian women seldom wear hats. *Tocoyales*, ribbons or strands of wool, may be twisted into a woman's braids. In Santiago Atitlán, a long ribbon is wound around itself to form a sort of halo headdress. Jewelry is worn when a woman can afford it. Colonial silver coins are frequently seen on women's necklaces, but cheap beads of plastic or aluminum are more common. Indian women traditionally go barefoot, but plastic shoes have now become the norm for town wear. And it's not at all rare to see an Indian woman on her way to the capital wearing high-heeled or platform shoes with an otherwise impeccably traditional outfit.

Music

Guatemala's traditional instrument is the marimba. It looks somewhat like a xylophone, and may be of African origin. In the original *marimba de tecomates,* the sounding elements are gourds of different sizes. Indian musicians in the highlands often play the marimba alone, bringing out plaintive and hollow sounds with two rubber-tipped sticks.

The marimba has been transformed in modern times into another version, with a double keyboard and sounding tubes made of hormigo wood. The modern marimba, sometimes in several sections, is played by two or more musicians accompanied by a brass band. Marimba "orchestras"—large bands—roam the country in buses, playing a busy schedule at fiestas in all the departments. They perform for many hours in front of the city hall and roam the streets on a flat-bed truck with hardly any rest, then pack up and hurry off to their next engagement. Their modern amplifiers inundate a town with blaring sound into the early hours of the morning. The recordings of the most popular groups are heard endlessly on the radio.

Almost every town has its own small marimba orchestra, if not two or three. No festive occasion is complete without a marimba. For private parties, a band is brought in to play for guests. And on a birthday, or when leaving for a trip, or on an anniversary, or at any other excuse for celebration, a Guatemalan will often wake up at dawn to fireworks followed by the tinkling sounds of a modern marimba and the brass of the accompanying band. For a foreigner who receives the traditional birthday treatment, it's an experience to be remembered, pleasantly or otherwise.

Other native instruments are used almost exclusively by Indians on ceremonial occasions. The *chirimía*, a sort of flute with the melancholy sound of an oboe, is the standard melodic accompaniment for cofradía processions. Rhythm is provided by the *tun,* a hollowed and sealed section of log. Slits are cut in the top so that two notes can be sounded with a rubber-tipped stick. A more familiar kind of drum is the *tambor*, consisting of an animal skin stretched over a cylindrical piece of wood. Gourds filled with seeds, turtle shells and a variety of other rhythm instruments are used regionally to accompany dances.

Fiesta Dances

Many visitors show up at fiestas expecting to see a graceful and disciplined show of native dancing. What they find is something quite different from the artsy adaptations of Indian ritual dances sometimes performed for paying customers. The spectacles that go on at fiesta times in Indian towns are dances only in part. They are also gaudy folk operas without singing, drunken orgies of stumbling and bumping, and endurance marathons.

The performers of Indian dances, all men, dress in grotesque, padded costumes rented for the occasion. They dance for hours and even days at a time with hardly a break, completely covered with costumes and masks, suffering and suffocating through the performance. Alcohol serves to relieve the trials of the participants somewhat, and also to loosen up the show. Toward the end of the fiesta, the dancers struggle to stay on their feet.

The steps of the fiesta dances are simple, even clumsy, and are performed to the accompaniment of drum beats and occasional melodic notes from a flute. There is no tradition among Guatemala's Indians of graceful social dancing on which to draw. One dance is distinguished from another not by the steps, but by the theme, usually an event of some historical significance, or a ritual whose meaning has been lost.

In a few of the more traditional towns, such as Todos Santos, the dances are taken seriously. It's a great honor to be selected for one of the dance teams, and one which involves great sacrifice in time for rehearsal and money to rent the costumes. But in most Indian towns, the costumes are cheap, and the dances are performed as a revel, or sometimes not at all.

The dances represent epic struggles. In the Dance of the Conquerors, the performers put on masks featuring the pink skin and large noses of the white man. The yellow hair of the Spanish invaders sticks out as long sisal fibers from under velvet hats. The mask is often smaller than a man's face, so cloths around the mask as well as gloves are used to cover the dancer's brown skin. Indians who usually go barefoot or in sandals must have their feet bound in ill-fitting boots. As if to represent the resignation of Indians to their lot in life, the Spaniards always triumph.

Some of the other dances seen at fiesta times are the Dance of the Bullfighter, depicting the combat between matador and bull; the Deer Dance, possibly of pre-Conquest origin, depicting the hunt, with performers dressed in animal skins and carved masks; the Dance of the Moors, celebrating the victory of the Spanish Christians; and the Dance of the Volcano, reenacting a battle between the Spanish and Indians near the volcano Agua during the Conquest.

One of the rarer dances is the *Palo Volador*, or Flying Pole, sometimes seen in Chichicastenango at fiesta time. A long pole is set up in front of the church, and two ropes long enough to reach to the ground are attached to a frame at the top. Two men climb up, set themselves in the loops at the ends of the ropes, and swing out from the pole. As the ropes unwind, the performers swing farther and farther out until they finally come to earth. Obviously of pre-Conquest origin, the dance is similar to one performed in Mexico which is related to the Aztec calendar and sun-worship rituals.

Ceramics

Indian pottery is strictly utilitarian. Items such as incense burners, *comales* (large pans for cooking tortillas), and water jars are molded by hand without the aid of a wheel, sometimes using an old pot or a straw model as a form. Pots are baked on open fires, and waterproofed with corn paste or a glaze. Specialty ceramic items are made in a few towns. Chinautla, near Guatemala City, is known for its white ceramic figures and jars. Antigua produces small glazed animal figures. Totonicapán is the largest ceramics center, producing a wide variety of glazed and colored household objects. In these places, the potter's wheel and kilns are used.

Pottery has suffered something of a decline in recent years. Frequently seen these days is a water jug with a traditional narrow neck and two handles—but made out of brightly colored plastic.

Baskets

There's an endless variety of baskets in Guatemala, used as hampers, strainers, baby cribs, and for any number of other purposes. But their main use is for marketing. Ladino women prefer a model with a handle. Indian women, who carry their loads on their heads, use baskets without handles.

Mats

Petates, or mats, may be room dividers, sunshades, door mats, or platforms for cleaning beans and coffee. Most often, they're stacked in Indian homes to form beds. Many are woven from straw or from *tules,* reeds which have a soft fiber in their stalks. But some in Alta Verapaz are sewn from palm fibers.

Sculpture

Many of the masks used in fiesta dances are roughly carved from wood, painted over, and decorated with rope fibers. The sculpturing of large figures for churches declined after the colonial period, as patronage of the arts decreased. But in Indian homes, figures of saints found their way into household shrines, replacing the stuccoed skulls of ancestors that held places of honor before the arrival of Christianity. Small figures of saints, often with many gory details of their martyrdom, as well as old masks, are highly prized by collectors.

A Second Introduction

What follows is a guide to many of the towns of Guatemala, as well as major archaeological sites, hot springs, and other points of interest to the visitor. The places described are grouped by region, roughly in the order in which you would reach them if travelling from Guatemala City. For each town, information is given on such basics as altitude, population, market days, and the language spoken, if there is a significant Indian population. When the meaning of the name of a town is of some interest, it is given within quotation marks after the town name. Kilometer markers along the highways are given as an aid to drivers.

I've noted the percentage of Indian population in many towns in the western highlands and Alta Verapaz. Now, this may seem to be a rather crude statistic, but it gives some indication of how traditional a town is, whether native-style clothing is worn, and whether the local culture is likely to be especially interesting. In many cases, it prevents the overuse of such phrases as "fine weaving" or "faithful to old customs." I've avoided going into too much detail on traditional dress or local crafts and religious practices unless they're especially noteworthy. It's not that such things aren't important, but they can be remarked upon to excess when dealing with a country with so many cultural riches.

The mention of a language is a rough measure of cultural identity beyond village limits. It would be misleading to say that the inhabitants of a town belong to one tribe or another. Over the centuries, each Indian town has developed its own culture, with a separate dialect, characteristic family names, patron saint, style of clothing, economic specializations, and even physical type after many years of inbreeding. Indians identify with their towns rather than with the pre-Conquest tribe that spoke their

39

language.

In many cases, population figures are given for both a town *(cabecera)* and the township *(municipio)* of which it is the center. In most Indian townships of the highlands, the majority of the population lives in outlying settlements, and comes to the town center only on market days and for fiestas. At other times, the town center is likely to have the appearance of a ghost town. If possible, visit an Indian town on a market or fiesta day. Use the calendars at the end of the book for planning. Note also that some of the smaller Indian towns don't have market days.

Population figures are taken from the 1981 census. The population of Guatemala is growing at a rate of just over three percent a year, but the rate in Guatemala City is much higher. All geographical information is taken from publications of the Military Geographic Institute of Guatemala.

Figures are expressed in the metric system, with equivalents in miles or feet sometimes given in parentheses. To convert meters to feet, multiply by 3.28. To convert kilometers to miles, multiply by 0.62, or about five-eighths.

Some additional explanations and disclaimers:

About Hotels: The rates I give are those approved by the Guatemala Tourist Commission. Taxes totalling 17 percent are included. These rates are representative of what you will pay if you book through a travel agency or hotel chain, or travel at Christmas or Easter. In the case of many moderate and better hotels, you can get lower rates—as much as 40 percent off—if you reserve directly with the hotel, either before you travel or from within Guatemala. Always request the hotel's special rate.

Though I haven't listed every hotel in every town, I've tried to give a range, from *pensiones* with no more than a bed and table in the room, to first-class establishments. In general, I'd plan to spend the night in towns for which accommodations are listed. When travelling to towns with limited accommodations, it is advisable to phone ahead to reserve, when telephone service is available. You can find accommodations in many of the smaller towns, but they'll usually be far from luxurious. In any small town, the place to go for information about lodging or anything else is the city hall (*municipalidad*). Don't be afraid to ask questions. Officials will usually go out of their way to be of assistance.

About Prices: These are given in U.S. dollars, based on recent exchange rates, and should be taken as approximate. Many budget hotel rates have not caught up with the decline of Guatemala's currency, and will no doubt rise by small amounts. But Guatemala has always been an inexpensive country for the traveller, and I think you'll still find costs quite reasonable. A 7 percent sales tax ("I.V.A.") applies to meals and most other purchases.

About Schedules: I've given these to show the ease or difficulty of getting around by bus, boat and train, and to help you plan your time. Schedules are subject to change, of course, but many are determined by traditional trading patterns and have not altered in twenty years. Whenever possible, verify departure times the day before you travel.

Much of the coverage in this book is of the obvious and accessible places. But I've also included towns that few tourists ever get to, and places that I especially like for one reason or another. I have my biases, of course, but I've tried to keep my partiality within acceptable limits.

I wouldn't take a trip through Guatemala by starting on the first page of the travel section of this book and blindly following it in order from place to place. Before you set out, take a quick read through the coverage of towns, take a few notes on the places that seem to interest you, plan some itineraries using the schedules given, and, above all, read the chapters on practical information and transportation at the back of the book. I've tried to include the practical information that most visitors will need, or at least to indicate where to obtain it. But if I've missed, don't hesitate to write to me, and I'll try to make changes in future editions.

Guatemala City

Population: 754,243; Altitude 1499 meters; Fiesta: August 15

Guatemala City was founded early in 1776 after war and earthquakes had forced the abandonment, in succession, of the three colonial capitals known today as Tecpán Guatemala, Ciudad Vieja and Antigua Guatemala. Colonial administrators laid out the city of New Guatemala of the Assumption in the fertile Ermita Valley. According to some sources, they thought that the ravines surrounding the site would absorb the shocks of earthquakes, and thus protect the city from the destruction that had befallen their previous capitals.

If that was their belief, they were dead wrong. An earthquake damaged the city in 1830, and a new pair of tremors on Christmas Day 1917 and January 24, 1918, destroyed the city almost completely. Because of the destruction early in this century, no colonial buildings remain, except for a few sturdy churches. The earthquake of February 4, 1976, wrought heavy damage and caused loss of life in a few of the outlying areas. But by and large, the newer buildings of the central city survived unscathed, or with only minor damage.

Old timers and not-so-old timers remember with much affection the Guatemala City of a few decades ago, precisely because so much of what they knew has given way to urban expansion. The capital was a sleepy backwater, with no industry to speak of. Physically, it developed no distinctive public architecture, and there was nothing left of its colonial heritage. After 1917, the attractive tile roofs, which had crashed down and crushed heads during the earthquake of that year, gave way to corrugated sheet metal on the houses of those who could afford it. Most buildings downtown were nondescript adobe or brick structures faced with

42

cement plaster.

Nevertheless, the city was a pleasant place, with tree-shaded residential neighborhoods, quiet streets, and few vehicles. People referred to locations by neighborhoods, and not by the zone numbers used today. There were the Parroquia, or parish, the oldest part of the city; El Gallito, the little rooster; Reformita; the Villa de Guadalupe; Tívoli; and the areas in the central city known as El Amatle (the amatle tree), Las Cinco Calles (the five streets), and El Botellón (the big bottle). The streets bore names, not numbers: Avenida Central, Calle del Hospital, and Calle del Tuerto (street of the one-eyed man).

The quaint street names exist now only in memory, though the old names for neighborhoods and intersections still survive in everyday usage, if not on official maps of Guatemala City. A zone numbering system came into use decades ago, making it easier for outsiders to find their way around in the metropolis. The population of the capital grew from 112,000 in 1924 to 284,000 in 1950, and today, including adjoining municipalities, it is over a million. With growth to the north limited by canyons, Guatemala City has expanded to the south and west. New residential neighborhoods have been built in what once were corn fields. Concrete-and-glass skyscrapers of government agencies, private offices and hotels dot the cityscape. Shanty towns have mushroomed in gullies wanted by nobody but the poor. Factories are sprouting up on the outskirts of town, and the urban ills of congestion, pollution and cacaphony have attacked the central core.

In many ways, Guatemala City is everything that the rest of the country is not. Most of it is not especially attractive (though there are a number of pleasant residential and commercial areas), while the countryside of Guatemala is everywhere breathtaking in its mountains, forest, lakes and volcanoes. The people of the capital live the relatively fast-paced life of a commercial center, dress in western business clothing, and are aware of a larger world outside their country. In the countryside, the pace is slower, trade retains a social as well as economic value, traditional Indian clothing is still seen, and the people generally see themselves as part of the smaller world of their own town and a few nearby villages. Although Guatemala is not very big, many of the people of the capital know relatively little about the ways of the countryside. And it's not unusual to see a country person in Guatemala City going about wide-eyed and having a bit of

Guatemala City

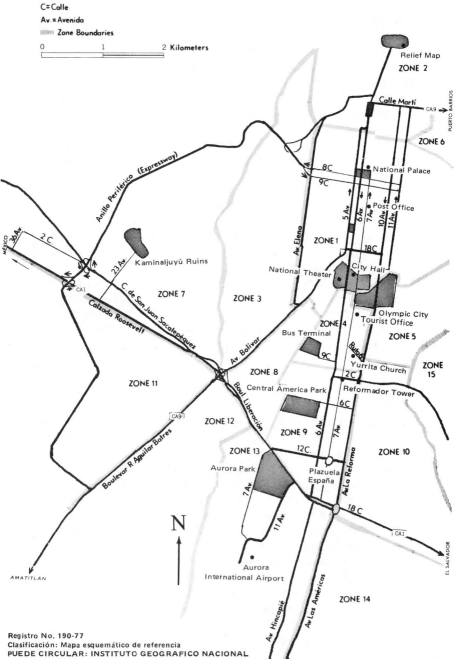

C = Calle
Av. = Avenida
Zone Boundaries

0   1   2 Kilometers

Relief Map
ZONE 2

Calle Martí
CA9
PUERTO BARRIOS
ZONE 6

Anillo Periférico (Expressway)

8C
9C
National Palace

36 Av.
MÉXICO
2 C
23 Av.
Kaminaljuyú Ruins
C. de San Juan Sacatepéquez
CA1
Calzada Roosevelt

5 Av.
6 Av.
7 Av.
10 Av.
11 Av.
Post Office
Av. Elena
ZONE 1
18C
National Theater
City Hall

ZONE 7   ZONE 3

Olympic City
Tourist Office
ZONE 4
Bus Terminal
9C
Ruta 6
Yurrita Church
ZONE 5
Av. Bolívar

ZONE 15

ZONE 11
ZONE 8
Central America Park
Blvd. Liberación
2C
Reformador Tower
6C

CA9
ZONE 12

6 Av.
7 Av.
ZONE 9
ZONE 10

Boulevar R. Aguilar Batres

ZONE 13
12C.
Aurora Park
Plazuela
España
7 Av.
11 Av.
Av. La Reforma
18 C

N

CA1

EL SALVADOR

AMATITLÁN

Aurora
International Airport
Av. Hincapié
Av. Las Américas
ZONE 14

Registro No. 190-77
Clasificación: Mapa esquemático de referencia
PUEDE CIRCULAR: INSTITUTO GEOGRAFICO NACIONAL
Guatemala, 16 de marzo de 1977

difficulty in managing things as he tries to take care of business that he has with the government, or some matter of trade.

Guatemala City is called "Guate" (Gwah-teh), "Guatemala," and *"la capital"* by locals. For the visitor, it's the center from which to go out and see the archaeological sites spread around the country, the colonial city of Antigua, and the many Indian villages easily reached during one-day trips from the capital. Mercifully, there isn't much in the way of obligatory sights to see in the capital. But there are good food and entertainment, excellent hotels, and markets and shops full of handicrafts. And of course, Guatemala City is the center of the government, economy and culture of the country, so you're bound to understand more of Guatemala by spending some time there.

Layout

Guatemala City is large, but quite manageable. The streets are logically numbered, and the places to which a visitor might go are concentrated in a few zones of the city.

The commercial sections of the city are zones 1, 4 and 9, along the north-south axis of 6 and 7 avenidas. Office buildings and hotels line these streets, forming the backbone of the city. To the north and northwest, steep canyons bring the city to a dead end. The industrial areas and residential sections spread out to the east, south and southwest.

When locating an address in Guatemala City, always check the zone number first on a map. The same street numbers are repeated in different zones. Once you have the zone, finding the building is easy. The address of the Hotel Pan American, for example, is 9a Calle 5-63, Zone 1, indicating that it's on 9a Calle (Novena Calle, or Ninth Street) between 5a Avenida and 6a Avenida (Sexta Avenida, or Sixth Avenue)

Numbers of streets from 1 to 10 bear the suffix "a" after the number (1a, 2a, etc.), indicating the equivalent of "first," "second," etc. To simplify matters, I've dropped the suffixes in all addresses that follow. To confuse thing slightly, there are also capital-letter suffixes. 6 Avenida "A", for example, is a short street parallel to 6 Avenida, between 6 Avenida and 7 Avenida.

Only a few streets bear names instead of numbers.

A street map of the city is available without charge at the tourist office.

HOTELS

Most of the moderate and better hotels are in zones 4, 9 and 10. These are the more pleasant areas of the capital, with good restaurants and interesting shopping. The hotels in these zones are good bases for rest and relaxation between excursions into the countryside, and the rates, for what you get, are generally reasonable.

Almost all inexpensive hotels are located in Zone 1, the congested old central area. With many Central Americans on the move, demand for low-priced accommodations exceeds supply, and if you arrive late in the day, you may find no rooms available, or no single rooms, or only undesirable rooms. Budget travellers, take note. Unless you are willing to pamper yourself a little, you are likely to find Guatemala City a trying place to visit. Choose your room early in the day, and enjoy a few good meals, or make nearby Antigua your base.

If you don't have a pre-paid package that includes accommodations, and will be traveling at a busy time of year (December 15 through Easter, and August), you might want to reserve a room for at least your first night in Guatemala City. Most travel agents in the United States and Canada can reserve rooms in the larger and more expensive hotels, or you can use toll-free telephone numbers. You'll have to write directly to smaller hotels.

Currently, there is plenty of excess capacity in moderate and higher-priced hotels, and some will give you a discount when you reserve directly or arrive without reservations. Simply ask for the special rate. I don't guarantee that this practice will continue, but it doesn't hurt to ask.

If you arrive by plane, the airport branch of the tourist office will phone around to find a room for you in town.

Better Hotels – Zone 4

Hotel Conquistador Sheraton, Vía 5 4-68, tel. 64691, 312222. U.S./Canada Reservations 800-325-3535. 170 rooms. $50-$90 single/$60-$90 double.
One of the best-run hotels in Guatemala, where attention is paid to many small details. Recently renovated and redecorated. The entry is a dramatic, multi-level atrium, where orchids are always

in bloom and the garden café is always open. All rooms in the two towers have individual air conditioning, balcony, and cable television with U.S. programs. Some suites with kitchens. Other facilities include the Restaurante de las Espadas and the Cueva de los Capitanes night club (see restaurant listings), a bar with entertainment and daily happy hour, travel agency, bookshop, garage, pool, meeting rooms, and a number of shops. Good value and central location.

Better Hotels – Zones 9 and 10

Each of the following hotels in this category, except where indicated, has a pool, one or several restaurants, bar, travel agency, shops, and car-rental service. Rooms have color television with U.S. programs via satellite, balconies, and air conditioning.

Hotel Camino Real-Biltmore, Avenida Reforma 14-01, Zone 10, tel. 681271. U.S./Canada reservations 800-228-3000. 430 rooms. $94 single or double, up to $900 for certain suites.
The largest luxury hotel in the city, with some of the best facilities, located in the most pleasant upper-class residential and commercial area. Good restaurants, entertainment at several bars, multiple swimming pools, tennis courts and gym, meeting rooms. Well managed.

Hotel El Dorado Americana, 7 Avenida 15-45, Zone 9, tel. 317777. U.S. reservations: 212-757-2981. Canada: 416-967-3442. 250 rooms. $94/$105.
Also well managed, with good, reasonably priced restaurants, and excellent sports facilities (tennis courts, two pools, two gymnasiums, steam baths).

Hotel Guatemala Fiesta, 1 Avenida 13-22, Zone 10, tel. 322555. 205 rooms. $64 to $140 single/$73 to $140 double.
Modernistic, with slightly garish rooms. Facilities include a gym and sauna. Usually very quiet.

Hotel Cortijo Reforma, Reforma 2-18, Zone 9, tel. 66712. U.S. reservations 800-223-6764, 212-758-4375. 150 suites. $41-49 single/$49-$56 double, $56-61 triple, more for larger suites.

A modern hotel consisting entirely of multi-room suites with balconies. Good value for parties of three or more, though the location is a few blocks from points of interest. No pool.

Moderate Hotels – Zone 1

"Moderate" covers a lot of territory pricewise, from $35 down to $10 for a single room, but I am categorizing by what you get, as well as what you pay.

Hotel Pan American, 9 Calle 5-63, tel. 26807,533991. 60 rooms. $35 single/$43 double.
Located a block from the main square, the Pan American is a long-standing favorite of the foreign community in Guatemala. The atmosphere is one of elegance well retained from the past, especially in the high-ceilinged lobby, and the service and food are excellent. Rooms are old-fashioned and comfortable, with t.v. Noise is a problem on the 6 Avenida side.

Hotel del Centro, 13 Calle 4-55, tel. 81281, 81519. U.S. reservations tel. 212-687-4422. 60 rooms. $35/$41.
Similar to modern Spanish hotels in decor—lots of wood and lamp fixtures. The rooms are comfortable. Restaurant, garage, pleasant rooftop terrace, and t.v. in the rooms.

Hotel Ritz Continental, 6 Avenida A 10-13, tel. 81674, 21078. U.S. reservations: 402-498-4300. Canada: 800-268-7041. 250 rooms. $35 to $70/$47 to $140.
Large and centrally located. Rooms are comfortable, not luxurious, with balconies, satellite television programming, colonial decor. Pool, game room, shops, garage, restaurants, and a rooftop bar with good views of the city. Ask for the special rate—$29 single, $35 double, with a welcome cocktail thrown in.

Hotel Guatemala Internacional, 6 Avenida 12-21, tel. 84441. 18 furnished apartments. $20 and up per unit.
In the heart of the city, and good for the price. Kitchens, cable t.v.

Posada Belén, 13 Calle A 10-30, tel. 513478, 29226. 10 rooms. $10/$15.

Best of the smaller hotels and guest houses in Zone 1, a tranquil home decorated with colonial-style wrought iron, plants, and handicrafts from around the country. The friendly management is helpful in planning trips (they'll even arrange a full-week tour if you write in advance), and keeps a library for guests. Good beds, and a very quiet location. Meals are served.

Hotel Centenario, 6 Calle 5-33, tel. 80381. 43 rooms. $12/$18.
The rooms are cramped and the atmosphere is sterile, but the place is clean, the sauna is a nice feature, and you're right on the main square, if that's what you want.

Hotel Maya Excelsior, 7 Avenida 12-46, tel. 82761. 108 rooms. $11 to $15/$14 to $19.
The Maya has seen better days—the wallpaper is peeling, some of the rooms are musty, and the restaurant is closed. But you won't find indoor parking, a pool and a sauna elsewhere at this price. Central location near the post office. Furnished apartments available for less than $200 per month.

Moderate Hotels – Zone 4

Hotel Plaza, Vía 7 6-16, tel. 63626, 310396. 57 rooms. $21/$26.
This is a good buy for its facilities (American motel-style rooms, pool, squash court). Located near some of the larger shopping complexes. Street noise can be a problem.

Moderate Hotels – Zones 9 and 10

Hotel Villa Española, 2 Calle 7-51, Zone 9, tel. 323362, 323381. 67 rooms. $21 single/$26 double.
Tiers of rooms in a Mediterranean-style building above a courtyard. Not bad for the price. Restaurant, bar.

Residencial Reforma (La Casa Grande), Avenida Reforma 7-67, Zone 10, tel. 310907. 28 rooms. $22 single/$26 double.
A guest house in a Moorish-style mansion, a block from the U.S. embassy. Good value.

Apartotel Alamo, 10 Calle 5-60, Zone 9, tel. 319817. 14 units.

$33 single/$40 double, lower by the month.
Modern apartments, but no restaurant or similar facilities found in hotels in this price range.

Hotel Residencial Carrillon, 5 Avenida 11-25, Zone 9, tel. 324267. $17 single/$22 double.
Modern, small hotel, quite reasonable for this area.

Budget Hotels – Zone 1

You generally won't have a private bathroom at a budget hotel, unless a range of prices is indicated. In that case, the higher price gets you a private toilet and shower.

Hotel Colonial, 7 Avenida 14-19, tel. 22955, 81208. 42 rooms. $9 single/$16 double.
Comfortable, old-fashioned ambience, spotless rooms with comfortable beds. Most rooms with private bath. A good value. Breakfast is available.

Hotel Ritz, 6 Avenida 9-28, tel. 536346. 16 rooms. $5 single/$8 double.
Up one flight of steps, as centrally located as you can get, pleasant little courtyard, but dreary rooms. Those on the 6 Avenida side fill up with traffic fumes. Hack, hack.

Hotel Berlin, 11 Calle 6-33. 8 rooms. $4/$7.
Pensión-type rooms off a courtyard.

Hotel Lessing House, 12 Calle 4-35, tel. 513891. 7 rooms. $6/$8.
A good, small hotel. Breakfast is available.

Mansión San Francisco, 6 Avenida 12-62, tel. 25125. 40 rooms. $8/$11.
Clean and recently refurbished. Furnished apartments are available.

Posada Real, 12 Calle 6-21, tel. 513786. 13 rooms. $4/$7.
Simple, central, slightly shabby, one flight up.

Chalet Suizo, 14 Calle 6-82, tel. 86371. 25 rooms. $3 to $4/$5 to

$6.
An old favorite among young travellers. Some of the rooms are
new and airy, others are stifling, so make sure you look before you
pay. Nice atmosphere, with a number of foreign guests usually
sharing experiences in the courtyard.

Hotel Spring, 8 Avenida 12-65, tel. 26637. 58 rooms. $4 to $5/$6
to $8.
Large rooms in this big old hotel, though some have unvented
showers that send out floods of steam. Another favorite of young
and young-at-heart visitors. Convivial.

Hogar del Turista, 11 Calle 10-43, tel. 25522. 14 rooms. $4 to
$5/$7 to $8.
A plain, German-managed pension. Good value. Guests are
expected to take their meals in the dining room.

Hotel El Virrey, 7 Avenida 15-46, tel. 28513. 60 rooms. $6 single
or double.
Central, only the rooms in the top tier are pleasant.

One of the many clusters of inexpensive hotels, in the vicinity of
15 Calle and 7 and 8 avenidas, includes these four, among others:

Hotel Bilbao, 15 Calle 8-45. $4 to $5/ $6 to $8. Bare and
adequate.
Hotel San Diego, 15 Calle 7-37, tel. 22958. 16 rooms. $3 to
$4/$5 to $7.
Hotel Fénix, 7 Avenida 15-81, tel. 516625. 18 rooms. $4/$6.
A nice old hotel with an air of faded glory.
Hotel Ajau, 8 Avenida 15-62. tel. 20488. $5 single or double, $8
with private bath. Clean, old, well-kept.

Along 9 Avenida is another cluster of inexpensive hotels, all of
recent vintage, patronized largely by Central American
businessmen. All have small rooms, usually with private baths.
There's always lots of activity in the lobbies, and the neighborhood
is a noisy, late-hours area. But rates are reasonable, rooms are
clean, and at least one of them usually has a vacancy. These
hotels are reluctant to rent rooms to singles.

Hotel Centro América, 9 Avenida 16-38, tel. 83941, 83821. 52

rooms. $3 to $4/$6 to $8.
Hotel Belmont, 9 Avenida 15-30, tel. 534662, 81467. 62 rooms.
$4 to $6/$6 to $10.
Hotel Capri, 9 Avenida 15-63, tel. 513737, 28191. 18 rooms. $3
to $5/$6 to $8.
Hotel España, 9 Avenida 15-59, tel. 29113. 74 rooms. $3 to $4/$4
to $6.
Hotel Gran Central, 9 Avenida 15-31, tel. 29514. 78 rooms. $2
to $4/$3 to $5. Older than the others.

Another cluster of more basic lodging places is in the vicinity of
16 Calle and 6 Avenue. The **Pensión Luna,** 6 Avenida 15-50, has
sagging beds in a few large rooms, and friendly owners. Knock
hard. On 16 Calle between 6 and 7 avenidas, rooms at the **Hotel
Mundial** and the **Mansión Mundial** are dismal. Those at **Casa
Washington,** at the corner of 6 Avenida, are better, especially the
outer ones with balconies. The rate at all of these establishments
is about $2 to $3 per person. The **Hotel Hernani,** 15 Calle 6-56,
tel. 22839, is slightly better than these, at about $4 per person.

Budget Hotels – Zones 9 and 10

Alameda Guest House, 4 Avenida 14-10, Zone 10, tel. 680152. 7
rooms. $7 to $12 single/$11 to $14 double.
A converted residence behind a high walls, like all the homes in
this fashionable neighborhood. For travelers with more taste than
money.

Other Hotels: The hotels and guest houses listed above are
convenient to places of interest, but there are others scattered
throughout Guatemala City. A partial list is available from the
tourist office. If you have a car, you might want to try one of the
motels along Calzada Roosevelt, the highway leading westward
out of the city. Most of these cater to the tryst trade, but many
are luxuriously furnished, and the price for a double room is rarely
higher than $15.

RESTAURANTS

The variety of restaurants in Guatemala City sometimes seems to be endless. There are seafood houses, American-style steak houses, Chinese eateries, Italian, German, Mexican and Spanish restaurants, and even a very few places serving native Guatemalan specialties.

Most of the inexpensive eateries are in Zone 1, while the more formal restaurants are clustered in zones 4, 9 and 10; but you'll find a range in prices, and good value for your money, in all areas.

The prices given below are generally for lunch or dinner, and are for a meal appropriate to the establishment. You wouldn't order just a cup of coffee in an elegant restaurant, or a seven-course dinner at McDonald's. Prices will be higher with a mixed drink. And the tab will skyrocket if you order an imported wine. Sales tax ("I.V.A.") is additional. Steak, poultry and fish are generally the best value. Shrimp and lobster are generally twice the price of other items on the menu.

Zone 1 - Downtown

Elegance and Tradition: The restaurant of the **Hotel Pan American,** 9 Calle 5-63, offers good food at unexpectedly reasonable prices. The dining room has a colonial decor, and includes such native touches as fiesta masks and waiters dressed in the men's outfit of Chichicastenango. The menu changes daily, but generally includes both American-style entrees served with soup, and one or two native dishes, as well as sandwiches. A buffet of native-style food is offered on Thursday, Friday and Sunday at lunch. Even if you're not looking for a full meal, you might stop in for a pastry and a cup of coffee. Open at 6 a.m. for breakfast (they have waffles). Highly recommended. Lunch or dinner $4 to $6, breakfast or sandwiches $2 and up.

Hotels: Also a haven from the noise and bustle of downtown is the main restaurant of the **Hotel Ritz-Continental,** 10 Calle at 6 Avenida A. There's nothing special about the ambience, but the food is good, and reasonably priced, especially the lunch special. Recent example: filet mignon, salad, desert and glass of wine for about $4. Prices are slightly higher in the Candilejas restaurant of the **Hotel del Centro,** 13 Calle at 5 Avenida. But a budget traveler can usually find one or two low-priced, filling items in any hotel restaurant. A club sandwich is often a good bet.

Italian Food: The small **Bologna,** 10 Calle 6-20, serves pasta, pizza and meat dishes, usually to a full house. Arrive early for lunch or dinner. From $2. For cheap Italian food, there is no end of pasta and pizza outlets. At **Al Macarone,** 6 Avenida 9-27, the decor is garish lavender, the service is slow, but the food isn't bad. Pizza and burger combinations for $1 and up. They have branches around town. A similar chain is **A Guy From Italy,** with one branch at 12 Calle 6-23.

Chinese Food: Many of the Chinese restaurants in Zone 1 are near Concordia Park, at 14 Calle and 6 Avenida. One of the better ones is **Canton,** 6 Avenida 14-20. Chow mein, chop suey, soups and sandwiches are on the menu, along with the usual long list of beef and seafood dishes and such favorites as hamburgers. Remember to order your rice separately, since it isn't included in the price of a meal at Chinese restaurants in Guatemala. (You do get porous white bread.) $4 and up, sandwiches from under $2. Another fairly good Chinese restaurant is **Fu Lu Sho,** on 6 Avenida at the corner of 12 Calle. This is a hangout, with the dining area open to the street and food served until midnight. $3 and up. **Ruby,** 11 Calle 6-56, serves the usual Chinese dishes as well as a filling non-Chinese lunch for less than $2.

Seafood and Spanish Food: Altuna, 5 Avenida 12-31, is a thoroughly enjoyable place for a long lunch. You can eat in the pleasant bar in the center of the restaurant (the converted patio of a large old home), or in one of the small dining rooms that surround it. The shrimp, paella and meat main courses are all excellent, and the waiters are friendly and efficient. $4 and up. Closed Sunday.

German Food: A favorite of the German community is the multi-level **Baviera,** at 11 Calle 6-55. There are daily specials, such as sauerbrauten and roast pork, as well as wurst, sandwiches on black bread, and pastries. Portions are on the small side. Lunch or dinner $2 and up, breakfast also. For less gemutlichkeit, try **Delicadezas Hamburgo,** at 15 Calle 5-34, on Concordia Park.

The set lunch is filling, and there are sausages, cakes, and fresh fruit drinks. $2 and up.

Mexican Food: El Gran Pavo, 13 Calle 4-41, is genuinely Mexican, which means that the food is longer on sauces and shorter on cheese and other garnishes than the Mexican-American cookery you may know. The locale is authentic, with arches between rooms, mariachi music, and an open fire. Plates of tacos and enchiladas for under $2, mole and grilled meats $4 and up. More for snacking is **Los Cebollines,** 6 Avenida 9-75.

Fast Food has come to dominate the eating scene in Zone 1 in the last few years, and in some ways, it's not such a bad thing. The food is sanitary and reasonably priced, and if you're hungry, relief is at hand. Service in many a more traditional eatery is exasperating. Here's a selection:

Multirestaurantes, 6 Avenida and 10 Calle on the lower level of the Plaza Vivar building, is the most interesting fast-food outlet. Choose from Chinese (chow mein, chop suey), Guatemalan (tacos, enchiladas), Italian (pizza) and American (burgers, fries) counters. You can easily assemble a meal for under $2.

McDonald's, on 10 Calle between 5 and 6 avenidas, offers Big Macs, French fries and the like. $1 and up. There are also several McDonald's clones, such as **Burger Shops,** 6 Avenida 13-40.

Pollo Campero, specializing in fried chicken, has branches throughout the city. In Zone 1, you'll find one at the corner of 9 Calle and 5 Avenida; and another at 6 Avenida and 15 Calle. Both have parking lots. The chicken is spicier than the American fast-food variety. A complete lunch of chicken, fries and Coke goes for less than $2. **Cafetería Los Pollos,** a chicken outlet on 6 Avenida between 14 and 15 calles, is worthy of mention mainly because it stays open 24 hours. Also less than $2 for a meal. Unique among fast-food chains, Los Pollos has branches outside of Guatemala City.

In the Centro Capitol, a shopping and cinema complex on 6 Avenida between 12 and 13 Calles, you'll find a **Wimpy's, Al Macarone, Pizza Hut,** and several other places at which you can eat for as little as $1. There are also Donkey Kong parlors.

Native Food: For Guatemalan cooking, try **Los Tecomates,** 6 Avenida 15-69. The restaurant is cramped and unpretentious, but authentic. Often there's often some meat smoking over a charcoal grill right outside the door. I like few things better than to attack a huge, slightly tough piece of *carne asada* (grilled beef) served with tortillas. Los Tecomates offers such a feast, as well as rabbit in wine and a mixed grill, served with a small salad, for $2 and up. Also slightly larger than a hole in the wall is **Ranchón Antigueño,** 13 Calle 3-50, where local-style grilled meats with fried plantains and beans go for less than $2. Consider as well **Las Salsas,** in the Multirestaurantes fast-food emporium.

Pastry Shops: A number of places serve pastries as well as complete meals. **Alemana,** at 7 Avenida 9-58, features a daily bargain lunch for about $2, including everything from soup to dessert, and inexpensive breakfasts. **Lutecia,** at 11 Calle 4-40, near the Bank of America, also has a few breakfast specials for less than $2. The atmosphere is something like that of a European tea room. For good black bread, and danishes, try **Jensen,** at 10 Calle 6-66, in the same. building as the Hotel Ritz Continental. There's a branch in the Etisa building on the Plazuela España in Zone 9.

Bars with Food: The **El Zócalo** bar, at 18 Calle 4-39, is a cavernous, busy and noisy place, heavy on local color. Order a beer, and you'll be served a mountain of *bocas* (snacks) that will include a bowl of soup, a pile of tortillas, and assorted bits of meat. The long, long menu includes hamburgers, spaghetti, steak, shrimp and paella. A marimba band entertains every day. Enter through the long corridor from the street. Lunch or dinner from $2, beer and double shots of rum for well under $1. Nearer the Central Park, in the arcade running off 6 Avenida between 8 and 9 calles, is **El Portal,** an old and woody drinking place, with mementos hung on the walls. Glasses of beer or shots of rum served with bocas for less than $1, light meals for $2.

Inexpensive Food: If you've read this far looking for inexpensive food, you haven't been paying attention. But here are a few additional choices. A number of restaurants on 11 Calle between 7 and 8 avenidas serve businessmen's lunches for $1 and up, as does **La Selecta,** 14 Calle 6-24, just off Concordia Park. The best cheap food is in the central market, however. Enter along 8 Calle near 8 Avenida, and follow the aroma of charcoal down to the eateries on the lower level. Squeeze in with the locals on a bench at a rough-hewn table, and fill up with stuffed peppers, grilled meat, omelettes, *pacaya*, plantains stuffed with beans, stew or *chuchitos,* all cooked before your eyes and served on enameled plates. Wash it all down with coffee or a soft drink, and pay with your spare change.

Zone 4 – Sheraton Area

French Food: One of the better restaurants in Guatemala City is **Estro Armónico,** at Vía 4 4-36, opposite the Sheraton. Unpretentious on the outside, but inside this is a lovely arched locale with an open fire. Try a tomato stuffed with shrimp as an appetizer, or leek, turtle or mushroom soup, then choose from daily specials that might include steak in bearnaise sauce or Tahitian shrimp. The sauces and vegetables are artfully prepared. I take issue only with the herbed margarine. From $8.

Restaurante de las Espadas, in the Conquistador Sheraton Hotel, Via 5 4-68, with a separate entrance on Via 4. The extensive menu includes nicely prepared tournedos and filet of beef, curried shrimp, native-style steak, and filet of fish with corn. $5 and up for most items, or you can have a lasagna or large sandwich for less. Dinner is sometimes accompanied by music. Hearty breakfasts are served from 6 a.m. for about $2.

Spanish Food: One of the best bargains in town, and perhaps in all of Central America, is the **Alicante,** a simple, open-to-the-street restaurant at 7 Avenida 7-16. You're sure to think there's some mistake in the prices. The daily luncheon special includes soup, a main course, dessert, coffee, and a cold glass of wine, all for less than $2. And the food is good. There are also steaks and paella, and fish and egg dishes, similarly inexpensive. The atmosphere is more pleasant at the wooden tables on the balcony.

Seafood: Auto Mariscos, at Vía 9, 5-04 (a couple of blocks from the Triángulo office building on 7 Avenida), is a big, U.S.-style drive-up seafood house, brightly lit and short on atmosphere, but with very good food, including shellfish soup, paella, shrimp and lobster in various guises, and a salad bar. Choose beer rather than the house wine. $5 and up, less for the kids' menu. Similar seafood is available in a more elegant atmosphere at **Delicias del Mar,** Vía 5 3-65, near the Sheraton. $6 and up.

Inexpensive Food: There's a cluster of cheap eateries near the Zone 4 Shopping Center (Centro Comercial), at 24 Calle and 6 Avenida, including a **Pizza Hut, Pollo Campero** and **A Guy From Italy.** Just up 6 Avenida is **Rostipollo Chapín,** where a whole barbecued chicken can be had for $4. And there are luncheon specials at other small restaurants on Vía 1 near 6 Avenida.

Zones 9 and 10 - Zona Viva and Nearby

The Zona Viva, or Lively Zone, centered on the Hotel Camino Real, is where Guatemala's upper crust shops, dines, and otherwise entertains itself. The prices are sometimes un-Guatemalan, but they generally fall as you move toward the edges of the area.

French Food: At **Le Rendez-vous,** 13 Calle 2-55, Zone 10, the dining is bistro-style on the patio and inside. Popular and pricey. $6 and up for a light lunch of an attractive salad or a croque monsieur and a drink, $12 for anything substantial. At **Palo Alto,** 4 Avenida 13-65, Zone 10, the fare is mainly meats in sauces. $12 and up, evenings only. **Siriaco's,** 1 Avenida 12-16, Zone 10, more French-influenced than French, serves quiche, small steaks and salads in a pleasant art-gallery atmosphere drooping with plants. $8 and up. **Martin's,** 13 Calle 7-65, Zone 9, an excellent restaurant of long standing, serves items usually not seen in these parts. Specialties include broiled salmon, frog's legs, lamb and lobster, all with organ music. $6 and up.

Steaks: Don't hesitate to order steak in Guatemala City. When it's aged and cooked right, Guatemalan beef is marvelous, and at these steak houses, it comes in large portions. Figure $5 or more for a steak and a beverage.
Peña de los Charangos, 6 Avenida 13-60, Zone 9. Gaucho ambience, with music.
Hacienda de los Sánchez, 12 Calle 2-10, Zone 10. Pleasant, open-air pavilion.
El Rodeo, at 7 Avenida 14-84, Zone 9. Rustic and woody. Seafood, too.

Native Food: El Parador, Reforma 6-70, serves tacos, enchiladas, and marinated meats cooked on an open grill. A marimba band usually plays. Similar are **Nim-Guaa,** at Reforma and 8 Calle; and **Los Antojitos,** Reforma 15-02. Meals $4 and up at any of these. If you hesitate to eat native-style snacks in the markets or on a bus, try **El Tamal,** 6 Avenida 14-49, Zone 9. Tamales, tacos, chuchos and similar items cost 40 cents or less, to eat in or take out.

Mexican Food: El Gran Pavo, 12 Calle and 6 Avenida, Zone 9, is a branch of the restaurant with the same name in Zone 1, though less atmospheric.

Seafood: Puerto Barrios, 11 Calle and 7 Avenida, Zone 9, is an attractive seafood house done up to look like a Spanish galleon. $10 or so for shrimp, excellent stuffed fish, or steak. You won't find a place like this in the real Puerto Barrios. At **El Arrecife,** 13 Calle 2-60, Zone 10, a set lunch with sea bass or breaded shrimp (or grilled steak, if you choose,) runs less than $5. There's live music weekends and weekday evenings. Closed Monday.

Oriental Food: Palacio Royal, at the corner of 7 Avenida and 11 Calle, Zone 9, is the best Chinese restaurant in Guatemala City. The decor is genuinely oriental, and the menu is in Chinese as well as Spanish and English, a good sign. Listed are the usual chow mein, rice and fried wonton, as well as eggplant stuffed with shrimp, crab claws, duck in sweet and sour sauce, and many other specialties. The soups are excellent. Ask about items that may not be on the menu. $7 and up. Also good is **Celeste Imperio,** 7 Avenida 9-99, Zone 4. More moderately priced, despite its location in the heart of the Zona Viva, is **Excellent,** 13 Calle at 2 Avenida. Many, many Chinese plates to choose from. $5 and up. **Sho-gun,** 1 Avenida 13-27, features teriyakis, tempuras and other Japanese dishes. $12 and up. **Renu's,** a Thai restaurant at Reforma 7-45, has some interesting items, including beef in peanut sauce, chicken in ginger, and curried fish. $5 and up.

Family Restaurants: NAIS, 7 Avenida 6-26 and 5 Avenida 12-31, Zone 9, is similar to Lum's and other family-style restaurants that you'll find on suburban strips in the States. The specialties are tenderloin strip steaks, chicken, fondues and burgers. Fairly good, and reasonable at $3 and up for a meal. Similar in atmosphere is **Dixieland BBQ,** Reforma 9-74. Big sandwiches are

$2, BBQ ribs, chops and steaks $5. Good food, slow service.

Hotels: The **Camino Real,** 14 Calle and Reforma, has several restaurants. In La Ronda, the cuisine is French and excellent. $12 and up. The Cafetal coffee shop is good for elegant sandwiches with trimmings, salads, and native-style dishes. $7 and up. The restaurants in the **El Dorado** are also first-rate, and more moderately priced. In El Galeón, large deli sandwiches and pasta cost less than $3, and main courses less than $5. A buffet is available at lunch. Over in the Italian-style Café-Bar, hefty sandwiches are served.

Kosher Style: La Miga de Yaacov, 7 Avenida 14-46, Zone 9, is a take-out deli. So where else will you find pastrami, salami and bagels? Closed from noon to 2 p.m.

Fast Food: The **Pollo Campero** chicken restaurant at 7 Avenida and 10 Calle, Zone 9, has a kids' play area. A **McDonald's** is at 14 Calle and 7 Avenida, Zone 9. **Multirestaurantes** has a large outlet at Reforma 13-59, near the Camino Real, and nearby is **Pizza Hut,** Reforma 15-54.

Inexpensive Food: In the office-shopping building at Reforma and 12 Calle, Zone 10, the **Casting Cafe** serves a $1 lunch special, and there are similar deals to be had in other office buildings in this area.

Bars and Night Life

Bars, discotheques, cozy clubs, restaurants and sleazy strip joints stay open into the early hours in Guatemala City. The nighttime scene is lively, and whatever it is you're looking for can be found. Here's a selection of places in addition to the bars and restaurants with entertainment mentioned above:

Some of the hotels are good bets for lively but hassle-free drinking, entertainment and dancing. In the **Sheraton** in Zone 4, the Refugio bar often has live guitar music or a chanteuse in the evening. Happy hour is from 5:30 to 8 p.m. Downstairs in the Sheraton, La Cueva de los Capitanes is a full-fledged night club, with live music and dancing, from 9 p.m. into the wee hours, Tuesday through Sunday. In Zone 10, the Lobby Bar of the **Camino Real** sometimes has a piano player, a jazz singer, or some other pleasant surprise.

In the Zona Viva of Zone 10, **Dash Disco** is downstairs in the shopping complex at 12 Calle and 1 Avenida, Zone 10. **Le Pont Disco,** 13 Calle 0-48, Zone 10, is attached to the Fiesta Hotel. **Safari,** 3 Avenida 11-65, Zone 10, is a popular night club.

Many a bar in Guatemala City is a low-down place in which to get smashed. More yuppie-style places in which to get smashed include **El Establo,** Avenida La Reforma 14-34, pleasantly decorated with beamed ceiling, dim light, gardens and Spanish-style furniture; and **El Mostachón,** in the Plaza Montúfar shopping center on 12 Calle near 6 Avenida, Zone 9.

Mariachis: At night, stop by the Trébol, the cloverleaf intersection of Avenida Bolívar and Carretera Roosevelt, and you'll see mariachi bands in full Mexican outfits. The music is loud and brassy. Listen to a few tunes, and watch as locals drive up and haggle over the price of a song with one of the bands. The neighborhood around the Trébol is somewhat on the rough side, so go in your car or a taxi, or don't go.

GUATEMALA CITY ZONE BY ZONE

Guatemala City is divided into 20 zones, but only those that contain museums, government offices, parks, monuments, hotels and restaurants that might interest most visitors are included here.

Of the places mentioned below, the most important are within a few blocks of the National Palace in Zone 1. These can be seen in a day before you make forays into the countryside. Later on you can pick and choose among the sights that especially interest you.

ZONE 1

Zone 1 is the old downtown area of Guatemala City, with its center at the **Central Park (Parque Central).** (In any Guatemalan town, the main square is called the parque). The executive branch of the national government, the congress, and many hotels and businesses are located in this area.

The Central Park, between 6 and 8 calles, is technically two parks. To the west of 6 Avenida is **Parque del Centenario;** to the east, the **Plaza de Armas.** In the early days of Guatemala City, the park was a market, surrounded by the Palace of the Captains-General (where independence was declared in 1821), the mint, and lesser government buildings. All fell in the 1917 earthquake. The Plaza de Armas had a facelift of sorts recently, and an official garage now stands under its barren surface. Parque del Centenario is currently being renovated.

Now standing on the north side of the park is the **National Palace,** the center of the government of Guatemala. Built from 1939 to 1943, it was the last great public project of the dictator Jorge Ubico, who was overthrown not long after its completion. Though structurally it consists of reinforced concrete filled in with brick, the palace is faced with light green stone, with a mishmash of classic and colonial decorative elements. Inside, the palace is far more pleasant and attractive than on the outside. The interior gardens and beams carved with coats of arms bring to mind the Moorish palaces of southern Spain. Around the two main interior stairways are a number of murals by Alfredo Gálvez Suárez depicting the history of Guatemala, from the semi-mythical times of the Popol Vuh to the wars between the Spanish invaders and the native kingdoms to the formation of a new society during the colonial period. Thrown in with these subjects is the unlikely theme of Don Quixote.

On the second floor is the **Reception Hall (Sala de Recepción),** a magnificent wood-panelled room with great chandeliers, used for state occasions. Stained glass windows depict the history of Indian and colonial Guatemala. But the most unusual feature is the stuffed quetzal—the bird that is Guatemala's symbol of national independence—which forms part of the coat of arms behind the rows of flags. If the Reception Hall is closed, ask one of the guards to let you in and to turn on the lights.

The **Cathedral (Catedral Metropolitana),** located on the east side of the Central Park, was begun in 1782 and finished in 1815. Bell towers and domes were added later. Built in the massive baroque style that was meant to resist earth tremors, the Cathedral has a bare white interior of little interest but for a number of altars covered with gold leaf. Some of the figures of saints were originally in the Cathedral of present-day Antigua. Adjacent to the Cathedral is the tile-roofed, colonial-style **Palace of the Archbishop.**

On the block behind the Cathedral is the modern **Central Market (Mercado Central)**, which replaced the old market that was destroyed inn the 1976 earthquake. A modern, low-slung concrete structure, the market starts with a pleasant plaza at street level, and continues for several stories *below* ground. Visitors will be most interested in the scores upon scores of stalls on the upper levels where Guatemala's fine textiles, baskets, pottery, and other handicrafts are sold. But don't stop there. Onward and downward, vendors of pots and pans, meat, fruits, furniture and spices attract local customers, and some of their wares are worthy of your attention as well. Down on the first level are the eateries.

Almost all of the vendors at the Central Market are permanent vendors, who buy their wares from country people and middlemen. There are several other large markets around the city, including the sprawling terminal market in Zone 4.

On the opposite side of the square from the Cathedral is the **National Library (Biblioteca Nacional),** a massive rectangular building which houses the General Archives of Central America on its first floor. While the library is not especially attractive, it features an intricate modernistic relief sculpture by Efraín Recinos on its main entrance stairway.

The stretch of 6 Avenida south of the square is the commercial heart of the city, lined with shops, slot machine parlors, movie houses and offices, and with restaurants and hotels located along the cross streets. 6 Avenida still retains a bustling, prosperous air, but on nearby streets you'll note the ills that afflict many an aging urban core. Bus after bus roars down an avenue, belching diesel exhaust from a poorly tuned engine, leaving hacking pedestrians and blackening buildings in its wake. Horns blare, trash is dropped in the streets, contaminants burn the eyes. Many a business and government agency has moved out of the central city, and many a street peddler has moved in to set up a stand and squeeze still more space from the congested sidewalks. Zone 1 is far from abandoned. A number of hotels and restaurants and shops maintain high standards. Still, in some establishments, floors crack, paint peels, nothing is repaired or replaced, and the clients have gone elsewhere.

Walking up 6 Avenida, with stops to look in shop windows along the way, you'll come to the **Church of San Francisco,** at the corner of 13 Calle. Built in an Italianate neoclassic style, the church is noted for its collection of paintings of martyrs, which is open daily except Monday from 8 a.m. to noon and 3 to 6 p.m. The great windowed dome makes the interior of the church especially light.

At the next street, 14 Calle, is **Parque Concordia,** another public square. At one corner is the headquarters of the National Police, built in the style of a Renaissance palace. Sometimes you'll see a new car on display in the park. It's the first prize in a charity raffle. Tickets for the national lottery are also available at the booths here.

Places in this part of Zone 1 that you may have to visit include the **Post Office,** at 7 Avenida and 12 Calle. You can't miss the Egypto-Moorish-baroque arch of the post office over 12 Calle. The long-distance department of **Guatel,** the telephone and cable company, is a block away at 8 Avenida and 12 Calle, and the **Immigration Department (Migración)** is at the same intersection, at the opposite corner.

The **Railroad Station** is located at 18 Calle and 9 Avenida, near the square where the first bullring of Guatemala City was sited. The station is quite attractive, a grand, Caribbean-style, tin-roofed building with classical elements. A second story of wooden columns and clapboard siding sits on a brick base. 18 Calle in this area is the busiest shopping street in the city, lined with shops and open-air stalls offering low-priced goods of all kinds.

At 7 Avenida above 21 Calle is the **Civic Center (Centro Cívico),** a complex of modern buildings housing offices of the city and national governments. The **City Hall (Municipalidad)** features a highly geometric interior mural by Carlos Mérida called *The Mestizo Race of Guatemala.* Mérida, Guatemala's leading modern artist, lived and worked for many years in Mexico. The outside relief sculpture on the east end of the building is by Dagoberto Vásquez. The combination of murals and sculpture with architecture in this and the other buildings of the Civic Center is a conscious attempt to revive the ancient Mayan tradition of integrating art with construction.

The other buildings in the Civic Center are those of the Social Security Institute (IGSS), with a relief sculpture by Roberto González Goyri depicting the Conquest and the bloody clash of European and indigenous cultures; the Bank of Guatemala, also with relief sculptures by González; and the towers of the Supreme Court, the National Mortgage Bank and the Ministry of Public Finances.

Overlooking the Civic Center is the **San José Fortress,** a massive old defensive work. It's also a nice park, with carefully manicured lawns and flower beds, and cannon placed here and there along the ramparts. At the top stands the indoor-outdoor **National Theater** complex, which is skillfully integrated into the old structures. From the theater area you can look out over the inner zones of the city, and onward to the wealthier residential areas on the hillsides to the southeast, to cultivated mountainsides, and, on a clear day, to the irregular outline of the volcano Pacaya to the south. The gates of the fortress are usually closed, but the guard will let you in if you can get his attention.

On the west side of Zone 1 is the **National Museum of Popular Arts and Crafts (Museo Nacional de Artes e Industrias Populares),** at 10 Avenida 10-72. On display are a number of huipiles, or women's blouses, silverwork, pottery, paintings by Indian artists, fiesta masks, and ceramic and other objects used in native religious ceremonies. The collection is relatively slim, considering the artistic wealth of Guatemala, and you can get a better sampling of native arts by visiting the handicraft stalls of the central market. But a few of the huipiles are in styles that are rarely seen today. Hours are from 9 a.m. to 4 p.m. Closed Monday and from noon to 2 p.m. weekends. Small admission charge.

The **National History Museum (Museo Nacional de Historia),** which houses a limited collection of paintings and artifacts of Guatemalan history, is located at 9 Calle 9-70. If you drop in, take a look at Edward Muybridge's 1875 photos of Totonicapán. Many a highland town has a similar appearance today. Hours are 9 to 4, with a break from noon to 2 p.m. on weekends.

The small **Church of San Miguel,** 10 Avenida and 10 Calle, is noted for its statuary and richly gilded retables, though it suffers from a new, white appearance that came with post-earthquake repairs. Note the engaged "cushioned" (accordion-fold) columns on the facade.

The **Church of Santo Domingo,** 12 Avenida and 10 Calle, is one of the finer ecclesiastical structures in the city, finished in white and pastel cream stucco. It has two attached squat bell towers, one of which held the first public clock of Guatemala City. Inside is a large niched retable.

Farther north, at 11 Avenida and 5 Calle, is the domed **Church of La Merced.** The baroque exterior, with its neoclassical columns, has been undergoing extensive repairs. The interior is richly decorated with noted paintings and statuary.

One last place that you might want to check out in Zone 1 is the **Ermita del Carmen,** a church located five blocks east and five blocks north of the Central Park, atop a hill. The area is somewhat run down today, but it is the oldest part of the city, the Barrio de la Parroquia, having been settled as the village of La Ermita long before the capital was moved to its present site. The original church was built early in the seventeenth century, destroyed in the 1917 earthquake, rebuilt, and damaged again in the 1976 quake. It's a rather simple and heavy whitewashed baroque structure, with a gilt altar and short bell tower. From the hilltop you can look out to the newer parts of the city. Despite the seedy aspect of the Parroquia neighborhood, the area is looked upon affectionately by residents of the city. Nobody is more genuinely Guatemalan than a person born in the Parroquia. From the northeast corner of the park in which the church is located, you can catch a number 2 bus back toward the east side of Zone 1, or on to Zone 4 or Zone 9 if you're headed that way.

ZONE 2

Zone 2 is a pleasant old residential area just north of the city center that has changed little over the years.

The **Relief Map of Guatemala** in Minerva Park is the main attraction in this part of town. Measuring about 2500 square meters, it has a vertical scale more than twice that of the horizontal scale, so that the mountainous terrain of the country is shown quite clearly, though with a distortion that gives the volcanoes a strange, skinny appearance. Climb up to the viewing platforms, and you'll be able to trace the places you've been to and will be going to. The map was finished in 1905, and includes running water in all the rivers.

Minerva Park is a pleasant and quiet place, with a baseball field and strolling paths. The area used to be known as the Hipódromo del Norte for the horse-racing track that was located here, and which has passed into memory. Canyons surround the park on three sides. Watch your step at the edge.

To get to Minerva Park and the relief map, take bus 1 north along 5 Avenida in Zone 1 to the end of the line.

ZONE 4

Zone 4, together with the adjacent Civic Center of Zone 1, is Guatemala City's midtown commercial area, less congested than the old town. A railroad line divides the two zones. Most of the streets, except for through arteries, are called *vías* and *rutas.*

Just past the railroad line from the Civic Center on 6 Avenida is the **Centro Comercial de la Zona 4,** a shopping center and office complex. Most people wouldn't consider this a tourist attraction, but I find it interesting to wander the corridors, peer into shop windows, and probe the aisles of the supermarkets to see what people are buying and how much they're paying. While most people in the city don't make their purchases in such shopping centers, you can get a sense of what kinds of material things the middle classes in Guatemala aspire to own, and what's within the reach of their pocketbooks.

A block to the east, on 7 Avenida, is the office building of the **Guatemala Tourist Commission,** where you can pick up a map, brochures, and ask questions at the first-floor information desk. Nearby is the sports complex known as **Olympic City (Ciudad Olímpica),** consisting of a stadium, gymnasium, swimming pool, tennis courts, and an indoor arena. Guatemalans are more obsessed than most peoples with sports, and what may seem to be an inordinate amount of space in the newspapers is devoted to the reporting of athletic events, especially the outcomes of soccer matches.

Farther south on 7 Avenida, at the intersection of Vía 8 past the Sheraton Hotel, are two more shopping center-office complexes called **El Triángulo** and **El Patio.** El Triángulo is a common reference point for giving directions in the city. Across the way is El Pueblo, my favorite supermarket, where you'll find bargains galore if you can shoehorn your way in.

The **Yurrita Church,** also called **Nuestra Señora de las Angustias,** is located on Ruta 6 a block east of the Triángulo. Architecturally, it's one of the more interesting (or strange) of the city's churches, with twisting columns and concrete grillework that give it an appearance much like that of a medieval European fortress. It was built as a private chapel by a rich philanthropist before being opened for public worship. Inside is a fine carved altar.

Up Ruta 6 from the Yurrita Church, across Avenida La Reforma at the corner of 1 Calle, in Zone 10, is the **Botanical Garden (Jardín Botánico)**, my favorite oasis in the capital. The garden features a selection from Guatemala's incredible variety of trees and plants. If you're interested in flora, this is the place for an overview before going out to the countryside to identify plants. Signs are in Spanish and Latin, though you should have little trouble in figuring out many of the English names. Even if you don't care about plants and flowers, the garden beats most of the city parks in landscaping and tranquility. Open Monday through Friday 8 a.m. to 3 p.m., closed December 1 to January 15. Enter through the building on Calle Mariscal Cruz (0 Calle). Also here is the small **Natural History Museum (Museo de Historia Natural** of the University of San Carlos, open weekdays from 8 a.m. to noon and 2 to 6 p.m. The exhibits, mainly of stuffed animals, are similar to those in the Natural History Museum in Aurora Park. Buses 2 and 14 pass the botanical garden.

West from the Triángulo, at 4 Avenida and 9 Calle, are the **Bus Terminal** and **Terminal Market.** The Terminal is a large lot covering several city blocks, jammed with buses that run to all parts of the country. Wedged between the buses, and scurrying for safety when the buses start moving, are hundreds of sellers of vegetables and fruits, dressed in the outfits of their towns. When you become familiar with the costumes of the different parts of the country, you'll appreciate the great distances that Indian traders travel with their wares. Here you'll see men of Sololá with great bundles of onions and garlic, women from San Pedro Sacatepéquez with baskets of cherries, and men of Nahualá in long woolen skirts, delivering *metates,* grinding stones.

Catching a bus at the terminal is vastly confusing. Some buses park in the main lot, others on the streets in the wholesale area to the south. But if you stand in one place, somebody will eventually come up to you, ask where you're going, and point the way. Fortunately, most buses to points of interest for visitors leave from elsewhere in the city.

Despite the madness and rush of the outside vendors, things are more organized on the two levels inside the market building, and in the temporary stalls that have sheltered vendors during continuing renovations. Here you'll find vegetables and herbs, flowers, handicrafts, cheap luggage, saddles and other leather products, hammocks and rope, baskets, piñatas, tropical birds, utensils made from scrap metal, and a thousand other items which you may or may not recognize. Butchers and grocers, merchants of beans, rice and wheat, sellers of every product that a working resident of Guatemala City might need for his daily life, offer their wares.

It takes a thick skin to penetrate the shabby area outside the Terminal, and the standard handicrafts of interest to visitors are available in greater quantities at the Central Market and elsewhere. But the Terminal is a fascinating display of penny capitalism. Any city bus marked "Terminal" will take you there. Buses back to Zone 1 pass outside the market along 4 Avenida.

ZONES 9 and 10

Zones 9 and 10, Guatemala City's uptown, include the major luxury hotels, several museums, and the more tony restaurants and shops.

At the northern end of Zone 9, the main landmark is the **Tower of the Reformer (Torre del Reformador)**, Guatemala's answer to the Eiffel Tower, at 7 Avenida and 2 Calle. Dedicated to President Justo Rufino Barrios, it can be seen from almost any point in the city. The bell on top is rung only on June 30, the anniversary of the Liberal triumph in the 1871 revolution.

Avenida La Reforma, a wide, tree-lined thoroughfare a block east of 7 Avenida, forms the boundary between zones 9 and 10. Along it are embassies, residences of the wealthy, and apartment and office buildings.

On the top floor of the office building at Reforma 8-16 is the **Museo Popol-Vuh,** a museum associated with Francisco Marroquín University. Pre-Columbian sculpture and pottery from all parts of Guatemala are on display. There are also colonial ceramics, religious sculpture and paintings; and traditional native outfits. Hours are Monday through Saturday 9 a.m. to 5:30 p.m., and there is an admission charge. In the same building, in office 322, is the Asociación Tikal, where William Coe's guide to Tikal is available.

Just east of Reforma, from 12 to 14 calles in the vicinity of the Hotel Camino Real, is the area called the Zona Viva, or Lively Zone, where the city's most fashionable boutiques, trendiest discos and most expensive restaurants are clustered. Upscale Guatemala City is tree-lined, clean, and more low-key than lively.

A few blocks east of Reforma, at 4 Avenida 16-27, Zone 10, is the **Museo Ixchel,** which houses an outstanding display of Indian textiles.   Included are many old-style town outfits and exquisite ceremonial costumes, which the visitor would not usually have the chance to see on excursions to Indian villages.   Techniques of weaving and the evolution of native styles of dress are explained. Also on display are paintings by Carmen Pettersen of Indians in their traditional outfits.   A stop here is highly recommended for anyone interested in Guatemala's native peoples and crafts. Hours are 9 a.m. to 5:30 p.m. daily except Sunday, and there is an admission charge.

The main street of the district, after Reforma, is 12 Calle, also known as Calle Montúfar. At its junction with 7 Avenida is the **Plazuela España,** a busy traffic circle. The fountain in the center of the plaza was originally the base for an equestrian statue of King Charles III of Spain. The statue was destroyed by a mob when Guatemala declared its independence, and President José María Reyna Barrios later had the fountain hidden.   The fountain was rediscovered in 1935 and placed in its present location.   Farther east on 12 Calle are a number of shopping centers, stores and restaurants.

At the southern end of Zone 9 is the **Obelisk (Obelisco),** a monument to Guatemala's independence, at the intersection of Boulevard Independencia and Avenida Reforma.

Bus 2 from along 8 Avenida in Zone 1 runs out along Reforma. Bus 5, which runs along 6 Avenida to 12 Calle, Zone 9, also stops within a couple of blocks of most of the above-mentioned places.

ZONE 13

Out in Zone 13 in the southern part of the city are the airport and the attractions of Aurora Park. The airport is mentioned in the city directory, below.

Aurora Park on Boulevard Liberación is a pleasant place to spend an afternoon. Along the northern rim of the park are the remains of a colonial aqueduct. The park entrance is marked by a huge statue of Tecún Umán, the national hero of Guatemala who was slain in single combat with the Spanish conqueror Pedro de Alvarado. Just inside the entrance and to the left is the zoo, which features lions, leopards, crocodiles, monkeys, peccaries and roving photographers. Out in back are rides for the kids.

The **Museum of Natural History (Museo de Historia Natural)** has an excellent collection of stuffed birds, including macaws, owls, and, of course, the rare quetzal, Guatemala's national symbol. The museum is a good place for bird watchers to familiarize themselves with the local species. There are also jaguars and reptiles (also stuffed), some of them in displays featuring mockups of the animals' natural environments.

The **National Museum of Archaeology and Ethnology** houses an extensive collection, only part of which is on display at any one time. There are plaster models of archaeological sites, a carved wooden lintel from Temple IV of Tikal on which the glyphs standing out more clearly than in most stone sculpture, stone masks, stelae, and pottery and many other artifacts. Many of the native outfits on exhibit were gathered thirty years ago, and are no longer in everyday use in Indian towns.

Next door is the **Museum of Modern Art (Museo de Arte Moderno)**, which houses a large mural by Carlos Mérida, one of the few modern Guatemalan artists to achieve an international reputation. There are also attempts by other artists at impressionism and cubism, but the visitor will probably appreciate more the representative works showing Guatemala's natural beauty and Indian life.

Hours at all the museums in Aurora Park are 9 a.m. to 4:30 p.m. every day except Monday. On weekends there's a break from noon to 2 p.m. There is a nominal admission charge to the archaeology museum. To reach the park, take bus 5 or 6 from along 8 Avenida in Zone 1, or bus 5 on 6 Avenida in Zone 4 or Zone 9.

ZONE 7

One of the major ancient cities of Mesoamerica, **Kaminaljuyú,** flourished within the limits of what is now Guatemala City. In the past few decades, most of the hundreds of mounds that once made up the great ceremonial center have been destroyed to make way for housing and commercial development. Some of the treasures of pottery and jewelry have been recovered and placed in the custody of the National Museum of Archeology and Ethnology. But an untold amount was carted off by private collectors, or else now lies buried beneath the houses of Guatemala's middle class.

Kaminaljuyú—Hill of the Dead—predated the great Mayan centers of the Petén. Through studies of the structures and

71

artifacts unearthed here, archaeologists have concluded that Kaminaljuyú was inhabited about 2000 years ago by a people skilled at sculpture and pottery, and who used glyph writing. The styles of certain artifacts—tripod cylindrical vases and pieces with images of a god very similar to the Mexican Tlaloc—indicate a close relationship with Teotihuacán in central Mexico. It's possible that Kaminaljuyú became a southern outpost of Teotihuacán, or of a related center.

What today seem to be small hills scattered over the landscape are the remains of temple platforms, covered over with dirt and vegetation. The temples were set about patios and plazas, and each was built over a burial or a row of burials.

Situated on a broad plain, Kaminaljuyú differs from the archaeological sites of a much later period in that it was not a defensible place. Utatlán, Mixco Viejo and Iximché were all built after the period of migrations from Mexico (about 1000 A.D.), when the highland nations were engaged in continuous warfare. These later cities were located on hilltops or on narrow tongues of land surrounded by canyons. But it would seem that the era when Kaminaljuyú thrived was a time of peace.

The excavations at Kaminaljuyú have been closed recently, and you should not visit the site unless you first verify that restoration work has been completed. Take bus 17-Kaminaljuyú from 4 Avenida and 17 Calle in Zone 1, or along 6 Avenida in Zone 4, or drive west along Calzada Roosevelt and turn right along 23 Avenida to the site.

ZONE 15

For a glimpse of some of the best and worst areas of Guatemala City, board bus 1 at the corner of 14 Calle and 10 Avenida, on the east side of Zone 1. The buses on this line are rarely crowded, despite the general disrepair of public transport in Guatemala City. You'll follow 12 Avenida southward. As you cross a bridge, look to your left, to a vast canyon where almost every inch of space is taken up by shacks of tin and scrap wood precariously clinging to the mud of the slopes. There are other such miserable squatter settlements in some of the canyons that ring the city.

The bus continues past a large military base (Campo de Marte), then down through another, unpopulated canyon, and up into a city of Frank Lloyd Wright-ish houses protected by barbed wire and shards of glass embedded in high walls. Despite appearances, most of the residents are not wealthy by the standards of the developed world, but in a country where many are poor, self-protection is inevitable. And in Latin America, in any case, family life typically unfolds out of public view.

You'll pass the American Club with its vast green spaces and tennis courts, the estates of private schools, and finally proceed down wide, tree-lined Boulevard Vista Hermosa. Ahead, on the hillside, are some of the better residential areas.

Get off the bus at the Super Centro Vista Hermosa, a shopping mall, and take a look at the stores, among them a gardening center, a cosmetics boutique, and others more run-of-the-mill. Occasionally you'll hear English and other non-local languages, but this is no foreign colony.

Continue your tour with a stroll outside. There are more stores, some typical of Guatemalan neighborhoods and others catering to the special interests of the bourgeois. Residential streets are uncongested, atypically quiet. When you've satisfied your curiosity about the other half, catch bus 1 heading the other way.

GUATEMALA CITY DIRECTORY

Here's a compendium of practical information about the capital:

Airport

Aurora International Airport, serving international flights and Aviateca flights to Flores, is located on the south side of Guatemala City in Zone 13.

When arriving on a flight, you'll first pass a desk staffed by a representative of the tourist office. You can pick up a tourist card here, if you don't already have one, and book a room in town. A Banco de Guatemala booth, for changing money, is open to meet most flights. Next come the immigration formalities, after which you pick up your baggage and go through what is usually a cursory customs inspection. Outside the door are taxis and the booths of the car rental companies. Bus 5, on the street outside the terminal, will take you to zones 9, 4 or 1, though it's usually a squeeze to get any luggage on. There are no limousines or collective buses to hotels. If the lower-level exchange booth is closed, take the outside stairway to the bank on the second level.

When taking a flight out of Aurora Airport, enter on the third level of the terminal via the driveway. Check in with your airline, and if you're taking an international flight, pay your exit tax (about $10), then go down to the second level, where you'll go through immigration formalities when your flight is announced. On the second floor are the cafeteria, duty-free shopping counters (low cigarette and liquor prices), handicraft shops, slot machines, a post office, a telephone-telegraph office (Guatel), and a branch of the Banco de Guatemala (hours: weekdays 7:30 a.m. to 6:30 p.m.; Saturdays, Sundays and holidays 8 a.m. to 11 a.m., and 3 p.m. to 6 p.m.). When the bank is closed, try to exchange money at one of the shops. Duty-free liquor and cigarette prices are especially low.

To get to the airport terminal, catch bus 5-Aeropuerto on 9 Calle between 6 and 7 Avenidas, along 7 or 9 avenida in Zone 1, or along 6 Avenida in zones 4 and 9. Taxis cost about $8 from Zone 1, slightly less from Zone 4 or Zone 9.

Service to Flores on Aerovías and Tapsa is provided from hangars on the east side of the airport, along Avenida Hincapie (see below). Bus 20 from downtown passes nearby, but since flights depart early, a taxi is a better bet.

Airlines

The main airlines operating to Guatemala City are:

Aviateca, Plaza Vivar, third floor, 10 Calle and 6 Avenida, Zone 1, tel. 64181, 320302.
COPA, 7 Avenida 6-52, Zone 4, tel. 316813, 318443.
Eastern, airport, tel. 317455 to 7
Iberia, 10 Calle 6-80, Zone 1, tel. 536555
KLM, airport, tel. 370222.
LACSA, airport, tel. 373905
Mexicana, 12 Calle 4-55, Zone 1, tel. 518824.
Pan American, 6 Avenida 11-41, Zone 1, tel. 82181.
SAHSA, 12 Calle 1-25, Zone 10, tel. 321071.
TACA, 10 Calle 5-00, Zone 1, tel. 80061 to 4.

Service to Flores (for onward travel to Tikal) is provided several times a week by Aviateca, and daily by Aerovías, Avenida Hincapie and 13 Calle, Zone 13, tel. 319663, and Tapsa, Avenida Hincapie, tel. 314860. A new route from Guatemala City to Flores, Belize and Cancún is projected.

See the "Getting to Guatemala" chapter for additional information about airline service.

Automobile Rental

Some of the conditions of car-rental in Guatemala are onerous. All companies charge a deductible of about $1800, only half of which can be covered by locally purchased insurance. Verify that your own policy will cover the deductible, or consider hiring a taxi for your excursions.

Rates vary from company to company, but are generally 25 to 50% higher than those in the U.S. and Canada. Among the companies are Tabarini (2 Calle A 7-30, Zone 10, tel. 316108), Avis (12 Calle 2-73, Zone 9, tel. 316990), National (7 Avenida 12-64, Zone 1, tel. 514952), Hertz (7 Avenida 14-76, Zone 9, tel. 312421) and Budget (tel. 316546). Some of these have agencies in the larger hotels and at the airport.

In the United States or Canada, call the toll-free numbers for Budget, Hertz or National/Tilden to reserve a car and confirm the latest rates.

Banks

Banking hours in Guatemala City are generally from 8:30 or 9 a.m. to 2:30 or 3 p.m., Monday through Friday. Some banks have after-hours windows open to 4:30 p.m. Most, but not all, commercial banks will cash a travelers check for you. If you can't find a place to cash a travelers check on a weekend, try the airport branch of the Banco de Guatemala. Downtown main offices of some banks are:

Banco de Guatemala, the national bank, Civic Center, Zone 1.
Bank of America, 5 Avenida and 10 Calle, Zone 1.
Lloyds Bank, 8 Avenida 10-67, Zone 1.
Banco Agrícola Mercantil, 7 Avenida 9-11, Zone 1
Banco Internacional, 7 Avenida 11-20, Zone 1.

A dozen other banks are listed in the telephone book under Bancos. Street money changers congregate around the post office in Zone 1, though the stores along 12 Calle nearby are a safer bet.

Books and Magazines in English and Other Languages

Zone 1: Arnel, 9 Calle 6-65, down a few steps from the street, has an excellent selection of books and magazines in English,

French and German. Prices are lower than at other bookstores. Zone 4: The IGA (Instituto Guatemalteco Americano) has a small book shop in its school at Ruta 1 and Vía 4, and there's a selection in the shop of the Conquistador Sheraton Hotel. Zones 9 and 10: The Book Nook in the Hotel Camino Real carries paperback bestsellers and one of the best magazine selections. For a larger choice of books, try La Plazuela at 12 Calle 6-14, where used books can also be traded; Geminis, at 6 Avenida 7-24; Cervantes, Reforma 13-70; and the large Tuncho bookstore on 12 Calle in the Plaza del Sol shopping center. Zone 15: Vista Hermosa Book Shop, 2 Calle 18-48, is well-stocked with all kinds of titles that you'd expect to find in an American bookstore, including children's books. Bus 1 from Zone 1 stops in front of the entrance.

Time and **Newsweek** are available at most of the large hotels and at many street newsstands. The **Miami Herald,** the **New York Times** and the **Wall Street Journal** are also distributed, usually the day after publication. You can find them at the Camino Real and Pan American hotels, among other places.

Local Buses

City buses run from about 4 a.m. to about 10:30 p.m., depending on the route. The fare is ten centavos during the day, more on some routes and after 8 p.m. and on holidays. Low city bus fares are a sacred cow, and attempts to raise them have periodically provoked mass protests. Most buses are clunkers, and service is insufficient. At rush hours, passengers hang precariously from the front and rear doors.

Bus stops are generally poorly marked, but one telltale sign is a newspaper-and-candy stand accompanied by a lineup of people.

If you choose to ride the buses, youl'll probably shuttle between zones 1, 4 and 9 on these lines:

Bus 2: Along 8 Avenida in Zone 1, Civic Center, along 6 Avenida and Ruta 6 in Zone 4, along Reforma in Zone 9 to the Obelisk. Also along 10 Avenida in Zone 1 to Reforma.

Bus 14: Same route as bus 2 as far as the Obelisk.

Bus 5: Along 8 Avenida and 4 Avenida in Zone 1, Civic Center, 6 Avenida in zones 4 and 9, 12 Calle in Zone 9 to Aurora Park. Bus 5U continues to the University of San Carlos in Zone 12. Any bus marked "Bolívar" takes a different route, going to Aurora Park by way of Avenida Bolívar. Bus 5-Aeropuerto continues to the airport.

Other buses for the major attractions are listed in the zone-by-zone guide.

Don't blame me if your bus doesn't appear where it's supposed to in Zone 1. The municipal government periodically orders route changes in an effort to decongest the city. Ask a cop or hotel clerk for directions.

Route numbers on buses are generic, and there are assorted variations. Bus 2A, for example, follows a different route from bus 2. Any bus with a sign reading "Terminal" will pass the inter-city bus terminal in Zone 4.

At night, after the buses have stopped running, you can get around by ruleteros, taxis and microbuses running along fixed routes until about 2 a.m. You're mainly interested in the ones following the same route as bus 2. Fare is 25 centavos and up, depending on the distance. To catch a ruletero, stand on a street corner and wait for a microbus, or for a taxi with its inside lights on. The driver or his helper will shout "Parque" or "Villa" or whatever the final destination is. If the driver shouts "taxi," he's not running on a regular route, and you'll have to negotiate your fare.

Buses to Mexico and Central America

Obtain your visa or tourist card at the consulate of Honduras, El Salvador or Mexico before leaving Guatemala City.

Bus companies operating to Talismán El Carmen (see index) on the Pacific coast route, will sell through tickets to Mexico City for $30 or so. The trip takes about 24 hours.

To go to Mexico via the mountain route (Comitán, San Cristóbal de Las Casas, etc.), see listings for La Mesilla.

To reach Honduras, take a bus to Esquipulas. There's frequent service from 19 Calle 8-18, Zone 1. Local buses provide service onward from Esquipulas to the borders of Honduras and El Salvador nearby.

Direct service from Guatemala City to San Salvador is available from Transportes Melva and Transportes Pezzarossi. Departures from the bus terminal in Zone 4 about about every hour from 6 a.m. to 2 p.m. Also Tica Bus, 9 Avenida 15-06, Zone 1, tel. 23432, one early departure, with pickup at your hotel.

Business Hours

Most stores and other places of business open at about 9 a.m., then close for a couple of hours starting at 12:30 or 1 p.m. They close for the day at 6 p.m. Few stores remain open during the lunch hour. On Saturdays, stores are open only during the morning. Offices of the government work a continuous eight-hour day, usually to 3:30 p.m., Monday through Friday. However, if you show up at a government office during lunch hours, you may find that the official you have to deal with is out.

Churches

There's no problem in finding a Catholic church anywhere in Guatemala. Here are some of the non-Catholic places of worship in the capital:

Baha'i, 3 Calle 4-54, Zone 1, tel. 29673.
Union Church of Guatemala, Plazuela España, Zone 9, tel. 316904.
St. James' Episcopal, Av. Castellana 40-06, Zone 8, tel.720852.
Latter-Day Saints (Mormon), 12 Calle 3-37, Zone 9.
Shaarei Binyamin Synagogue, 7 Avenida 13-51, Zone 9.
Magen David Synagogue, 7 Avenida 3-80, Zone2, tel. 20932.
Lutheran Church, 4 Calle 2-55, Zone 9, tel. 66652.

Doctors

If you need to see a doctor, call your embassy and get a list of approved doctors who speak your language. In an emergency, try the Centro Médico, a private hospital with an excellent reputation, located at 6 Avenida 3-47, Zone 10 (tel. 323555 to 323559). The Centro Médico has a 24-hour emergency service, and a staff of specialists in a number of fields. Note also that several pharmacies are open 24 hours on a rotating basis *(de turno)*. Check the list posted at the nearest pharmacy.

Driving

If you're driving your own car, make sure it's parked in a garage or a protected lot overnight, and, preferably, in the daytime as well.

Traffic lights are turned off after 8 p.m. When they're off, and during the day at intersections that don't have signals, traffic on avenidas has preference over traffic on calles. Be ready to brake for drivers ignoring the rules.

Embassies and Consulates

Most of the addresses given below are for consulates. For countries not listed, see the blue pages of the telephone directory under "Cuerpo Diplomático" and "Cuerpo Consular." Best time to visit any consulate is on a weekday morning. Many are closed afternoons and weekends.

Belgium, Reforma 13-70, Zone 9, tel. 316597.
Canada, 7 Avenida 11-59, Zone 9, tel. 321411.
China (Taiwan), 7 Avenida 1-20, Zone 4, tel. 324888.
Costa Rica, Reforma 8-60, Zone 9, tel. 320531.
El Salvador, 12 Calle 5-43, Zone 9, tel. 325848.
France, 16 Calle 4-53, Zone 10, tel. 373639.
Germany (West), Av. Américas 15-00, Zone 13, tel. 64695.
Holland, 15 Calle 1-91, Zone 10, tel. 374092.
Honduras, 15 Calle 9-16, Zone 10, tel. 371921.
Israel, 13 Avenida 14-07, Zone 10, tel. 371334.
Italy, 8 Calle 3-14, Zone 10, tel. 62128
Japan, Ruta 6 8-19, Zone 4, tel. 319666.
Mexico, 13 Calle 7-30, Zone 9, tel. 63573.
Nicaragua, 2 Calle 15-95, Zone 13, tel. 65613.
Panama, Via 5 4-50, Zone 4, tel. 320763.
Spain, 4 Calle 7-73, Zone 9, tel. 318784.
Sweden, 4 Avenida 12-70, Zone 10, tel. 62467.
Switzerland, 4 Calle 7-73, Zone 9, tel. 313725.
United Kingdom, Vía 5 4-50, Zone 4.
U.S.A., Reforma 7-01, Zone 10, tel. 311541.
Venezuela, 8 Calle 0-56, Zone 9, tel. 316505.

Entertainment

Concerts and sporting events are advertised in the Prensa Libre newspaper. See also Movies, below.

The city has two especially interesting performance areas, the National Theater in the San José fortress, and the Teatro Abril, at 9 Avenida and 14 Calle, a recently restored neoclassical building which makes extensive use of such fine local materials as marble and mahogany.

Gambling

There's no big-time gambling in Guatemala. Content yourself with the slot machines in the arcades along 6 Avenida in Zone 1, and with the lotteries. Lottery tickets range in price from 10 centavos to a couple of quetzales. The payoff ranges from getting your money back (less a small tax) to a small fortune. Winning numbers are published in the newspapers the day after the drawing. Lottery-ticket sellers are ubiquitous, but in case you don't run across one, try the booths in the Rubio arcade off 6 Avenida between 8 and 9 calles, or at Concordia Park, 6 Avenida and 14 Calle, both in Zone 1.

Laundries
Your hotel can arrange to do your laundry, but prices are often outrageous, so check first. There are plenty of commercial laundries and dry cleaners around town, many with rapid service. If you prefer to put your stuff in the machines yourself, try the laundries at 4 Avenida 13-89, Zone 1; and Ruta 6 7-53, Zone 4, opposite the Triángulo building.

Libraries
For books in English, try the library of IGA (Instituto Guatemalteco Americano) at the corner of Ruta 1 and Vía 4 in Zone 4. The collection is on a par with that of a high school library in the States, though there's a good selection of current American newspapers and magazines. To borrow books, you'll have to become a paying member.

For serious research, there's the Biblioteca Nacional on the Central Park; the library of the Banco de Guatemala in the Civic Center (best reading room in town); and the poorly catalogued Sociedad de Geografía e Historia, in the basement of the National Library. Most of the books are in Spanish, of course.

If your interest is textiles, try the library of the Museo Ixchel, 4 Avenida 16-27, Zone 10, where you'll find a large photo and manuscript collection, as well as textile samples and material on weaving techniques.

In Antigua, the library of the Centro de Investigaciones Regionales de Mesoamérica (5 Calle Oriente no. 2E, Apartado Postal 336), collects journals dealing with Guatemalan archaeology and ethnology, as well as books covering all aspects of Guatemala.

Maps
Serviceable maps of Guatemala and of the capital are available from the office of the Guatemala Tourist Commission in Zone 4. For detailed maps, go to the Military Geographic Institute

(Instituto Geográfico Militar) at Avenida Las Américas 5-76, Zone 13. The institute publishes a good general map of Guatemala, a number of geological maps, and detailed maps of the country in 250 small sections. If you're planning to do any hiking in the countryside, these detailed maps are a must. Many are not available to the general public, but can be consulted at the institute. From Zone 1, take bus 20; or bus 2 or bus 14 to the Obelisco.

Movies

Admission charges range upward from about 50 cents U.S., depending on the movie house and the feature. Current attractions are listed in the daily newspapers. Addresses of cinemas are rarely given, so ask at your hotel. Many movie houses are located along 6 Avenida in Zone 1. Sound tracks are usually in the original language, with subtitles in Spanish.

Post Office

The main post office is located at the corner of 7 Avenida and 12 Calle, Zone 1. To mail a letter, go to one of the counters on either side of the stairway that faces the entrance. Have your letters weighed and buy the proper postage. Deposit letters along the wall to the right. To mail a package, go all the way to the rear, where you'll see a Parcel Post sign in English. To pick up General Delivery mail, look for the *Lista de Correos* sign to the right of the stairway. To send telegrams within Guatemala, turn right just inside the entrance. See also the practical information section of this book.

Shopping

For some general comments about what's available for purchase in Guatemala, and about bargaining in the markets, see Shopping and Bargaining in the practical information section of this book.

In Guatemala City, the main attractions are handicrafts, especially fabrics woven by hand in the various regions of the country. It would take much time and searching to visit all the towns where the best *huipiles* (blouses), *pantalones* (trousers), *camisas* (shirts), *fajas* (sashes), *individuales* and *servilletas* (place mats and napkins), *ponchos* (blankets), and *caites* (sandals) are made, but these items from all parts of the country are available in Guatemala City's markets and handicraft stores, along with pottery, incense burners, baskets from El Salvador, clay pipes,

81

wooden statues, and countless other articles. The prices, of course, are a bit higher than at the point of origin, but not that much higher, for a Guatemalan trader does not usually make allowance for the time and trouble it takes to seek out and transport goods. The main center for native articles is the Central Market, where a visitor can spend many an hour gazing at and bargaining over the wares. Also interesting, if you can put up with the smells and confusion of the neighborhood, is the Terminal Market in Zone 4, where merchandise is more utilitarian. The National Handicraft Market, off the beaten track in Aurora Park near the airport, in Zone 13, is targeted at tourists.

Much of what you'll see in the markets is also available in handicraft stores (*tiendas típicas*, or typical shops), where you can sometimes bargain. Some stores specialize in better-quality weaving, which the owners must search out or contract for, and the prices are fixed and higher. Among stores with a good selection of textiles are Lin Canola, 5 Calle 9-60, Zone 1, near the Central Market; and Sombol, at Avenida La Reforma and 13 Calle, Zone 9. And there are many, many others. In some stores you'll find fine native textiles made up into stylish garments that can be worn at home and work in North America and Europe, which is often not the case with garments bought in the markets. You pay for the styling, of course, but usually not excessively. Among such shops are Dzunún, 1 Avenida 13-29, Zone 10, in the Zona Viva (also an art gallery and somewhat avant-garde), and Brigi, in the Triángulo building in Zone 4.

Antiques—coins, ironwork, furniture and statues of saints—can also be found at some of the shops in Zone 1, especially 4 Ahau, 11 Calle 4-53, and in shops on 12 Calle between 3 and 5 avenidas. Nice to look at, even if you decide you can't lug the items home. Another locale for old items is along 5 Avenida between 8 and 10 calles. Beware of items of recent manufacture, and of pre-Columbian artifacts, which could be confiscated at U.S. customs.

Don't overlook non-handicraft items. Cotton towels and bathrobes from El Salvador in attractive patterns are available at a fraction of what you would pay at home. Visit a supermarket if you have the time and stock up on coffee. Café León, Café Mocca and BBB are good brands of ground coffee. A few stores have whole beans, which are less subject to losing their flavor (coffee is packed in cellophane). Also pick up peppers, hot sauces and exotic canned items, such as hearts of palm. Save your liquor

purchases for the duty-free shop at the airport, where good local
rum goes for about three dollars per bottle.

Taxis

Cabs have no meters, so many drivers will try to charge you
more than the going rates. Even if you're not taken, you'll find
that fares are quite high for this part of the world. There's little
competition from the overworked public transit system.

Always agree on the fare before you get in. A trip of a few
blocks will cost a couple of dollars. Figure about two dollars per
kilometer for longer runs, and $8 from the airport to any hotel,
even those only a kilometer or two away. If you bargain hard, you
may ride for less. Ask for advice about fares at your hotel, or
from residents.

Taxis are hard to spot. They look like other cars, except that
their license plates begin with "A." Best place to pick one up is in
front of the major hotels, or at the taxi stands located at the
Central Park or Concordia Park (15 Calle and 6 Avenida) in Zone
1. The alternative, if you're carrying luggage, is to telephone a
taxi stand. Some of the numbers are: 80531, 534124, 29290
(Central Park, Zone 1); 26213 (Concordia Park, Zone 1); 62882
(Conquistador Sheraton Hotel); 67216 (Bus Terminal); 681872
(Hotel Camino Real); 61686, 61975 (Airport).

Ruleteros—jitney taxis running along fixed routes—are
mentioned in this section under Buses.

Telegrams

Telegrams within the country should be sent from the main post
office, 7 Avenida and 12 Calle. The cost is quite low, about 3
cents U.S. per word. Telegrams for foreign countries are handled
by Guatel, 8 Avenida and 12 Calle.

Telephones

Coin telephones are in short supply. Good places to find them
are pharmacies, the lobbies of some hotels, and outside the Guatel
building on 7 Avenida between 12 and 13 calles, Zone 1. Place
coins of 5, 10 and 25 centavos on the rack to be swallowed as
required. Long-distance calls within Guatemala can be dialed
direct from coin telephones, and this is often easier than going
through a hotel operator. Use 25-centavo coins in this case. Dial
0 plus a six-digit number.

Many small stores will rent their telephones to you at charges higher than those at coin phones.

Long-distance calls to foreign countries, and to places within Guatemala that don't have automatic telephone service, can also be dialed direct (have a pocketful of coins!), or placed from your hotel or from the offices of Guatel: 8 Avenida and 12 Calle, Zone 1; Avenida La Castellana and 39 Calle, Zone 8 (near the bus terminal); and at the airport.

You may see a listing such as this for a telephone number: 456722 a 8, or 456722 to 8. This means that all the six-digit numbers from 456722 to 456728 will connect you with the place indicated. You'll have to dial them individually if one of the numbers is busy.

Some emergency and service numbers:

120: Police
121: Long distance within Guatemala
122: Volunteer Fire Department (Bomberos Voluntarios)
123: Municipal Fire Department (Bomberos Municipales)
124: Telephone number information
125: Red Cross (Cruz Roja)
126: Time of day
127: International Telegrams
171: International long distance
174: Information for international long distance

Tourist Office

For travel information, stop by the information desk at the Guatemala Tourist Commission (Instituto Guatemalteco de Turismo), 7 Avenida 1-17, Zone 4 (south of the Civic Center), or phone 311333 (to 47). Free maps are available, and personnel at the reception desk will attempt to answer your questions. Hours are 8 a.m. to 4:30 p.m. on weekdays, to 1 p.m. on Saturdays.

Trains

Passenger service is provided from the station at 18 Calle and 9 Avenida, Zone 1, to Puerto Barrios on the Caribbean and Tecún Umán on the border with Mexico. Service is slow—both trips take all day—with many stops at intermediate stations. But if you're a train freak, you'll want to buy your ticket, pack a hamper of food, and enjoy the ride. These trains may not operate for much longer.

Trains for Tecún Umán, operating by way of Escuintla,

Escuintla, Mazatenango and Coatepeque, leave twice weekly (recently on Tuesday and Saturday) at about 7 a.m. A train for Puerto Barrios, operating by way of El Progreso, Zacapa and Quiriguá, leaves three times weekly (recently Tuesday, Thursday and Saturday) at 7 a.m. In both cases the fare is less than $3. Return trains operate the same days. Trains have occasionally operated from Zacapa to San Salvador. Verify all schedules before you travel.

Water

The tap water in Guatemala City is chemically treated and safe to drink. If you don't like the taste, stick to bottled mineral water or beer. Some parts of the city suffer from periodic water shortages, but the better hotels have their own water-storage and purification systems.

Weather

Average daily high temperature during the year in Guatemala City is 25° Centigrade (77° Fahrenheit). Average low is 13° C (55° F). Warmest time of the year is April, when the average high is 27° C (80° F) and the average low 15° C (59° F). The coldest time is December, with an average range from 23° C (73° F) down to 12° C (54° F). In other words, temperatures are mild, and don't vary too much during the year. Occasional cold and windy spells occur in November and December. Rainfall is another matter. From November through April, there's hardly any rainfall at all. June and September are the wettest months of the rainy season in the capital, with about 260 mm (10 inches) of rain. Even in these wet months, it only rains two out of three days, and then for only a few hours.

ONE-DAY TRIPS FROM GUATEMALA CITY

Listed here are some of the places which you can conveniently reach during one-day excursions from the capital. Tikal, Antigua, Lake Atitlán and other spots are worth stays of at least a few days. But if you're in the country for only a short time, and want to get to know a variety of places, you might have to content yourself with short trips from Guatemala City.

The available means for reaching each place and returning in a day are given in parentheses. For details, consult the index. The

85

list is *more or less* in order of interest.

Tikal (plane)
Antigua (bus, tour, car)
Lake Atitlán (tour, car)
Chichicastenango (tour, car)
Quiriguá (tour, car)
Copán, Honduras (tour, car)
La Democracia, Escuintla (bus, tour, car)
Río Dulce (as part of a Quiriguá tour)
San Pedro Sacatepéquez (bus, car)
San Juan Sacatepéquez (bus, car)
Mixco Viejo (tour, car)
Iximché (bus, tour, car)
Pacaya Volcano (bus, tour, car)
Amatitlán (bus, tour, car) Puerto San José (bus, tour, car)

TOURS AND TRAVEL AGENCIES

Whether or not you take a tour depends on how much time you have, the money you have to spend, and whether you're up to traveling around the country on ordinary buses. The latter can be uncomfortable and disconcerting if you're alone and find it difficult to be continuously among people who don't speak your language.

It also depends on where you're going. For travel to the scenic highlands of western Guatemala, it's more enjoyable, and usually cheaper, if two or more persons share a rented car and make overnight stops in Antigua, Panajachel and Chichicastenango. On the other hand, tours are a good bet for long one-day trips from Guatemala City to the Pacific Coast, Copán and Tikal.

Tour prices don't vary too much from one company to another. Some samples of approximate prices for tours lasting a day or less: Guatemala City, $15; Antigua, $15 to $25; Mixco Viejo, $30; Chichicastenango and Lake Atitlán, $30; Quiriguá and Río Dulce, $50; Copán, $60; Tikal, $150.

When a tour covers a few towns or archaeological sites and includes overnight accommodations, the price rises considerably. Examples: Chichicastenango–Lake Atitlán–Antigua (two days), $100; Tikal (overnight), $200.

Among the companies offering tours and other travel services are:

86

Panamundo Guatemala Travel Service, 7 Avenida 14-44, Zone 9, tel. 313188. Good for fishing and archaeological tours, as well as standard destinations.
Clark Tours, 7 Avenida 6-53, Zone 4, tel. 310213. Most experienced travel agency.
ECA Tours, 5 Avenida 13-16, Zone 9, tel. 310540.
Turismo Kim' Arrin, Vía 5 4-50, Zone 4, tel. 324931
Ney's Tours, 13 Calle 0-56, Zone 10, tel. 370884.
Maya Tours, 6 Avenida 9-62, Zone 1, tel. 84479.

American Express has a representative agency at Reforma 9-00, Zone 9, tel. 311311.

NEARBY TOWNS

The department of Guatemala includes sixteen minicipios, or townships, besides Guatemala City. A few towns and one major archaeological site in adjacent departments are also readily accessible from the capital.

MIXCO
Population 11,544 (township 197,741; 11% indigenous); Altitude 1739 meters; Languages: Spanish, Cakchiquel and Pokomam; Fiestas: last Sunday of January and August 4; "Cloud-covered place"

Mixco was founded in 1525 after the Spanish conqueror Pedro de Alvarado laid siege to and captured the Pokomam capital now known as Mixco Viejo. The Indian survivors of the battle were forced to migrate to the present-day site of Mixco, where the Spanish would better be able to control them. For centuries, Mixco was a majority Indian town, but it is now part of the metropolitan area of the capital, its population consisting mainly of working-class Ladinos.
Corn and beans are raised in the few parts of the township that remain rural, and in the urban areas there's some light industry. The land here is craggy and broken. The most outstanding feature of Mixco is the large domed church, which travelers can readily see as they pass through on the way from Guatemala City to the western highlands. Mixco was the scene of bloody battles during

the civil war of 1829, and suffered severely during the 1976 earthquake.

SAN PEDRO SACATEPEQUEZ
Population 5358 (township 12,471; 93% indigenous); Altitude 2102 meters; Languages: Cakchiquel and Spanish; Fiesta: June 29; Market: Every day, but especially Friday. Kilometer 20.

San Pedro Sacatepéquez is an agricultural center whose farmers sell their produce in the markets of Guatemala City. The textiles woven here are particularly beautiful, especially the women's huipiles, which from a distance appear to consist of hundreds of bright watercolor splotches painted on cloth. The region was occupied by the Sacatepéquez nation at the time of the Spanish conquest, hence the name Sacatepéquez became attached to many towns in the area. The market is worth a visit.

Buses run frequently to San Pedro from the terminal in zone 4.

SAN JUAN SACATEPEQUEZ
Population: 6726 (township 49,848; 85% indigenous); Altitude 1845 meters; Languages: Cakchiquel and Spanish; Fiesta: June 24; Market: Every day, but especially Friday and Sunday; Kilometer 31.

Largest Indian township in the department of Guatemala, San Juan, like San Pedro, supplies produce to the capital. Terraced slopes planted to a variety of flowers, for sale in the markets of Guatemala City and for shipment abroad by air, make the area around San Juan particularly colorful. Women's huipiles are woven in purple and yellow, and many bear the figures of two-headed eagles and horses. Women will often wear a second huipil to ward off the morning and evening chill.

Buses run frequently to San Juan from the terminal in Zone 4.

The hills along the road from Guatemala through San Pedro and San Juan are thickly forested, and many residents of the capital drive out this way to spend weekends at their country homes, or to enjoy the scenery and a meal at one of the roadside restaurants. A few kilometers after San Juan, where the dirt road leads off toward Mixco Viejo, the landscape starts to change. Vegetation is less abundant, except in river valleys, and the terrain is more broken. The high ridge of the Sierra de Chuacús is visible to the north. There are only scattered small settlements along the winding road.

MIXCO VIEJO RUINS
Kilometer 60

Mixco Viejo was the capital of the Pokomam nation, one of the warring peoples of pre-Conquest Guatemala. Dramatically set on a hilltop that commands the surrounding valleys, the city was a ceremonial center and also a bastion of defense.

Spanish forces laid siege to Mixco in 1525. For three months they tried to starve the warriors in the fortress, but the Indians held out, receiving supplies, according to legend, through a secret tunnel. Finally, the allies of the Pokomams abandoned the fight and revealed to the Spaniards the entrance of the tunnel. Alvarado blocked the supply route, and managed to storm the fortress by way of the only other access, a narrow and treacherous trail. The inhabitants were evacuated to the present-day Mixco near Guatemala City, and the fortress destroyed.

The site consists of pyramids, observation and defense platforms, ball courts, altars and walls. The buildings date from the fourteenth and fifteenth centuries, but older walls have been found under the platforms in the area called Group A. Many pyramids show Mexican stylistic elements that were typical of the period just before the conquest, such as double stairways and twin, flat-roofed temples. No tombs have been found at the site, and archaeologists suggest that bodies might have been cremated, which would have been an unusual practice in the highlands. One of the more interesting details is a ballcourt marker in Group C, a copy of the original, which is in the shape of a snake with a human head in its mouth.

Excavations at Mixco Viejo were begun in 1954 by a team of archaeologists from the Museum of Man in Paris. Most of the structures were rebuilt, but the restoration work collapsed during the 1976 earthquake. New restoration work has been underway. A plaster model at the site gives an idea of what archaeologists think Mixco viejo looked like when it was occupied.

Despite the damage wrought by the 1976 earthquake, there's much to see at Mixco Viejo, and the setting is spectacular. If you're driving, it's an easy trip via San Juan Sacatepéquez, though the last part of the route is unpaved and winding. Turn left at the junction just after kilometer 59.

Buses of the La Fortuna line leave from the terminal in Guatemala City for Mixco Viejo at 10 a.m. Before you go, verify that the bus will return the same day. The bus drops you at the junction near kilometer 59 at 1 p.m. From there you have to walk uphill another kilometer to the ruins. To return, walk back to kilometer 58 to catch the bus, which might leave as early as 3 p.m. Obviously, this doesn't give you much time. On the other hand, if you've got the equipment, the ruins are an ideal place to camp out. Nobody minds if you unroll your sleeping bag under one of the thatched shelters, as long as you leave the site clean. It's a lovely place for watching the sunset and sunrise, and for thinking yourself back into the times when religious rituals were performed at the temples here. Water and soft drinks are available at the site, but bring your own food.

CHUARRANCHO
Population 4122 (township 6744; 81% indigenous); Altitude: 1350 meters; Languages: Cakchiquel and Spanish; Fiesta: June 29.

Chuarrancho is a very poor and quite traditional Indian town, whose inhabitants are devoted to farming, woodcutting and making charcoal. Nearby is Cerro Las Minas, a hill where ceremonies are performed to seek rain in time of drought. The hill is sacred, and its sides are not cultivated for fear of causing the earth to rumble.

South of Guatemala City

AMATITLAN
Population 20,407; Altitude 1190 meters; Fiesta: May 3; "Place of the amate trees"; Kilometer 25

Located along the shore of the lake of the same name, Amatitlán is a favorite weekend resort for residents of Guatemala City. The lake—11 kilometers long, 3.5 kilometers wide, with a maximum depth of 40 meters—is a beautiful sight, with hills on the north and the volcano Pacaya towering over to the south. Hot springs bubble up from the earth all over the area, and at many points along the highway to Escuintla, you'll see steam coming out of the ground. But the lake has not been dealt with kindly by recent generations. A railroad crosses it at the center, its narrowest part, and a power plant belches smoke along its shore.

Its waters are polluted.

Most of the area along the shore is privately owned and occupied by houses of the wealthy. One of the few places where visitors may approach the waterside is near the town of Amatitlán, at a small rocky beach lined with cheap eateries, and where boats offer rides on the lake. Bathhouses nearby offer one-hour sessions in hot tubs for a dollar or so. A highway circles the lake, and makes for a pleasant drive.

The area around Amatitlán was occupied before the Conquest. There are ruins about one kilometer east of the town center, consisting of mounds and the remains of ball courts, which appear to have been occupied from 500 to 800 A.D. The area produced cochineal during colonial times, and the town is now a processing center for coffee, sugar and dairy products.

From the shores of the lake, you can take an aerial tramway to United Nations Park (Parque Naciones Unidas), or you can drive up. The main asset of the park is the panoramic view of the lake far below. It's also somewhat of a lovers lane. Pleasant for a picnic and for hiking, though you'll have to search around for the parts that are uncrowded and unlittered. Small admission fee.

Trailer Parks

The nearest trailer parks to Guatemala City are along the highway outside Amatitlán. Thermal swimming pools are located near or on the sites of all three. Rates run from 50 cents for backpackers to several dollars for motor homes.

La Red Trailer Park, kilometer 33. If you're not staying at the park, you can use the pools for a small fee.
Las Hamacas, kilometer 32. Pools are also available here for day use.
Auto Mariscos, kilometer 33. Several hookups behind the seafood restaurant.

Buses for Amatitlán leave frequently from the corner of 20 Calle and 3 Avenida, Zone 1, Guatemala City. Trains for Tecún Umán also stop here.

SAN VICENTE PACAYA
Population 3483; Altitude 1625 meters; Fiesta: January 22

A small town in a coffee-growing area, San Vicente Pacaya is located on the slopes of the Pacaya volcano, which is the main attraction. The volcano is active, and from time to time spews lava from its cone. A trail starting near the school leads up the volcano's slopes, and on a clear day, when the volcano is belching, you can. see some pretty nifty fireworks. It's a nice climb even when the peak is shrouded in clouds. The newer cone of the volcano can be viewed from the old cone above it. Try to find out before you come out whether the volcano has been acting up. You might ask the drivers of the buses for San Vicente Pacaya at the bus terminal, or simply look south on a clear night.

Buses for San Vicente Pacaya leave from the terminal in Zone 4 in the late morning and return the next day. It's more convenient to go in the early morning, either by driving or by taking an Escuintla bus to the junction for San Vicente and walking up to town. This will give you time to climb on the slopes before returning to Guatemala City in the evening.

PALIN
Population 8362 (township 14,140; 37% indigenous); Altitude 1148 meters; Languages: Pokomam and Spanish; Fiesta: July 30; Market Days: Wednesday and Friday; "Wind-blown place"; kilometer 40

On the slopes of the volcano Agua, Palín is a center for the production of furniture and toy marimbas. In its plaza is a massive centuries-old ceiba tree, and nearby is a colonial church. Palín used to be known for the fabrics woven by its women, but native weaving has now all but disappeared. A dirt road leads from Palín to Antigua. Along the way is a branch road which climbs the slopes of Agua. Best strategy is to visit Palín on a Wednesday, the busier market day, while on the way to the Pacific lowlands.

Buses: Take any Escuintla bus from the terminal in Zone 4. Also train service on the Tecún Umán line.

North of Guatemala City:

CHINAUTLA
Population 2027 (township 41,682; 9% indigenous); altitude 1220 meters; Languages: Spanish and Pokomam; Fiesta: December 6

Chinautla, just a few kilometers north of Guatemala City, is a quiet, rural place. The only access is by a dirt road that winds through a narrow, forested canyon. The town is little more than a wide spot in the canyon, and, over the years, it has been hit hard by floods, as well as by the 1976 earthquake. The village was originally populated in colonial times by Indian allies of the vanquished inhabitants of Mixco Viejo.

Chinautla is famous for its cream-colored pottery, particularly pieces in the form of angels and doves, and pieces with plant motifs in red and gray, though the industry has been in decline. To the southwest are the remains of a pre-Conquest City, surrounded on three sides by canyons. Finds of obsidian and flint arrowheads suggest that battles took place there.

There isn't much to do in town, but getting here is a pleasant and quick trip by bus, and worth it just for the ride through the canyon. Take bus BC from the Central Park in Guatemala City to the market on Calle Martí in Zone 6, and catch a bus from there for Chinautla. There's one at 7 a.m. and then about every hour from noon to 5 p.m. Buses for San Antonio Las Flores, a hamlet farther up the road, will also take you to Chinautla.

Southeast of Guatemala City:

SAN JOSE PINULA
Population 5296; Altitude 1752 meters; Fiesta: March 19

An agricultural town most noted for Pavón, the penal farm on its outskirts, The church is said to have been built over an old silver mine. If you're going out to see a friend in prison, you'll find direct buses from the terminal in Zone 4. If you want to see Pavón from the inside, read "How to Get into Trouble" in the chapter of practical information.

The Western Highlands

The western highlands are the most densely inhabited part of Guatemala, and the home of most of the Indian population. Stretching from Guatemala City to the border of Mexico, the area includes the great mountain peaks of the Sierra Madre and the Cuchumatanes range, and temperate and near-tropical valleys. Guatemala's chain of volcanoes runs parallel to the Pacific, forming the southern rim of the region.

In the western highlands is the most dramatic scenery of Guatemala, including Lake Atitlán, surrounded by volcanoes and precipitous mountains, one of the most beautiful lakes anywhere. Roads climb to frosty heights, drop down in a few kilometers to plateaus planted with corn and wheat, and plunge into narrow valleys, their sides carpeted with trees, streams rushing through at the bottom. Spotted here and there through the landscape are clusters of whitewashed adobe houses with red tiled roofs, little hamlets of people dressed all alike in traditional clothing.

The highlands are naturally forested. But over the years, the stands of cypress, cedar, oak and pine have been thinned out and cut down to create small corn patches. In the process, many of the wild animals that once roamed the area have disappeared. At the higher altitudes, the land is bare and cold, and used for the grazing of sheep. But lower down, the climate is the eternal springtime about which Guatemalans boast. In the rainy season, from May to October, the hills are green with maturing crops. After the harvest is in and the rains cease, wildflowers bloom at the roadsides, and the green of the fields gradually fades to golden brown, except in the forests and in a few places where the water of streams is diverted to irrigate vegetable plots.

Most of Guatemala's rivers rise in the western highlands. Those flowing into the Pacific are all relatively short. The rivers running down the northeastern slope wander long distances to the

Caribbean, and across the western border and north to the Gulf of Mexico.

Much of Guatemalan history has unfolded in the countryside and towns of the area. The pre-Columbian nations made war upon each other, and finally fell one by one to the Spanish invaders. Colonial Antigua endured for 200 years as one of the great cities of America, ruling over an empire that stretched to Panama. Indians subjected to the rule of outsiders slowly adapted to a new way of life, and from time to time rose up in rebellion against their masters. Revolutionaries plotted against the authoritarian regimes of Guatemala in the nineteenth century, marched through the highlands, and made their triumphant entry into the capital.

The highlands shake and rattle and change, slowly and suddenly. Earthquakes come periodically as the underlying structures of the land shift. Minor tremors are a feature of everyday life. Long-dormant volcanoes awake, blow off their tops, and show a new form when they settle down again, and other volcanoes stay in continuous eruption. Hot water and steam seep out of the earth at innumerable points.

But despite the inevitable activity of the earth, the sense of the highlands is one of tranquility, of small rural towns and much tradition and color and set ways in the people. Men walk along the roadsides carrying heavy bundles as they make their rounds from market to market, as their fathers and grandfathers did. The old tend flocks of sheep, and in the fields, one sees the same laborious clearing and planting and cultivation by hand that has gone on for centuries.

Highway Notes

The main route from Guatemala City westward through the highlands is the Inter-American Highway, CA-1. Except for a few stretches, it's a winding road, climbing from one valley up over a pass and down to the next valley and the next major town. The road is in good condition, paved and four lanes wide to the junction for Antigua, then two lanes wide to the border. The scenery is breathtaking everywhere.

The steep grades require frequent gear shifting. Nighttime travel can be difficult, especially in the mountain heights where fog rolls in and reduces traffic to a crawl. The best plan is to confine your driving to the daylight hours and early evening.

To get out to the Inter-American Highway from Guatemala

City, follow any avenida southward to Boulevard Liberación, turn right, and keep going. From Zone 1, you can also follow 8 Calle westward onto the Periférico, the expressway that rings the city. Take the Mixco exit onto Calzada Roosevelt, an extension of Boulevard Liberación.

The Inter-American Highway climbs out of and overlooks Guatemala City before dropping down to San Lucas Sacatepéquez at kilometer 30. Here, a branch road snakes south through a canyon to Antigua. The main road continues toward Lake Atitlán and Chichicastenango.

ANTIGUA GUATEMALA

Population 15,801 (township 27,258); Altitude 1530 meters; Fiestas: Holy Week, July 25; Market: Every day; Kilometer 45

In a valley surrounded by mountains, and by the towering volcanoes Agua, Fuego and Acatenango, lies Antigua Guatemala. Today it is a pleasant city of cobblestone streets, houses and businesses with colonial-style facades and tile roofs, and of restored and vegetation-covered ruins of churches, palaces, convents and mansions. Just over 200 years ago, it was Santiago de los Caballeros de Guatemala, along with Lima and Mexico City one of the major centers of Spanish power in the Americas. A teeming city of more than 60,000 people, Santiago was full of political intrigue, wealth and miserable poverty, noble ideals and pervasive corruption. As capital of the Kingdom and Captaincy-General of Guatemala, it was the home of an elite of civic officials and ecclesiastical princes who enriched themselves, the Church and the crown, as they exploited the riches of the hinterland and the labor of the native peoples.

Santiago de los Caballeros was founded amid disaster, lived an existence of intermittent calamities, and ended in catastrophe. The previous capital had been located at the place now called Ciudad Vieja, on the slopes of the volcano Agua. On the night of September 10, 1541, shortly after the news of the death of Pedro de Alvarado had arrived from Mexico, after fires had raged through parts of the city, after Alvarado's widow had seized power, and torrential rains had battered Santiago for three days, an earthquake shook the capital and caused the volcano Agua to release the water dammed up in its crater. The city was washed away.

The survivors founded the new Santiago on March 10, 1543, in the neighboring Panchoy valley. In 1566 it received the title *Muy Noble y Muy Leal Ciudad de Santiago de los Caballeros de Guatemala,* Most Noble and Loyal City of St. James of the Knights of Guatemala. Churches and convents grew in number and opulence. The city's illustrious residents included Bishop Francisco Marroquín, a defender of the rights of the poor and founder of the first school in the capital; Friar Bartolomé de las Casas, missionary and promoter of laws to protect the Indians; the historian and chronicler Francisco Antonio de Fuentes y Guzmán;

97

and the poet Rafael Landívar. A printing press, the third in the Americas, was installed in 1660, and a newspaper, the *Gazeta de Goathemala,* began publication in 1729. The University of San Carlos, sixth in the hemisphere, was founded in 1681. By 1773, the city had 38 churches, as well as monasteries, convents, and numerous other ecclesiastical structures.

But for all its cultural progress and growing wealth, Santiago lived through few long periods of peace. The early bishops and friars concerned with the conditions of the people gave way to those more preoccupied with ministering to the wealthy and administering the riches of the church. The Church orders battled each other for power. A growing class of native-born merchants, deprived of the privileges of the Spanish-born, clashed with civil and Church authorities. Drought and epidemic cut into the population, crime rose steadily, riots broke out, the volcano Fuego erupted intermittently and poured out lava and ashes, and more than a dozen earthquakes left many of the inhabitants buried in the wreckage of their houses.

In June 1773 the final catastrophe began. A series of earthquakes shook Santiago, and many of the citizens abandoned the city for the countryside. The tremors continued into the next month, and on July 29, a sharp shock forced most of the remaining population into the streets. Shortly afterward, a new tremor greater than all the others left the city in ruins. Aftershocks continued for months, rains melted adobe walls, food and water were in short supply, and disease ravaged the survivors.

Amid the rubble of the capital, the Church and civil officials battled for supremacy. The governor, Martín de Mayorga y Mendiente, set about finding a new site for the capital, while Archbishop Pedro Cortez y Larraz sought to have Santiago rebuilt. Mayorga moved the government to the neighboring Ermita valley in September 1773, and in January 1775 formally ordered the abandonment of Santiago. Nevertheless, reconstruction had already started, and the archbishop refused to budge. The king of Spain finally approved the relocation of the capital in July 1775, and on January 2, 1776, the city of New Guatemala of the Assumption was formally founded. Mayorga ordered that doors, gratings, balconies, beams and everything else that was moveable be taken from Santiago to build the new capital.

Most of the inhabitants eventually relocated, though Santiago was never entirely abandoned. For a while, the city was important in the production of cochineal, a dye made from an insect which fed on the cactus cultivated in the area. A new prosperity and a rise in population came late in the nineteenth century, with the introduction of coffee cultivation to the region. People began to refer to the city as Antigua Guatemala—Old Guatemala—which in time was adopted as its official name. Some of the old mansions were repaired and reoccupied, and in the twentieth century, as Guatemalans began to appreciate the esthetic values of the old city, hardly changed since its destruction, major restoration work began, finally converting Antigua into today's living colonial monument.

Layout

Streets in the central part of Antigua are for the most part numbered. East-west streets are called *calles.* They bear the suffix *poniente* or *oriente* depending on whether they're west or east of the Cathedral. North-south streets are *avenidas* and carry a suffix of *norte* or *sur* (north or south). As a point of reference, the Cathedral is on the east side of the central park, or main square. Some streets are also marked with old colonial names.

Tourist Office

The tourist office in Antigua should be one of your first stops. Mr. Benjamín García López, who's often at the desk, will give you a map of the city and orient you to the major colonial monuments, tell you ghost stories, mention any new restaurants and hotels that have opened, try to find you a room in a private home when the hotels are filled up, and in general will make you feel at home. The tourist office is on the ground floor of the Palace of the Captains-General, not far from the Cathedral on the south side of the central park.

HOTELS

Ramada Antigua, 9 Calle and Carretera Ciudad Vieja, tel. 320011. 155 rooms. $36-$59 single/$42-$59 double.
Located on the road to Ciudad Vieja, in a modernesque-colonial complex. Farther from the center of town than other hotels (a walk of ten minutes or so), but the facilities are the best in Antigua: extensive gardens, two pools, tennis courts, a children's play area, sauna, numerous shops, and a large restaurant and bar.

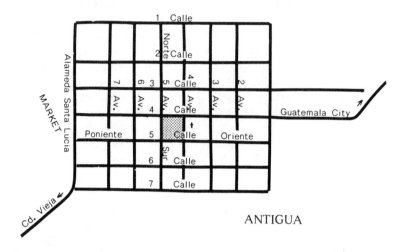

ANTIGUA

Every room has a fireplace, and views to the surrounding misted volcanoes are enchanting. Recommendable as a base for travel around Guatemala, or simply as a winter vacation resort.

Hotel Antigua, 8 Calle Oriente and 4 Avenida Sur, tel. 320331. 60 rooms. $56/$70.
Distinguished , colonial-style, with extensive gardens, fireplaces in all rooms. Lovely atmosphere. The hotel comes alive on Sunday, when a luncheon buffet of native and American food is accompanied by marimba music. Pool, restaurant, bar, shops, parking.

✳ **Posada de Don Rodrigo,** 5 Avenida Norte No. 9, tel. 320291. 33 rooms. $21/$28.
This comfortable inn, near the center of town, is a restored and historic colonial house, the Casa de Los Leones, named originally for the lions sculptured in stone by the doorway. The furnishings and decorative details around the several cobbled and gardened patios are worth a look even if you're not staying here. Restaurant, bar. Good value.

El Rosario Lodge, 5 Avenida Sur and 9 Calle Poniente, tel. 320336. 36 rooms. $7/$8.
Tranquil location on the edge of a coffee and orange farm. Plain, comfortable rooms, some with fireplaces. A few efficiency

apartments are available by the month. Restaurant, parking.

Hotel Aurora, 4 Calle Oriente No. 16, tel. 320217. 36 rooms, $12/$14.
A well-kept, family-run establishment in a large old home with courtyard. Colonial atmosphere, good value. Breakfast served.

Casa del Patio, 5 Avenida Norte No. 37, tel. 320003. 9 rooms. $12/$16.
Neat rooms off the patio of a large restored house, decorated with colonial-style furniture and weaving arts. Fireplaces. May not be open—check first at tourist office.

Hotel Los Capitanes, 5 Avenida Sur No. 8, tel. 320581. 34 rooms. $4 per person.
Located above a large restaurant and movie house, noisy at times, but good for the price.

It's hard to go wrong at any of the hostelries offering budget rooms in Antigua. A sampling:

El Descanso, 5 Avenida Norte No. 9. 14 rooms. $3 to $5 double.
Relatively new, rooms are small but quite clean.

Casa de Santa Lucía, Alameda Santa Lucía Sur No. 5. 10 rooms. $6 double.
Small, comfortable rooms with private baths. On the edge of town near the bus terminal and market.

Pensión El Arco, 5 Avenida Norte No. 28. $2 per person with shared bath.
Simple, clean lodging, pleasant atmosphere.

Others inexpensive lodging places, $2 to $3 per person, are Posada de Doña Angelina, 4 Calle Poniente No. 33 (better rooms with private bath are upstairs); Hospedaje El Pasaje, Alameda de Santa Lucía No. 3; Hotel Plácido, Avenida del Desengaño No. 25 (out on the Chimaltenango road, but rooms face a nice courtyard); Posada El Refugio, 4 Calle Poniente No. 32; Posada Las Rosas, 6 Avenida Sur No. 8. Last and least, basic but honorable, is Posada La Antigueñita, 2 Calle Poniente No. 25, just $1 per person.

RESTAURANTS

You can eat and drink to your heart's content in Antigua, usually at insignificant expense. A selection from the bounty of restaurants:

Doña Luisa's (Pastelería y Panadería de Doña Luisa Xicotencatl), 4 Calle Oriente No. 2. Reuben sandwiches, Polish plate, chili con carne, baked potatoes, excellent bread and pastries, and assorted other down-home specialties. Here at Antigua's most convivial restaurant, you'll run into that fellow or lady whose acquaintance you last made in Katmandu (or was it La Paz?). Ample seating at courtyard tables, and upstairs for good volcano views. $2 and up. Also baked goods to take out.

Zen, 3 Avenida Norte No. 3. An excellent and authentic small Japanese restaurant. Teriyaki and other beef, shrimp and chicken dishes, all steaming hot. $2 to $5. Closed Wednesdays.

El Sereno, 6 Calle Poniente No. 30. Perhaps the classiest restaurant in Guatemala. Exquisite atmosphere in a meticulously restored colonial mansion: beamed ceilings, decorative plantings, flowing fountain, roaring fire, subdued lighting, glowing candles, classical music, the works. The food is not quite up to the environment, but still well prepared. The vegetables are a good point. A changing daily menu includes soups, creative salads, a choice of French- and native-style main courses. Lunch at noon, dinner 6:30 p.m., closed Monday and Tuesday, small children forbidden. $20. Telephone 320073 to reserve.

Welten, 4 Calle Oriente 21A. A courtyard restaurant with lots of ferns, ironwork, and colonial-style furniture. Adaptations of classic Italian cuisine include fettucine with macadamia sauce, chicken breast in wine, spezzatino, and saltimbocca, all quite tasty. $10 to $15.

El Palomar, 5 Calle Oriente No. 3, just up from the square, is yet another pleasant courtyard restaurant, where you dine under massive archways. Plain French-style food (medallions of beef, fondue bourguignone). $6 and up.

Also good bets for atmospheric dining are some of the hotels. At

102

Posada de Don Rodrigo, 5 Avenida Norte No. 9, you have a choice of American-style steak and native dishes. $4 to $6. In the **Hotel Antigua,** 4 Avenida Sur and 8 Calle Oriente, service is faultless. $6 and up for lunch or dinner, buffet on Sundays.

At **Casa de Café Ana,** in the Rosario Lodge, 5 Avenida Sur at 9 Calle Poniente, the food is good and the portions are large. Complete breakfasts and lunches are prepared at meal times (starting at 7:30 a.m., 12:30 p.m. and 6:30 p.m.), a la carte Guatemalan specialties and meats at other hours. Pleasant, quiet. Less than $2 for the set meal.

At **La Fonda de la Calle Real,** 5 Avenida Norte No. 5, the specialty is fondue, a rarity in Guatemala. They also have grilled sandwiches, salads and soups. Pleasant atmosphere, with small tables, an open fire at the entrance, and live music on weekends. Portions are small, best for snacks. $2 to $4.

Emilio, 4 Calle Poniente No. 3, and **Gran Muralla,** 4 Calle Poniente No. 4, both offer Chinese food, as well as hamburgers, steak and other "international" dishes. Lunch or dinner $2 to $5. The chow is better at Emilio. La Estrella, 5 Calle Poniente No. 6, also serves Chinese food.

Café Café, in the patio at 5 Avenida Norte No. 14. Native specialties such as stuffed peppers and pepián, and sandwiches. $2 to $4. Pleasant.

La Cenicienta, 5 Avenida Norte No. 9. Strictly desserts, and good ones: apple pie, carrot cake, brownies. $1 with coffee.

El Capuchino 6 Av. Norte £10. Italian-style. Pizza and pasta, as well as steak, shrimp and sandwiches. $2 to $8.

For inexpensive meals, try the San Carlos restaurant, your basic Guatemalan eatery, on the north side of the central park, next to the corner pharmacy. Complete breakfasts and lunches run $2 or less, and there are enchiladas and tamales and other such snacks. The restaurant in the Hotel Los Capitanes, 5 Avenida Sur No. 8, is a local late-hours hangout, and inexpensive. Cafetería Los Pollos, 5 Calle Poniente and 7 Avenida Sur, is open 24 hours for lovers of fried chicken. The eateries in the market, near the bus station, also dish up simple, filling, cheap meals. Several ice cream stores in the vicinity of the main square will be amply visible as you wander the streets.

Bars: The El Tarro Bar, one block in from the tourist office on 4 Avenida Sur, open until the last person leaves, is heavy on the blues. Other current drinking spots are the Mío Cid Bar, 5 Calle Oriente at 3 Avenida Sur, heavy on the wrought iron; and Los Encuentros, at 4 Calle Oriente and 1 Calle, heavy on the wood. Or try the Posada de Don Rodrigo, the Hotel Antigua or the Ramada (where the peanuts at the bar are unusually excellent) for a civilized drink.

COLONIAL ANTIGUA

Antigua is a city of monuments of the colonial past, both restored and in decaying ruins. The harshness of the 1773 disaster has been softened by time and creeping vegetation, creating the tranquil anachronism of Antigua today, set almost in a pocket of time in a green valley watched over by volcanoes and mountains.

Antigua is an eighteenth-century city. Though it lived as Santiago de los Caballeros for more than 200 years, much of the early architecture was lost to intermittent earthquakes or modified over the years. Buildings partially destroyed by tremors were rebuilt in then-current styles. Most of what is left today was built after the 1717 earthquake, in the colonial-late baroque style.

The rebuilders of the city in the eighteenth century thought they had learned their lessons from the early disasters. Structures went up with massive walls of brick and rubble to resist the vibrations of earth tremors. Buildings were kept low to prevent walls from toppling. Short bell towers were set firmly into churches, or separated from them entirely. The squat, heavy aspect of the city was relieved by the flamboyant decorations of the Churrigueresque style that were worked into the plaster and stucco that covered walls. Delicate flowers in relief, flutings on columns, plaster statues of saints in niches in the façades of churches all hid the underlying massiveness of the buildings in an interplay of light and shadow, as did the wooden grilles and carved

104

stone portals of private homes. Fountains, spacious plazas and an orderly plan of wide streets added to the sense of openness.

The most interesting parts of Antigua are in most cases on the outside of the surviving buildings. The interior decorations of the churches, the massive altarpieces that complemented the decoration of the entranceways, have been lost. Floor plans are basic, rectangular, with one or three naves. The development of architecture in Antigua concentrated not on the shape of the space enclosed, but on decorative detail, and on modifications to keep buildings from tumbling. The latter turned out, in many cases, to be not very successful.

Listed below is a selection of the most important monuments of the city, along a route that can be covered in from one to a few days, depending on how long you linger at each place. With continuing reconstruction work, an exhibition room or some other part of a monument may be closed from time to time.

Museums and restored buildings are generally open daily except Monday from 9 a.m. to 4 p.m. (with a break on weekends from noon to 2 p.m.). There are nominal admission charges to some museums. The grounds of unrestored ruins are open from 8 a.m. to 5 p.m., closed on Mondays.

Start at the central park, with a look at the restored fountain in its center. In colonial times, the plaza was a place for assembly and public functions, for bullfights, tournaments, whippings and hangings, and for the daily market. This was a bare, open stretch of land, without the shade trees and benches that now make the plaza a pleasant place in which to sit and watch the passing scene. On three sides of the square, the facing sidewalks are sheltered by restored colonial archways.

The **Ayuntamiento (City Hall),** on the north side of the square, was the headquarters of the city government of Santiago de los Caballeros, and now houses the government of the present-day city. On the façade is the coat of arms of Santiago, showing St. James on horseback riding above three volcanoes, the central one in full eruption.

Part of the Ayuntamiento now houses the **Museum of Santiago,** a collection of artifacts depicting aspects of daily life in the colony. On exhibit are colonial ceramics and modern copies, ironwork, tools, uniforms, silver articles, paintings, musical compositions on parchment, and a sword that was used by Pedro de Alvarado. The great siege cannon on display was taken from Fort San Felipe on the Río Dulce. In the rear is a two-story prison that functioned until 1955.

Next door is the **Museo del Libro Antiguo (Old Book Museum)**, in the part of the Ayuntamiento that housed the first printing press of the Kingdom of Guatemala. On display are assorted imprints, and illustrations of the progress of printing.

The **Palace of the Captains-General**, on the south side of the central park, was the headquarters of the government of the colony. Its façade is a two-story archway, now restored, extending the entire length of the block. The upper level was used by the nobility to watch spectacles in the plaza. Inside were the residence of the captain-general, courts of law, and the royal treasury.

The original building was damaged during the intermittent earthquakes that preceded the destruction of Santiago, and a new building was completed in 1764. It crumbled in the 1773 earthquake.

The front of the palace is now occupied by the local police detachment, the tourist office, and offices of the government of the department of Sacatepéquez, of which Antigua is the capital. Few signs remain in the ruined interior of the grand salons from which a kingdom was ruled. Visitors may enter the courtyard, and climb to the second floor of the restored part of the palace.

What now remains on the east side of the central park is the shell of the second **Cathedral** of Santiago. The original building, financed partly by Bishop Marroquín's sale of what remained of the cathedral in the former capital, was started in 1543, and rebuilt late in the seventeenth century, after earthquakes had caused much of it to fall. The second building was a maze of naves, chapels, domes, arches and belfries, lit by dozens of windows, its altars inlaid with precious metals, its columns sheathed in tortoise shell. The walls and niches were decorated with numerous paintings and statues of saints.

Beneath the floor of the first Cathedral were buried the remains of Pedro de Alvarado, his wife Beatriz de la Cueva, Bishop Francisco Marroquín, Bernal Díaz del Castillo, and other dignitaries and dastardlies of the early years of the colony. The exact location of the tombs was lost after the partial collapse of the building.

The Cathedral's present façade is a composite of elements taken from the wreckage of the colonial building. Behind the façade, one of the chapels has been reconstructed as the Church of San José. Inside is a statue of Christ by Quirio Cataño, who also sculptured the Black Christ of Esquipulas. The remainder of the Cathedral is a vast jungle of ruined arches, rubble, broken columns and crumbling walls.

The **University of San Carlos de Borromeo**, on 5 Calle Oriente facing the Cathedral, is a beautiful building in the Moorish style. The rooms are set off an arched passageway around the patio and central fountain. The arches are ornamented with curves and points and flutes, and the walls facing the courtyard are covered with geometrical decorations. The basic architectural plan, with a relatively bare façade facing the street and most of the decoration in the courtyard, was used in many houses in Santiago. The building, which has survived with relatively little damage over the years, was the second home of the university, completed about ten years before the destruction of Santiago. The present doorway dates from 1843.

Founded in 1681, the University of San Carlos was where young men of the colony studied law, medicine, languages, theology and philosophy. Many of the graduates went on to high positions in the Church and civil hierarchy. As an extension of the Catholic church, the faculty of the university was composed of members of the religious orders. Processions and ceremony were a part of academic life, along with rigorous training of the mind.

Today the university houses the **Colonial Museum**, an exhibition of art from the colonial period and depictions of life in old Guatemala. A good part of the collection consists of paintings of religious personalities and saints, as well as wooden statues of saints, which are still a form of popular art in rural Guatemala. In Room 4 is an interesting diorama of a university classroom in colonial times, in which two students present a thesis and refutation, while the professor supervises the action from a pulpit. Room 5 features a large mural of a university graduation, as well as some recreations of colonial activities: blacksmithing, sculpture, pottery-making and evangelizing among the Indians.

Up the street a couple of blocks from the museum, on the left side of 5 Calle Oriente between 2 and 1 avenidas, is the **Bernal Díaz del Castillo House.** Díaz was a soldier in Mexico and Guatemala, and in his later years, while living in retirement in Guatemala, he wrote a history of the conquest of New Spain, having been dissatisfied with the versions of the wars that others had told. For many years he was also a councilman of Santiago de los Caballeros. Farther up the street, on the right-hand side at the corner of 1 Avenida, is **Casa Popenoe,** a restored colonial mansion, which is open for visits daily except Sunday from 3 to 3:30 p.m.

Turning right on 1 Avenida and continuing two blocks, you come to the **Church and Monastery of San Francisco.** The partly restored church was as large as the Cathedral, its columns and arches towering in a combination of massiveness and grace. Next to the church, the monastery was the headquarters of the Franciscan order, which patronized the arts and science.

One of the Franciscan friars, Pedro de Bethancourt, is buried in a chapel adjoining the church. He is revered today as a healer of the sick. Brother Pedro founded a hospital, and is credited with having turned many a sinner from evil ways.

Down 7 Calle to 2 Avenida, then one block north to 6 Calle, are the **Church and Convent of Santa Clara.** The convent was founded by nuns who came from Puebla, Mexico, in 1699. It fell in the 1717 earthquake, and the second convent was completed in 1734. The church and the cloisters in two arched rows face inward to a large patio with a fountain at the center, forming an enclosed space that afforded the sisters plenty of privacy. The size of the buildings and the expanse of the gardens amply convey the idea that life in the convent was not especially burdensome. The order of Santa Clara was composed largely of the daughters of well-to-do families. They are said to have baked excellent bread.

Four blocks north on 2 Avenida, at the corner of 2 Calle, are the ruins of the **Church and Convent of Las Capuchinas,** completed in 1736. This was another place where the sisters lived in splendor. The cells are built around a unique circular patio. Each had its own toilet, an incredible luxury for the time. The daily chores of the sisters are said to have included tending their gardens and doing the laundry of the priests of Santiago.

The **Church of La Merced,** at 1 Calle Poniente and 6 Avenida Norte, now largely restored, is a massive structure with a Churrigueresque façade of arches, winding stems of stuccoed flowers and vines, and lace-like patterns. The designs cover almost every square inch of the central section, and of the niches where figures of saints are placed. The church and monastery, home of the Mercedarian friars in Guatemala, were completed a few years before the 1773 earthquake, and suffered little damage while the rest of the city fell around them.

The **Church and Monastery of the Compañía de Jesús,** on 6

108

Avenida Norte between 4 and 3 calles, were the center of the Jesuits in Guatemala. Completed in 1626, the church featured large windows and finely carved doors. It is now mostly rubble, though the cracked façade remains standing, with headless statues of saints in the niches. For many years, the monastery adjoining the church formed part of the Antigua market, and was subdivided into shops and areas for selling meat, vegetables and handicrafts. The painted signs of the merchants remain on the walls.

The **Church of San Jerónimo**, at the corner of 1 Calle Poniente and the Alameda de Santa Lucía, near the bus terminal, is a small building in ruins, set next to a monastery whose thick walls surround a central fountain. The church was built in 1757 and closed a few years later, when it was discovered that the Mercedarians had never obtained a building permit. It was later used as the royal customhouse.

The ruins of **La Recolección** are down the dirt street next to San Jerónimo. With the exposed brick work of great columns and arches, one might think oneself in the ruins of ancient Rome. But a glance upward to the coffee and shade trees all around, and the volcanoes towering overhead, reminds the visitor that this is the New World. The setting of the church and monastery is probably the most magnificent in Antigua.

The church was founded early in the eighteenth century on the outskirts of town, since Santiago was already quite closely built, and there was some opposition to the establishment of yet another ecclesiastical structure in the city. The two-story monastery included a large library, medical facilities and study areas. The church, of which not much remains, was a treasure house of works by European and Guatemalan artists.

On the opposite side of the market and bus terminal from La Recolección is the **Monument to Rafael Landívar.** Though not a colonial structure, it's built in the old baroque style. Landívar, a Jesuit who composed his verse in Latin, was Guatemala's finest poet of the colonial period. He wrote his greatest work, *Rusticatio Mexicana*, in Italy, after the Jesuits had been expelled from Spanish America in 1767. The house where Landívar lived is around the corner on 5 Calle Poniente.

On the way back toward the central park, on 5 Calle Poniente at the corner of 7 Avenida Norte, is the **Church of San Agustín.** The site had been originally occupied by the convent of Santa Catarina. Because of its relatively modest size and the great buttresses against its walls, the church survived the earthquake of

1773. But subsequent earthquakes have left it mostly in rubble, with only the façade intact.

ANTIGUA DIRECTORY

Banks: Lloyds Bank, at the northeast corner of the central park, open 9 a.m. to 3 p.m.; Banco de Guatemala, on the west side of the central park, open 8:30 a.m. to 2 p.m., to 2:30 p.m. on Fridays; Banco del Agro, also on the park.

Bicycles are rented at 6 Avenida Sur No. 6. Go inside the auto repair shop. Motorbikes are also available.

Books in English, including guides and other titles on Guatemala and Central America, are available at Casa Andinista, 4 Calle Oriente No. 5A (opposite Doña Luisa's), along with newspapers and magazines. I recommend that you stop in to pick up a copy of *Antigua Guatemala: City and Area Guide,* by Mike Shawcross. It contains a wealth of detailed practical and background information of interest to all visitors. Books are also available at Un Poco de Todo on the east side of the central park.

Buses leave from the terminal and market three blocks west of the central park. For service to villages near Antigua, see "Nearby Towns," below.

Buses for Antigua leave from 15 Calle between 3 and 4 avenidas, Zone 1, Guatemala City, about every hour, from 7 a.m. to 7:45 p.m. On weekends, the service is every half hour. There are additional departures from 18 Calle and 4 Avenida, and from the bus terminal in Zone 4. Buses leave Antigua for Guatemala City from 6 a.m. to about 7 p.m.

To connect with buses heading for the western part of Guatemala (Lake Atitlán, Chichicastenango, Quezaltenango and Huehuetenango), take a bus to Chimaltenango. Departures are from the bus terminal about every 45 minutes, from 6:30 a.m. to 5:30 p.m.

Candy: A store selling traditional native candies is located at 4 Calle Oriente No. 11. The same family has run the business for many years, and the sweets are well known throughout Guatemala.

Coffee: The Antigua area produces some of Guatemala's finest coffee. Coffee trees are small and delicate, and are shaded by taller trees. They're planted on almost all available flat land around Antigua and in many places within the town. The small white flowers bloom at the beginning of the rainy season, after which the green berry (called the *cereza,* or cherry, in Spanish) develops and ripens to a deep red. The bean is inside, under the skin of the berry and an inner skin. The harvest takes place at the close of the rainy season.

Cultural Resources: Assorted places not mentioned elsewhere include CIRMA, a resource center and library specializing in Middle America, at 5 Calle Oriente No. 2E; Casa de la Cultura, next to the Cathedral, which sponsors art exhibitions, talks, and musical performances; Alliance Française, 3 Calle Oriente No. 19A; Istituto Italiano, 4 Calle Oriente No. 21; and Casa K'ojom, Calle Recoletos No. 55 (near Alameda de Santa Lucía), where there is an exhibition on native music, open daily except Monday.

Doctors: Dr. Aceituno, a general practitioner, has his office at 2 Calle Poniente No. 7, tel. 320512. He speaks English.

Entertainment: Nights are quiet during the week in Antigua, which is very conscious of its role as a cultural center. There's not much to do except sit and converse over coffee or a drink, or go out to a movie. Weekends are livelier, however, with many visitors driving into town from Guatemala city.

There are two cinemas in Antigua, the Imperial, on the west side of the central park, which has been closed recently, and the Colonial, in the same building as the Hotel Los Capitanes, south of the central park on 5 Avenida Sur, the roof of which is said to leak during heavy downpours. Admission to most movies is a dollar or less. Check the posters in the lobbies to see what's playing, and to get starting times.

Chamber music and classical marimba concerts are held intermittently throughout the year. Check with the tourist office to see if any are on tap, as well as for any other special events. There are also open-air concerts on Sunday mornings and some evenings on the central park.

Marimba concerts are usually given on weekend afternoons at the Hotel Antigua.

A disco operates in the Hotel Ramada.

Fiestas: The traditional fiesta of Antigua on July 25 honors St. James the Apostle, the patron saint of the city. The biggest religious celebrations, however, take place between Ash Wednesday and Easter Sunday.

On Sundays during Lent, processions from the churches of Antigua and from nearby villages wind their way through the streets of the city. On Fridays, vigils are kept at special altars.

The celebration of Holy Week (Semana Santa) starts with processions and vigils on Palm Sunday. On the night of Holy Thursday, elaborate carpets of flowers and colored sawdust are laid out in the streets. On Good Friday, a solemn procession reenacts the progress of Christ to his crucifixion. Penitents carry on their shoulders the heavy platform bearing the image of Jesus and the cross. During the morning, the members of the procession dress in purple, but after 3 p.m., the hour of the crucifixion, they change into black. Funereal music accompanies the ceremonies, which are attended by the devout from all over Central America.

The major Good Friday procession leaves the church of La Merced at 8 a.m. A few blocks from the church, it passes through the Calle Ancha over some of the most beautiful sawdust carpets.

Colorful processions also take place in Antigua at Corpus Christi and during the days preceding Christmas.

Groceries: One particularly well-stocked store with cheeses, meats, liquors and the usual staple items is located at 6 Avenida Sur No. 1. There are similar but smaller stores in the area, and in the market as well. The Troccoli hardware store, at 5 Avenida Norte and 6 Calle Poniente, has a good selection of liquor.

Guides are ubiquitous in Antigua. Ask for credentials, or hire one at official rates through the tourist office. If you go shopping with a guide, he'll get a cut from the merchant, and the price to you will be higher.

Houses for Rent: You can sometimes pick up leads from the tourist office or resident foreigners.

Language Schools are Antigua's growth industry. More than a dozen schools offer instruction in the Spanish language. Through them, you can arrange to board with a Guatemalan family. Among the schools are Proyecto Lingüístico Francisco Marroquín, 4 Avenida Sur No. 4; Tecún Umán Linguistic School, 6 Calle Poniente No. 34; and Centro Internacional de Español, 4 Avenida Norte at 2 Calle Oriente. For complete listings, see *Antigua Guatemala: City and Area Guide.* Also see "Study Programs" in the chapter of practical information. Fees range up to $450 per month all inclusive, a bargain.

Laundry: Coin-operated washers and dryers are available at Lavarápido, 5 Calle Poniente No. 7A.

The Market is located at the bus terminal, three blocks west of the central park. Every day is market day, but business is busiest on Mondays, Thursdays and Saturdays. Before the 1976 earthquake, the market was held in and around the old Jesuit monastery. The new location is considerably more ample, if less central, with large sections set aside for handicrafts of various sorts, as well as groceries, fruits and vegetables. Enter and wander about at your leisure. This market is less ordered than most, having taken root on a "temporary" site.

Post and Telegraph Office: On the Alameda de Santa Lucía at 4 Calle Poniente, opposite the market.

Pottery Factory: The Montiel factory uses traditional techniques to produce glazed pottery in Antigua's distinctive style. Clay is ground by large stone wheels turned by hand, and pottery wheels are operated by foot power. The factory once had many employees, but as cheaper pottery and plastic vessels came into use, business declined. It's now operated as a small family enterprise. To reach the factory, go north on 6 Avenida Norte to the diagonal street on the edge of town, about six blocks from the central park. Go left one block on the diagonal street, then turn right, and walk up to number 20. If you get lost, ask for the "fábrica de loza Montiel." You're welcome to examine the techniques, and to buy if you wish.

Ceramic birds are a specialty of the Ródenas family. One workshop can be visited at 1 Calle del Chajón no. 21 (a couple of blocks north of the market, near La Recolección), and other family members work elsewhere in the neighborhood.

113

Shopping: The specialties of Antigua are textiles from nearby towns, available at the market, at handicraft shops around town, in the weaving market next to Compañía de Jesús (6 Avenida Norte at 4 Calle Poniente) and in the village of San Antonio Aguas Calientes; ceramics, at the market, handicraft shops, and at the workshops mentioned above; antiques, at some of the handicraft stores; carved jade, at several shops; and silver jewelry, at the factory in San Felipe de Jesús.

Most shops that cater to visitors are located on 5 Avenida Norte and 4 Calle Oriente. Some, such as Colibrí, 4 Calle Oriente No. 3B, benefit development or aid projects. Jade is sold at several factory showrooms along 4 Calle Oriente, one near the park, another above 1 Avenida. Un Poco de Todo, on the square, sells rubbings of Mayan and colonial monuments. Several interesting shops are away from the town center, among them Concha's Foot Loom, 7 Calle Oriente No. 14; Casa de Los Gigantes, 7 Calle Oriente No. 18; and Casa de Artes, 4 Avenida Sur No. 11, near the Hotel Antigua, which has some of the highest quality artisanry, paintings and antiques.

Swimming: The Hotel Antigua and the Ramada Antigua will let you use their pools for a fee if you're not a guest. For a hot-springs swimming pool, see San Lorenzo El Tejar, listed below under "Nearby Towns."

Taxis are abundant around the central park. The tourist office will advise you on what is a fair rate to Guatemala City or any of the neighboring villages.

Telephones: The office of Guatel, the telephone company, is at the corner of 5 Avenida Sur and 5 Calle Poniente, on the central park. Pay phones are located next to the San Carlos restaurant and along the arcade on the central park.

Public Toilets: Across from Lloyds Bank, at the northeast corner of the central park.

Travel Agency: There's one upstairs in Un Poco de Todo, on the west side of the park.

Trips from Antigua: Check out "Nearby Towns," below. If you rent a car, or can get a few persons together to hire a taxi, you can also use Antigua as a base for most of the day trips listed in the Guatemala City section. You'll probably find Antigua a more pleasant place in which to stay. If you're traveling by bus, you can visit Chichicastenango or Iximché and return to Antigua in the evening.

Views: For a panorama of Antigua, walk or drive up to Cerro de la Candelaria, the hill north of town. Follow 1 Avenida Norte as it winds upward. The trip takes about 10 minutes by car from the central park, or about 25 minutes on foot. Best time is around noon, when there are no shadows to obscure details.

Volcanoes: Agua, south of Antigua, measures 3766 meters (12,356 feet) above sea level. An earthquake in 1541 caused water dammed in its crater to wash away the second capital of Guatemala, now known as Ciudad Vieja. The peak can be reached from the village of Santa María de Jesús.

Fuego and Acatenango lie southwest of Antigua. Acatenango is the one to the north. Fire-scarred Fuego, measuring 3763 meters (12,346 feet), was in eruption at the time of the arrival of the Spanish, and still belches fire, lava and ash intermittently. Its continuing activity has caused its profile to change over the years. Acatenango measures 3975 meters (13,042 feet).

Of the three volcanoes, Agua is the easiest climb. From its summit, the Pacific Ocean can be seen clearly to the south across the coastal plain, as can the peaks of the chain of volcanoes stretching from Mexico to El Salvador. For more details about climbing these volcanoes, see Mr. Benjamíin García at the Antigua tourist office, consult the Antigua guide by Mike Shawcross, or inquire at the Asociación de Andinismo, 6 Avenida Norte No. 34.

Weaving Schools have operated from time to time in Antigua. Check with the tourist office. If there are no formal programs at the time of your stay, you should be able to find a teacher by inquiring of the handicraft sellers on the plaza of San Antonio Aguas Calientes (see below).

NEARBY TOWNS

San Felipe de Jesús, a suburb of Antigua, is the site of a white Gothic church containing a famous image of Christ. On the first Friday of Lent, the image is the goal of pilgrims who seek cures of their illnesses. There's also a factory where silver articles are made, located about two blocks from the central park. Visitors are welcome to watch the craftsmen at work. Children outside will try to hustle themselves as guides, but there's no need for them.

Buses operate to San Felipe about every half hour from the Antigua terminal. Last return bus is at about 6 p.m. The walk to San Felipe takes about 25 minutes, following 6 Avenida northward out of Antigua.

San Juan del Obispo, a picturesque little town to the south of Antigua, is the site of the palace of Francisco Marroquín, first bishop of Guatemala. The palace is easily seen from many points within Antigua. San Juan offers good panoramic views of Antigua and the surrounding area. Small buses operate to San Juan every half hour from the Antigua terminal. If you're walking back from Santa María de Jesús, you'll pass this way.

SANTA MARIA DE JESUS
Population 8287 (98% indigenous); Altitude 2050 meters; Languages: Cakchiquel and Spanish; Fiesta: January 2

Santa María de Jesús, on the slopes of the Agua volcano, was founded shortly after the Conquest, and populated with Indians of the Quiché nation brought from the area of Quezaltenango. It was moved up to its present site early in the eighteenth century, after a flood destroyed the original village.

A picturesque town with many thatched houses, Santa María is one of the few places in the region where some of the men as well as the women wear the traditional town outfit. Men's shirts are red, with woven figures of flowers and animals.

Santa María is the usual starting point for climbing the Agua volcano, and a guide can sometimes be secured by inquiring at the city hall.

Buses for Santa María leave from the Antigua terminal about

every hour from 10 a.m. to 5 p.m. The last bus returns from Santa María at 6 p.m. It's also a pleasant walk downhill for about 10 kilometers along the dirt road back to Antigua, through forests, meadows, and, finally, coffee plantations in the area of San Juan del Obispo, with many impressive views along the way. The road beyond Santa María continues to Palín on the highway to the Pacific. It's best driven in a jeep. A branch road climbs part way up the volcano Agua.

CIUDAD VIEJA
Population 9435; Altitude 1519 meters; Fiesta: December 8

After the Cakchiquel revolt in Iximché early in the colonial period, the Spanish relocated their capital to the Almolonga valley at the foot of the volcano Agua. The valley was chosen for its abundance of pasture lands and forests, fertile soil, water supplies, and deposits of lime from which mortar could be made.

The second Santiago de los Caballeros de Guatemala, founded in 1527, was quickly built up along the traditional Spanish plan, with a cathedral, palace of the captains-general and city hall grouped around the main square. Religious orders established monasteries and convents, and the Mexican Indian allies of the Spanish were granted lands on the outskirts of town.

In September of 1541, a driving rainstorm lashed the city for many days, shortly after Doña Beatriz, widow of Pedro de Alvarado, had taken over the reins of government from her late husband. On the night of September 10, an earthquake struck, and a natural dam on the slopes of the volcano Agua collapsed, sending an avalanche of water and mud to destroy the capital. Doña Beatriz and hundreds of Spaniards and Indians were killed. The disaster was said to have been divine retribution for the excess show of mourning put on by the widow. Santiago de los Caballeros was eventually relocated to the place now called Antigua.

Not much remains of the Old City. The first mass in the capital is said to have been celebrated under a tree that still shades the central park. A colonial church also stands, but the original cathedral was washed away in the 1541 disaster. Recent archaeological investigations indicate that the center of the old capital might have been at San Miguel Escobar, two kilometers east of today's town center.

SAN ANTONIO AGUAS CALIENTES

Population 3698 (96% indigenous); Altitude 1550 meters; Languages: Cakchiquel and Spanish; Fiesta: June 13

San Antonio Aguas Calientes, like the surrounding small towns, is a center for the cultivation of corn, beans and coffee, as well as citrus and vegetables. But the attraction here is the weaving, some of the best in Guatemala in terms of tightness of the weave, designs and color combinations. Characteristic designs include flowers and geometric shapes, usually done on an orange background. Local huipiles, napkins and wall hangings are displayed for sale all over town, along with pieces from other parts of the country.

The main activity for visitors to San Antonio is to admire and buy textiles at the open stands on the plaza. If you're going to be around for a while, you can contract with one of the women for weaving lessons.

Buses operate from Antigua to San Antonio Aguas Calientes by way of Ciudad Vieja about every hour, starting at 7 a.m. The last return bus leaves San Antonio at 5 p.m. The walk from Ciudad Vieja (dusty in the dry season) takes about 45 minutes.

Santa Catarina Barahona (population 1437, 96% indigenous; altitude 1459 meters; languages Cakchiquel and Spanish; fiesta January 15) adjoins San Antonio Aguas Calientes, and the women wear similar outfits. A few blocks from the square is a small swimming pool fed by a cold stream, usually open on weekends.

Alotenango (population 6751, 87% indigenous; altitude 1388 meters; languages Cakchiquel and Spanish; fiesta September 29) is a prosperous coffee-producing center near Ciudad Vieja.

Toward Guatemala City:

SANTA LUCIA MILPAS ALTAS

Population 1186; Altitude 2100 meters; Fiesta: December 13; Kilometer 34 (junction)

A small agricultural town, where some inhabitants cut firewood and manufacture charcoal.

118

SAN LUCAS SACATEPEQUEZ
Population 3825; Altitude 2063 meters; Fiesta: October 18; Kilometer 30

San Lucas Sacatepéquez existed at the time the Spanish arrived, but was moved to its present location a couple of decades after the Conquest, with its population augmented by Indians brought from Rabinal. In 1871, it was the site of a great battle in which Liberal revolutionaries defeated government forces.

San Lucas is important nowadays as a junction for Antigua on the Pan American (Inter-American) Highway. On weekends, residents of the capital on excursion crowd the numerous restaurants and the roadside market.

You'll notice a few motels in the area. In Guatemala, as elsewhere in Latin America, many motels are locales for romantic trysts, and don't cater to the family trade. Which is why they're usually not mentioned in travel literature.

Along the Pan American Highway (CA-1)

SUMPANGO
Population 9484 (township 13,072 (96% indigenous); Altitude 1900 meters; Languages: Cakchiquel and Spanish; Fiesta: August 28; Market Days: Tuesday and Saturday; "Place of the Skull Chapels"; Kilometer 45

Founded long before the Conquest, Sumpango was probably a Toltec center before it was absorbed into the Cakchiquel domains. The name of the town derives from the Toltec custom of enshrining skulls of sacrificed prisoners in a chapel. More traditional than many Indian towns in the region, Sumpango was heavily damaged in the 1976 earthquake.

SANTIAGO SACATEPEQUEZ
Population 6522 (township 9658; 90% indigenous); Altitude 2080 meters; Languages: Cakchiquel and Spanish; Fiesta: July 25; Market Day: Saturday

A hillside agricultural town north of the Pan American Highway, Santiago Sacatepéquez is best known for its celebration of All Saints' Day, November 1. In addition to the usual festivities in the town graveyard, the men fly gigantic circular paper kites with intricate designs, which take months to make. When a kite becomes shredded after repeated crashes, its skin is burned, leaving the bamboo frame for re-use the following year.

Between Antigua and Chimaltenango:

JOCOTENANGO
Population 6668; Altitude 1540 meters; Fiesta: August 15

Adjoining Antigua, Jocotenango is a center for processing coffee beans grown in the area. There's an Adventist herbalist institute at Calle Real No. 30, if you're interested in natural cures, massages and steam baths. Closed Saturdays.

San Lorenzo El Tejar, part of the township of Pastores, is the site of a small and pleasant hot-springs swimming pool. To get there, take any Chimaltenango bus from Antigua, and ask to be let off at San Luis Las Carretas. From there, it's a walk of about two kilometers to the pool. Ask for the *balneario.* If you're driving, take the right-hand fork at San Luis Las Carretas. Admission is less than a dollar, hours are 9 a.m. to 5 p.m.

PARRAMOS
Population 3069 (township 3921; 60% indigenous); Altitude 2225 meters; Languages: Cakchiquel and Spanish; Fiesta: December 28; Market Day: Sunday; "Among the branches"

Parramos has the reputation of producing the best black beans in Guatemala, as well as excellent coffee.

Laguna de los Cisnes (Los Aposentos) is a small lake alongside the highway, just before the climb to the city of Chimaltenango. A weekend resort for the less well off, it has rowboats available for rent, and some snack stands.

CHIMALTENANGO

Population 14,967 (township 27,017; 66% indigenous); Fiesta: July 26; Market Days: Every day, but especially Monday and Thursday; "Place of the wall of shields"; Kilometer 55

Situated on the continental divide, Chimaltenango was an important town of the Cakchiquel kingdom before the Conquest. The present city was founded by Pedro de Portocarrero in 1526. In 1527 and 1541, Chimaltenango was considered as a possible site for the capital of Guatemala. Today, it is a busy trading center, home to some light industry (sawmills, a thread factory), and capital of the department of Chimaltenango. It's also headquarters for a number of foreign evangelical missions, which run schools and churches, and are active, with some success, in converting the inhabitants from their traditional religion.

The department of Chimaltenango was one of the worst-hit sections of Guatemala in the 1976 earthquake. Chimaltenango, San Martín Jilotepeque, Tecpán, Patzicía, Patzún and smaller towns on or near the major fault line were flattened. For weeks after the disaster, as relief organizations went into action, the dust of crumbled adobe bricks drifted over temporary cardboard and tin shelters erected by the survivors. What walls remained standing began to melt in the rains of May, and weeds sprouted in abandoned patios and dirt floors.

The rubble is long gone, but the area has been permanently altered. Traditional and attractive—but structurally dangerous— homes of adobe with heavy tiled roofs have been replaced by safer houses of wood and concrete blocks, with tin overhead.

Buses leave frequently for Chimaltenango from the corner of 20 Calle and Avenida Bolívar, Zone 1, Guatemala City. Last bus about 4 p.m. Buses run from Chimaltenango to Antigua about every 45 minutes, the last at 5 p.m.

EL TEJAR

Population 3251 (township 4265; 44% indigenous); Altitude 1765 meters; Languages: Spanish and Cakchiquel; Fiesta: January 20; "Tile-making place"; Kilometer 51

El Tejar, east of Chimaltenango, is unusual in that it grew on

121

the basis of industry, rather than as an agricultural or administrative center. After the destruction of the second Santiago de los Caballeros (Ciudad Vieja), bricks and roof tiles were in short supply, and El Tejar was established as a brick-making center because of the availability of suitable clay. The industry still thrives, and brick kilns can be seen on either side of the Pan American Highway as you pass through. El Tejar is also a truck stop, with numerous roadside cafes.

Two towns west of Chimaltenango and just off the Pan American Highway are noted for fine weaving:

COMALAPA
Population 11,362 (township 20,422; 96% indigenous); Altitude 2115 meters; Languages: Cakchiquel and Spanish; Fiesta: June 24; Market Days: Tuesday and Friday; "Place of the comales" (pans for cooking tortillas); junction kilometer 64, then north about 15 kilometers.

In 1526, after the Cakchiquel revolt in Iximché, the Spanish established temporary headquarters near Comalapa.

SANTA CRUZ BALANYA
Population 2443 (township 3607; 95% indigenous); Altitude 2060 meters; Languages: Cakchiquel and Spanish; Fiesta: May 3; Balanyá, "tiger river"; junction kilometer 76

TECPAN GUATEMALA
Population 5977 (township 29,564; 90% indigenous); Altitude 2286 meters; Languages: Cakchiquel and Spanish; Fiesta: October 4; Market Days: Thursday and Sunday; "Royal Court of Guatemala"; Kilometer 88

First Spanish capital of the Kingdom of Guatemala, Tecpán is one of the more important market centers of the highlands. The surrounding plain is a major wheat-growing area, and in the town are flour mills, as well as sawmills for processing lumber from nearby forests.

IXIMCHE RUINS

Located about three kilometers from Tecpán, at Pueblo Viejo, Iximché was the capital of the Cakchiquel nation when the Spanish arrived in Guatemala. Of the archaeological sites in the highlands, it is the one that suffered the least destruction during the Spanish conquest and in succeeding centuries.

Iximché was founded around 1470, when the Cakchiquels began a period of conflict with the Quichés. A fortified capital (like others of the same period in the highlands), it was surrounded by deep ravines and a man-made ditch which isolated the ceremonial centers and dwelling places of the nobility from the plebeians who lived outside. Although the Cakchiquels were almost always at war, construction and expansion of the capital continued until the arrival of the Spanish, through the levying of labor and material contributions on subject tribes.

The Cakchiquels received the Spanish peacefully in 1524, and Pedro de Alvarado established Tecpán Guatemala nearby as his headquarters for governing the colonial Kingdom of Guatemala. The Cakchiquels had been allies of the Spanish against the Tzutuhils and the Quichés, but in the face of demands for treasure by Jorge de Alvarado, they rose in revolt, and waged a guerrilla war against the Spaniards until 1530.

The site of Iximché consists of four large ceremonial plazas and two smaller plazas, each with one or two temples, house platforms, smaller ceremonial structures, and, in two cases, ball courts. The plazas were built with slight inclines to allow for drainage. The substructures of stone and mortar have survived the highland climate over four centuries, and are now partially restored. But the adobe superstructures, which were probably roofed with straw or some other perishable material, have largely melted away.

Visitors to Iximché can see the remains of murals painted on the stucco that covered the buildings. Archaeologists attribute the three layers of mortar and paving to the practice of repaving streets and plastering over and repairing walls whenever a king died.

The largest complex at Iximché is the Palace, consisting of altars and a nucleus of houses around a patio. Knives, grinding stones, *comales* for cooking tortillas, and other implements of domestic life have been found here, but all have been removed. Nearby is a pyramidal base with a stone block, used for sacrifices. Like the Aztecs and many other tribes of Mesoamerica, the Cakchiquels tore out the hearts of their victims.

Among the artifacts excavated at Iximché are large cylindrical incense burners, ceramic objects of various types, obsidian knives, skulls of beheaded humans, and a flute made from the femur of a child. These are illustrated in a guide book in Spanish by Jorge Guillemín, available at the site.

Visiting hours at Iximché are 9 a.m. to 4 p.m.

Buses directly to or passing Tecpán operate frequently from the corner of 20 Calle and Avenida Bolívar, Zone 1, Guatemala City, from 6 a.m. to 4 p.m. Travel time is about two hours. For first-class service, take a Quezaltenango bus (see Quezaltenango listings).

From Tecpán, you'll have to walk (or drive) to the ruins. Ask for Iximché or Pueblo Viejo. It's a pleasant hike along a winding dirt road through corn fields and forests.

After your visit, flag down a bus for Guatemala City on the Pan American Highway. If traveling westward, make sure you get back to the highway by 3 p.m.

Food: No food is available at the ruins. Stock up on snacks before you set out. You can stop at one of the roadside restaurants near Tecpán, kilometer 87. If you're continuing westward, try Cafetería Chichoy, at kilometer 102 on the south side of the highway, for inexpensive Guatemalan home cooking, and a look at the handicrafts of a widow's cooperative.

Highway Notes

West of Tecpán, the Pan American Highway climbs through forested countryside. There are only scattered small settlements along the road at these altitudes, up to 3000 meters above sea level. Along the way are junctions for roads to Godínez and the coast (kilometer 117), Chichicastenango (kilometer 127), and Panajachel and Lake Atitlán (kilometer 130).

Back at kilometer 69, another road cuts south from the Pan American Highway toward Lake Atitlán, passing through Patzicía and Patzún. This route, with many hairpin turns, steep grades and unpaved stretches, is not recommended for travel beyond Patzún.

PATZICIA

Population 7628 (township 12,386; 86% indigenous); Altitude 2131 meters; Languages: Cakchiquel and Spanish; Fiesta: July 25; Market Days: Wednesday and Saturday; "Place of the water dog"; Kilometer 70.

The Declaration of Patzicía in 1871 set down the programs of the Liberal revolutionaries and recognized Miguel García Granados as president. Patzicía was also the site of Indian riots in 1940.

PATZUN

Population 9802 (township 23,430; 92% indigenous); Altitude 2234 meters; Languages: Cakchiquel and Spanish; Fiestas: May 20 and Corpus Christi; Market Days: Tuesday, Thursday and Sunday; "Place of the daisies"; Kilometer 83

Patzún is noted for its Corpus Christi celebrations in June, when the Indian religious brotherhoods form processions through streets decorated with carpets of colored sawdust, flowers and pine needles. The women's huipil, still widely worn, is bright red, embellished with embroidery around the neckline. Lovely embroidered cloths, sold as wall hangings, are also made in town.

LAKE ATITLAN

Aldous Huxley once called Atitlán the most beautiful lake in the world, and only a few hard souls have been known to disagree with that judgment. Located about 65 kilometers west of Guatemala City in a straight line, or more than double that distance via the winding mountain roads, the lake is a gem in its natural beauty, in the flora and fauna of its waters and the surrounding area, and in the rich traditional Indian life of the villagers who live along its shores. Three volcanoes—San Pedro, Tolimán and Atitlán—tower over the southern shore, while mountains rise to a thousand meters above the northern rim.

Thousands of years ago, the eruptions that formed the volcanoes closed off several river valleys, and in the process created Lake Atitlán. New eruptions sealed the lake's river outlet about 500 years ago, and today, the lake drains through underground seepage into rivers leading to the Pacific.

The lake's surface is 1562 meters (5125 feet) above sea level, though the figure varies somewhat from year to year, as the waters rise and fall. The maximum recorded depth is 324 meters (1063 feet), but the waters are probably deeper in parts. The length is 18.5 kilometers, the width varies from 7 to 12 kilometers, and the total surface area is 130 square kilometers (50 square miles). Eighteen small islands dot the surface, but some disappear during years of high water.

The area around Lake Atitlán is a region of brilliant natural color. The shades of the sky vary from sunrise to sunset. The lake is a light blue when the *Xocomil* (Sho-ko-mil) wind blows up from the coast in the late morning, a deep blue when the sky is cloudless, and a gray sea when the evening fog rolls in. Everywhere are the colors of wildflowers along the roadsides, white coffee flowers or red coffee berries, and the hibiscus and bougainvillea and countless other plants cultivated in gardens.

Twelve villages (or more, if some of the smaller hamlets are counted) line the shores of Atitlán. Their inhabitants are for the most part descendants of the Cakchiquel and Tzutuhil nations that inhabited the area at the time of the arrival of the Spaniards. Some of the villages are modern in the manner of other highland settlements, with many of the inhabitants speaking Spanish, traditional native dress going out of fashion, and orthodox

126

Catholicism and Protestantism replacing the old religious organization. But in a few of the villages, a visit by an outsider is still a rare event. Life goes on much as it has for centuries. Men till fields of corn and patches of vegetables, and raise coffee, avocados, anise, onions and strawberries as cash crops. Women weave and tend to household chores in tile-roofed, whitewashed adobe homes. In many ways, the lake villages represent the great spectrum of life styles seen in the Indian towns of all of western Guatemala today.

While some natives use *cayucos*, dugout canoes with sides built up of rough planks, the lake figures little in the daily life of the people who live along its shores. Most will trudge along a lakeside trail with their cargo on their backs, in the manner of the people of other highland towns, rather than use a canoe. Few natives ever learn to swim, and there are hardly any legends about the lake. Fish has never been an important part of the Indian diet, and the stocking of the lake with black bass some years back nearly wiped out the native fish population.

Hotels and restaurants are concentrated in Panajachel, on the northern shore. Good roads allow day excursions from Panajachel to Chichicastenango, Quezaltenango, smaller highland towns, and the Pacific lowlands.

As for the name . . . Atitlán signifies "place of much water," or simply "lake," in Nahuatl, the language of the Mexican Indian allies of Pedro de Alvarado.

Highway Notes

From Guatemala City, the easiest route to Lake Atitlán is via the Pan American Highway. A road winds southward from the junction at kilometer 130 to Sololá, and then down a steep grade to Panajachel. Total distance is about 147 kilometers. Along the way, at kilometer 120 on the Pan American Highway, a roadside rest area affords breathtaking views to the lake far below and the volcanoes beyond. At kilometer 117 on the Pan American Highway, Las Trampas, is the junction for a scenic, winding road to Panajachel via Godínez, above the eastern end of the lake. Total distance via this route is about 160 kilometers. The narrow old road via Patzicía and Patzún, through several canyons, is in a near-abandoned state and should be avoided. From the coast highway, an excellent paved road starts at kilometer 113, and continues to San Lucas Tolimán on the southern shore of the lake, and Godínez on the north side.

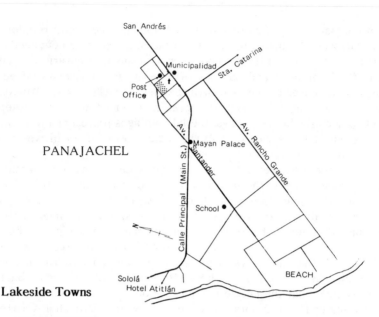

PANAJACHEL

Lakeside Towns

PANAJACHEL

Population 3403 (township 4862; 70% indigenous); Altitude 1573 meters; Languages: Cakchiquel and Spanish; Fiesta: October 4; Market Day: Sunday; "Place of the white zapote" (a fruit tree); Kilometer 121 (via Patzún)

Located in a broad river delta, Panajachel is the main center from which to see the lake area. It has a number of hotels and restaurants covering a wide range of prices and service.

During the period of the Spanish conquest of Guatemala, the shores of the lake near where the Hotel Tzanjuyú now stands were the scene of the great battle in which the Spanish and their Cakchiquel allies defeated the Tzutuhils. The Franciscans set up a church and monastery in Panajachel soon afterward, and used the town as a center for converting the Indians of the region to the Catholic faith. The original façade of the church still stands, and is one of the gems of the colonial churrigueresque style in Guatemala.

Old-timers remember Panajachel as a sleepy village with a couple of small, elegant inns. No more. At its center, Panajachel is a typical highland town, where shops, pool hall and eateries are huddled one against another in similar thick-walled adobe buildings. Along several streets toward the lake are

128

substantial vacation homes behind stone walls, each with a family of caretakers who cut the grass with machetes and keep the bougainvillea trimmed for when the owner shows up. On another street is an informal bazaar where native peddlers and visitors on indefinite stays offer textiles and trinkets, among dust and paper kicked up by the late-morning wind. Advertising signs, concrete-block hotels, and mini-shopping centers have sprouted, along with rickety plank buildings that see alternating service as handicraft shops, eateries and lodging places. Some gringos say that other gringos have spoiled Panajachel, but Guatemalans flock to town on weekends to take it all in.

Along the back paths, where the native inhabitants live in small adobe houses and cultivate irrigated plots of vegetables, Panajachel is timeless. Many women still wear the traditional red huipil and blue skirt, and a number of men use the old-style *ponchito,* a short blanket-skirt, over white pants. Despite the evident influence of tourism, agriculture is still the main occupation of the townspeople, and when seen from the approach roads winding down the mountainsides, the coffee plantings and vegetable patches give Panajachel the appearance of a great garden.

Layout

Though not very large in population, Panajachel is quite spread out, in contrast to other highland towns, and you're bound to do a bit of walking to get from place to place. The streets have various formal and informal names, but none are posted. The road from Sololá, which is the main street, enters Panajachel near the lake, then angles away from the water toward the town center. The major reference point for getting your bearings is the Mayan Palace Hotel, at the intersection of the main street and the street leading to the beach (Avenida Santander).

Across the river from the center of Panajachel is the neighborhood called Jucanyá ("across the river" in Cakchiquel), a quieter and mostly Indian area. The road that fords the river (starting at the bakery on the main street) continues to the lakeside villages of Santa Catarina Palopó and San Antonio Palopó.

In addition to the streets in Panajachel, a network of narrow trails makes it possible to get from one place to another without seeing anything more than Indian houses and coffee trees along the way.

129

HOTELS

Hotel del Lago. Tel. 621334. 100 rooms. $30 single/$40 double.
A multi-story resort hotel on the public beach, with bar, swimming pool, shops. All rooms have lake views.

Hotel Atitlán, Tel. 621429. 44 rooms. $58/$67.
On the edge of a coffee plantation two kilometers from town (toward Sololá) in a colonial-style building. Away-from-it-all atmosphere and excellent volcano views. The bar is especially pleasant. Beach and tennis courts, but no pool. Getting to town is an up-and-down hike, or a drive.

Cacique Inn. Tel. 621205. 30 rooms. $19/$22.
At the entrance to town on the Sololá side. Pool, fireplace in each of the large, attractive rooms. Good food.

Hotel Tzanjuyú. Tel. 621309. 32 rooms. $15/$19.
An older hotel, not without elegance, at the entrance to town from Sololá. Swimming pool, bar and extensive bare grounds. The large corner rooms have the best views. Food not great.

Hotel Monterrey. Tel. 621126. 30 rooms. $6/$12.
Neglected hotel of recent vintage, but right on the lake, with views, gardens.

Hotel Playa Linda. Tel. 621159. 15 rooms. $12/$17.
On the rocky public beach. All rooms have terraces facing the lake.

Paradise Inn. 7 rooms. $12/$17.
Nice compound near the lake. From the beach, follow the river.

Hotel Visión Azul. Tel. 621426. 16 rooms. $20/$25.
Off the Sololá road. Attractive rooms, all with lakeview terraces. Beach, pool, horses for rent, and coffee shop. Coffee plantation next door. Get written confirmation of the rate.

Mayan Palace Tel. 621028. 24 rooms. $5/$9.
Nice rooms for the price, but the hotel is on the main street at the noisiest intersection in town.

Hotel Rancho Grande. Tel. 621554. 7 rooms. $12/$20.
Comfortable rooms in cottages on well-tended grounds edged with bougainvilleas. The price includes an enormous breakfast. Good value. At the midpoint of Avenida Rancho Grande. (This is a classy neighborhood, by the way. The author lived next door for a number of years.)

Hotel Regis. Tel. 621149. 19 rooms. $10/$15.
On Avenida Santander. Spacious grounds with children's play area. Well-maintained rooms in an older building, many with fireplaces.

Hotel Galindo. 10 rooms. $7/$14.
On the main street. The flowered courtyard is the nice feature here. The hotel also has cottages near the lake, each with two bedrooms and kitchen.

Mini Motel Riva Bella. Tel. 621353. 7 rooms. $5/$9.
Near the Texaco station on the main street. Comfortable rooms for the price, but the location has no advantages.

Fonda del Sol. Tel. 621162. 10 rooms. $3 per person, $5 with private bath.
Pleasant woody rooms above the restaurant of the same name. On the main street.

Hotel Maya Kanek. Tel. 621104. 28 rooms. $4 per person, or less with shared bath.
On the main street in the center of town. Hot water and protected parking—good features for a budget hotel.

Las Casitas. 18 rooms. $3 per person.
Pleasant compound next to the town hall.

Cheap Hotels: It's easy to find lodging for $2 per person at any of the places that advertise their "rooms." Best of these budget pensions are Rooms Santander and Mario's Rooms, both on Avenida Santander. There are others on Avenida Rancho Grande, the next street over. In the center of town, you can stay at the Hotel Panajachel for $2 per person.

131

Elsewhere around the lake, there is a fine, secluded little hotel in San Antonio Palopó, and there are basic pensions in Santiago Atitlán, San Lucas Tolimán and San Pedro La Laguna. The Hotel Santa Catarina, a couple of kilometers beyond the village of the same name, has operated intermittently.

Camping is usually permitted at the public beach, though policy changes from time to time. Negotiate for trailer parking space at hotels with ample grounds, such as the Visión Azul.

RESTAURANTS

El Bistro, at the end of Avenida Santander, is a delightful eating place. Sit in one of the inside rooms, or, preferably, at a table in the garden, among herbs planted by the owner-chef. The menu varies, but you may find steak au poivre (excellent!), fettucine Alfredo or another homemade pasta, or lake bass. Salads are safe and creative, and big enough for two. Special meals can be arranged. $5 to $10, half portions available. Lunch at 1 p.m. No kids allowed at dinner (from 7:30 p.m.).

La Fontana. Attractive locale, open-air and inside dining overlooking the main street. Very good Italian-style food. Nice pastas for $2, sirloin steak and fondues about $7. Half portions may be ordered.

El Patio. Popular and informal, inside-outside, in the Patio shopping area on Avenida Santander. Char-broiled steaks, cassoulet, Chinese chicken and other interesting plates for $2 to $4, sandwiches and breakfast for less.

La Laguna. Dining on the porch or inside a large house set back from the main street. Steak in various forms, chicken and shrimp, $4 and up, sandwiches $2.

Blue Bird, on the extension of Av. Santander. The daily complete meal goes for $2, and there are salads, sandwiches, pies, and cheap breakfasts. A favorite of budget travelers.

Comedor Hsieh, down the street from the Blue Bird. Vegetarian. Daily specials, for about $2, include lasagna, curried vegetables, pizza and stuffed peppers. Also breakfast combinations, yogurt, granola and sandwiches.

La Unica, a.k.a. The Deli. Pastrami and Virginia Ham sandwiches, bagels, falaffel, mousse, all nicely done. $2 and up. In a courtyard off the main street, opposite the Centro de Salud (health center).

At the beach, Comedor El Cisne, opposite the Hotel del Lago, serves a complete meal including dessert and weak coffee, for $2, and well worth it. Open late. Nearby, Los Pumpos and Brisas del Lago offer sandwiches and light dinners. Also inexpensive. Pleasant to sit outside at these two places and watch the volcanoes, the lake and sunset.

Other spots include the Fonda del Sol, on the main street. Good food, no surprises, $3 to $4; Sicodélico, on Avenida Santander, not great, but open 24 hours; the Rancho Grande Inn, where a huge breakfast is served graciously for $3; Villa Martita, next to the Bistro, $3 or less for a Guatemalan-style meal; and, cheapest of all, the hole-in-the-wall eateries in back of the market.

BARS

On the side street leading from the Mayan Palace to the center of town is **Posada del Pintor,** a.k.a. Circus Bar. Live music with your drinks. The food is quite good: goulash soup, steak, pasta and pizzas, mostly for less than $3. This establishment's name honors Hannes Wiemann, a German painter who spent his last years in this house. Just up the street, **Tex Saloon** serves drinks on the patio, along with chicken-fried everything in Tex-sized portions at Guat-style prices. $2 and up. Ask for Tex.

The Last Resort, off Avenida Santander near the elementary school, is Panajachel's most venerable non-traditional watering hole. Drinks for about a dollar, and generous meals of lake fish, chicken and ribs for $3, as well as sandwiches and pizza. Down by the beach is **Past Ten,** a late drinking and dancing spot.

I don't vouch for the service, and drinks are more expensive than elsewhere; but one of the pleasures of Panajachel is to walk out to the Hotel Atitlán at sunset, and sip your drink in the bar or on the terrace as you look over gardens to the lake, the mist, and the clouds folding over the ridge between volcanoes in the distance. Surely one of the better views from any bar.

PANAJACHEL-LAKE ATITLAN DIRECTORY

Bank: Banco Agrícola Mercantil, in the same building as the Mayan Palace Hotel. Open 9 a.m. to 3 p.m. weekdays. Cash your travelers checks here. There's also a branch of the Banco de Guatemala in Sololá, but there are no other banks in the lake region. Make sure you have sufficient cash before setting out for nearby towns.

Beach: The public beach, which is the edge of the wide delta of the Panajachel River, is where visitors go for sunning and swimming and volcano-watching, where locals wash themselves and park their cayucos (canoes) for the night, where drivers bathe their buses, and where the ladies from Santa Catarina press their woven wares upon you. The beach is never dull, but nor is it an idyllic, sun-drenched, endless stretch of white sand. Pebbles, rocks, and plain old dirt are ample, driving rains rut the surface, and drainage ditches make some sections of the beach less than savory.

Best time to swim is in the morning, before the Xocomil wind comes up and turns the water choppy. The water's cold (this is a high mountain lake), but it becomes quite tolerable, even refreshing, once you go under. Changing rooms are available for a few cents.

Parking is permitted at the beach, with a small fee imposed when there are enough visitors to make it worth sending somebody to collect (usually on weekends). Camping is sometimes permitted, sometimes discouraged.

A private and cleaner beach, at the Hotel Visión Azul, is open to visitors for a fee of about 50 cents. Campers can also rent space.

Bicycles are rented just off the main street near the Mayan Palace Hotel; and at a location down the street from the Last Resort bar, off Avenida Santander.

Boats: There's scheduled service from Panajachel to Santiago

134

Atitlán (daily at 9:30 a.m. from the public beach) and to San Pedro La Laguna (daily at 3:30 a.m. and 3 p.m. from the Hotel Tzanjuyú). More details are given in the listings for each of these towns, below. You can make a one-day circle trip by boat from Panajachel to Santiago Atitlán to San Pedro and back to Panajachel. Or you can go by bus to San Lucas and Santiago Atitlán and continue by boat. Boats operate more frequently on fiesta days.

Rowboats can be rented at the boatyard at the foot of Avenida Santander. Go out in the morning, when the waters are calm. Motorboat tours to lake villages, and water skiing, can be arranged at the same place. Group trips are also available at the Hotel Atitlán, the Hotel Tzanjuyú, and the Hotel del Lago (more expensive), and from the boatyard of Mr. Rosales across the river, near the cemetery (cheaper). And you can sometimes barter with the owners of canoes and motorboats at the public beach to take you to Santa Catarina Palopó and San Antonio Palopó.

Books, new and used, are sold and traded at The Book Exchange, on the main street near the Fonda del Sol, as well as at the chocolates shop on the corner opposite the Mayan Palace.

Buses will stop for you anywhere on the main street, but the main unofficial bus stop is in front of the Mayan Palace Hotel.

Guatemala City to Panajachel: Transportes Higueros from 17 Calle 6-25, Zone 1, at 4 a.m. and 3:30 p.m., not reliable. Transportes Rebuli from 20 Calle and Avenida Bolívar approximately every hour from 6 a.m. to 4 p.m. Fare on either line under $2. There is no first-class bus service. To travel part of the way in more comfort, take a Quezaltenango bus from Guatemala City and change at Los Encuentros. Travel time from Guatemala City is about four hours.

Panajachel to Guatemala City: Transportes Higueros at 5:30 a.m. and 5:30 p.m.; Rebuli about every hour from 5 a.m. to 2 p.m., to the Zone 4 terminal.

To Chichicastenango, Quezaltenango, Huehuetenango and Mexico: Take any Guatemala City bus and connect at Los Encuentros. There are also several direct buses for Quezaltenango from 5:30 to 6:30 a.m. For Antigua, take a Guatemala City bus and connect

135

at Chimaltenango.

To Sololá: Take a Guatemala City bus, or one of the rickety vans or station wagons that operate every hour or so.

Direct buses to San Lucas Tolimán and the coast highway at Cocales pass through about every hour, more frequently before 8 a.m. Connect at Cocales for lowland destinations and the Mexican border. The 7 a.m. bus connects at San Lucas with a bus for Santiago Atitlán.

Doctors: For emergencies, try the health center (Centro de Salud) or the national hospital in Sololá. Dr. Hernández has his clinic near the Texaco station.

Entertainment: The best entertainment after a days's swimming or marketing is to watch the sunset, or the coastal lightning reflected against distant clouds during the rainy season (a show!). Movies are shown occasionally at the auditorium next to city hall, with Mexican thrillers (e.g., Saint Against the Mummies of Guanajuato) predominating. Also video movies, usually in English, in the Casa de Pays in the Hotel Maya Kanek and next to the El Patio restaurant.

Fishing: It's a big lake, but except for some large-mouth and small-mouth bass, the fish are small. Hooks and line can be purchased at any general store. You might catch some crappies or tilapia if you drop your line near shore; the black bass are farther out, and are usually speared by natives.

Houses for Rent: Rents range from $10 to several hundred dollars per month, according to amenities and what the traffic will bear. Most quarters are secured simply by asking around. Try any of the compounds of bungalows. Well-equipped units at Bungalows Guayacán go for $150 per month.

Laundry: If your hotel doesn't do laundry, or if you don't like the price, try any of several ladies who will pound your linens into cleanliness at a set price per dozen (a dozen anything, handkerchiefs to jeans). Look for the laundry sign on Avenida Santander, or ask somebody who's been around town a while.

Market: The market is on the main street at the eastern end of town, just past the town hall. Market day in Panajachel is Sunday, but things are also fairly busy on Saturdays. On these days, stalls are rented by vendors of textiles from all the major highland towns, as well as spice and kitchen-utensil merchants, itinerant shoemakers, and sellers of fish and pineapples and assorted other exotic produce from all corners of the republic. On non-market days, there's always a good selection of local produce in the morning.

Market days at towns readily accessible from Panajachel are: Sunday, Chichicastenango, Nahualá; Tuesday, Sololá, San Lucas Tolimán; Thursday, Chichicastenango; Friday, Sololá, Santiago Atitlán, San Lucas Tolimán; Saturday, San Lucas Tolimán.

Post Office-Telegraph-Telephones: The post office is located along the side street by the Catholic church, near the town hall. Try to mail packages early in the morning. Domestic telegrams are handled next door. For telephone calls and international telegrams, go to the Guatel office, in the red-brick building on Avenida Santander. Look for the microwave tower. Coin phones are located outside Guatel, and next to city hall.

Shopping: Native textiles are the local specialty, in the market of Panajachel, in the many handicraft stores in town, and in the markets of Sololá and Santiago Atitlán. Non-traditional arts and crafts include imaginative hand-painted t-shirts at Faces, next to the Hotel Galindo; oil paintings of village scenes and of the lake, some quite good, some not so good; and assorted bead necklaces, silver jewelry, and sketches by itinerant artists.

Taxis park near the post office. Dial 621571 to call one to your hotel.

Tourist Office: On the main street near Avenida Santander. Limited information. Unofficially, information and useful services are available at El Toro Pinto, opposite the Texaco station.

Trips from Panajachel: See the listings for other lakeside towns and nearby towns, below.

Volcanoes: Three volcanoes tower over the south shore of Lake

Atitlán. Look at them, and you can read the history of the lake, which was formed by their eruptions. San Pedro, to the southwest of Panajachel, rises to 3020 meters (9909 feet) and can be climbed in a day, starting from the town of San Pedro La Laguna. To the southeast is Tolimán with its twin craters, one at 3134 meters (10,283 feet), the other at 3158 meters (10,361 feet). Behind Tolimán, to the south, is Atitlán, the highest of the lake volcanoes, at 3535 meters (11,598 feet). Atitlán last erupted in 1853. Steam still seeps from the craters of both Atitlán and Tolimán. The climb to the top of either, starting at the town of San Lucas Tolimán, usually requires an overnight stay at the crater or in the saddle between the volcanoes.

Between Tolimán and the lake is Cerro de Oro, a volcanic mound. Its crater once held a Tzutuhil fortress, but is now given over to corn and bean cultivation. Cerro de Oro can be climbed in less than an hour.

Weather: During the rainy season, from May to October, temperatures will reach about 81° Fahrenheit (27° Centigrade) during the day. At night, there are usually enough clouds lingering to hold in the warmth of the day, but the temperature may drop to as low as 54° F (12° C). A sweater will come in handy. During the dry season, daily highs range from 73° to 84° F. (23° to 29° C.), but at night, the mercury can fall to the high thirties and low forties F (3° to 5° C). Frigid winds are common at night during the dry season, so a couple of sweaters or a coat are necessary. Above the lake, around Sololá and at the higher altitudes, frost is common early in the morning in the dry season. I have even seen snow flurries along the Pan American Highway late at night in February.

What to Do: Aside from people-watching and shopping, appreciation of beauty is the main activity for visitors to Panajachel. One can easily spend a number of days observing the nuances of color in the sunset or the waters of the lake, or staring at the clouds rolling overhead and creeping around the peaks of the volcanoes. If you don't feel like leaving, but don't know what else to do, here are some suggestions: Wander along the back paths of Panajachel. Visit one of the nearby towns by car, by bus, or on foot. Take a walk on the trails along the lake, or into the mountains. Take a bus ride to Cocales, down through a landscape that changes from cool highland to coffee slopes to sugar and

138

citronella fields to steaming cattle pastures, the coastal flats and sea often visible in the distance. Climb a volcano; swim; rent a boat, or take a ride on one of the scheduled boats.

Winds: Of the many currents that blow across the lake from the surrounding valleys, the most constant is the Xocomil, "the wind that carries away sin" (in Cakchiquel). The Xocomil rushes up late every morning from the coast, and suddenly turns the waters of the lake from calm to choppy. Afternoon winds usually blow in from the north, bringing rain from May to October. Winds on the lake are ever-shifting, which makes sailboating difficult.

SANTA CATARINA PALOPO
Population 1049 (99.9% indigenous); Altitude 1580 meters; Language: Cakchiquel; Fiesta: November 25; Palopó, "Among the amates" (wild fig trees)

A small and picturesque hillside farming town four kilometers from Panajachel. The inhabitants of Santa Catarina, unlike the people of other lake villages, were once dependent on fishing for cash income. The industry was wiped out by the introduction to the lake of black bass, which preys on smaller fish and is itself difficult to catch by traditional methods. The people have now turned to vegetable gardening, migratory work, and, most visibly, to selling their weaving in Panajachel. Both men and women still wear traditional dress.

Santa Catarina is reached by car or on foot from Panajachel, or by buses for San Antonio Palopó. For a more interesting approach, take a bus toward Godínez from Panajachel, and get off after San Andrés Semetabaj, at the convent on the right side of the road. A trail leads downward, at first steep and narrow, then gentler and wider through Santa Catarina's terraced, irrigated garden plots. Allow an hour for the descent, then another hour back to Panajachel.

SAN ANTONIO PALOPO
Population 1834 (99% indigenous); Altitude 1600 meters; Language: Cakchiquel; Fiesta: June 13

Another, larger village of adobe houses climbing the hillside from the lake shore. Onions and anise are the cash crops here, in addition to the staples of corn and beans. Traditional men's dress includes a long *rodillera,* or blanket-skirt, and a turban-like headdress worn only on holidays.

Several daily buses run to San Antonio from Panajachel, at about 6 a.m., 9 a.m. and 3 p.m., and usually return immediately. More buses on Friday and Sunday. A good plan is to go by bus and take a leisurely walk back. You can also drive, or take a Cocales bus to Godínez and take a trail down. This is a walk of about an hour, with spectacular lake views along the way.

There's one lodging place in San Antonio, the away-from-it-all **Terrazas del Lago,** hewn into the hillside at the water's edge. Ferns, avocados and bougainvilleas abound. The nine rooms are modern. $11 single/$15 double, slightly more for the front room with the best views. Simple meals. A chat with Feliks, the owner, is always worthwhile. Walk along the shore from where the road ends.

SAN LUCAS TOLIMAN
Population 6067 (82% indigenous); Altitude 1591 meters; Languages: Cakchiquel and Spanish; Fiesta: October 18; Market Days: Tuesday, Friday and Sunday; Tolimán, "place of the reeds"

A commercial center where locally grown coffee is processed, and where trucks plying the highway from the highlands to the coast are serviced. The church dates from early in the colonial period. Traditional houses are of bamboo or of rock, though the use of wood and concrete block in some of the newer buildings gives San Lucas an appearance similar to that of many coastal towns.

Transportation and Accommodations: From Panajachel, buses for Cocales stop near San Lucas. Buses for Santiago Atitlán from Guatemala City pass through San Lucas at approximately 9 a.m., 2 p.m. and 6 p.m. There are several combination eateries and pensions near the square.

Highway Notes
The road along the south shore of the lake between San Lucas Tolimán and Santiago Atitlán is unpaved, narrow and rutted. It passes through a boulder-strewn area with vegetation less

140

abundant than along the north shore of the lake, where there is some year-round irrigation. Beyond Santiago Atitlán, the road is in fair condition in the stretch where it climbs through pine forest along the southern slopes of the San Pedro volcano. After San Pedro, the route is mostly level, through San Juan La Laguna to San Pablo La Laguna.

CERRO DE ORO
Population 2367; Altitude 1590 meters; Languages: Cakchiquel and Spanish

A small settlement near the Cerro de Oro volcanic mound. Though part of the Tzutuhil-speaking township of Santiago Atitlán, most of the inhabitants are descendants of migrants from Patzicía, and speak a Cakchiquel dialect. The church has an interesting modern mural showing Christ dressed in the purple-and-white trousers of Santiago Atitlán.

Cerro de Oro is three kilometers down a side road from the road between San Lucas and Santiago Atitlán.

SANTIAGO ATITLAN
Population 14,152 (township 19,652; 95% indigenous); Altitude 1592 meters; Language: Tzutuhil; Fiesta: July 25; Market Day: Every day, but especially Friday.

Santiago Atitlán, largest and most traditional of the lake towns, is a collection of stone and bamboo huts with thatched roofs, crowded along winding paths. At the time the Spaniards arrived, the capital of the Tzutuhil nation was located across the bay on the hill called Chuitinamit, at the base of the San Pedro volcano. Nothing remains of the fortress, but the area where the common people lived is today's Santiago Atitlán. During the early part of the colonial period, the town, then known as as Santiago Chiyá, or Santiago-by-the-water, was an important missionary and trading center. The large white church dates from that time.

An unusual figure in the traditional religious life of Atitlán is Maximón, said to represent a combination of Judas, Pedro de Alvarado, and the traditional god Mam. While many other towns in the highlands have a Maximón, who is the object of scorn during Easter celebrations, in Atitlán the figure is revered. This heresy

141

was the cause of friction between the bishop of Sololá and the people of Atitlán in the 1950s, and only at the intervention of the president of Guatemala was Maximón restored to his traditional place in the local ritual. Maximón is usually kept locked up under the care of a religious brotherhood, but he may be seen, complete with a cigar stuck in his wooden face, during colorful Holy Week celebrations.

The traditional textiles of Santiago Atitlán are highly regarded. Men wear striped purple-and-white trousers, though these days they usually dress in western-style shirts. Women's huipiles are also in purple and white, and covered with delicately woven and embroidered figures of birds and animals. The unusual halo-style headdress, consisting of a long ribbon wound around the crown, is pictured on Guatemala's 25-centavo coin. Fine samples of Atitlán weaving (huipiles, trousers and, occasionally, shawls) are on sale in the booths along the side of the market (which is an all-woman operation), as well as in some stores.

There's not much of a beach in town, but if you walk in the direction of San Pedro, the road runs along the water and you can jump in off the rocks.

Out of town, toward San Lucas, is the preserve of the pok, or Atitlán Grebe (podilymbus gigas), a flightless waterbird found only on Lake Atitlán. The pok has been threatened in recent years by the large-mouth bass, which feeds on the young of the species and competes for its food, and by the over-cutting of reeds, to which nests are anchored. An underwater fence keeps fish out of the preserve, which also has a small swimming beach. The entrance road is identified by a sign reading "DIGESA."

Transportation: From Panajachel, boats leave daily for Santiago Atitlán, from both the Hotel Tzanjuyú (9 a.m.,) and the Hotel del Lago (9:30 a.m.). You have about an hour to spend in town before departure for Panajchel at 11:30 a.m. or noon. Fare is about $2 each way from the public beach, more from the Tzanjuyú.

Boats leave for San Pedro at noon and 4 p.m.

Rebuli buses leave Guatemala City (20 Calle and Avenida Bolívar, Zone 1) at 6 and 11 a.m., and 3 p.m. From Atitlán, departures for Guatemala City are at 4 and 7 a.m., and 1 p.m., via San Lucas and the coast highway.

Accommodations: The Chi-nim-ya on the lake front offers plain, decent rooms for less than $2. For the same price, you can stay at

142

the Pensión Rosita, just off the main square. There is a pleasant little diner near the dock, with basic meals for a couple of dollars. Cheaper and less inviting places are up the street.

Beyond Santiago Atitlán, at the gasoline station, the road divides. The way to the left is past the small hospital of the Catholic mission, and onward to Chicacao, down toward the coast. The route is passable only in the dry season. Views to the coastal lowlands from a lookout point are excellent. To the right, the unpaved main road climbs through pine forests on the south side of the San Pedro volcano, before winding down into the town of San Pedro La Laguna.

SAN PEDRO LA LAGUNA
Population 5597 (98% indigenous); Altitude 1610 meters; Languages: Tzutuhil and Spanish; Fiesta: June 29

Under the volcano of the same name, San Pedro is a densely populated little town that looks like a small city. Houses are built close upon one another, and the spires of a number of evangelical temples rise up along with the old white Catholic church. *Pedranos* have always been considered somewhat different from the people of neighboring villages. They're aggressive in commerce, and over the years, have bought up much of the land in nearby San Juan. They've taken to using horses and mules to carry cargo, instead of their own backs, and, most significantly, a good many have converted to evangelical Protestantism. The rituals of folk Catholicism have disappeared from San Pedro, and have been replaced by guitar strumming and the singing of hymns at prayer meetings. A modified version of traditional clothing is still the norm, however. Men wear white trousers with broken blue stripes, and shirts made locally from cloth woven of tie-dyed thread on foot looms. The shirts are also sold in other towns of the lake region and throughout the country. The women's huipil is cut from machine-made cloth.

San Pedro is altogether a pleasant place, where foreign visitors are hardly even noticed, and many an impecunious outsider has settled in for months on end. In addition to subsistence agriculture, the cultivation of coffee and avocados, and the manufacture of shirts, there's a factory on the beach northeast of town that produces hand-knotted wool rugs, many with designs

143

taken from Mayan glyphs.

Accommodations: Hospedaje Chuasinahu, on the beach northeast of town, is the best of several pensions. $1 per person, or $2 with your own toilet. Clean. There are several simple diners on the main street, opposite the square.

Transportation: Boats from Panajachel (Hotel Tzanjuyú) daily at 3:30 a.m., stopping in San Pablo and San Juan on the way out, leaving San Pedro at 6 a.m. for Panajachel. Also at 3 p.m. direct to San Pedro, leaving San Pedro at 4 p.m. for Panajachel, with stops in San Juan and San Pablo. Fare about $2. The dock is northwest of the center of San Pedro. These boats mainly serve people from San Pedro heading to the the markets of Panajachel and Sololá, which explains the schedule.

Boats leave for Santiago Atitlán at 7 a.m. and 2 p.m. from the beach northeast of town.

SAN JUAN LA LAGUNA
Population 2068 (99% indigenous); Altitude 1580 meters; Languages: Tzutuhil and Spanish; Fiesta: June 24.

A small town about two kilometers beyond San Pedro, specializing in the cultivation of coffee and in the weaving of *petates* —mats—from reeds harvested in shallow waters.

From just beyond San Juan, a steep trail leads to Santa Clara La Laguna and Santa María Visitación, villages high above the lake. The dirt road along the shore passes Cristalinas beach, the most pleasant place on the lake for a swim. Only a few people are seen around the beach, tending waterside vegetable plots or gathering reeds to dry on the shore. Ducks paddle about the water, and the hill called Cristalinas juts up behind.

SAN PABLO LA LAGUNA
Population 2811 (99.7% indigenous); Altitude 1650 meters; Language: Tzutuhil; Fiesta: January 25

The major activity in San Pablo is the twisting of the fibers of the maguey plant into rope, and making the rope into hammocks and bags. Ropes in the process of being twisted and braided are stretched out all over town. The maguey plant requires little attention, and there's relatively less cultivation of corn and beans than in other lake towns, so many men end up sitting around with not much to do.

The colonial church, in ruins for many years, has been rebuilt, retaining only its original facade.

The road around the lake comes to an end at San Pablo, and the following three towns are reached by trail or boat.

SAN MARCOS LA LAGUNA

Population 927 (99% indigenous); Altitude 1660 meters; Language: Cakchiquel; Fiesta: April 25

San Marcos, a town of thatched mud-and-bamboo houses, has been ravaged repeatedly over the years by floods pouring down from the mountains towering to the north. After the flood of 1950, when much of the town washed into the lake, most houses were moved to two hills overlooking the old town center. The cultivation of fruit trees and maguey plants, and cattle raising, are the main activities.

TZUNUNA

Population 739; Altitude 1600 meters; Language: Cakchiquel; "Hummingbird of the water"

Tzununá produces some of the best citrus fruits of the region. The town also was heavily hit in the 1950 flood, and most of the people built new mud-and-bamboo houses on higher ground. Few of the inhabitants venture far from their homes, and the women turn and hide their faces when a stranger passes.

SANTA CRUZ LA LAGUNA

Population 535 (99% indigenous); Altitude 1660 meters; Language: Cakchiquel; Fiesta: May 10

A picturesque and poor hamlet of adobe houses, isolated on a hillside, accessible by a difficult trail from Panajachel.

Towns Above the Lake

SOLOLA

Population 6286 (township 29,188; 90% indigenous); Altitude 2113 meters; Languages: Cakchiquel and Spanish; Market days: Tuesday and Friday; "Sap of the elder: or possibly "bat river"; Kilometer 129

Situated on a ridge high above Lake Atitlán, Sololá is one of the major market centers of the western highlands. On Tuesdays and Fridays, the plaza and the streets leading to the large market building are filled with people who have journeyed from all over the region to sell their produce and buy their necessities. Many can be recognized by their town outfits: men of San Antonio Palopó and Nahualá in long woolen skirts, women of Chichicastenango in huipiles covered with floral designs, and, most of all, the people of Sololá and the surrounding settlements, the women in huipiles of red stripes and pinstripes, and men in pants of the same material, wearing short blanket skirts and waist-length woolen jackets in the old style of Spanish officers. The jackets bear a stylized bat on the back, symbol of the last ruling dynasty of the Cakchiquel nation.

Founded in 1547, Sololá is the the capital of the department of the same name. The ruins of the original settle, Tzoloyá, are a few kilometers north of the present town. The surrounding highlands produce wool, wheat, corn, barley, potatoes, onions and garlic. At the lower altitudes of the department, around Lake Atitlán and toward the coast, coffee and sugar cane are important crops.

Sololatecos are faithful to their old rituals. On Sunday mornings, cofradía (religious brotherhood) officers in top hats and black capes, with staffs of office in hand, march together from the square up to the church. Men, women and children kiss the hands of their respected elders, and at fiesta times, the processions of religious brotherhoods wind their way through the streets.

Accommodations: There are two small hotels a block above the square. Rooms about $2 per person. Better to continue to Panajachel.

Buses: Service to Panajachel and to Los Encuentros, on the Pan

American Highway, on crowded station wagons and vans, and on the larger Guatemala City buses. Allow a half-hour for the run between Sololá and Panajachel. Leave early to get to Sololá from Panajachel on a market day.

Bank: Banco de Guatemala, one block north of the square, on 7 Avenida.

CONCEPCION
Population 947 (99% indigenous); Altitude 2050 meters; Language: Cakchiquel; Fiesta: December 8

A farming village on the plateau directly north of Panajachel. The baroque colonial church has a small silver collection, which can sometimes be seen by tipping the caretaker. Reached by dirt road from Sololá, or by trail from Panajachel, with good views of the lake along the way.

SAN JORGE LA LAGUNA
Population 1087; Altitude 1800 meters; Language: Cakchiquel; Fiesta: April 24

Part of the township of Sololá, San Jorge is a picturesque village dominated by a white church, located just below the highway between Panajachel and Sololá. Once situated on the broad river delta below, San Jorge was moved up in the eighteenth century, after a flood. Though just off a busy highway, San Jorge sees few outsiders. A dirt road leads to the shores of the lake below.

SAN ANDRES SEMETABAJ
Population 984 (81% indigenous) Altitude 1960 meters; Languages: Cakchiquel and Spanish; Fiesta: November 30; Market day: Tuesday; Semetabaj, "glassy rock"; Kilometer 113

A village of skilled farmers, with a magnificent ruin of a colonial church, located eight kilometers from Panajachel.

SAN JOSE CHACAYA
Population 114 (59% indigenous); Altitude 2150 meters: Languages: Cakchiquel and Spanish; Fiesta: Tuesday of Easter Week.

A farming village with a colonial church, six kilometers from Sololá, reached by a dirt road that winds through a scenic area of forests and rushing streams.

SANTA LUCIA UTATLAN
Population 989 (township 10,358; 95% indigenous); Altitude 2491 meters; Languages: Quiché and Spanish; Fiesta: December 13; Market Day: Sunday; Utatlán, "place of bamboo"

Farther up the dirt road from Sololá, in an area of pine and oak forest, and wheat and corn fields. Pleasant views to towns in the valleys on either side of the road. Also reached by a branch road from kilometer 142 on the Pan American Highway.

Beyond Santa Lucía, a dirt road curves through the hilly plateau toward the twin villages of Santa María Visitación (population 745, 97% indigenous; altitude 2050 meters) and Santa Clara La Laguna (population 2447; 98% indigenous; altitude 2090 meters, market days Tuesday and Saturday). Both are Quiché-speaking, and Santa Clara specializes to some degree in basket weaving. At kilometer 152 on the way to Santa Clara, there's a cleft on the left side of the road, which affords dizzying views of San Pedro, San Pablo and Santiago Atitlán far below on the lake shore. A steep trail leads from Santa Clara down to San Juan La Laguna.

Nearby Towns

NAHUALA
Population 2314 (township 26,674; 99% indigenous); Altitude 2467 meters; Languages; Quiché and Spanish; Fiesta: November 25; Market Day: Sunday; "Place of magic"

Nahualá is the large town in this part of the highlands that has most stubbornly resisted the encroachments of the outside world. For many years, Ladinos and foreigners were not permitted to enter Nahualá, and all attempts to buy town lands or set up

148

missions were rejected. Attitudes have relaxed in recent years. A few Ladinos live in Nahualá, and an occasional visitor turns up for the market. The prohibition of liquor, in force for many years, has been lifted, though drinking is still looked down upon.

Half of the men of Nahualá are rumored to be *brujos*, traditional prayer men, though the figure is no doubt exaggerated. Folk-Catholic ceremonies are often seen on the steps of the town church, with candles, incense and muted supplications to the ruling gods and saints.

Along the Pan American Highway in the vicinity of the town, and in the surrounding hills, the men of Nahualá can be seen tending flocks of sheep, or carrying carved wooden furniture and grinding stones on their backs to markets all over the highlands. Their outfit consists of a long woolen skirt worn over short white pants, and an overshirt made of the undyed black wool of local sheep. Underneath, they wear striped red shirts, with embroidered patches sewn onto cuffs and collars. The white huipiles of the women often display figures of animals, including a two-headed eagle which is said to be copied from the emblem of the Hapsburgs who ruled Spain in the colonial period. All of the weaving in Nahualá is of fine quality, especially the men's blue head cloths.

Nahualá is well worth a visit on market day. In contrast to Chichicastenango and other towns more frequented by outsiders, Nahualá is subdued, with transactions carried out in soft murmurs. The visitor will feel strongly the gulf between himself and the traditional, mysterious ways of the townspeople.

To get to Nahualá, drive or take any bus heading west to Quezaltenango, as far as kilometer 155 on the Pan American Highway.

SANTA CATARINA IXTAHUACAN
Population 1396 (township 19,650; 99% indigenous); Altitude 2320 meters; Language: Quiché; Fiesta: November 25; Ixtahuacán, "cultivated land"

A sister town of Nahualá, located five kilometers to the southwest. The dress, customs and dialect of the two towns are identical.

CHICHICASTENANGO

Population 3199 (township 56,615; 97% indigenous); Altitude 2071 meters; Languages: Quiché and Spanish; Fiesta: December 21; Market Days: Thursday and Sunday; "Place of the nettles"; Kilometer 145

Santo Tomás Chichicastenango has long been one of the magical destinations of the Americas. A great market center for the Indians of the western highlands, it is inundated on Thursdays and Sundays with traders who bring their produce, textiles and handiwork from all the towns of the region. It is also a place where the traditional, mystical ways of Guatemala's indigenous peoples still visibly hold sway.

In former times, traders would carry their wares for hours along dirt roads or back paths to reach Chichicastenango, often setting out the day before the market and sleeping out on the plaza. Visitors from the outside had to face grueling hours on dusty roads from the capital to get to see the great market, the mix of pagan and Catholic ritual amid clouds of incense at the Santo Tomás church, the rolling hills and steep canyons of the forested and farmed countryside often shrouded in mist. Now many traders come in the buses that choke the streets to the east of the square, and visitors can arrive in comfort over paved roads from Guatemala City. The isolation of Chichicastenango is a thing of the past, and much of the market is now given over to goods made for the tourist. But the excitement of market day, the folk Catholicism so strange to the visitor, and the splendor of the setting all remain.

Years before the Conquest, the site of Chichicastenango was a Cakchiquel settlement called Chaviar. The Cakchiquels moved their capital to Iximché at the start of their period of war with the Quichés, who had their capital at Cumarcaj, or Utatlán, twenty kilometers from Chaviar. When Alvarado and the Spanish laid waste to Utatlán in 1524, refugees migrated to the area of the former Cakchiquel town, which the Spanish, adopting the name given to the place by their Mexican allies, called Chichicastenango, after the greenish-yellow spiny plant that grows all over the area. The Quichés called their settlement, and still call it, Siguán Tinamit, "the town surrounded by canyons."

On a market day, Chichicastenango may not appear to be the traditional town that it is said to be. Some of the tourist trade is dominated by Ladino merchants, and the presence of large numbers of foreigners arriving on tour buses takes away much of the atmosphere that is present on non-market days. But a glimpse through the crowds reveals much that is foreign to the western world. The *Masheños*, the people of Chichicastenango, have remained faithful to most of their old ways.

Chichicastenango still maintains a separate government for its Indians. A first and second mayor and councilmen, as well as an Indian court, take care of matters that concern the Indian community exclusively. Operating parallel to the Indian government is the religious organization based on cofradías, groups of men devoted to a particular saint. Duties in the cofradías are alternated with service in the government, as a man slowly but steadily rises in position in each.

The cofradías and *chuchkajaues*—native prayer men—have always been more important than the institutional church in the religious life of Chichicastenango. While baptisms take place in church, and are all-important in setting a person on the proper course in life, marriages and funerals are under the charge of chuchkajaues.

The cofradías number fourteen. The most important is the cofradía of St. Thomas, the patron saint of Chichicastenango. On the day of the saint of each cofradía, the saint's image is carried in procession, and installed in its place of honor in the house of the new cofradía chief, or *alcalde*.

All the cofradías participate in the feasts of the more important saints. Images of the major saints bring up the rear of the processions. The cofradía officers wear ceremonial jackets over their regular outfits, and carry *varas*, staffs of office capped with silver suns and wrapped in ritual cloths. The beat of the *tun* (a drum) and the melody of the *chirimía* (a flute) provide musical accompaniment. Every few steps, the procession comes to a halt and a rocket bomb is fired from a launching pipe. Candles, incense burners, feathers and fruit decorate the thrones of the saints.

The processions are only the visible part of the activities of the cofradías. All during the year, the head of a cofradía hosts meals for his members. At fiesta times, the cofradía dresses up its saint and members drink heavily. The expenses born by a cofradía leader are heavy, sometimes running into more than what he earns in a year, and so he often must go into debt to finance his position of honor.

The chuchkajaues, or prayer men, act as mediators between

individuals and the saints and idols. In the folk Catholicism of the highlands, the saints and idols are seen very much as active powers who can intervene in the world to set things right or punish wrongdoers. A prayer man, phrasing things in the proper way, can appeal to an idol for help, ask for forgiveness, seek a cure for illness, or give thanks for a bit of fortune. By using a kit of seeds, a chuchkajau can tell the future. The ceremonies of chuchkajaues take place at the church, at household shrines, and at stone idols set up in the hills outside town. When the ceremony is held at an idol, a sacrificial chicken may be thrown in with offerings of candles, flowers and liquor.

While the religious and community life of Chichicastenango are strong, some traditional elements are fading. The men's outfit is going out of use. This consists of black woolen knee pants with seams open from below the thigh, a red sash, a black woolen jacket with embroidered trim and designs in red, and a red *tzut*, or scarf, around the head. These days, the old style of clothing is seen only on the older men, some chuchkajaues, and the employees of the Mayan Inn. (It is also worn by employees of the Hotel Pan American in Guatemala City.) Most women still wear a huipil of hand-woven cotton, completely covered with geometric designs and figures of flowers and plants. The shoulders bear small round sections of black satin or rayon, and the collar section is in the form of pointed spokes, like the rays of the sun. The skirt, secured by a sash, is of striped blue cloth woven on foot looms, with a horizontal embroidered band around the middle. A headcloth is used as a cushion on which to place baskets and jugs of water.

The Market on Thursdays and Sundays is the principal attraction for most visitors. The specialties are Chichicastenango huipiles (women's blouses), sashes, carved and painted boxes, and masks. But handicrafts from all over the highlands are brought to town for the benefit of tourists. The selection is better than in other markets, but asking prices are higher, so be prepared to bargain hard.

Visitors arriving early on market day will see the roads crowded with Indians carrying heavy loads of produce, pottery and dismantled furniture on their backs. By late morning, the central plaza is a packed madhouse of vendors, natives doing their shopping, and tourists bargaining for handicrafts while roving sellers approach them with cheap jewelry. The jostling and the frank commerce can be unsettling at times, and it takes patience and detachment to wade through all that is available, decide what you really want, and try to strike a deal. By late afternoon, most of the vendors are packing up, and peace returns to the plaza, amid the litter and discards of the day's commerce.

With all the noise and madness of market day, and all the merchants from outside who come to town, it's often difficult to see through the activity and focus on the town itself. Visitors might want to arrive a day early or stay for a day after the market to get a picture of Chichicastenango at peace.

The Church of Santo Tomás on the east side of the plaza is a whitewashed colonial structure, built around 1540. On the steps, prayer men burn copal resin on a stone platform, and estoraque, another resinous incense, in hand-held burners. The altarpieces inside are of wood and silver, decorated with faded paintings and statues of saints.

The impressive part of the church is not its physical structure, but the ceremony that takes place amid clouds of incense on the front steps and around low wooden platforms placed along the aisles. After burning incense on the front steps, a chuchkajau enters with his client, and stops at the door to explain the purpose of the ceremony to the guardian spirits of the church. Prayers are said at the altar railing, and then at the platforms, each of which is associated with a specific group of ancestors. Candles, flowers and liquor are offered to the souls residing in each area. The chuchkajau, using the exact combination of words appropriate for the act, calls on the saints, the souls of the departed and the lords of all the natural forces of the Indian universe to hear his plea.

To the side of the church is a former monastery, now used for church offices. Laid out in its garden is a model in concrete of the ceremonial staff of the St. Thomas cofradía.

In the parish archives, the Spanish priest Francisco Ximénez discovered the manuscript of the Popol Vuh, the sacred book of the Quichés, early in the eighteenth century. Regarded as a masterpiece of American indigenous literature, the Popol Vuh consists of two parts. The first reads somewhat like the Christian Bible, and tells through allegory, poetry and symbolism the early history of mankind. Man was created from a paste of corn, according to the Popol Vuh, after initial attempts using wood and clay produced excessively rigid and fragile human beings. The

153

second part is an account of the wanderings of the forebears of the Quiché nation, from their ancestral home in the Toltec lands of Mexico to the highlands of what is now Guatemala, and the establishment of a powerful kingdom. This part seems to have a strong factual basis, at least to the extent that historians and ethnologists can compare it with archaeological evidence and the few other written accounts available to them.

Visitors to the church should enter by the side door through the monastery, and stay off the front steps so as not to interrupt the ritual. Sunday mass starts at about 8 a.m., and is attended by the members of the cofradías, who arrive early and sit near the altar.

El Calvario is the chapel on the west side of the plaza. Inside is a figure of Christ in a glass case. Incense is burned on a stone platform at the top of the steps, and rituals similar to those of the Santo Tomás church take place inside.

The Museum is located on the south side of the plaza and contains the jade collection of Ildefonso Rossbach. Rossbach came to Guatemala as an accountant, studied for the priesthood in the United States, and returned to Guatemala to serve in Chichicastenango until his death in 1944 at the age of 74.

In addition to the jade, there are ceramic figures, household objects, incense burners, and a stuccoed cranium that probably once stood in a household shrine. Almost all the pieces are from the department of Quiché, and a few are thought to date from before the time of Christ. Most of the exhibits bear no explanatory captions, but if you have any questions about a particular piece, one of the attendants will give you some background.

The museum is open every day except Tuesday from 8 a.m. to noon and from 2 to 5 p.m. On market days, it often stays open past noon.

The Cemetery is located down the hill from and two blocks west of the plaza. Richer families bury their dead in above-ground vaults near the entrance, but most Indians end up under a whitewashed mound of earth with a bit of food and drink in their coffins and a wood or stone cross, if anything, to mark the grave. There's a small chapel at the front of the cemetery, and at the rear, the yellow burial vault of Father Rossbach.

The cemetery is a quiet place, except on All Saints' and All Souls' days, when families come out to remember the dead with drinking and eating. Cemeteries in the highlands are also the places where men of black magic place curses on people in the deep of the night.

Pascual Abaj, or **Turkaj,** is a stone idol located on a hilltop about a kilometer from town. In local religious practice, idols complement the saints as representations of the natural forces that govern the world. Unless a ceremony is in progress, with candles and incense burning and perhaps a chicken being sacrificed, the shrine itself, a stone figure surrounded by stones, with an incense-burning platform nearby, won't seem particularly impressive. Views of Chichicastenango and the surrounding valleys from the hilltop, however, are excellent.

The shrine was attacked by orthodox Catholics during the religious conflicts of the fifties, and the idol was damaged, but it has now been patched up with reinforced concrete.

To reach the idol, take the street that leads south from the plaza between the church and the museum, turn right at the first corner, and follow the road down the hill and out of town. About halfway along, the trail passes through the yard of a man who takes care of the masks and costumes used for fiestas. If there's anybody around, you may be able to look at the collection.

Fiestas are the times of year when the cofradías honor their saints and install new officers. Most of the ritual takes place in the house of the outgoing head of the cofradía, amid food and drink. The saint is brought to the church the night before the day dedicated to him, and the next morning is carried in procession after mass, and later placed in the house of the new cofradía head.

The fireworks specialists, responsible for all the noise of the celebration, have their own guardian figure called Tzijolaj, a small horse and rider carried by one of the members of the fraternity as he dances about. Tzijolaj, who may represent St. James, is a messenger who communicates between man and the governing forces of the universe. Tzijolaj is thought to have originated at the time of the Conquest, when men on horses were taken by the natives to be gods.

At major fiestas, young men dress up in elaborate costumes to perform traditional dances. The special dance groups train in

155

preparation for the festivities, but in the end, drunkenness and long hours of dance without rest cause the steps to deteriorate into stuporific stumbling and fumbling. Among the dances performed in Chichicastenango are the Dance of the Bulls, representing the contest between matador and bull; the Dance of the Conquest, in which the native nations are defeated by the gaudily dressed conquerors; and the Dance of the Mexicans.

The feast of St. Thomas, starting on December 14 and culminating on December 21, is the main Chichicastenango fiesta. Processions and liquor and dances also appear during Holy Week (Easter), at Christmas, on All Saints' and All Souls' days (November 1 and 2), at the October harvest festival, on Corpus Christi, and on the feast days of the saints of each of the cofradías, most notably January 20, March 19 and June 24.

HOTELS

Mayan Inn. 30 rooms. $28 single/$33 double. Tel. 561176 (60213 in Guatemala City)
One of the best hotels in the country, in two traditional tile-roofed buildings west of the square. Furnished with antiques and antiquities gathered from all over the country. Pleasant gardens, and views to the surrounding valleys from the terraces. Horseback trips and car tours arranged. Also a good place to hear the marimba, Guatemala's best-known native instrument, usually played on market days in the courtyard of the bar. Add about $15 per person for three meals.

Hotel Santo Tomás. 25 rooms. $30/$37
On the entrance street, next to the Chevron station. A pleasant, relatively new hotel in tasteful colonial style. All rooms have fireplaces.

Pensión Chuguilá. 23 rooms. $4 to $7/$6 to $12.
North of the square on the street leading through the arch. A pleasant, traditional place built around a courtyard. Many rooms have fireplaces. Good value. Add about $6 for three filling meals.

Maya Lodge. 10 rooms. $5 to $6/$8 to $9. Tel. 561167 (29367 in Guatemala City).

On the square, simple and clean. Meals available for less than $3.

For cheaper rooms, try the Casa de Huéspedes Girón on the street one block north of the square, where rooms go for $4 per person, less with shared bath. Cheap rooms are in short supply, so if you're on a tight budget, plan to see Chichicastenango on a day outing from Guatemala City or Panajachel, or continue to Santa Cruz del Quiché or Quezaltenango for the night.

RESTAURANTS

Inexpensive and moderately priced meals are available at the Maya Lodge, on the square, and at the Pensión Chuguilá. For more elegant dining, try the Mayan Inn and Hotel Santo Tomás. For cheap food, go to the booths in the market, or the small eateries on the entrance street east of the plaza.

Services: The Banco del Ejército is on 6 Calle, the main street, about a block from the square. Telephone calls can be made at the Guatel office on the entrance street, next to the pig market. The post office is nearby.

Transportation: To drive to Chichicastenango, follow the Pan American Highway (CA1) to Los Encuentros junction at kilometer 127. Turn right for the road to Chichicastenango. Near kilometer 135, there's a small turnout on the left where you can stop to look down on Chichicastenango. In the distance is the city of Santa Cruz del Quiché, on its own hilltop. Beyond this point, the road descends into a canyon on switchbacks, and climbs back up to the plateau on which Chichicastenango sits. A small parking fee is collected on market days at the town entrance.

Buses of the Masheña and Reina de Utatlán lines leave from the terminal in Zone 4, Guatemala City, about every hour on market days, about every two hours on other days. Take any bus marked Quiché or Chichicastenango. For a comfortable ride part of the way, take Rutas Lima (8 a.m. from 8 Calle 3-63, Zone 1) and connect with another bus at Los Encuentros.

Many local buses also operate from Chichicastenango to Los Encuentros, where connections can be made for Guatemala City, Panajachel and Quezaltenango. Don't start out too late in the day. Los Encuentros is a lousy place in which to get stuck. It's

2600 meters high, and cold and windy in the early morning and from the late afternoon on. The temperature drops below freezing at night in the dry season. There's a small restaurant at the gas station.

Almost all travel agencies in Guatemala City offer tours to Chichicastenango, usually including a stop at Lake Atitlán in the package.

SANTA CRUZ DEL QUICHE
Population 8966 (township 35,301; 79% indigenous); Altitude 2021 meters; Languages: Quiché and Spanish; Fiesta: August 18; Market: Every day, but especially Thursday and Sunday; Kilometer 164

Capital of the department of El Quiché, Santa Cruz del Quiché is a well-kept and quiet place. The streets are frequented by people from the surrounding towns bringing their produce to market, and a few women hurrying along, their busy fingers twisting straw into the braids from which hats will be sewn. Quiché is a transfer point for travelers going by bus to towns to the east and north, especially Nebaj. Visitors will find that prices in the market are more reasonable than those in Chichicastenango. Crocheted shoulder bags, made in nearby towns and by the inmates of the local jail, are a good buy. The colonial church might also be worth a glimpse.

Accommodations: There are a few small pensions in Quiché. For a basic room, try Posada Calle Real, 2 Avenida 7-36, Zone 1; Hospedaje San Pedro, 0 Avenida 9-02, Zone 5; or Hotel San Pascual, 7 Calle 0-43, Zone 1. All are near the bus terminal, and all charge $2 per person or less. On the far side of the square from the bus terminal, meals are available at Lago Azul (tablecloths!), 0 Avenida 2-12, and Comedor Las Rosas, 1 Avenida 1-28.
There's a branch of the Banco de Guatemala on the main square.

Buses leave the terminal in Guatemala City for Chichicastenango and Santa Cruz del Quiché about every two hours, and every hour on Thursdays and Sundays. Last bus from Quiché to Guatemala

City about 3 p.m.

A bus leaves for Nebaj daily except Sunday at 9:30 a.m. from the Quiché terminal, 1 Avenida and 10 Calle, Zone 5. There may be other buses during the morning for Nebaj, San Juan Cotzal and Chajul. On Wednesdays and Saturdays, the bus for Nebaj from Guatemala City stops near the main square at about 11 a.m. The trip takes five hours. There are other buses for Huehuetenango via Sacapulas, and for Zacualpa and Joyabaj (see below).

UTATLAN RUINS

The Utatlán ruins are located about three kilometers west of Santa Cruz del Quiché via a dirt road. Utatlán, or Cumarcaj, as the inhabitants called it, was the pre-Conquest capital of the Quiché, the most culturally advanced of the highland nations. Surrounded by deep canyons and approachable only by steep steps and a narrow causeway, Utatlán was the center for the royal court and priests. The common people lived outside the fortress.

In 1524, Tecún Umán, one of the Quiché rulers, was killed in single combat by Pedro de Alvarado near the present site of Quezaltenango. The Quiché lords invited the Spanish to their capital, planning to trap them inside and burn them alive. Alvarado discovered the plot, had the Quiché nobility burned, and destroyed the city. Some of the stones were removed and used to construct the city of Santa Cruz del Quiché. Tecún Umán is still honored as the native hero of Guatemala. Large statues of him stand in Guatemala City's Aurora Park, and outside Quezaltenango.

Because of the intentional destruction of the fortress, not much remains of Utatlán for the visitor to see. The structures, all of which were once covered with several layers of plaster, are in a sad state of ruin. The pyramids, like those at Zaculeu and Rabinal, were sloped structures, ending in vertical top sections. One of the interesting features of the site is a tunnel to a burial chamber. Bring a flashlight or candles.

The department of El Quiché is one of the largest in Guatemala. In the south, near the Pan American Highway, the climate is temperate, with warm days and cold nights. To the north, toward the great ridge of the Cuchumatanes Mountains, which cross the department from west to east, the countryside becomes

159

increasingly dry, and pine forest gives way to scrub and cactus in the valley of the Río Chixoy. Over the mountain ridge, the valleys are lush and green, with some rainfall throughout the year. The area to the north of Nebaj is sparsely populated. The land gradually slopes downward toward the dense jungles of the Petén. Some military presence remains in the northern part of El Quiché following the unrest of the early 1980s.

East of Santa Cruz del Quiché

The scenic road to the east of Santa Cruz del Quiché traverses a rolling countryside of forests, corn fields and pastures, to the towns of Chinique, Zacualpa and Joyabaj. Buses leave Santa Cruz del Quiché for Joyabaj approximately every two hours from 10 a.m. to 5 p.m. Buses leave from Joyabaj for Quiché at dawn, and from early to mid-afternoon. If you start from Chichicastenango or Santa Cruz del Quiché in the morning, you'll have a couple of hours to spend in Zacualpa, which has the most interesting market of the towns out this way, before catching the last bus back.

CHICHE
Population 1020 (township 12,642; 94% indigenous); Altitude 2001 meters; Languages: Quiché and Spanish; Fiesta: December 28; "Place of trees"

Chiché is a sister town of Chichicastenango, and once formed part of the same township. The local dress and dialect are identical to those of Chichicastenango, though the town itself is hardly as picturesque.

CHINIQUE
Population 872 (township 5690; 72% indigenous); Altitude 1921 meters; Languages: Quiché and Spanish; Fiesta: January 15

A village where mats and hats are woven. There are warm springs for bathing about a kilometer away, indicated by a sign along the highway.

ZACUALPA
Population 1382 (township 13,746; 90% indigenous); Altitude 1500 meters; Languages: Quiché and Spanish; Fiesta: 40 days after Good Friday; Market Days: Thursday and Sunday; "The hiding place"

Zacualpa's women weave some of the most beautiful huipiles of Guatemala, in striking red, with the upper section covered by closely formed designs in purple. Nearby are the ruins of a pre-Conquest settlement, a defensive site typical of the fourteenth and fifteenth centuries. There's evidence that the inhabitants of this old city burned their dead, which would indicate that they were infiltrated by foreign ideas. Some effigy urns and tripod vases with legs in the form of human figures have been excavated from the mounds, but no reconstruction has been carried out.

JOYABAJ
Population 2458 (township 35,719; 75% indigenous); Altitude 1433 meters; Languages: Quiché and Spanish; Fiesta: August 15; Market Day: Sunday; "Among the stones"; 50 kilometers from Santa Cruz del Quiché

Heavily damaged in the 1976 earthquake, Joyabaj is an agricultural town, with some manufacture of brown sugar and turpentine. Nearby, in the mountains, are the remains of Samaneb, capital of the realms of the Rabinal Achí, one of the branches of the pre-Conquest Quiché nation.

North of Santa Cruz del Quiché
The road toward Sacapulas and Nebaj winds down through increasingly bare and sparsely populated country, toward the looming east-west ridge of mountains that blocks the passage of rain clouds over much of the valley. The road finally reaches the Río Chixoy, or Río Negro, one of the feeders of the Usumacinta River, which flows along the Mexican-Guatemalan border and on into the Gulf of Mexico. Farther to the east, the muddy river has been harnessed to provide electrical power.

161

SACAPULAS
Population 1700 (township 20,744; 94% indigenous); Altitude 1196 meters; Languages: Quiché and Spanish; Fiesta: August 4; Market Days: Thursday and Sunday; "Crumbled grass"; 48 kilometers north of Santa Cruz del Quiché

Dry and sun baked, Sacapulas is a town of whitewashed houses along the rocky bed or the Chixoy River in a near-desert area, at the base of an eastern spur of the Cuchumatanes mountains. The women wear white lace huipiles, and an unusual headdress, with pompons, that might make the visitor think he had wandered into a thirties dance hall. Women of some means are given to wearing silver ornaments, especially bunches of rings as a neck pendant. A dark salt cake is produced from deposits along the river.

The original town, called Lamak, was located 28 kilometers northwest of the present site. Destroyed in one of the pre-Conquest wars, its inhabitants dispersed to the present-day towns of Aguacatán, Cunén, Uspantán and Sacapulas. The Spanish friar Bartolomé de las Casas was active in converting the Indians of the area to Catholicism soon after the Conquest, and the bridge over the river is named for him. Near the town are some hot springs. The local people don't sit in them, but perch alongside the hot pools and use basins to scoop out water and pour it over themselves. They don't mind if you join them.

Accommodations: A small pension west of the bridge provides inexpensive lodging. Buses passing through Sacapulas stop across the bridge, where local women sell peanuts, drinks and light meals from open stands.

From Sacapulas: Sacapulas is a way station for travelers going to and from Cobán, Huehuetenango, Nebaj and Santa Cruz del Quiché. West of town, the dirt road follows the Río Chixoy, then climbs up into forested mountains and on to Aguacatán and Huehuetenango. There are usually two buses a day for Huehuetenango.

To the east, from across the river, the road winds onward to Cobán, with a branch a few kilometers out of Sacapulas for Nebaj. A bus for Nebaj passes through Sacapulas at about noon.

There are several daily buses for Santa Cruz del Quiché. To reach Cobán by bus, you'll usually have to stay overnight in Cunén or Uspantán.

Highway Notes

If you're driving through the north of the department of El Quiché, be warned that the roads are unpaved, rutted, winding and narrow, with many blind curves. If you come across a vehicle traveling in the opposite direction (a rare occurrence), one of you will have to back up to a wide spot to allow the other to get by. This is a hairy experience in stretches where the road hangs along the side of a mountain, with a sheer drop of a thousand meters to the valley floor. Sound your horn at blind curves, and make sure your car is in good condition. Remember that the vehicle going uphill has the right of way.

Between Sacapulas and Nebaj, the road ascends to the top of a ridge, with alternating glimpses along the way, as the road winds back and forth, to Sacapulas and Cunén in their separate valleys, increasingly farther below. Immediately over the summit, the scene changes dramatically, from the dry scrub forest on the south side to the rich green to the north. Here, up and down the valley, are pastures for grazing cattle, dense pine forests, and patches of corn.

NEBAJ

Population 4491 (township 18,134; 88% indigenous); Altitude 1907 meters; Languages: Ixil and Spanish; Fiesta: August 15; Market Days: Thursday and Sunday; 85 kilometers from Santa Cruz del Quiché

Located in the corner of a long valley, isolated by mountains, Nebaj has the spiritual and provincial air of a place remote from the capital, quite different from the towns nearer Guatemala City which are modernizing quickly and perhaps a bit too imperfectly. The people are simple country folk who still look at visitors in a wide-eyed manner. The air is brisk in the morning, the adobe houses are neatly laid out, with smoke seeping out from open cooking fires inside and blackening the whitewash, and the atmosphere is usually somewhat misty and mysterious, with patches of clouds moving here and there around the mountains above. Always there are the women going about in their beautiful everyday clothing.

For the visitor, there's hardly a thing to do except watch the

163

inhabitants as they go about their marketing and weaving, engage in conversation with them (both you and most of the townspeople will most likely be speaking in broken Spanish, so you'll be on equal terms), and shop for the weaving of Nebaj, which is outstanding.

The women's outfit of Nebaj took first place in the native-costume competition of the Miss Universe pageant of 1975. It consists of a huipil with woven tiers of geometric designs on a red and white background, and dancing figures of birds and animals. The huipiles are worn with red skirts. A long striped cloth twisted and braided around the crown complements the women's natural, round-faced beauty. The men's outfit—hand-woven white pants, flat-brimmed hat, and a short red jacket modeled after the kind worn by Spanish officers—has pretty much gone out of use, though the jacket is seen occasionally on some of the older men. The wool for the red jackets and the black trim used to be prepared in Germany especially for the towns of Nebaj, Chajul and San Juan Cotzal. One townsman says that it was of such quality that it never lost its original color, even when the jacket was in rags. The demands of modern times have kept the factory in Germany from attending to the textile needs of a few small Guatemalan towns, and most of the men now dress in drab western clothing.

The market in Nebaj is held in a new building one block east of the bare old colonial church. It's mostly a food market, and to buy a huipil, a sash, a tzut or a tightly made bag, you'll have to walk around town and wait until somebody invites you to his or her house to look at some items. Across from the market is an expert hat maker, who for a moderate fee will make a hat to measure and block it into any style you can explain. Hats are sewn up from long strands of braided palm fiber.

A little bit away from the town center are some pre-Conquest burial mounds. To reach them, walk three blocks from the plaza in the direction opposite from the church, then take a left turn and follow the path out of town. The mounds are along the right side. It's difficult to spot them if you're not used to unrestored ruins. They appear to be little more than hillocks with trees growing on top, but if you look at the surrounding relatively flat ground, you'll realize that the mounds seem out of place as natural features. Archaeologists digging in the burial chambers under the mounds unearthed large clay urns, with covers decorated with jaguar heads. The area around the mounds is sacred, and is used for folk-Catholic prayer ceremonies, or costumbres.

Farther along, the wide path past the mounds leads up one of the mountains flanking Nebaj to a height of 2300 meters, and down into a peaceful Alpine valley to a hamlet called Acul. As happened elsewhere in this zone in the 1980s, the population was relocated to an army-controlled site. Past Acul is the Finca San Antonio, a farm owned by a family of Italian origin, where Emmentaler cheese of excellent quality is made. You can buy the cheese at a fair price. It's also possible to drive to Acul via a circuitous route, but the walk is a more interesting excursion.

For an easier walk, take the Chajul road to a stream on the edge of town, then follow a side road along the stream to a waterfall two kilometers away, passing under tree branches laden with bromeliads.

Accommodations

For the best place to stay, ask for *la pensión de las tres hermanas*. Rooms go for a couple of dollars per night, with the usual bare furnishings, but sufficient blankets to ward off the night chill. Meals are inexpensive, with a reduced price if you don't order meat. It's rather pleasant to take your breakfast in the dark kitchen next to the wood-burning stove, warming yourself with a cup of steaming coffee while you wait for your eggs and beans. The local police and storekeepers often come in for a bite to eat. Sleeping rooms are around a flower-planted courtyard, with a big *pila* (sink) in the center. The toilet is an outhouse, but better kept than many a flush toilet elsewhere. It's a sign of the times that a local woman appears in the morning in huipil and headdress to sell yogurt to lodgers. If all rooms are taken, try the less-charming Pensión Las Gemelitas a few blocks away.

Buses for Nebaj leave the terminal in Guatemala City Wednesday and Saturday at 6:30 a.m., arrive at about 4 p.m. On other days, travel via Santa Cruz del Quiché. At least one bus leaves Santa Cruz del Quiché daily, except Sunday, at about 9:30 a.m. Buses leave Nebaj for Guatemala City Monday and Thursday at 3 a.m.; and for Santa Cruz del Quiché at 1 a.m.

About five kilometers north of Nebaj is a military airstrip, at La Pista, open to civilian aircraft (in case you charter a plane this way).

SAN JUAN COTZAL

Population 2006 (township 10,944; 95% indigenous); Altitude 1800 meters; Languages: Ixil and Spanish; Fiesta: June 24; Cotzal, "to the warm lands"; 20 kilometers from Nebaj.

The people of San Juan Cotzal specialize in the cultivation of the maguey plant and in weaving rope products from its fibers. The road to the town is winding and difficult, but scenic. San Juan Cotzal's traditional huipil is similar to that worn by the women of Nebaj, with more blue and green tones. Nebaj, San Juan Cotzal and Chajul are the only towns in Guatemala that use the Ixil language.

CHAJUL

Population 3465 (township 15,713; 81% indigenous); Altitude 1991 meters; Languages: Ixil and Spanish; Fiesta: Second Friday of Lent; "pitch pine"

A traditional and charming town specializing in weaving and basket-making. A rustic figure of Christ of Golgotha in the colonial church is the object of pilgrimages on the second Friday of Lent. The statue is guarded by two figures of soldiers.

The women of Chajul wear huipiles of white or red with scattered figures of animals woven into the cloth. Their pierced ears are decorated with strands of yarn onto which old coins are threaded.

There is bus service several days a week for Cotzal from Santa Cruz del Quiché via Nebaj, recently on Tuesday and Friday at noon, returning Wednesday and Sunday mornings. You might also try hiking to Chajul or Cotzal from Nebaj, either by following the road or by venturing onto the foot trails, which take some hilly shortcuts. Bring a sleeping bag if you intend to stay the night. Rooms may be found at one basic pension in Chajul, or by asking around in Cotzal, though neither town receives many visits from outsiders.

CUNEN
Population 1577 (township 12,732; 86% indigenous); Altitude 1827 meters; Languages: Quiché and Spanish; Fiesta: February 2; 20 kilometers from Sacapulas.

A patchwork quilt of lush green fields spreads over a valley above Cunén, whose houses huddle around a colonial church. Basic lodging is available at a pensión on the main street east of the church. Buses leave early in the day for Cobán and Sacapulas.

USPANTAN
Population 3209 (township 42,685; 74% indigenous); Altitude 1837 meters; Languages: Quiché and Spanish; Fiesta: May 8; Market Days: Thursday and Sunday; 43 kilometers from Sacapulas.

Another town on the road to Cobán, specializing in the manufacture of rope and mats. Uspantán was conquered by the Spaniards, along with Nebaj and Chajul, in 1530. All survivors of the bloody battles were condemned to slavery.

Highway Notes
The unpaved 100-kilometer stretch of road from Sacapulas to San Cristóbal Verapaz can be driven in about five hours. Most of the route is through relatively dry river valleys hemmed in by mountains. But there are also irrigated bottom lands planted with sugar cane and bananas; narrow damp canyons rich in plant and bird life; and the lush rain forest of Alta Verapaz. Travel by bus requires an overnight stop in Cunén.

QUEZALTENANGO

Population 62,719 (township 72,922; 50% indigenous); Altitude 2333 meters; Languages: Spanish and Quiché; Fiesta: September 15; Market: Every day; "Place of the quetzal"; Kilometer 201

Quezaltenango is on the surface a provincial sort of place, with narrow streets winding up and down hills, a scarcity of traffic in the center, and a peaceful and dignified air. Yet the city is the second largest in Guatemala, the hub of the highlands, the center for trade between the coast and the highlands, and for the movement of the produce of the area to the capital.

The area around Quezaltenango was inhabited by the Mam nation until two centuries before the Spanish conquest, when the Quichés took over the region. The Quichés called their walled city Xelajuj, "under the ten hills," and today most Guatemalans refer to the town as Xela ("SHAY-la").

It was near Xelajuj that the Spanish under Pedro de Alvarado defeated the forces of Tecún Umán. In what was to become a pattern, the old Indian city was abandoned, and the new city of Quezaltenango was founded nearby as a center of Spanish power.

Quezaltenango was to become a rival of Guatemala City. In the years after Central American independence, when travel was difficult and regionalism was stronger than it is today, Quezaltenango first declared its allegiance to Mexico, then finally joined the Central American Federation as capital of the state of Los Altos. Los Altos was incorporated into Guatemala in 1840, but in 1848, another attempt at secession was put down by armed force.

Late in the nineteenth century, much of the Pacific slope of Guatemala was planted in coffee, and Quezaltenango grew as a commercial center from which the beans were shipped to Pacific ports. Foreign traders moved in to take charge of the commerce of the town, and many of Guatemala's richest families trace their wealth to the trade boom of those days. The city's expansion was halted suddenly by the earthquake of 1902, which destroyed Quezaltenango and brought ruin to its merchant class.

The city was rebuilt, and a railroad was constructed to facilitate commerce between highland and coast. The railway was washed out in the thirties and never reconstructed, but a toll auto road eventually took its place. Quezaltenango recovered

168

from the disasters, but was never again to rival Guatemala City.

Today, Quezaltenango is a city proud of its cultural heritage. Many of Guatemala's best writers, musicians and scholars have lived there, and are honored with statues in front of the municipal theater. The neoclassical architecture preserved from the beginning of the century gives the town a dignity that contrasts sharply with the helter-skelter construction of Guatemala City and coastal towns. Quezaltenango's setting is one of grandeur, under cultivated hills and the perfect cone of the Santa María volcano.

Quezaltenango is one place where many an Indian has prospered in commerce. In other highland towns, business is often the exclusive realm of Ladino merchants. But many of the stores in Quezaltenango are tended by women in huipiles and pleated skirts of foot-loomed material, working not as hired hands, but as owners.

If there is an eternal springtime in Quezaltenango, it's felt for only a few hours a day. Nights are cold, and during the dry season, the temperature sometimes drops below freezing. Throughout the year, people arise late in order to avoid facing the morning chill, and only by midmorning has the sun warmed the air sufficiently for the inhabitants to go about without wraps. In the evening, a crispness returns to the air, and the *Quezaltecos* don sweaters and shawls again.

The department of Quezaltenango has been one of the more densely populated areas of Guatemala since colonial times. The highland parts are given over to the cultivation corn and wheat, and to sheep grazing. Textiles are woven in great quantities, using techniques ranging from the backstrap looms of small towns to the foot looms of Salcajá to the modern machine looms of the town of Cantel. The Pacific slope is largely planted in coffee, while the lowland parts of the department, around Coatepeque, are areas of large-scale sugar and cotton farming. All around the city of Quezaltenango, the earth's depths open to the surface through hot springs and active volcanoes.

Highway Notes

Beyond Nahualá (kilometer 155), the Pan American Highway twists and climbs to frosty altitudes of over 3000 meters, through bare, sheep-grazing country. This area is often shrouded in fog at night. The road is in excellent condition, but poorly tuned cars will huff and puff on the way up. The road winds down from the

169

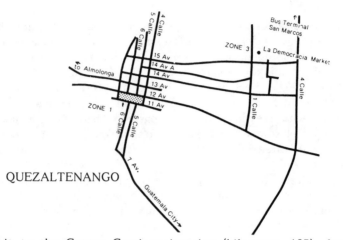

QUEZALTENANGO

summit to the Cuatro Caminos junction (kilometer 185), from which the white church of San Francisco El Alto is usually visible, far above the highway. Roads from the junction lead to Totonicapán and Quezaltenango. The junction for San Francisco El Alto and Momostenango is a few kilometers up the Pan American Highway. If you're going to either of the latter two towns, take the second turn for an easier climb from the highway. The main highway continues over another mountain pass to Huehuetenango.

The branch road to Quezaltenango passes through Salcajá. A few kilometers before entering Quezaltenango is the junction called Las Rosas. A sharp turn at the police post takes you around the prison farm (granja penal) and onto the paved highway to Cantel, Zunil, and onward down to the coast. There's a small toll for automobiles beyond Zunil. At El Zarco junction, the road joins the Pacific Highway.

HOTELS

Dial 061 plus the local number to reach these hotels from outside Quezaltenango.

Pensión Bonifaz, 4 Calle 10-50, Zone 1, tel. 4241. 53 rooms. $20 single/$25 double. In Guatemala City, tel. 80887.
Quezaltenango's dowager hotel, colonial-style and elegant, with impeccable service, pleasant public rooms, and roof terrace for

170

views of the city. Excellent restaurant, bar, protected parking. The portable room heaters are welcome on cold highland nights. Highly recommended.

Centroamericana Inn, Blvd. Minerva 14-09, Zone 3, tel. 4901. 12 rooms. $7/$10.
Near the Democracia market, with neatly furnished rooms in a rambling compound of spruced-up wood and stuccoed buildings.

Hotel del Campo, Las Rosas junction, tel. 2064. 100 rooms. $11-15/$14-21.
A modern roadside motel, at the junction for the highway to the coast. Warm pool. Rooms are clean and plain, and apartments are available for larger groups. Suitable if you have a car (as is the hotel at Las Georginas hot springs, mentioned a few pages ahead).

Hotel Modelo, 14 Avenida A 2-31, Zone 1, tel. 2715. 24 rooms.$8/$14.
Nice colonial-style hotel popular with businessmen.

Casa Kaehler, 13 Avenida 3-33, Zone 1, tel. 2091. 6 rooms. $8 double.
Small and cozy. Knock on the door to get some attention from the lady who runs the place.

Casa Suiza, 14 Avenida A 2-36, Zone 1, tel. 4350. 12 rooms. $4/$7, or slightly less sharing bathroom.
A good, small, older lodging place, with rooms around a courtyard.

Hotel Kiktem Ja, 13 Avenida 7-18, Zone 1, tel. 4304. $7/$9.
Colonial-style, thick-walled, musty, with a few ghosts. Good value.

Hotel Canadá, 4 Calle 12-22, Zone 1, tel. 4045. 37 rooms. $3/$5
Largest of Quezaltenango's budget hotels, a cavernous old place with rooms off balconies above the courtyard. Some rooms have fireplaces, the others are often uncomfortably cold.

Hotel Radar 99, 13 Avenida 3-27, Zone 1. 15 rooms. $3 per person, less with shared bathroom.

171

Smallest of the budget places, and relatively clean for the price. Try to get one of the two quiet rooms on the top level, where there's a terrace for sitting around and looking out to the city and hills. I don't know where the hotel's name comes from.

Other cheap hotels, $2 per person or less, are the Pensión Andina, 8 Avenida 6-07, Zone 1, tel. 4012; Hotel Capri, 8 Calle 11-39, Zone 1, tel. 4111; and Casa del Viajero, 8 Avenida 9-17, Zone 1.

RESTAURANTS

Pensión Bonifaz, just off the square, offers the most elegant dining in town. The cream of Quezaltenango society gathers at the Bonifaz; often a few older German-Guatemalan ladies are here at midday, remnants of the old foreign commercial elite of coffee country. Table d'hote lunches and dinners, as well as a la carte main courses, salads and sandwiches, all served by women in native outfits. Food preparation is good, but the atmosphere is the main asset. Even if you're on a budget, you might want to stop in for coffee, a pastry, and impeccable service. Breakfast $3, lunch or dinner $4 and up.

Early risers heading to nearby markets may have trouble finding breakfast. Most restaurants in Quezaltenango take their time in opening. However, the dining room of the **Hotel Modelo** starts serving at 7:15 a.m., and offers eggs, pancakes and juices at reasonable prices—$2 and up—in a pleasant atmosphere. Also open early is the **Capri,** at 11 Avenida and 8 Calle, just down from the central park. The cooking is native style: eggs will be served with tortillas, meat will be garnished with a topping of tomatoes and onions. Smoky atmosphere, brick walls, big wooden chairs, and locally woven tablecloths. Less than $2 for breakfast, lunch or dinner. Another good choice is **La Polonesa,** 14 Avenida A 4-71, near the post office. They serve hearty breakfasts of bacon, eggs, toast and coffee, as well as hamburgers and sausages. About $2.

For quick eats, try **Pizza Grizzly,** 14 Avenida 3-39. Burgers and pizza, Less than $2. There are many other small eating places along 14 Avenida.

For fair Chinese food, try **Shanghai,** 4 Calle 12-22. $3 and up, less for non-Chinese items.

Bars: Tecún, in the passageway off the central park, at 12 Avenida 4-32, is a cavernous, down-at-the-heels bar with decaying wooden tables and two juke boxes (called rockolas in Guatemala). Beer, rum and little plates of stuffed peppers, spaghetti and eggs are served. Drinks less than $1. Definitely a place in which to get smashed. At 1 Calle and 14 Avenida, opposite the municipal theater, **Taberna Don Rodrigo** serves up burgers, coffee and draft beer. Less than $2 for a light meal with beer.

Inexpensive Food: Down from the main square, you can buy cheap little snacks cooked in the open outside the Mercadito (see next page). You'll find similar tasty tidbits at La Democracia, the market in Zone 3. Especially good are the elotes, chewy ears of field corn cooked over charcoal and rubbed with lime and salt. Also, don't pass up the opportunity to assemble a picnic feast for pennies. Suggestions: fresh fruits from the market; warm French bread made in local bakeries; and cheese from the Xelac cooperative, available at supermarkets near the market and main square. Top it off with ice cream from Helados La Americana, 14 Avenida 4-35, a few steps from the main square.

Around the Central Park

Quezaltenango possesses one of the most attractive main squares in Guatemala, lined with buildings from early in the century. Officially called Parque Centro América, the square is a rectangle a few blocks long, sloping uphill to the north. In it are stone benches and fountains and statues, and all around are stone-faced buildings in the neoclassical style, with triangular pediments, fluted columns, and a Moorish octagonal window thrown in here and there. Standing along with these dignified buildings housing government offices, banks and the cultural center, are the Cathedral with its colonial baroque facade, the old market with its massive, fortress-like walls, a couple of tall (three stories, which is tall for these parts) old brick commercial buildings, and some newer nondescript store structures. There are always people sitting out on the stone benches of the park watching the passing scene, and traffic is usually light. The air often has a bite to it, which seems to slow things down.

173

The **Cathedral,** on the east side of the park, presents an old and florid façade with a squat bell tower alongside. This front wall is all that remains of the original building, which fell down some time ago. In back is a newer building, bubbling with domes.

The **City Hall (Palacio Municipal),** on the next block up from the Cathedral, is one of the main neoclassical buildings on the square, complete with Corinthian capitals on its columns. If the gray stone on the outside looks somewhat forbidding, take a look at the beautiful gardens in the courtyard.

The **Natural History Museum** is located on the south side of the park in another neoclassical building called the **Casa de Cultura del Occidente (House of Culture of the West).** There are a number of small exhibits here, some of them rather trivial, such as a mirror shattered by lightning. But most of the displays are interesting, and include pottery from the Pacific lowland area, pre-Columbian ceramics and jade, native costumes, stuffed animals and birds, herbs and mushrooms, a pickled human brain, and blurbs for local industries. This mishmash of subjects is not all natural history, but it's a fun collection of manageable size, in a dusty, small-city museum. Exhibitions of paintings are often held in the salon next to the museum entrance. Open Monday through Friday 8 a.m. to noon and 2 to 6 p.m.

Also in the Casa de Cultura is the **Tourist Office.** The local delegate of the tourist commission keeps extensive files on bus schedules, local cultural events, and new restaurants. A city map is available. Hours are 8 a.m. to noon and 2 to 6 p.m., Mon.-Fri.

Behind the museum is the **Mercadito,** the old little market which nowadays is mainly a place where women peddle cheap meals. The main market is in Zone 3. Across from the Mercadito is the **Centro Comercial Municipal,** a modern three-story shopping center, and in between is a public amphitheater built into the slope.

Elsewhere in Quezaltenango

All over Quezaltenango there are gray old classical buildings and monuments to architectural whimsy. Mansard roofs sit on plain stone-faced buildings, tile roofs on classical structures, great steep fenestrated tin roofs on three-story wooden houses with porches poking out. There are even some Tudor beam-and-stucco buildings. On a side street near the square, an old arched bridge serving absolutely no purpose crosses the roadway. It's all part of the charm of the city.

As solid and stolid as some of the buildings in Quezaltenango appear to be, they are rather basic structures of brick and concrete, and the apparently massive stonework is only a thin facing. Older buildings with thicker walls did not survive the periodic earthquakes.

The **Municipal Theater (Teatro Municipal)** is a few blocks up from the square, at 1 Calle between 14 Avenida and 14 Avenida A. It's another of the neoclassical buildings, with Doric capitals on its columns. The plaza in front is decorated with busts of local artists and scholars.

The **La Democracia Market** is in Zone 3, seven blocks north and three blocks west of the central park. It's a big old building from the thirties, with many sellers of vegetables, cloth and groceries stationed inside.

A few blocks from La Democracia Market, at 4 Calle and 15 Avenida, is the **Church of San Nicolás**, a gray Gothic structure with flying buttresses of reinforced concrete, looking somewhat like an illegitimate offspring of the cathedrals of northern Europe.

Just over a kilometer to the west, along 4 Calle, is **Minerva Park**, a large, green, tree-shaded area, pleasant for spending a free afternoon. Right in the middle of 4 Calle, at the entrance to the park, is the **Templo de Minerva.** A glut of such temples was erected throughout Guatemala during the reign of Estrada Cabrera, who figured himself a promoter of education, and dedicated monuments to the appropriate Roman goddess. The one in Quezaltenango stood incomplete for decades, but the finishing touches were put on a few years ago.

To reach Minerva Park, take bus 6 from the central park.

Nearby, off 4 Calle, are the main market of Quezaltenango, and the terminal from which buses leave for the small towns of the department of Quezaltenango, the coast, and other parts of the highlands. If the main square of the city is deceptively quiet, the frenzy of activity at the bus terminal and market gives some idea of the commercial importance of Quezaltenango.

QUEZALTENANGO DIRECTORY

Banks: Several are located around the Central Park, including Banco de Guatemala and Banco del Occidente.

Buses: Most buses leave, rather inconveniently, from the terminal out in Zone 3. Few buses leave after 4 p.m. To reach the bus terminal, take bus 2 or 6 from the central park. First-class buses to Guatemala City and buses for towns nearby leave from locations nearer the central park.

Guatemala City to Quezaltenango: First-class service on Rutas Lima (8 Calle 3-63, Zone 1) 7:45 a.m., 3, 4:30, 8 p.m.; Galgos (7 Avenida 19-44, Zone 1): 5, 8:30, 11 a.m., 2:30, 5, 7, 9 p.m.; Américas, 2 Avenida 18-47, Zone 1, five daily departures. Second-class service on Tacaná (2 Avenida 20-49, Zone 1).

Quezaltenango to Guatemala City: Bus stations for this route are along 7 Avenida, a few blocks east of the square. Rutas Lima (2 Calle 1-07, Zone 2), 5:30, 8 a.m., 2:30, 8:30 p.m. Galgos (2 Calle 5-66, Zone 2), 5, 8:30, 10 a.m., 12, 5, 7 p.m. Also América (2 Calle 3-33, Zone 2), five daily departures, and Tacaná, four daily second-class buses from the Zone 3 terminal.

Panajachel (Lake Atitlán): From the terminal at noon and 1:30; Higueros (12 Avenida and 7 Calle off the central park): 4 a.m. and 3:30 p.m. Chichicastenango: direct buses from the terminal at 1:30 and 2 p.m. At other times, take a Guatemala City bus and transfer at Los Encuentros for Panajachel or Chichicastenango.

San Marcos: Rutas Lima: 11:45 a.m., 8:30 p.m. (both first class); various companies from the bus terminal about every two hours.

Huehuetenango: Rutas Lima: 5 a.m. (continuing to La Mesilla and Mexican border), and from the terminal about every hour. Or take a bus from behind the Centro Comercial near the Central Park to Cuatro Caminos, and flag down a bus on the Pan American Highway.

Tecún Umán/Talismán/Mexican Border: two daily buses from the terminal, or by changing buses at Coatepeque on the Pacific highway. Rutas Lima has a direct early-morning bus to Talismán.

For other schedules, see listings for nearby towns, below.

Camping: If you're driving a camper or towing a trailer, check at the tourist office to find out if you'll be allowed to pull into

176

Minerva park for the night. Space might be available next to the Panchoy restaurant on the San Marcos road.

Doctors: Try Dr. Isaac Cohen, 17 Avenida 1-36, Zone 3, tel. 4698; or Dr. Oscar Macal, 1 Calle 16-43, Zone 1, tel. 2247. Both speak some English.

Entertainment: Movies are shown at the Cadore, 13 Avenida at 7 Calle, a block from the central park, and the Roma, 14 Avenida A A-34, near the municipal theater. Mexican flicks predominate.

On Sunday mornings, the Trencito Estrella, a train of cars pulled by a tractor, takes kids and grownups on rides around town, starting at the Municipalidad on the park. Nominal fare.

Groceries: In addition to many small shops around the city, the best-stocked place is Minimercado La Democracia, on 15 Avenida across from the market in Zone 3. Near the central park, try the La Selecta and Metro Centro supermarkets, both at the corner of 4 Calle and 13 Avenida. A large, modern shopping center is located at 4 Calle and 24 Avenida in Zone 3, on the way to Minerva Park.

Hikes: See the listings for nearby towns and hot springs, below.

Hospital: The best is the Hospital Privado, Calle Rodolfo Robles 23-51, Zone 1, tel. 4381.

Insurance: If you've just driven from Mexico, buy liability coverage at Granai y Townson, 14 Avenida 3-31, Zone 1, upstairs.

Language Study: S.A.B.E., 1 Calle 12-35, Zone 1; International Language School, 3 Calle and 15 Avenida, Zone 1; and International School of Spanish, 8 Avenida 6-33, Zone 1, offer immersion programs that includes room and board with a local family. See "Language Study" in the Compendium of Practical Information at the end of this book.

Laundry: For coin-operated machines, try Minimax at the corner of 1 Calle and 14 Avenida.

Mexican Consulate: In the Pensión Bonifaz, just up from the central park. Open weekdays 8 a.m. to noon and 2 to 5 p.m.

Stop in if you need a Mexican tourist card.

Post Office–Telegrams: The post office is at the corner of 15 Avenida and 4 Calle, Zone 1. Local telegrams are sent from here, international ones from the telephone office.

Shopping: There are many handicraft stores in the Centro Comercial (shopping center) just down from the central park. Most feature merchandise from the Quezaltenango region. A large Artexco (handicraft cooperative) outlet is located at 7 Avenida and 16 Calle on the road out of town toward the Pan American Highway. Take a Las Rosas city bus from the square. A handicraft market operates the first Sunday of every month on the square, and there is a handicraft exhibition, locally touted but similar to other shops, at 14 Avenida 3-36. You also shouldn't miss the Democracia market in Zone 3. It's one of the largest and most varied in Guatemala, good for many hours of prowling, gaping at strange wares, and admiring the fruits and vegetables, along with the crafts. And, of course, the nearby towns are full of handicraft specialties.

Taxis: For $2 or less, you can reach any destination in town. The tourist office will advise you about fares if you want to hire a taxi to one of the nearby towns. To call a taxi to your hotel, dial 8121.

Telephones: For long-distance calls, the Guatel office is at the corner of 15 Avenida A and 4 Calle, Zone 1. Telephones in Quezaltenango are reached from elsewhere in Guatemala by dialing 061 plus the four digits of the local number.

Tours/Travel Agency: SAB Tours, at 1 Calle 12-35 (tel. 2042), sells airline tickets, makes reservations for travel within Guatemala, and offers local tours in cars and minibuses.

Views: To look out over Quezaltenango and the surrounding area, climb to the top of the hill called El Baúl, where there's a park. Bus 3 will take you from the main square to near the base of the hill; or take a taxi.

Volcanoes: The major volcano in the area is perfectly formed Santa María, 3772 meters (12,376 feet) high, which peeks out over the ridge to the south of Quezaltenango. A crater on its slope, Santiaguito, was formed in 1902, and is in constant eruption. For a view of the fireworks, take a bus from the Zone 3 terminal to Llanos del Pinal, or else drive there by following 8 Calle and Diagonal 11 west from the central park. From Llanos del Pinal, take the trail near the military reserve (polígono de la brigada militar). You can climb a ridge and look down into the crater. Best time for viewing is just before dawn.

A couple of other high peaks south of Santa María are Zunil and Santo Tomás. A few years ago, the National Geographic Institute stripped these mountains of their status as volcanoes. The institute decided that what appear to be craters are in fact eroded peaks.

NEARBY TOWNS AND HOT SPRINGS

LOS VAHOS

These are naturally heated steam baths in the hills overlooking Quezaltenango. If you're driving, follow the road toward Almolonga and Zunil. About 200 meters past the sign reading "Límite Urbano Quezaltenango," there's a dirt road to the right leading up to Los Vahos. You can also take an Almolonga bus to the junction, and then continue on foot for three kilometers. The branch road winds up through corn and wheat fields and pine forests. At the first fork, bear to the right, and at the next fork, go left. From here onward, there are views to the city of Quezaltenango far below. In the rainy season, these hills are often blanketed in fog. The baths, at the end of the road, are small steaming rooms, with cold showers in the outer chambers. There's an hourly charge of about $2 per person, and though there's no snow to jump into after your sweat session, the air outside is usually cool and bracing.

179

ALMOLONGA

Population 7148 (township 8018; 99% indigenous); Altitude 2251 meters; Languages: Quiché and Spanish; Fiesta: June 29; Market Days: Wednesday and Saturday; "Where the water springs up"

A picturesque town with an old colonial church, set in a long, narrow valley. Vegetables for the Quezaltenango market are grown here in intensively irrigated plots.

LOS BAÑOS

Two kilometers beyond Almolonga, Los Baños is the site of a couple of hot baths. Both have seen better days. The paint on the buildings is cracking and the roofs are rusted. But you forget all that when you soak in the sulfurous waters. The Cirilo Flores baths charge about a dollar for a 45-minute session in a concrete tub built into the floor of a small room, more for a larger room and tub. The charge is the same no matter how many people crowd in. Buy a ball of pig-fat soap for a few cents, and scrub away. There's no sex discrimination here. Your party simply buys a ticket, chooses a room, enters and locks the door.

At the El Recreo baths, a run-down hacienda-type compound across the road, the charge is about a dollar for a one-hour bath.

Just past the bath houses is a running hot brook where local women do their laundry. You might want to walk from Los Baños down the quiet narrow valley to Zunil, three kilometers away.

Frequent buses for Almolonga and Los Baños run from the Zone 3 terminal in Quezaltenango. These stop at the corner of 10 Avenida and 10 Calle in Zone 1.

ZUNIL

Population 4205 (township 7009; 92% indigenous); Altitude 2077 meters; Languages: Quiché and Spanish; Fiesta: November 25; Market Day: Sunday

A picturesque little town dominated by an old white church with a beautifully ornate façade. Vegetables are cultivated in irrigated patches along the river, where hot springs bubble up here and there.

To the right of the church is the local weavers' cooperative, where shirts, shawls, wall hangings and lengths of material are on sale. Some of the clothing is cut in western styles. Zunil's shawls, in bright purple, are unusually wide, so that when draped around a woman's shoulders, they reach all the way to her ankles.

After a look at the cooperative, and perhaps a quick dip in one of the hot pools (not the river—it's said to be polluted), there's not much to do but sit around the plaza and watch the women fetch water from the central fountain, using lengths of bamboo as conduits. The water is carried in those now-ubiquitous narrow-necked plastic jugs in bright colors. The women balance them perfectly on their heads, and never lose a drop.

Zunil is at the junction of the road from Quezaltenango via Almolonga, and the paved highway from Quezaltenango via Cantel. The latter highway continues to the coastal lowlands. Buses for Zunil by either road operate about every half hour from the terminal in Quezaltenango. You can catch these as they leave town from the foot of 13 Avenida, Zone 1. Try a circle trip to Zunil with a stop at Los Baños, and another at Cantel on the way back.

FUENTES GEORGINAS

The Fuentes Georginas are hot springs located eight kilometers from Zunil along a dirt road winding up the mountain called Zunil. The road starts on the opposite side of the highway from town.

The spa was built during the presidential term of Jorge Ubico, and named in his honor. The grounds here are the best example of public landscape gardening in Guatemala. A few hot springs swimming pools lined with cut rock are open for general swimming, and cabins are available, each with a large hot-springs tub and fireplace. Stepping out from a dip into the sometimes biting air can be a refreshing and shivering experience.

The cabins are rented for about $8 double, and can be cold when no firewood is available. A restaurant serves sandwiches, but you would do well to pack some food of your own. There's a small charge to use the pools for the day. Campers may park for the night.

No buses serve the Georginas. Drive, take a taxi from Quezaltenango, or walk from Zunil. It's a mild uphill grade all the way, through lush countryside, but don't attempt the walk if you're not used to the altitude. There isn't enough traffic to count on hitching a ride.

CANTEL
Population 2491 (township 16,561; 93% indigenous); Altitude 2370 meters; Languages: Quiché and Spanish; Fiesta: August 15; Market Day: Sunday; Cantel, a tree with yellow flowers.

Most of the people of the township till their crops, but the center is much a company town, the domain of the great Cantel textile factory, a complex of several old white buildings rambling over a hillside. Cantel produces simple cloth for the Indian trade, much of it the heavy white *manta* used for making trousers. A textile cooperative sells the work of independent local weavers.

SALCAJA
Population 7426 (township 10,143; 32% indigenous); Altitude 2322 meters; Languages: Spanish and Quiché; Fiesta: August 25; Market Day: Tuesday; "Bitter white waters"

Salcajá was one of the first towns founded by the Spaniards after their early battles with the Quichés. The original town, several kilometers north of the present site, was populated by Spaniards, their Tlaxcalan allies, and some forcibly settled Quichés. A few of the current inhabitants claim to trace their descent from the Spanish captain Juan de León Cardona, who was left in charge of the settlement. The church of San Jacinto was among the very first temples erected by the Spanish.

Today, Salcajá is Guatemala's cottage-industry weaving town par excellence. Look into almost any doorway, and you'll see clacking foot looms on which *jaspé* fabric is produced. The looms are operated exclusively by men, who control the warp strands by means of pedals, while with their hands they pass the woof strands, attached to sticks. The warp threads are tie-dyed to achieve intricate patterns, and stretched out between poles everywhere around town to dry. Through some doorways, you may see raw cotton being beaten and cleaned by hand, and thread being spun on wooden spinning wheels.

A couple of kilometers past Salcajá, on the left side of the road leading to San Cristóbal Totonicapán, is the Xelac dairy cooperative. If you're driving, you might want to stop and try the excellent cheese and butter. The Xelac sign bears the standard double pine tree symbol of the cooperative movement. Many of the cooperatives in Guatemala were founded with the aid of missionaries and foreign assistance programs.

SAN CRISTOBAL TOTONICAPAN
Population 3416 (township 19,970; 93% indigenous); Altitude 2330 meters; Languages: Quiché and Spanish; Fiesta: July 25; Market Day: Sunday

Like Salcajá, San Cristobal Totonicapán is an important center for weaving textiles in wool, silk and cotton, and also produces fine pottery. The colonial church has a unique altar of silver and glass, which is considered one of the gems of surviving colonial art. The annual fiesta is noted for its large cattle market, and masks and costumes for fiesta dances are made here and used throughout the country. Take a look at the costume workshop (La Morería) at 5 Calle 3-20, Zone 1. The town center is a kilometer from the Cuatro Caminos junction on the Pan American Highway.

TOTONICAPAN
Population 7478 (township 62,407; 95% indigenous); Altitude 2495 meters; Languages: Quiché and Spanish; Fiesta: September 29; Market Days: Tuesday and Saturday; "At the hot waters"

Pre-Conquest Totonicapán was the second city of the Quiché nation after Utatlán. The present site of the city, in a valley carpeted with pine and oak trees, was founded by the Spaniards, who moved in Tlaxcalan Indians from Mexico, as well as Quichés from the old site of the town.

In 1820, Totonicapán was the center of an Indian revolt. The mayor was forced to flee, and the leader of the rebellion, Atanasio Tzul, was crowned king.

Today, Totonicapán is the capital of one of the smaller departments in the country. Where other towns specialize in one or two articles, the artisans of Totonicapán have mastered a variety of crafts. Here there are tanneries, kilns for firing pottery, and furniture workshops. But Totonicapán is best known for its elaborately patterned huipiles and lengths of skirt material, which are sold in markets all over the highlands. The town is also

183

the site of a warehouse that rents out costumes used in fiesta dances. The masks are made here and in San Cristóbal Totonicapán.

Totonicapán has two main squares. One is dominated by the neoclassical municipal theater, the other is surrounded by more modern structures.

About a kilometer from the center of town is a communal hot bath. The sign outside advises that the facilities are free to all, but that bathers must provide their own shorts. It's a pleasant walk out this way, along 9 Avenida from the new clock and bell tower, following the signs pointing toward a hamlet called Alaska. You can take a quick look in through the door to the great steaming pool, and then perhaps continue onward to sit on the old stone bridge over a stream where women wash their clothes.

SAN FRANCISCO EL ALTO
Population 3404 (township 25419; 99% indigenous); Altitude 2610 meters; Languages: Quiché and Spanish; Fiesta: October 4; Market Day: Friday; Kilometer 190

Located high on a bluff overlooking the broad valley of Quezaltenango, San Francisco is the most picturesque town in the region. From the plaza, the volcanoes Santa María and Cerro Quemado and the peak of Zunil are easily seen. On rainy season afternoons, the white colonial church is often visible above the clouds from the Cuatro Caminos junction on the Pan American highway far below, making a stunning sight. The harvest at the end of the rainy season is followed by an elaborate thanksgiving in the church, and in mountain shrines outside the town.

The Friday market is one of the best in the country, attended by traders from as far away as Cobán. It begins early, and by noon, the plaza starts to quiet down again. There's usually a good selection of blankets from Momostenango. At fiesta times, San Francisco is the site of a great fair that includes considerable cattle trading.

Buses run frequently from behind the Centro Comercial on the central park of Quezaltenango to Salcajá, San Cristóbal Totonicapán, Cuatro Caminos junction on the Pan American Highway, Totonicapán and San Francisco El Alto. Many of the buses are converted panel trucks, and the seating is claustrophobic and conducive to back pains. You might want to wait for one of the larger buses, or else share a taxi.

MOMOSTENANGO
Population 6094 (township 53,418; 99% indigenous); Altitude 2204 meters; Languages: Quiché and Spanish; Fiesta: August 1; Market Days: Wednesday and Sunday; "Place of the altars"

Momostenango, reached by a good dirt road from San Francisco El Alto, is where most of Guatemala's heavy woolen Indian blankets are woven on large foot looms, both in town and in rural settlements nearby. Sheep and goats raised in the hills provide the raw material, and hot springs in the area are used for washing finished blankets.

In the hills around Momostenango are altar mounds composed of broken pottery. On Guaxaquib Batz (literally "Eight Monkey"), which occurs every 260 days in the traditional tzolkin religious calendar, these mounds are the scene of a New Year purification ritual, during which pottery broken during the year is offered to the gods. The observance begins with long hours of prayer outside the church on the eve of Eight Monkey, the worshipers bringing incense and candles, and pine boughs with which the altar mounds are to be decorated. At dawn the next day, the devout head for the mounds, each of which is attended by a prayer man who receives them individually or in small groups. The pottery offering is placed on the mound, and amid incense and drinking of liquor, the prayer man communicates the wishes of the supplicants to the gods. The larger altars are reserved for the use of the senior prayer men.

A number of stores in Momostenango advertise themselves as blanket factories, but are only middlemen. The cooperative near the center of town offers a good selection of blankets at fixed and reasonable prices. About a kilometer from the town center is a factory where visitors can see the process of making blankets, from the preparation of the wool to weaving on large looms to final combing. Visitors are welcome, but are expected to make a purchase. Ask for the *fábrica*.

Near the factory are the *Riscos*, a set of pillars and shallow caves formed in volcanic ash by erosion. Interesting for a short walk. Spotted among the many canyons surrounding Momostenango are a number of hot springs. Visitors may camp at

Palá Chiquito, a hot spring about six kilometers from the center of town. The road is often impassable during the rainy season.

Momostenango has more than its share of bothersome kids who chase after visitors and offer themselves as guides. Best way to deal with them is to ignore them.

Bus service to Momostenango isn't the greatest. From the terminal in Quezaltenango, buses leave daily about every hour between 11 a.m. and 4:30 p.m. Buses leave Momostenango for Quezaltenango before 9 a.m., and several times in the afternoon. On Sundays, there are extra buses in the morning from Quezaltenango. The market starts early, so the best strategy is to take the 6 a.m. bus on Sunday morning, and to try to get out on one of the early afternoon buses. Otherwise, share a taxi from Quezaltenango, or from the Cuatro Caminos junction, or drive.

San Bartolo (population 874, altitude 2370 meters), a small town near Momostenango, was the scene of a revolt against President Carrera in 1855. After the revolt was suppressed, the heads of the rebel chieftains were displayed in the plaza of Momostenango.

OLINTEPEQUE
Population 2690 (township 11,962; 92% indigenous); Altitude 2341 meters; Languages: Quiché and Spanish; Fiesta: June 24; Market Day: Tuesday; "Place of the trembling hill"

A textile-weaving town just north of Quezaltenango on the old road to Huehuetenango. Legend has it that the nearby Xequijel River was stained red with the blood of Quiché warriors in the first great battle of the Conquest (Xequijel means "under blood"). Other versions say that the battle took place elsewhere, at Llanos del Pinal. The soldiers of the Conquest were fortune hunters and promoters of Christianity, and not especially good keepers of records, which has created all sorts of problems for present-day historians trying to sort out the events and locales of that time.

Buses for Olintepeque run frequently from the market in Quezaltenango.

OSTUNCALCO

Population 7124 (township 23,298; 83% indigenous); Altitude 2502 meters; Languages: Mam and Spanish; Fiesta: February 2; Market Days: Thursday and Sunday; "Place of the cave houses"

San Juan Ostuncalco is located west of Quezaltenango on the paved highway to San Marcos, in a wheat-growing area dotted with family compounds of adobe farm houses. The major industry here is the manufacture of furniture from willow wood and rope. The chairs, made in dozens of family workshops, are comfortable and quite reasonably priced, though some of the colors are gaudy. Local men use a wide sash instead of a belt.

Located 15 kilometers from Quezaltenango, Ostuncalco is served about every half hour by buses from the Quezaltenango terminal. It's also a pleasant walk to the town over a winding road without too many grades.

CONCEPCION CHIQUIRICHAPA

Population 2819 (township 8055; 99% indigenous); Altitude 2502 meters; Languages: Mam and Spanish; Fiesta: December 8; Chiquirichapa, "creek of the cicadas:

A sister town of Ostuncalco, located about two kilometers away via a dirt road. Furniture of willow and rope is made here also.

SAN MARTIN SACATEPEQUEZ

Population 1813 (township 9764; 94% indigenous); altitude 2490 meters; Languages: Mam and Spanish; Fiesta: November 11; Market Day: Friday.

This town is more familiarly known as San Martín Chile Verde, after the green peppers grown nearby. Basket weaving and farming are the main occupations. The men of San Martín wear one of the most unusual native outfits in Guatemala: trousers and knee-length tunics of a white cotton cloth with red pinstripes. Both sleeves and cuffs are covered with multicolored designs, and a long red sash is worn around the tunic.

Overlooking the thatched-roof, mud-and-sticks houses of San Martín is the Chicabal volcano, rising to 2900 meters. The ascent is not difficult, but the cone is often shrouded in dense fog during the rainy season, making it easy for climbers to lose their way. In the crater of the volcano is a small lake, the locale of traditional sacrificial ceremonies performed by native prayer men throughout the year, but especially at the fiesta of the Holy Cross on May 3.

Buses leave the Quezaltenango terminal for San Martín about every 90 minutes from 5 a.m. to 4 p.m. If you feel like stretching your legs, take a bus to San Juan Ostuncalco and walk the five kilometers on to San Martín. It's downhill all the way, as the road descends into a narrow valley, the sides of which are covered with corn and maguey. Beyond San Martín, the dirt road drops through coffee country, and eventually joins the coast highway.

Past San Juan Ostuncalco, the paved road out of Quezaltenango winds through a forested area, up to and along a ridge above a wide valley, and finally descends to the village of Palestina de Los Altos. In contrast to the towns nearer Quezaltenango, many of the houses here are built of mud and sticks, and have roofs of straw or of wooden shingles. About 10 kilometers beyond Palestina and the end of the descent from the mountain pass are the twin towns of San Pedro Sacatepéquez and San Marcos.

SAN PEDRO SACATEPEQUEZ
Population 11,414 (township 37,452; 44% indigenous); Altitude 2350 meters; Languages: Spanish and Mam; Fiesta: June 29; Market Days: Thursday and Sunday; Kilometer 241

Not to be confused with the place of the same name near Guatemala City, San Pedro Sacatepéquez in the department of San Marcos is a busy little town of narrow streets, situated in a peaceful valley. The area was granted to the Indian chieftain Pedro de Sacatepéquez shortly after the Conquest in return for his services to the Spaniards, hence the name. The main industry is the weaving of textiles, many of which are similar to those of highland villages farther to the east. But the specialty is a silk-like fabric of artificial fiber used by local women for their skirts, usually of a yellow color with crossing tie-dyed strands. The local cloth is displayed at booths in the market next to the square, and at stores nearby.

The central park of San Pedro is unusually large, surrounded by

188

pastel buildings, including the church and city hall, in a subdued wedding-cake style. It's altogether a pleasant place in which to sit around in the evening, under the wooden clock tower of the city hall.

The road through San Pedro was once the main route to Mexico. But highways to Huehuetenango and through the lowlands have made San Pedro something of a backwater. Which means that the visitor can appreciate the mountain scenery and climate, visit nearby hot springs, and go out to some little-visited mountain villages with the near certainty of running into few of his countrymen.

SAN MARCOS
Population 6963 (township 19,963; 22% indigenous); Altitude 2398 meters; Languages: Spanish and Mam; Fiesta: April 25; Market Days: Tuesday and Friday

Capital of the department of the same name, San Marcos was settled by the Spanish immediately after the Conquest. The town center is about two kilometers from that of San Pedro Sacatepéquez, and disputes about the boundary line between the two townships have arisen on and off over the years.

Along the divided boulevard linking the two towns is the Palacio Maya, the outstanding architectural gem of the area, and perhaps the masterpiece of weird architecture in all of Central America. The building, housing the government of the department, is a monolithic thirties structure, cleverly disguised to resemble a Toltec-Maya temple. The Toltec-Maya of the Yucatán didn't leave any architectural remains in this area before the Conquest, but later architects made up for the omission with this structure. Heads of serpents peek out at the corners of the building, corbeled arches frame the windows, and flutings of the kind seen at Chichén-Itzá decorate the walls. In the top center of the facade is a clock with Mayan glyph numerals, and snakes for hands. Well worth a long, incredulous look.

The center of San Marcos is more subdued. Wooden and stucco-faced buildings surround the sloping central square, which is graced with a central band shell. There's a rinky dink natural history museum on the park, intended mainly for local school children, and if you're lucky enough to find the caretaker, you might get a look at the few exhibits inside. Also on the square is a branch of the Banco de Guatemala, and just up the street, the modern market and bus terminal.

The department of San Marcos stretches from the highlands to the Pacific Ocean, and includes the two highest volcanoes in Central America, Tajumulco (4220 meters, or 13,846 feet, near the town of the same name) and Tacaná (4093 meters, or 13,429 feet, near the village of Sibinal and sitting squarely on the Mexican border). Tajumulco is thought to sit atop the remains of an older volcano, and has two peaks, the eastern one being higher. The best way to secure a guide and horse for the trip is to stop in at the office of the mayor in the towns near the volcanoes.

Much of the highland area around the departmental capital is planted in wheat, and some of the large ranches breed horses and cattle. Weaving of wool and cotton, and tanning of cowhides are specialties of many of the villages to the northwest of the city of San Marcos. To the west and south, the land slopes down through the coffee belt to the coastal plain.

Accommodations: The Pérez, on the boulevard leading into San Marcos, is by far the best hotel in the area. About $4 per person for a room with private bath. Hearty meals about $3 each. If the Pérez is full, try the Hotel Bagod in San Pedro, at the corner of 6 Calle and 8 Avenida. Clean and basic, about $3 per person with shared bath. The best meals are at the Hotel Pérez in San Marcos, though there are simple eateries around the squares of both San Pedro and San Marcos.

Around San Pedro and San Marcos: Movies are shown at the Cine Carúa near the Hotel Pérez in San Marcos and at the Cine T'Manek in San Pedro. You'll probably be more comfortable staying in San Marcos, though the shopping for handicrafts is better in San Pedro. Collective taxis provide a local rapid transit system between the two town centers.

Buses depart from the San Marcos market, and from the terminal a block from the square in San Pedro.

Guatemala City to San Pedro/San Marcos: Rutas Lima (8 Calle 3-63, Zone 1), 7:45 a.m. and 4:30 p.m., first class. Tacaná (2 Avenida 20-49, Zone 1), five daily departures.

190

San Pedro to Quezaltenango and Guatemala City (departing 15 minutes earlier from San Marcos): Rutas Lima at 5 a.m. and 6:30 p.m. Tacaná, five daily departures.

Buses to Malacatán, Tecún Umán and the Mexican border leave four times daily.

Trips from San Marcos and San Pedro Sacatepéquez

A couple of bathing areas are easily reached from San Marcos and San Pedro. The Agua Tibia baths are a pair of warm swimming pools where a stream has been dammed up. To walk here from San Pedro, take the street toward San Marcos, then turn left at the church with the large candelabra on its roof. Follow the path down one canyon and up the other side, through the neighborhood called Tenería ("tannery"), and down the next canyon to the pools. Total distance about two kilometers. If you're driving, take the Coatepeque road out of San Marcos to Tenería, turn right, and follow the road down the hill. The park around the pools is nicely landscaped, with plenty of geese flitting around the grass and in their own steaming pools. Idyllic. Admission costs a few cents.

The La Castalia hot baths are located about 12 kilometers from San Marcos on the road to Coatepeque. There's a steaming grotto, as well as some showers with water in temperatures varying from cold to boiling. There's no admission charge, and the place isn't maintained, but it's a nice excursion by car. If you have no car, take one of the Coatepeque buses, or try to hitch a ride on a truck.

To Tacaná

An unpaved road crosses the high, sheep-raising country northwest of San Marcos, ending at Tacaná, near the Mexican border. Out this way are the little-visited villages of Tejutla, Ixchiguán, San José Ojetenam and Sibinal. Each is a settlement of about a thousand people or less, with a much larger population scattered over the surrounding countryside of the township. Wool is produced in abundance, and in Tejutla, there are tanneries for processing hides. The great, green valleys; bare, frosty heights; and towering volcanoes combine to make some of the most stunning off-the-beaten-track scenery in all Guatemala.

From San Marcos, the road winds back and forth as it climbs through pine forests, affording glimpses along the way of the twin

191

towns of San Pedro and San Marcos farther and farther below. Volcanic peaks come into view. To the east, near Quezaltenango, are the cone of Santa María and the eroded top of Cerro Quemado. To the south, down a widening valley, is Lacandón, with the coastal lowlands stretching in the haze beyond it. Over a ridge, past the junction for the branch road to Tejutla, the route crosses a moonscape of scattered, wrinkled boulders on the slopes of Tajumulco. In the rainy season, patches of ice glisten on its slope, though the view is often obscured by clouds. In the dry season, the crater can be reached on foot in a few hours from a point near the kilometer 26 marker. (The climb starts at an altitude of 3100 meters; the crater is at 4225 meters.)

Past Tajumulco, broad valleys stretch away to the north. The road runs along a ridge through cold, rocky terrain inhabited by sheep, goats and a few shepherds, and up to the village of Ixchiguán, perched on a hillside more than 3050 meters (over 10,000 feet) above sea level. The concrete platform in its main square offers a view downward to an Andean bleakness on three sides. Beyond Ixchiguán is the pass called the Cumbre de Cotzil, the highest point on any road in Central America.

Tacaná (population 1334, altitude 2400 meters, "House of fire"), 73 kilometers from San Marcos at the end of the unpaved road, is more active commercially than the other towns of the area. There are no handicrafts of note, though a peculiarly Mexican undertone is present. Mexican musicians arrive at fiesta time (August 15), and there is some movement of people and goods throughout the year over the trails that run to the border. The majestic cone of the Tacaná volcano, second highest in Central America, towers to the south.

Buses leave San Marcos for Tacaná twice a day. The trip takes five hours. Simple overnight accommodations are available at a pension in Tacaná. If you have a rugged vehicle, you might want to take a day trip out this way. It takes about three hours to drive to Tacaná in a Jeep from San Marcos, or you can go only as far as the Cotzil pass and then turn back. Bring warm clothing.

HUEHUETENANGO

Population 12,422 (township 36,861); Altitude: 1902 meters; Fiesta: July 12-18; Market: Every day, but especially Thursday and Sunday; "town of old people"; Kilometer 262

The department of Huehuetenango is one of the richest in Guatemala in tradition and color. The vast majority of the people are indigenous, most speaking some dialect of the Mam language. The Mam kingdom covered the greater part of the western highlands centuries before the Conquest, until Quiché warriors pushed the Mam people back to the present-day departments of Huehuetenango and San Marcos. Now, living in the towns where the Spanish overlords concentrated their ancestors, many still follow their mixed pagan and Catholic traditions.

In the department of Huehuetenango are frosty mountain peaks and dry plains and dense jungle, ravines and valleys, lakes and vast forests. To the north of the city of Huehuetenango rise the Cuchumatanes mountains, highest in Guatemala, with frosty peaks over 3000 meters. It's too cold at the heights to plant many crops, and the inhabitants depend on sheep-raising. At lower altitudes, corn and highland fruits are grown, and in the hotter valleys of the department, sugar cane, tobacco and tropical fruit. There are deposits of lead, silver, zinc and copper, and also some gold. Mining is not significant at present, but in colonial times, mining and cattle were the principal sources of wealth.

Many of the towns of the department were reached by roads only in the last twenty years. Much traditional trade still takes place on market days, when men carry heavy loads for many kilometers over narrow, steep and winding trails in order to earn a bit of cash. Sometimes exchanges take place over the border with Indian towns in the Mexican state of Chiapas, whose peoples are closely related to those of Huehuetenango in language and heritage.

The city of Huehuetenango is a quiet and provincial sort of place, populated mostly by Ladinos. The area around the market is crowded with Indian traders from all parts of the department, often dressed in the colorful outfits of their home villages. Trucks filled with Indian workers on their way to plantations on the coast pass through at all hours. There's some light industry—flour mills, shoemaking and the like—but mostly, Huehuetenango is a trading center for handicrafts and agricultural

193

products moving out of the towns of the department, and cloth and thread and manufactured goods coming in.

The square is a quiet center of town life that has remained unchanged for many years. Archways shelter the sidewalks, a band shell looks out over the park from the second floor of the city hall, and a wedding-cake tower sprouts from the departmental government building to a height that must have seemed awesome many years ago. Laid out in one corner of the tree-shaded park is a relief map of the department, interesting for tracing the ups and downs of the winding roads going to the more isolated towns. The colonial church is off to one side, and on some central streets are schools and other buildings in the neoclassical style that was popular in the nineteenth century, after the Liberal revolution.

HOTELS

For a small city, Huehuetenango has more than its share of hotels and pensions, catering to border travelers, visitors from the outside, and traders heading to or coming from mountain villages. Many of the pensions are of the most basic sort, patronized by Indians for whom a quetzal is a significant expense. But with all the competition, hotels of every class are reasonably priced.

Hotel Zaculeu, 5 Avenida 1-14, tel. 641086. 18 rooms. $5 to $7 single/$7 to $10 double.
An old hotel with rooms opening off a flowered courtyard, and public areas decorated with regional handicrafts. Some rooms are relatively bare, others nicely furnished. The meals are not one of the hotel's good features. Beware early-morning bus noise on the street side.

Hotel Pino Montano. Tel. 310761 in Guatemala City. 18 rooms. $7 per person.
On the Pan American Highway at kilometer 259 (two kilometers past the junction for Huehuetenango). Accommodations are in semi-detached units on pleasantly landscaped grounds. Restaurant, pool under construction. This is your best bet if you have a car.

Hotel Mary, 2 Calle 3-52. 25 rooms. $3/$6
New, clean brick building. Some rooms with private bath. Good
buy.

Gran Hotel Shinulá, 4 Calle 2-20. 45 rooms. $3 per person.
Tiers of rooms above a busy street. Private bath.

Hotel Central, 5 Avenida 1-33. $2 per person.
Nice old place with large rooms. All rooms are bathless, but the
common sinks have hot water, which is often absent in cheap
hotels. You don't have to stay here to eat in the dining room,
which offers the best food bargains in town. Tasty, filling meals
go for just over $1. Breakfast is served at 7 a.m., lunch at 12:30,
dinner at 6:30 p.m.

Hotel Maya, 3 Avenida 3-55. $3 per person ($2 sharing bathroom).
A cement-block hotel, with small but well-lit rooms. Good
value.

Auto Hotel Vásquez, 2 Calle 6-67, tel. 641338. 20 rooms. $2 per
person.
Concrete block rooms, characterless. The name means it has
parking.

Other basic hotels with rooms for $2 per person or less are the
Posada Familiar, 4 Calle 6-83; Pensión Astoria, 4 Avenida 1-45;
Hotel Roberto's, 2 Calle 5-49; and Posada Española, 4 Calle 4-13.

RESTAURANTS

If you find a really good restaurant in Huehuetenango, let me
know. Meanwhile . . .

In the $3 range: The Regis Restaurant in the Hotel Mary, 2 Calle
3-52, is clean-looking and serves meals with beef or chicken as the
main course. Las Brasas, 4 Avenida 1-53, has a few Chinese items
on the menu.

In the $2 range: Pizza Hogareña, 6 Avenida 4-45, cooks up a fair
pizza, as well as spaghetti, and makes huge fruit drinks with
purified water. Maxi Pizza, 2 Calle 5-35, serves a set lunch and

sometimes has pizza. Cleaner than most. For a couple of pieces of fried chicken, try Rico Mac Pollo, on 3 Avenida next to the Hotel Maya. A couple of doors up the street, La Pradera sells ice cream, yogurt and other pasteurized milk products. The Restaurant Magnolia, at 4 Calle and 6 Avenida, is a big hangout where locals sit over beers late into the night. Open at about noon. Last and least is the Buen Samaritano, 4 Calle 3-30. Lunches and sandwiches, as well as ice cream, but watch out for the grease.

In the $1 range: The eatery of the Hotel Central, mentioned above, is Huehuetenango's budget food champion.

HUEHUETENANGO DIRECTORY

Banks: Change your travelers checks at Banco de Guatemala, 5 Avenida and 2 Calle. Open 8:30 a.m. to 2 p.m. (Fridays to 2:30 p.m.) If you're heading to Mexico, unload your extra quetzales here for dollars, if any are available. Rates over the border are less favorable.

Buses: Most buses leave from near the market, though there is the possibility that some services will relocate to a new market-terminal off the road to Guatemala City. For destinations not mentioned here, see individual town listings, or inquire at bus company offices along 1 Avenida between 4 and 1 calles, preferably the day before you travel.

Guatemala City to Huehuetenango: El Cóndor (19 Calle 2-01, Zone 1): five buses daily, including first-class buses at 8 a.m. and 5 p.m.; Los Halcones (7 Avenida 15-27, Zone 1): 7 a.m., 2 p.m.; Los Flamingos (6 Avenida A 18-70, Zone 1): 12:15 and 5:30 p.m.; Rápidos Zaculeu (9 Calle 11-42, Zone 1): 6 a.m., 3 p.m.

Huehuetenango to Guatemala City: El Cóndor (5 Avenida 1-15), five buses daily, including first-class buses at 8 a.m. and 2 p.m.; Los Halcones (7 Avenida 3-62), 7 a.m., 2 p.m.; Los Flamingos (4 Calle 1-51): 5 a.m., 12:30 p.m.; Rápidos Zaculeu (3 Avenida 5-25): 6 a.m., 3 p.m.

Quezaltenango: Rutas Lima (4 Calle 3-30), 3:30 p.m. (first

class). Other departures about every hour from market area.

La Mesilla/Mexican Border: Pick up your Mexican tourist card at the consulate in Huehuetenango. El Cóndor, 6 a.m. (first class), 3 p.m. Rutas Lima: 8 a.m. (first class). Other departures approximately every hour from along 4 Calle and 1 Avenida, until 2 p.m.

Sacapulas: 4:30 a.m. and 11:30 a.m. from 1 Avenida 2-46. Other buses operate to Santa Cruz del Quiché and Nebaj via Sacapulas.

Entertainment: Not much happens at night in Huehuetenango. Try a movie at the Cine Lili, 3 Calle 5-35. Films in English are often shown. If you're lucky, you might catch an evening band concert in the central park.

Groceries: For pasteurized milk, cheeses and cold cuts, try any of several small stores located on 3 Calle between 2 and 3 avenidas, or the Sáenz supermarket at 3 Calle and 5 Avenida on the central park, or the Comisariato in back of the pharmacy at 3 Avenida and 3 Calle.

Insurance: Automobile liability insurance is available at Granai y Townson, 5 Avenida 4-23.

Language Study: A language school that has functioned recently is Fundación 23, 7 Calle 6-27.

Mexican Consulate: In the Farmacia del Cid, 4 Calle and 5 Avenida. They charge a dollar or so for a tourist card. No telling what you'll be charged if you show up at the border without one.

Post Office–Telephones–Telegraph: 2 Calle 3-54. Go in back to mail a letter.

Shopping: Specialties in Huehuetenango are hand-woven huipiles, shirts, bags, sashes and other items of Indian clothing from all over the department. These can be found around the market, in the Artexco cooperative (look for the double pine tree sign on 4 Calle opposite the market), and in stores near the central park.

Taxis park near the central park. I can't imagine any need for a taxi to get around town, but you might want to hire one to go out to the Zaculeu ruins or to a nearby town. Always bargain on fares.

Trips from Huehuetenango

Most easily visited on round trips of a few hours from Huehuetenango are the ruins of Zaculeu and the towns of Chiantla and Aguacatán. Trips by bus to other towns will usually require an overnight stay, often in the most basic accommodations. The best way to get around is in your own vehicle, preferably a rugged one.

Numerous trails, combined with inadequate bus service and, in some cases, a lack of roads altogether, make trekking the most reliable way to reach some hamlets.

If you decide to go out on foot, make preparations appropriate to your destination. Santiago Chimaltenango and several other hamlets can be reached by climbing for a few hours from a paved highway. But for longer hikes, take camping equipment and a stock of food and water. Plot your route carefully, and inquire along the way as to conditions ahead. Check the detailed maps of the Military Geographic Institute.

After 1980, military operations and guerrilla activity made it inadvisable for outsiders to venture too far to the north or northeast of Huehuetenango. The situation is generally tranquil now, though if you are considering travel into the area, you might want to verify with a reliable, conservative source (such as your embassy) that there is no current danger.

ZACULEU

The ruins of Zaculeu are not particularly impressive. They cover a rather small area, and the reconstruction work, done under the patronage of the United Fruit Company, has left the structures looking as if they were erected just a few years ago.

Zaculeu shows much in common with other sites that flourished during the period of Mexican influence, a few hundred years before the Spanish conquest. It's essentially a defensive location, surrounded on two sides by precipices, and on a third by a river. The only access is by a narrow sash of land on the north. The artifacts unearthed at the site include effigy vases and large earrings made of copper and gold alloys, which are forms that

198

appear to have been brought from Mexico. These objects and some human remains may be seen in the museum at the site, open from 8 a.m. to noon, and from 1 to 5 p.m.

The structures of Zaculeu are built around a ceremonial plaza. The principal pyramid consists of seven stepped sections with vertical faces. The stairway on the west side is divided into two parallel sections. At the top are the remains of a one-room temple with a triple entrance. All of these architectural features are Mexican in character. Judging by the dimensions of the temple at the top of the main pyramid, the roof was probably not formed with a corbeled arch. The restoration has used beams and mortar, which may or may not have been the original type of structure. The walls are made of round stones covered with mortar.

The other major structure at Zaculeu is a pyramid on the east side of the ceremonial plaza. The remains of two rectangular platforms that were probably used for sacrifices and offerings sit in the center of the plaza. Similar platforms in the more remote parts of Guatemala are still used for religious ceremonies. There's also a ball court with a narrow central corridor, and sides with unpronounced slopes.

The overwhelming sense of bareness at Zaculeu is not entirely due to the nature of the restoration. There are no glyphs on the walls or columns, no great monoliths or sculptures in the ceremonial patio, no arches or causeways. The massive structures of Zaculeu were built with a maximum of human effort and a minimum of imagination.

It's not at all certain that the Mam people of the region were still using Zaculeu as a ceremonial center when the Spanish arrived. But because of the site's excellent defensive situation, it became a bastion against the forces of Gonzalo de Alvarado, and it was here that the Mam kingdom came to an end when hunger forced surrender to the besieging Spanish in 1525.

Station wagons for Zaculeu run about every half-hour from the corner of 4 Calle and 3 Avenida in Huehuetenango. Get off at the soccer field (cancha de fútbol). From there, it's a walk of about a half-hour to the ruins, down the road leading off to the right. Taxis will take you as well, or you can drive, following 6 Avenida out of town in the direction opposite from the road to Guatemala City.

199

CHIANTLA

Population 3853 (township 33,304); Altitude 1992 meters; Languages: Spanish and Mam; Fiesta: February 2; Market Day: Sunday

Chiantla, a few kilometers from Huehuetenango, is an important religious center. The town church holds an image of the Virgin Mary, before which the sick and lame crawl and pray for a miraculous recovery. The major pilgrimage to the shrine takes place on February 2. The market is busiest on Sundays, and is unusual for its built-in chapel.

Much of the countryside around Chiantla is relatively barren, and a good part of the land is given over to the grazing of sheep and cattle. The curing of hides and the production of saddles and harnesses are local craft specialties.

Buses for Chiantla stop at the central park in Huehuetenango, along 5 Avenida.

AGUACATAN

Population 1651 (township 21,960; 86% indigenous); Altitude 1669 meters; Languages: Aguateca and Spanish; Fiesta: 40 days after Easter: Market Days: Thursday and Sunday; "place of avocados"; 24 kilometers from Huehuetenango.

Aguacatán is an unusual place. The main street is a few kilometers long, with hardly a side street leading away from it. When you arrive, you might think that you'll never reach the town center. The women seem especially small, and the language, Aguateca, is spoken nowhere else.

In addition to the avocados that give the town its name, vegetables are produced in great abundance and variety, mostly in irrigated plots. The fertility of the land is almost legendary.

In the area of Aguacatán was a great pre-Conquest center known as Chalchitán. The unexcavated burial mounds of the old city can be seen a couple of kilometers north of town. There's also a lovely park and bathing area where the San Juan River gushes out of the ground at its source, at the base of a cliff. To reach the park, turn off the main road at the yellow "Río San Juan" sign by the school east of town. Take the first left, then turn right to the river, 1.5 kilometers from the main road.

Buses: To arrive in time for the market, take an early Sacapulas bus from Huehuetenango. There are also several mid-morning departures for Aguacatán from along 1 Calle. Continue on a later bus to Sacapulas and points beyond, or return to Huehuetenango.

TODOS SANTOS CUCHUMATAN
Population 1259 (township 12,130; 90% indigenous); Altitude 2450 meters; Languages: Mam and Spanish; Fiesta: November 1; Market Day: Saturday; Cuchumatán, "place of the parrot hunters," or possibly "joined together by force"

In its own enchanted valley high in the Cuchumatanes mountains, Todos Santos appears as if in a Shangri-La world. The trip to Todos Santos takes the visitor up from Huehuetenango on a twisting dirt road on the face of the mountain ridge, over the summit to a bare, frosty plain, and along a branch road down into a valley where sheep graze among twisted and stunted cedar trees rising out of the rocky earth. Gradually, houses appear more frequently, but many have roofs of shakes, instead of the red tiles more common in western Guatemala. There are stands of tall pines, and finally patches of corn, as the road winds down the widening valley into the town of Todos Santos.

Along the way, in the outlying settlements, appear Todos Santos people, impressive merely to look at. The men are tall, handsome, dignified, with an ease of manner that contrasts sharply with the humble aspect of Indian men of other areas. Their costume adds to their stature. Men's shirts are woven in heavy cotton, with big, red, floppy collars. Pants are long, in broad red and white stripes, and covered by black woolen breeches. A black capisayo, or cloak, with flappy arm flaps, may be worn as an overdress. A bandanna is usually tied around the head and capped with a round straw hat, with a leather belt around the crown. Sandals have a distinctive heel shelter.

Todos Santos sits amid mountains rising up to 3500 meters. Good pasture abounds, and sheep are kept at the higher altitudes of the township, in corrals built of stone. Mornings are cold, but by early afternoon, the chill has usually been burned off by the intense mountain sun.

Isolated for many years, the Todos Santos people kept their old ways, using the traditional 260-day religious calendar and performing prayer rituals at idols in the surrounding hills. Now that a passable road and bus service are available, the men range out to sell their women's weaving as far away as Guatemala City, and to work on lowland plantations. But wherever a Todos Santos man goes, he almost invariably retains the dress of his town. The world outside may be used as a source of cash, but it isn't allowed to interfere with tradition.

The market in Todos Santos is an open-sided structure, a quiet place even on a Saturday, when bargaining goes on in hushed tones. It's a center for friendly greeting and social contact, for most of the people of the township are isolated in hamlets in the surrounding hills for the rest of the week. Traders come in from neighboring valleys, trudging over mountain trails with their wares on their backs. Most notable are men of San Juan Atitán, dressed in red shirts with floppy collars, red headcloths, hats with ribbons, and short white pants.

To the south of town, up the ridge of mountains, are the burial mounds of Tecumanchún, a pre-Conquest ceremonial center. The mounds, now covered over by fir trees, are easily visible from the market.

By far the best time of the year to visit Todos Santos is during the annual fiesta, which starts on October 31 and lasts until November 5. The most unusual feature of the celebrations is a horseback marathon that takes place on November 1, All Saints' Day. Each participant takes a turn on horseback around a course running through the outskirts of town, pausing every time he completes a lap to swig down some liquor. When a man can no longer stay on horseback, his wife drags him away to sleep off the effects of the event. The traditional Dance of the Conquest is performed by a group of men that practices for months in advance.

Accommodations

Basic lodging is available for a couple of dollars per person at the Pensión Lucía and the Hospedaje La Paz, both within a block of where the bus from Huehuetenango stops. Meals are available at the Pensión Lucía, and at a small eatery above the market.

For shopping, you can try the craft cooperative, which has fixed prices. It's identified by a sign with the standard symbol of two pine trees. Another store, on the street above the market, sells local shirts, shoulder bags and huipiles. You can also wait for somebody to invite you to his or her house to see some weaving.

Buses leave from Huehuetenango (1 Avenida between 2 and 3 calles) for Todos Santos at 11 a.m. and 1 p.m.; from Todos Santos for Huehuetenango Sunday through Friday at 5 a.m. and 1 p.m. There may be an additional early-morning bus on Saturday, market day. Wear a few layers of clothing; it's cold on the way up. If the morning is clear, you'll get excellent views of the valley of Huehuetenango and the chain of volcanoes. Try to get a seat at the front of the bus, or next to a window.

The High Country

North from the junction for the branch road to Todos Santos, the main dirt highway continues through a little-visited but visually fascinating area, climbing and twisting from the plain through rocky grazing country and onward into misty evergreen forests in the highest parts of the Cuchumatanes, then dropping from the jagged peaks toward more gently rolling but still massive mountains overlooking temperate valleys. Aside from an occasional logging operation, there's little human presence in the cold, high forest, where the road is a one-lane ribbon of rock clinging to the mountainside.

Beyond the lofty summits, the highway passes through San Juan Ixcoy, Soloma, Santa Eulalia and San Mateo Ixtatán, each in its own valley, and comes to Barillas, a bruising eight hours by bus from Huehuetenango. The visitor would do well to stop for the night at Soloma, the halfway point, where there is a fairly comfortable hotel, and take a day trip from there to see the village of San Mateo Ixtatán and the variety of highland scenery along the way. Simple accommodations are available in the other small towns.

Buses leave Huehuetenango (1 Avenida between 2 and 3 calles) for Barillas at 1 a.m. and 11:30 a.m., and from Barillas at the same hours. Other buses go only as far as Santa Eulalia.

SAN JUAN IXCOY

Population 895 (township 9466; 93% indigenous); Altitude 2150 meters; Languages: Chuj and Spanish; Fiesta: June 24; Kilometer 323

A small town whose farmers specialize in the cultivation of

cherries, apples and other cold-land fruits, as well as corn and wheat. A revolt took place in San Juan Ixcoy in 1898 as a result of the mistreatment of Indians by Ladinos. Every Ladino in the town but one was killed on the night of July 17 of that year.

A pension in town serves poor meals, best tried only if you're desperately hungry, and also rents out rooms.

Beyond San Juan Ixcoy, the road continues beside a rushing stream through a valley bordered by rolling hills. At kilometer 330 is the junction for a side road to the village of San Miguel Acatán. The adventurous might try to hitch a ride on a truck going that way, and then continue on foot over a mountain ridge to Jacaltenango and back to Huehuetenango by road. Such off-road travel is best attempted in the dry season, though there is some rain throughout the year in these northern valleys. Beyond the junction, the main road ascends a steep mountainside and over into the next valley, where Soloma is located.

SOLOMA

Population 2975 (township 18,126; 93% indigenous); Altitude 2250 meters; Languages: Chuj, Kanjobal and Spanish; Fiesta: June 29; "Head of water"; Kilometer 335

Surrounded by wooded mountains, Soloma sits on an unstable stretch of land. Cave-ins have resulted in finds of old bits of wood, which have led geologists to conclude that the town was once the bed of a lake. Soloma has been ravaged periodically by disasters: repeated earthquakes, a great fire in 1884, and a smallpox epidemic in 1885. The area around the town is given over to the cultivation of grains and cold-land fruits. A great variety of medicinal and tanniferous plants flourishes in the countryside.

The women of Soloma wear an all-white huipil with lace layered around the neck, and often place another, longer huipil over their heads, which makes the town center look a spooky meeting place of nuns in white habits. Soloma is a commercial center for the northern part of the department of Huehuetenango, and so has a more "civilized" and built-up appearance than the smaller towns out this way. Overlooking Soloma is the cemetery, which from a distance appears to be a village in itself, with roofs constructed over groups of graves.

204

Accommodations: The Hotel Río Lindo is the best in the Cuchumatanes, with clean, airy rooms for about $3 per person, and warm showers available. Ask for extra blankets on crisp nights. Meals are served, or you can try a small eatery just off the square.

If you spend the night in Soloma, you can catch a bus going north early in the morning, spend a few hours in San Mateo Ixtatán, and return for the night to Soloma, or else continue to Huehuetenango. It's also pleasant to walk for a few hours to the north or south and then continue by bus. Confirm first that a bus will catch up to you.

SANTA EULALIA

Population 1217 (township 15,276; 99% indigenous); Altitude 2250 meters; Languages: Kanjobal and Spanish; Fiesta: February 12; Market Day: Sunday; Kilometer 348

This community is a trading center for the more remote towns of the department of Huehuetenango, and woolen garments and rope bags are made here. Rituals are held at caves and shrines outside town, one of which, Jolom Conob ("the village head"), has gained sufficient fame that a bus company was once named for it.

SAN MATEO IXTATAN

Population 1851 (township 16,048; 94% indigenous); Altitude 2250 meters; Languages: Chuj and Spanish; Fiesta: September 21; Market Days: Thursday and Sunday; Ixtatan, "At the salt waters"; Kilometer 378

The manufacture of a blackish salt from local spring water is the principal industry of San Mateo. The salt is said to have therapeutic properties. Woolen tunics (capisayos) widely used by men in the department are also made, but the women's huipiles are far more interesting. These bear heavily embroidered semicircular designs, mostly in red but with many other colors, covering the top part of the huipil. The rest of the long garment is usually left plain. Larger pieces with the traditional embroidered design are sold as tablecloths and wall hangings, and are made into shoulder bags. San Mateo's huipiles have come into

205

fashion in Guatemala City as well, where the unembroidered part is cut off, leaving a round poncho that reaches just to the waist.

In the center of San Mateo Ixtatán, down a hill from the market, is an old church where folk-Catholic prayer rituals are performed. About ten minutes from town, behind a school, are the remains of burial mounds and a ball court. Some of the stonework from the original structures survives.

BARILLAS

Population 3092 (township 32,734; 80% indigenous); Altitude 1400 meters; Languages: Chuj, Kanjobal and Spanish; Fiesta: May 3; Market Day: Sunday; Kilometer 405

Barillas has more in common with boom towns in the Petén than with the Indian villages of the northern part of Huehuetenango. Though hundreds of years old, Barillas has seen an influx of outsiders in the last few decades, as the area to the north and east, known as the Ixcán, has been opened up to farming. Instead of huddling around a square and church, Barillas spreads out in a beautiful valley, its wide, dusty streets running among scattered houses and empty lots. Formerly known as Santa Cruz Yalmox, the town was renamed to honor General Manuel Lisandro Barillas, a former president.

Much of the land around Barillas is low lying, and used for the cultivation of coffee, sugar cane, tobacco and fruits. Farther to the north, thick jungle grows along the rivers, which flow on toward Chiapas, in Mexico, and the Petén. Some of the rivers disappear into the ground, as in parts of El Quiché and Alta Verapaz. Rains throughout the year in the northern lowlands keep much of the land swampy. The tropical forest is rich in animal and bird life, including wild boars, tapirs, monkeys, herons and pheasants, and the quetzal is occasionally seen.

The end-of-the-road aspect of Barillas might have special interest for some visitors. A couple of pensions provide accommodations that are overpriced at $2 or so per person. The truly adventurous will pass up the next day's bus and trudge onward toward the lowlands to check out some deep sinkholes, and head downriver into the jungles on a boat. A road will eventually head eastward across the country. For now, roads from Barillas only reach the Ixcán River to the east, and the San Ramón River.

Toward the Mexican Border

From the plateau of the city of Huehuetenango, the Pan American Highway descends to the northwest, following the valley of the Selegua River. There is some cross-border traffic, of course. But the highway is also an important trade route for the little towns that sit just off it, and for the villages isolated in the mountains that tower to either side.

If you take a bus toward the border, you'll see Indians getting on and off along the way, carrying bundles wrapped in the sturdy cotton cloth called manta. Among the costumes the women wear will be red huipiles with white vertical and horizontal stripes from Santiago Chimaltenango, a village reached only by a foot trail running up from the highway; Colotenango huipiles with vertical red and white stripes; and the exquisite huipiles of San Pedro Necta, with horizontal stripes in red and brown on a white background. The bus trip provides an opportunity to see some of the costumes, and to look at the faces and gestures of people of formerly isolated cultures.

Direct buses for the border don't stray from the highway, and an exploration of towns along or accessible from the Pan American Highway will be made during day trips from Huehuetenango by bus or in your own vehicle.

SAN SEBASTIAN HUEHUETENANGO

Population 604 (township 9605; 95% indigenous); Altitude 1690 meters; Languages: Mam and Spanish; Fiesta: January 18; Kilometer 276

The original San Sebastián Huehuetenango, four kilometers east of the present location, was destroyed by a flood of the Selegua River in 1891. The old site is known as Toj Joj, and other ruins are located to the north of the present town. San Sebastián is thought to have been a large population center in pre-Columbian times. A small and pretty town, its people make their livings from agriculture, limestone and lead mining, lumbering, and the manufacture of rope.

Northwest of the turnoff for San Sebastián Huehuetenango, the Pan American Highway passes through a narrow canyon along the course of the Selegua River. Before the road was paved and the river tamed with rock jetties, the route was subject to frequent washouts during the rainy season. This part of the highway is known as El Tapón, the cork, or, figuratively, the bottleneck.

SAN JUAN ATITAN
Population 849 (township 7227; 98% indigenous); Altitude 2500 meters; Languages: Mam and Spanish; Fiesta: June 24

San Juan Atitán is located in the midst of pine, cypress and oak forests. Some of the inhabitants earn their living from lumbering; others from making rope and hats. Traders from San Juan Atitán are often seen in other towns of the department in their traditional dress of short white pants, shirt with a red floppy collar, an overshirt (capisayo) of black wool, a long red headcloth, and a round straw hat with a ribbon.

A jeep track leads up to San Juan Atitán from San Sebastián Huehuetenango, and is a good hiking route. Indians walk up in about two and a half hours, but it can take visitors up to double that time. If you don't plan to camp out, be back at the highway by 4 p.m. to catch the last bus to Huehuetenango.

CUILCO
Population 1067 (township 24,898; 46% indigenous); Altitude 1150 meters; Languages: Spanish, Mam and some dialects of Chiapas, Mexico; Fiesta: November 28; Market Day: Sunday; "Painted place"

Westernmost township of the department, Cuilco formerly included lands that are now part of Mexico. The town had a large population before the Conquest, and changed its location after the Spanish arrived. The ruins of the old town are known as Cuilco Viejo. Cuilco was the first stop of the invading Liberal army in 1871.

Cuilco lies 36 kilometers from the Pan American Highway at the end of a dirt road that branches off at kilometer 288, near Colotenango. The road passes through the villages of San Gaspar Ixchil and Ixtahuacán.

To Jacaltenango
At kilometer 314 on the Pan American Highway, an unpaved road leads northward to San Antonio Huista and Jacaltenango. These two towns have little to offer in terms of native crafts or

customs, but an excursion out this way in a jeep or pickup truck gives the visitor a glimpse of some magnificent scenery rarely seen by outsiders.

From the Pan American highway, the Jacaltenango road climbs steeply and winds around a bend into an area of coffee cultivation. As one slowly ascends along the side of a deep valley, little clusters of buildings, the processing centers of coffee plantations, become visible far below. Near them are open vats for washing coffee beans and great concrete drying platforms. Cattle graze on steep slopes on the opposite side of the valley. Here and there one sees women who have come to work on the coffee plantations, dressed in the outfits of towns of the region.

After following a ridge, the road creeps downward into another immense valley planted with sugar cane, corn, and more coffee, and looked over by mountains rising to more than 2900 meters. On a clear day one can see many kilometers down the valley to the flatter lands of the Mexican state of Chiapas. On the far side, the church and clusters of houses of San Antonio Huista poke out from the coffee and shade trees.

SAN ANTONIO HUISTA
Population 2632 (township 5964); Altitude 1250 meters; Fiesta: June 13; Huista, "place of the thorns"; Kilometer 349

San Antonio is a warm little town which has become a trading center for the formerly isolated villages of this part of the department of Huehuetenango. Farther down the valley is Santa Ana Huista, and a few valleys over, to the north, is Nentón, 37 kilometers distant. Both places are reached by a rutted track. A better road leads eastward over a pass to Jacaltenango. Relatively clean and simple accommodations are available.

JACALTENANGO
Population 4967 (township 18,012; 94% indigenous); Altitude 1438 meters; Languages: Jacalteca and Spanish; Fiesta: February 2; "Place of the huts"; Market Day: Sunday; Kilometer 361

Jacaltenango, 12 kilometers beyond San Antonio, is the center of a rocky coffee-growing region. In its more isolated days, it

209

was noted for its colorful folk-Catholic rituals, especially that of the Year Bearer. In accordance with the traditional 360-day secular calendar (as distinguished from the 260-day ritual calendar), a day was set aside, usually in May, to honor the lord of the new year. Turkeys and chickens were sacrificed to insure good fortune, and days were spent in intense prayer. As in other parts of Guatemala, the traditional ceremonies have been in decline.

Though old-style native dress has to a large extent been discarded, the women of Jacaltenango still weave sashes and belts, many of which turn up in stores and markets in all parts of western Guatemala. A Maryknoll Catholic hospital serves the town and also trains medical aides for the smaller hamlets of the region.

About ten kilometers up the valley from Jacaltenango, and almost a thousand meters higher, is Concepción (population 3107). Formerly part of the township of Jacaltenango, Concepción separated in the seventeenth century after a civil and religious dispute. Sheep are grazed in the colder altitudes near the town, and excellent honey is produced. Ajul, a nearby hamlet, has been the site of religious ceremonies and sacrifices since long before the Conquest. Some Jacalteca-speaking Indians still gather there in a cave to burn incense and send messages to the old gods.

The road ends at Jacaltenango, and visitors who arrive by jeep or pickup truck will have to turn back. The adventurous traveler might continue on foot on the abandoned track that winds high up the mountain ridge behind Jacaltenango and over toward San Miguel Acatán, which is on a spur of the road to Barillas. One can also reach Todos Santos by trail. Indian traders occasionally take these routes with heavy loads upon their backs. But with the expansion of truck and bus transportation to the more remote areas of Guatemala, these traders are becoming a vanishing breed. It's sometimes hard to find somebody to point the way or even to admit that a trail exists. For overnight accommodations, it's best to return to San Antonio Huista.

Buses leave Huehuetenango (2 Calle 2-45) at 5 a.m. and noon, and take about five hours to reach Jacaltenango. Departures from Jacaltenango are before dawn and in the late morning. In a pickup truck or jeep, the trip takes about three hours.

Buses from Huehuetenango also serve Nentón and the villages up in the northwest corner of the department of Huehuetenango.

It is possible to cross over into the Mexican state of Chiapas, but immigration services have lagged behind recent travel possibilities, and you might not be able to get your passport stamped.

LA MESILLA/MEXICAN BORDER
Kilometer 341

La Mesilla is the hamlet on the Guatemalan side of the border; a few kilometers down the road on the other side is Ciudad Cuauhtémoc, in the Mexican state of Chiapas.

If entering Guatemala at La Mesilla, you'll first go through immigration procedures at the station on the border. Tourist cards are sometimes available, but it's best to pick one up in advance at the Guatemalan consulate in Comitán. The customs post for baggage inspection is a couple of hundred meters up the road from the border.

Buses: To Huehuetenango: Various companies about every 90 minutes from 5:30 a.m. to 4 p.m. Travel time about three hours to Huehuetenango second class, 90 minutes on the 10 a.m. first-class bus. To Guatemala City and intermediate points: El Cóndor buses at 6 and 10 a.m., both first class. At other times, connect at Huehuetenango. Leave San Cristóbal de las Casas on the first bus of the day to meet the 10 a.m. bus. Guatemala City to La Mesilla: El Cóndor (19 Calle 2-01, Zone 1) at 4, 8 (first class) and 10 a.m. The 4 a.m. bus offers the best onward connections, or start later in the day from Quezaltenango or Huehuetenango.

On to Mexico
Buses for San Cristóbal and points beyond leave from the Mexican side at about noon. Others depart from the Mexican customs post about three kilometers up the road, and you'll have to walk or take a taxi to catch them. It's best to have a Mexican tourist card in hand. If you get stuck, a couple of rooms are available at one of the cafés opposite the main Mexican customs post.

The Pacific Lowlands

When Guatemalans talk about the *Costa Sur* —the South Coast—they refer not only to the great expanse of black volcanic beach along the Pacific Ocean from the Mexican border to El Salvador, but also to the wide lowland plain, broken by dozens of rivers, stretching more than 50 kilometers inland. This is a steaming area where temperatures above 100 degrees F (37 C) are not uncommon at any time of year, and where the humidity is high enough to keep anyone drenched in sweat. It's also an extraordinarily fertile land of lush, green, exuberant vegetation; of giant trees, exotic flowers and tropical birds in the brightest of colors.

The jungles of the lowlands were spotted here and there with settlements long before the Spanish conquest. There are probably more archaeological remains in the area than anywhere else in Guatemala. But the structures left by the early inhabitants were not especially durable, and have fallen prey to the humid climate, tropical vegetation, and, in recent years, the plows of large-scale agriculture

The Pipils, the major Indian nation of the area, migrated from Mexico and settled around the present-day cities of Santa Lucía Cotzumalguapa and Escuintla. Their kingdom, Panacat, stretched into El Salvador. The highland nations, coveting the coastal lowlands and their agricultural products (especially cacao beans, which were used as currency), alternately warred upon and allied themselves with the coastal peoples. By the time the Spanish arrived, much of the area was under the control of the Quichés and the Cakchiquels.

Alvarado at first joined forces with the Pipils, but this alliance, like all his others, dissolved into enmity and warfare. Eventually, the Spaniards destroyed the Pipil city of Iscuintepeque, predecessor of today's Escuintla.

212

After the Franciscans started missionary work among the coastal peoples, much of the land was used for indigo plantations and cattle ranching. Epidemics, hard labor and drunkenness among Indian workers led to the decay of agriculture, the depopulation of the area, and the loss of some of the early settlements to the jungle. Malaria, worms and other diseases and infestations resulted in much of the land remaining abandoned to jungle and swamps into the twentieth century, when better communications and measures to improve health conditions opened large areas to settlement and farming. A railroad began operation between Guatemala City and Puerto San José in 1880, and later was extended to the Mexican border. It facilitated the shipment of bananas from the United Fruit Company's plantations around Tiquisate to Puerto Barrios, after disease had damaged much of the company's original plantings in the Caribbean area. Today, the railroad has given way to the coast highway as the main carrier of traffic, and bananas have moved downward on the list of Guatemala's exports.

Indians from the highlands have traditionally cultivated small lowland plots on which they harvest two crops of corn a year. But the spread of large-scale agriculture has more and more crowded out small cultivators. Sugar cane, rice, cotton, cacao and rubber are the chief crops of the lowlands, and there are great cattle ranches. Just back from the plain, where the land rises, are the coffee plantations.

Travel Strategy for the Coast

The main attractions of the Pacific lowlands are long stretches of beaches of black volcanic sand, and some important archaeological sites. But even if you're not interested in the sun, near-deserted beaches, and the vestiges of pre-Columbian civilizations, you may want to drop down to the lowlands to see a Guatemala very different from the highlands—a land of ramshackle steaming towns, fat cattle lazing in pastures, and endless expanses of sugar cane.

The most economical way to travel around the lowlands is by bus, and it's acceptable enough to get on a bus in Guatemala City and head for one of the beaches and then return to cooler climes. But I wouldn't start out with the intention of hopping around from town to town in the lowlands by bus. I can think of few things more evaporating than to be crowded into one of Guatemala's ordinary buses in this hot area, with no chance to stop for a cold drink to pick up your spirit.

My best recommendation for lowland travel is to go by rented car or taxi. It's a sad fact that although Guatemala's Pacific beaches are pleasant for swimming and surfing, dining facilities and overnight accommodations are usually squalid, and most visitors would not want to risk missing the last bus out. Of the larger beach resorts with hotels near Puerto San José, only Likín is easily reached by bus. The archaeological sites around Santa Lucía Cotzumalguapa are a bit spread out, and without a vehicle you'd be trudging in the heat through sugar-cane fields and along back roads. The best alternative to a car is to take a day tour out of Guatemala City to La Democracia, Santa Lucía Cotzumalguapa and one of the Pacific beach resorts; or to take a bus and then hire a taxi locally.

One last possibility is to do part of your travel by train. Passenger trains leave Guatemala City for Escuintla, Santa Lucía Cotzumalguapa, Mazatenango, Coatepeque and Tecún Umán on the Mexican border twice a week. Fares are ridiculously low—a few dollars for the all-day trip to Tecún Umán—but comfort is not one of the attractions.

With a bit of good advice and preparation, an excursion to the lowlands can be pleasant and enlightening. Wear light cotton clothing, and don't forget your bathing suit. Even if you're not going to the beach, many of the motels and restaurants along the coast highway have swimming pools where for a fee (or sometimes for free if you take a meal) you can jump in and cool off after a day of sweltering heat. There's a certain similarity to the restaurants along the highway. Meals generally go for $4 or so, and the dining area is often an open bamboo pavilion with a thatched roof.

You should also be aware that malaria isn't unknown in these parts. During the dry season, when there's little stagnant water in which mosquitoes can breed, there's not much of a problem. And in the rainy season, the mosquitoes usually become bothersome only at night. If you stay at a hotel that's well sprayed with insecticides or screened in, then have no fear. You can minimize the risk of contracting malaria by limiting your lowland travel in the rainy season to day trips from the highlands, or by taking a preventive drug (see the practical information chapter).

Highway Notes

A good paved highway, CA2, runs through the lowlands between the borders of Mexico and El Salvador. It's known as the **Carretera del Pacífico,** or Pacific Highway. From Guatemala City, Highway CA9, which is an expressway part of the way, runs down to join the coast highway at Escuintla, and on to Puerto San José and the nearby beaches. To get on CA9, follow Avenida Bolívar or take the Periférico expressway out of Zone 1. Keep an eye out for the strange, gigantic painted quetzal on the rocks on the left side of the road, in the vicinity of kilometer 47.

A number of good paved roads branch from the Pacific Highway to the small beach towns mentioned below. The coast highway is also accessible by a toll road leading down from Quezaltenango to the El Zarco junction between Mazatenango and Retalhuleu, by a scenic road from San Lucas Tolimán on Lake Atitlán, and another paved road from Cuilapa on the highland route to El Salvador. A number of unpaved roads also descend from the highlands, the most interesting of these being the one between San Marcos and Malacatán. Magnificent scenery, but rough going in parts.

The Pacific lowland towns listed below are more or less in geographical order from west to east.

TALISMAN–EL CARMEN

This is one of the border–crossing points to Mexico. There are a few small eateries and a couple of rather basic lodging places. Immigration procedures take place at the international bridge over the Suchiate River, and customs inspection at the post about a kilometer uphill from the border. Have your Mexican tourist card in hand when you reach the border if you come from the Guatemalan side.

Buses

Guatemala City to Talismán: Running time is about five hours. Galgos (7 Avenida 19-44, Zone 1), 5:30, 10 a.m., noon, 3:30 and 5 p.m. Rutas Lima (8 Calle 3-63, Zone 1), 6:45 a.m. and 2:45 p.m. These first class buses connect with onward intercity buses on the Mexican side (through ticket to Mexico City $30, time 24 hours) and there are local buses for Tapachula. Also Unión Pacífico buses about every hour from 18 Calle and 9 Avenida, Zone 1.

To Guatemala City: Galgos, 5, 9 and 11 a.m., 3 and 5 p.m. Rutas Lima, 10:30 a.m. and 3 p.m. Use this bus to connect for Quezaltenango at El Zarco (also a direct bus at 8 a.m.). Or take a taxi to nearby Malacatán to catch a bus for San Marcos.

MALACATAN
Population 5594; Altitude 391 meters

An important commercial center because of its location near the border and along the road to San Marcos. There's little reason to stop in Malacatán, except to visit the Mexican consulate. Basic accommodations are available at the Hospedaje Santa Lucía and the Hotel América. Buses pass through Malacatán on the way from Tecún Umán to San Marcos, and other buses run to Coatepeque and Quezaltenango via the coast highway.

TECUN UMAN
Population 4125; Altitude 24 meters; Kilometer 245

A sweltering border town, formerly called Ayutla. Much of the land across the border was once part of Guatemala, and was known as Soconusco. That area was ceded to Mexico in the nineteenth century.

The railroad from Guatemala City has its terminal at Tecún Umán, making the town an important transit center. A long railroad and highway bridge crosses the Suchiate River to the Mexican town of Ciudad Hidalgo. From there, frequent local buses run to Tapachula, where connections can be made for Mexico City.

If you're driving, it doesn't much matter whether you cross the border at Tecún Umán or Talismán. Better first-class bus service into Guatemala is available from Talismán.

Buses
Guatemala City: Transportes Fortaleza, from Guatemala City (9 Avenida and 19 Calle, Zone 1) about every two hours from 5 a.m. to 5 p.m. From Tecún Umán: about every two hours until 4 p.m. Several daily departures to San Marcos. For Quezaltenango,

change buses at San Marcos, or at El Zarco junction.

Trains
Departures for Guatemala City Tuesday and Saturday at 6 a.m., arriving in Guatemala City in the evening. (By bus, the trip takes about five hours.) There was a time when this train was the main means of overland transportation from Mexico to Guatemala City, but hardly anyone takes it these days.

Hotels: Basic lodging at Hotel Don José, Hotel Blanquita and several other establishments. For better accommodations, continue to Coatepeque.

OCOS
Population 794; Altitude 4 meters

A small fishing port on the Pacific, south of Tecún Umán. Before the Conquest, the town was known as Ucuz, and was populated by Mam Indians.

Across the Río Naranjo from Ocós is the village of Tilapa, reached by a new paved road from the Pacific Highway. A small hotel offers basic rooms.

COATEPEQUE
Population 19,307 (township 50,106; 34% indigenous); Altitude 498 meters; Fiesta: March 15; Kilometer 214

A coffee-processing and commercial center just off the Pacific Highway, about 30 kilometers from Tecún Umán. If you're driving from the border, this is the first town with first-class hotel accommodations.

Hotels: Hotel Virginia, 15 rooms, on the highway at kilometer 220. $7 to $12 single, $10 to $15 double. Really a motel, with carports for each room and nice gardened grounds. The restaurant serves moderately priced meals. In the center of town, there's the Hotel Europa (6 Calle 4-01) with rooms for $3 to $5 per person; and the Posada Santander (6 Calle 6-43), $3 per person for a basic room.

Buses for Tecún Umán and Talismán stop at the bus terminal (the first-class buses stop at the square). Frequent service to Quezaltenango and Guatemala City. Two early-morning buses to San Marcos. Many buses to Guatemala City, and also a morning train twice a week.

SAN SEBASTIAN
Population 5869 (township 12,782; 58% indigenous); Altitude 311 meters; Languages: Cakchiquel and Spanish; Fiesta: January 18

The women of San Sebastián were once known for their habit of going around barechested, in contrast to the more modest Indian women of the highlands. These days, the laws have obliged them to put on blouses when they go out in the streets. The inhabitants raise vegetables for nearby Retalhuleu, and manufacture *panela*, cakes of hard brown sugar.

Motel La Colonia, on the Pacific Highway at kilometer 178. Telephone 710054. Cottages for $10 to $15 single, $15 to $20 double. Pool and parking, a la carte lunch and dinner.

RETALHULEU
Population 22,001 (township 46,652); Altitude 239 meters; Languages: Spanish and Quiché; Fiesta: December 8; "Sign on the earth"; Kilometer 184

According to one historian, soon after the Spanish conquest, the Mam people of this area complained to Pedro de Alvarado about encroachments made on their territories by the Quichés. Alvarado took a sword and drew a line on the ground to divide the territories, hence the name of Retalhuleu. The town is often called by its short name, Reu (RAY-ooh).

Retalhuleu, capital of the department of the same name, is relatively pleasant as lowland towns go, with a number of new public buildings around the downtown area, and elegant homes on the outskirts. The region is a rich sugar, cattle, cotton, rice and rubber area, and in town there's some coffee processing and small industry, especially the distilling of liquor. The people here are chauvinistic. A sign at the entrance to town reads "Bienvenidos a Retalhuleu, capital del mundo" ("Welcome to Retalhuleu, capital of the world").

Hotels: Hotel Astor, 5 Calle 4-60, $5 per person; Posada de Don José, 3 Avenida 5-14, $6 per person.

Buses: Frequent service to Retalhuleu from 19 Calle and 9 Avenida, Zone 1, Guatemala City. Frequent service from the terminal in Retalhuleu to Champerico on the Pacific, Quezaltenango, Mazatenango and Guatemala City.

CHAMPERICO
Population 6891; Altitude 5 meters; Kilometer 226

A honky-tonk port south of Retalhuleu on the Pacific, opened by President Miguel García Granados in 1872 to serve the developing coffee industry. The beach isn't much, and the town is sweltering, but a walk along the shore (or a drive, if you happen to have a dune buggy) will take you to some isolated stretches of sand.

Hotels: Hotel Miramar, 2 Calle and Avenida Coatepeque; Hotel Martita, good place for a shrimp lunch; Hotel Modelo, 5 Calle 4-53. All charge about $5 per person.

Buses: Frequent service from Retalhuleu and Quezaltenango.

EL ZARCO
Kilometer 175

Junction for the toll road to Quezaltenango.

CUYOTENANGO
Population 3977 (township 24,710; 41% indigenous); Altitude 334 meters; Languages: Spanish and Quiché; Fiesta: January 15; "Place of the coyote"; Kilometer 165

An old town with narrow streets, in an area where coffee, citronella, lemon tea and cacao are grown. You can often smell the scent of lemongrass as you drive along the highway.

219

Hotel Posada del Sol, east of town at kilometer 263 on the Pacific Highway. $8 per person. Swimming pool.

MAZATENANGO
Population 20,918 (township 38,181; 26% indigenous); Altitude 371 meters; Languages: Spanish and Quiché; Fiesta: During Carnival (Mardi Gras); "Place of the deer"; Kilometer 159

A bustling center for processing cottonseed, coffee and other agricultural products of the region; capital of the department of Suchitepéquez.

Hotels: Hotel Kakol Kiej, 7 Calle 2-10, Zone 2, $5 per person; Hotel La Gran Tasca, 7 Avenida Norte No. 10, $4 per person.

Buses: Frequent service via Retalhuleu buses; also trains several times a week.

CHICACAO
Population 5588 (township 28,786; 81% indigenous); Altitude 494 meters; Languages: Spanish and Quiché; Fiesta: December 19

A town north of the Pacific Highway, named for Francisco Chicajau, an Indian of Santiago Atitlán who once owned the land on which the town is built. Chicacao is in the middle of the belt of great coffee estates. Essential oils are also produced nearby.
Chicacao maintains a traditional trading relationship with Santiago Atitlán, and a dirt road, passable in the dry season only, links the two towns. During the rainy season, buses carrying traders and goods from Atitlán take the long way around by way of the highway from San Lucas Tolimán to the coast.

TIQUISATE
Population 12,096; Altitude 69 meters

Tiquisate (or Pueblo Nuevo Tiquisate to use its full name) was once the capital of the Pacific region of United Fruit's banana empire. Some of the land formerly planted in bananas has been converted to cattle pasture or divided up into small landholdings.

The former club for United Fruit employees, south of town, is now a moderately priced hotel. Pool and tennis courts, $4 per person. Back in town, the Hotel Oasis charges similar rates, and serves acceptable meals.

Buses: From Guatemala City (Tropicana company at the bus terminal) about every hour from 4 a.m. to 4:45 p.m. From Tiquisate about every hour from 4 a.m. to 5 p.m.

Two small Pacific coast beach towns, Semillero and Tecojate, are reached by bus or car from Tiquisate. There's not much in the way of facilities at either of these places, except for some simple thatched eateries, and cabanas where you can spend the night for a couple of quetzales.

COCALES
Kilometer 113

Junction for the scenic highway through coffee country to San Lucas Tolimán on Lake Atitlán, by way of Patulul.

SANTA LUCIA COTZUMALGUAPA
Population 14,624; Altitude 356 meters; Fiesta: December 25; Cotzumalguapa, "River of the rainbow"; Kilometer 89

Before the Conquest, Cotzumalguapa was taken from the Pipils by the Cakchiquels, who coveted its agricultural treasure of cacao. The Spanish tried to exploit the area, and founded their town of Santa Lucía on the site of the Indian village, but disease and drunkenness put an end to those first efforts.

Long before the Spanish conquest, this area was inhabited by a race of people who sculptured mysterious massive heads, discs, statues and humanoid figures. Today, these sculptures litter the sugar-cane fields of the area. Some are on the surface, some under the ground, covered by the sediment of the centuries. The mechanized plows of extensive agriculture have done more damage to the sculptures in the past few years than was done in the preceding millennium. Some of the sculptures have been removed to museums in Guatemala and Europe, or to the headquarters of the *fincas* (plantations) where they were discovered. A few remain in place, the areas around them cleared to prevent further damage. Some are still used by local Indians for religious ceremonies.

Several of the massive heads found around Santa Lucía are mystifyingly similar to the Olmec sculptures of south-central Mexico, though nobody seems to be able to explain what the Olmecs might have been doing here. The stylistic similarity may be a coincidence. The Olmecs are thought to have developed their civilization in Mexico before the great heads were carved in lowland Guatemala. The variety of the sculptures is also fascinating. There are heads and bodies in the simple Olmec-like style; stelae bearing the visages of Mexican gods; Mexican-style circle numerals, and depictions of Mexican clothing; great rocks carved on one flattened face; busy sets of intertwining figures in a Maya-like style; and faces with a personal detail that appears nowhere else in Guatemala. From this mixture, it appears that the rocks were carved over a long period, during which the people or peoples of the area were subject to many different cultural streams. The carving wasn't a very difficult task, given the availability of soft volcanic rock, which was easily worked with tools of obsidian and jade.

Near Santa Lucía are the archaeological sites known as El Baúl, El Castillo and Bilbao. The structures were stepped pyramids set on plazas paved with a slate-like stone. Although the pyramids have been excavated by archaeologists, they haven't been restored, so the sites appear to be nothing but lumps of earth. The pottery found at the sites, the architecture and the sculpture all indicate a developing Mexican influence. Many of the faces have deep incisions between the lash and pupil, a characteristic of central Mexican art, and there are depictions of the Mexican gods Quetzalcoatl and Tlaloc.

Going around the area of Santa Lucía Cotzumalguapa to gaze at the sculptures can be a trying experience, not only because of the heat, but because most of the sculptures are located in the middle of sugar-cane fields. It's easy to get lost in the cane and feel like an idiot. Follow the itinerary below carefully. If it doesn't seem clear to you, you might want to hire a local taxi driver to show you around. Or else take a tour from Guatemala City with a guide who knows where things are supposed to be. Good luck.

Start at Finca Las Ilusiones on the eastern outskirts of Santa Lucía. From the Pacific Highway, turn north in the vicinity of kilometer 88 onto a dirt road lined by scattered palm trees. Landmarks in the area are an Esso station on the north side of the road, and a soccer field. At the end of the road is the finca headquarters. Outside the buildings are copies of sculptures found in the area. There are more carved stones on the patio of one of the buildings. Others are in a little museum, which is open when you can find somebody to unlock the door.

From the finca, head back out to the highway, then on into Santa Lucía. In the square are several copies of monumental stones. They look like the real thing, but for telltale ends of reinforcing rods.

While in town, sample the local scene. A couple has wedding photographs taken in the central park. Men snooze under shade trees in the mid-day heat. Highland Indians stroll around, on break from work on surrounding fincas, where the law once forced them to work, and where necessity still makes them labor.

At the northern end of 4 Avenida is a dirt road leading a short distance to the entrance to the Bilbao site. Since 4 Avenida is a one-way street going south, you'll have to detour by another avenue to get to the northern end. The entrance to the area is usually fenced off, so if you're driving, park and continue on foot.

About 300 meters up the dirt road is a narrow path leading to the left (west) through the sugar cane. A few meters in is a small clearing with a carved stone. Back out to the dirt road, up another hundred meters or so, and on the left is another narrow path leading to a more interesting carved rock. This one was sculptured in relief on a face flattened at an angle—a task that required considerable skill. The relief, dating from about 600 A.D., shows, among other things, what might be a witch doctor with a puppet, a prince playing ball, local fruits whimsically depicted in the form of animals, and all kinds of other intertwining motifs. If you get lost while looking for the sculptures, ask one of the people in the area for the *piedra española* —the Spanish stone—which is what some of them call one of the larger rocks, though the Spanish can hardly claim any credit. There are other sculptures lying around, and with some hunting in the cane you might find one.

The next stop is the El Baúl archaeological site. By car, take the road west from the Bilbao site (not the road back to town), then turn right onto the wide road. If you get lost, ask for the road to Finca El Baúl. Make another right turn at the arrow pointing to Ingenio Los Tarros, at the junction just after a bridge. Stop where a road cuts off to the left. There's an entrance to the sugar-cane field just to the right, but don't enter in your vehicle unless it has four-wheel drive. This point is about four kilometers from town.

After following the track into the field, you'll come to a fork. Go to the right, then stop where the track starts to rise and another track leads off to the left. On foot, take the track to the left, up the tree-covered hill. Any time that you see a tree-covered hill in Guatemala where there shouldn't be a tree-covered hill, chances are that it's the remains of a temple or burial mound—which is the case here.

Up in a clearing, among the trees, you'll see some more great sculptures. The one on the left is a man with a large nose, about five feet wide and five feet high, and up to four feet thick. Its face is blackened from the smoke of coals and incense, for Indians use the site for prayer ceremonies. Opposite is another carved stone with many circular motifs. A reproduction of it stands in the central park of Santa Lucía Cotzumalguapa.

Return to the entrance to the field. Take the road that leads west from the one on which you came, for about two kilometers to Finca El Baúl. Occasionally buses run out to the finca from Santa Lucía. Here there's an open-air collection of sculptures gathered from the area. One is a great jaguar in a sitting position, looking somewhat like a cartoon figure, with some of the rock flaked off by the heat of incense fires that once burned before it. There are also cylindrical carved stones which possibly were used as some kind of calendar. One has been damaged from use as a washboard.

After a look at the sculptures, go back to town for a drink and some shelter from the sun and heat.

Accommodations

The Caminotel Santiaguito, on the Pacific Highway on the west side of town, is a palm-shaded oasis compound. Swimming pools, of course. $10 per person. Good food at the hotel's restaurant, a pleasant room with overhead fans. Try the orangeade. Meals about $4 and up.

Across the way from the Santiaguito is the lesser Hotel El Camino, $5 per person, where meals are also served. There are also inexpensive diners right in town.

Buses: Frequent service from the terminal in Zone 4, and from 19 Calle and 9 Avenida, Zone 1, Guatemala City.

After a visit to the ruins, you might want to stop at the museum in nearby La Democracia. Flag down any bus on the highway and take it to Siquinalá, where you can catch a bus to La Democracia.

LA DEMOCRACIA
Population 2788; Altitude 165 meters; Fiesta: December 31; Kilometer 90

La Democracia, a quiet town of wooden shacks, is the location of a collection of gigantic stone heads from the nearby Monte Alto archaeological site, and of an archaeological museum.

The sculptures, displayed on the central plaza around a great ceiba tree, may or may not have been the work of people of the Olmec culture. The Olmecs flourished in the area around Veracruz in Mexico more than a thousand years before Christ, and are thought to have been the progenitors of the later Maya and Toltec civilizations of Mesoamerica. The carved stones, however, may be up to 4000 years old. The similarity in styles, and the possibility that the stones predated Classic Olmec civilization, lead to the tempting alternative theory that the Pacific lowlands of Guatemala were the cradle of Mesoamerican civilization.

The enormous heads and fat-bellied, squatting grotesqueries of La Democracia are crude in technique. They wear frowns or expressionless faces, but they are nevertheless robust and lively. The fat figures may represent fertility, or the agricultural bounty of the region. One surprising recent discovery is that they were carved around natural magnetic poles in basaltic rock.

Inside the modern town museum is a varied collection of artifacts from the area: stone pieces that might have been used as yokes for beasts of burden or possibly as goals in ball games; large urns that might have held human remains; grinding stones, evidence of corn agriculture; effigy pottery, similar in style to pieces found at Teotihuacán and Kaminaljuyú; and stone sculptures, including some heads that were used in recent times as idols in Indian religious ceremonies. There are also some exhibits of local plant life. A set of paintings gives a general history of Indians in the Americas, but doesn't have much to do with the

225

material on display.

The museum is open from 9 a.m. to noon and from 2 to 5 p.m.; closed on Mondays and holidays. The guard will turn on the air conditioning when you enter, if it's working.

There are only a few simple diners around the square of La Democracia. Stop at one of the restaurants on the Pacific Highway, or else pack some sandwiches for the trip.

Buses for La Democracia and Sipacate leave from the terminal in Guatemala City about every half hour from 6 a.m. to 4 p.m.

From La Democracia, you can head for the Pacific at Sipacate (population 3200), a village where you won't find much except thatched shacks, a few open-air diners, cabanas where you can spend the night, and a black sand beach. You can also continue to Santa Lucía Cotzumalguapa (take a Guatemala City bus to Siquinalá, then catch a westbound bus), or else return to Guatemala City.

ESCUINTLA
Population 36,931; Altitude 347 meters; Fiesta: December 8; "Hill of the dogs"; Kilometer 58

Commercially and industrially, Escuintla is one of the more important cities of the Pacific lowlands. Located at the junction of the Pacific Highway and the road from Guatemala City, it's a center for processing the sugar cane, cottonseed, coffee, beef and other agricultural products of the area, and for the refining of petroleum. It's also the capital of the department of Escuintla, which stretches from the volcanoes near Antigua and Lake Amatitlán to the steaming coastal plain. The town's name refers to a species of dog raised for food in pre-Columbian times.

Physically, Escuintla is a dumpy place of wooden and cement-block houses, hot at all times, with an oppressive humidity. There's no reason to tarry long in town, but all around one can appreciate the luxuriant tropical vegetation, tall palms, dense forests in shades of green, banana trees with giant leaves (so large that they were once used as raincoats) and exotic flowers. Volcanoes and mountains tower above the city to the north.

Buses to Escuintla run frequently from the terminal in Guatemala City. Buses for all parts of the lowlands stop at the Escuintla terminal.

Hotels: Hotel Sarita, on the highway through Escuintla, tel. 380482, $10 per person; Motel Texas, near the Sarita, tel. 380183, $8 per person and a fair place to have lunch.

PUERTO SAN JOSE
Population 9795; Altitude 2 meters; Fiesta: March 19; Kilometer 109

San José is the complete sailors' port in the tropics, a seedy place of ramshackle houses and thatched huts, unpaved streets, and bars from one end of town to the other. The port is relatively new, having been opened to commerce in 1853. Freight coming to San José, which lacks a sheltered harbor, is transferred from ships to lighters, and unloaded at the long iron pier. The railroad, opened in 1880, made San José the main terminal for Pacific Ocean commerce. Before the port was opened, much of Guatemala's trade moved through the port of Acajutla in El Salvador.

Across the Chiquimulilla Canal from the town center is the honky-tonk bathing area lined with diners and cheap cabanas, many of them rotting wooden stilt structures. Puerto San José is fine for a quick look around, or if you want to mix in at the sailors' bars. Otherwise, you'd do better to take the sun at Chulamar, Likin, Iztapa or Puerto Quetzal.

Buses: There's frequent service to Puerto San José and Iztapa from the bus terminal in Zone 4, Guatemala City.

Hotels in Puerto San José and all along the coast are rather uninviting. Best in town is the Viñas del Mar ($5 per person). You can also stay in cubicles at any of several *casetas* for a few quetzales per person. About five kilometers west of San José via a sandy road is the Chulamar bathing area, reached by car or taxi only. Cabanas and bungalows (sleeping up to six) are available for prices starting at about $30 per day. Telephone 23886 in Guatemala City. An expensive hotel may have re-opened here at

227

the time of your visit. East of San José at kilometer 113 on the road to Iztapa is Likin, a planned community. On the surface, it looks like Florida, but it's strictly a local-style resort, quiet during the week and noisy on weekends. Bungalows rent from about $30 per day. Telephone 22190 in Guatemala City.

IZTAPA
Population 1593; Altitude: sea level; Fiesta: October 24; "River of Salt"; Kilometer 127

Iztapa was Guatemala's first port. In colonial times, Pedro de Alvarado had a fleet built here for an expedition to Mexico from which he never returned. In succeeding years, Iztapa failed to develop because of its unhealthy climate, and the main Pacific port was finally moved to San José in 1853.

The town that stands today is a quiet place, more pleasant and uncrowded than San José, with streets of sand and most of the buildings roofed with thatch. From the town center, you can take a boat for a few cents to the other side of the canal, where the beach, restaurants and cheap cabana hotels are located.

You can also hire a boat to take you through the Chiquimulilla canal. Running from Sipacate to the border of El Salvador, the canal is an intracoastal waterway, just inland from the ocean and navigable by small boats for most of the way. It's pleasant to cruise along, watch the birds amid the lush vegetation, and look out on the rice paddies of the area.

Near Iztapa is Guatemala's newest port, Puerto Quetzal, with modern ocean shipping facilities. There's also a beach there, which for now is less crowded than others in the area.

TAXISCO
Population 3591; Altitude 214 meters; "The prairie"; Kilometer 109

Now a cattle-raising center, Taxisco existed before the Conquest, and was mentioned by Alvarado in his letters to the Spanish king. Junction here for a branch road to the beaches around Monterrico.

MONTERRICO
Population 609

A small town on the Pacific. Catch boats here for the trip along the canal to Hawaii, a beach village three kilometers east of Monterrico. An idyllic spot, Hawaii even boasts some small sand dunes. Uncomfortable bamboo cabanas are available for rent, and there are few facilities. Bring supplies if you plan to stay the night.

The Reserva Monterrico is an area set aside to protect beaches of black volcanic sand, mangroves, lagoons and sea birds.

LAS LISAS
Population 835

Another idyllic tropical beach resort on the Pacific, about 20 kilometers from the border of El Salvador. Las Lisas is a favorite vacation spot for a few prosperous Guatemalans. The beach, separated from the mainland by the Chiquimulilla Canal, offers fair surfing. The beach huts, however, are primitive, and even the "high-priced" accommodations at about $5 per person provide only a cot with one sheet in a cubicle. Stop by on an uncrowded weekday, enjoy the coconuts, papayas and seafood, and continue on your way. A bus from Guatemala City (or your car) will take you as far as the canal, where you catch a boat for the beach.

CIUDAD PEDRO DE ALVARADO
Kilometer 166

A planned city at the border-crossing point for El Salvador. Most buses from Guatemala City to San Salvador take another highway to the north, but some local buses run to the border, if you have any reason to go that way.

In case you missed the symbolism, the city named for Tecún Umán, the native hero of Guatemala, is at the western end of the Pacific Highway, at the Mexican border. The city named for Alvarado, who vanquished Tecún Umán, is here at the opposite end of the highway.

229

The Inland Route to El Salvador

The towns mentioned below are not exactly in the Pacific lowlands. Rather, they're along or near the highways leading east from Guatemala City to El Salvador. I'm afraid there's no better place than this in which to mention them.

The eastern highlands are nowhere near as impressive as the mountains to the west of Guatemala City. These are older, worn, lower hills, mostly temperate in climate, planted in corn, beans and coffee, or used for grazing. The inhabitants of the area today include descendants of the Xinca, Pokomam and Pipil Indian nations, who long ago lost their native languages and styles of dress and mixed into the Ladino population.

The highway running east from Guatemala City is a good, paved, two-lane road, winding in parts, branching past Cuilapa into two routes, both of which lead to the border.

CUILAPA

Population 5669; Altitude 893 meters; fiesta: December 25; Kilometer 63

Capital of the department of Santa Rosa, and a center for processing sugar cane and coffee. A paved branch road leads from Cuilapa to Chiquimulilla and the Pacific Highway. Southeast of Cuilapa is the isolated mountain town of Santa María Ixhuatán (population 2396; altitude 1300 meters), where pottery is made.

EL MOLINO

A few kilometers past Cuilapa. Junction here for the shorter route to El Salvador, highway CA8, running southeast from highway CA1 to the El Salvador border at Valle Nuevo, kilometer 122.

JUTIAPA

Population 10,648; Altitude 906 meters; Fiesta: November 13; "Shrimp river"; Kilometer 118

A trading center in a relatively arid area that produces sugar cane, tobacco, coffee and dairy products. The volcanoes Suchitán (2042 meters) and Moyuta (1662 meters) are nearby, but they're

230

not very impressive when compared to those in the western part of the country.

Hotels: Posada Silvia, along the highway, $5 per person; Hotel España, $3 per person.

ASUNCION MITA
Population 8707; Altitude 470 meters; Fiestas: August 15 and December 8; Mita, from Mictlán, "Place of the dead"; Kilometer 145

Asunción Mita is located on a centuries-old trade route from Mexico down to Panama. The archaeological site above town shows some evidence of Mexican influence: effigy vases and vases of Mexican onyx. Rooms were roofed over, using corbeled arches in an architectural style similar to that of the Classic Maya sites. But the stones are set with clay instead of lime mortar, and faced with lava stone instead of limestone. It's assumed that the site flourished at about the same time as Copán, which is not far away in Honduras. The site was still being used as an Indian ceremonial center at the time of the Conquest.

LAKE GUIJA

A lake to the east of Asunción Mita on the border of El Salvador, reached by a poor dirt road. Covering 44 square kilometers, and with an unknown depth, Lake Guija was probably formed when a volcanic eruption closed off the channels of two rivers. There are some small species of fish in the waters.

SAN CRISTOBAL FRONTERA
Kilometer 166

Border-crossing point for El Salvador. The road continues to the cities of Santa Ana and San Salvador.

To the Caribbean

Northeast of Guatemala City is the long valley of the Motagua River, a near-desert region for almost 200 kilometers from the capital, then a lush, green, lowland area, where the river winds through cattle and banana country, to empty finally into the Caribbean at the border of Honduras. There are three main areas of interest for the visitor heading out this way:

—Cobán, the highlands of the department of Alta Verapaz, and the valley of the Polochic River.

—The Mayan ruins of Copán, across the border in Honduras, and a few nearby Guatemalan towns, including Esquipulas, a religious center for all Central America.

—The Caribbean lowlands, once the haunt of pirates, and today a developing vacation area of peaceful rivers, and jungles alive with bird and animal life.

Traveling out toward the Caribbean is easy. The paved Atlantic Highway *(Carretera al Atlántico)*, completed in the 1950s, runs from Guatemala City to Puerto Barrios, with branch roads to Cobán and Esquipulas. Bus service is frequent to all points mentioned below, except the Copán ruins.

Before the highway to Puerto Barrios was completed, the main route through the region was the railroad along the Motagua River. A train still operates a couple of times a week in each direction, passing through dozens of small settlements, snaking along the river valley, and crossing trestles over deep canyons.

The lowlands along the Caribbean are small compared to the Pacific lowlands, and though the temperature is often in the nineties (Fahrenheit), distances to be covered are relatively short,

232

so I wouldn't worry too much about the discomforts of bus travel. The rainy season isn't as well defined to the north and northeast of Guatemala City as in the western highlands or on the Pacific coast. Storms can blow in from the Caribbean at any time of day on any day of the year, bringing short and heavy downpours. Take along a raincoat or umbrella. Anyone spending a lot of time in the area, or staying in cheaper accommodations that might not be adequately screened, should take a malaria preventive.

Highway Notes

To get on the Atlantic Highway (CA-9) from Guatemala City, take any of the main avenues north to Calle Martí in Zone 2. Turn right, and follow Calle Martí over the Belice Bridge and out of town. The Belice Bridge, which crosses a deep canyon, is Guatemala's equivalent of the Golden Gate Bridge, the scene of an occasional suicide.

Down the road, at kilometer 16, is a toll booth. Stop and pay according to your destination. Hold onto your receipt and turn it in at the booth where you turn off.

The trip to the Caribbean is relatively smooth going. The highway is two lanes wide, well maintained, with few sharp grades or sudden curves down the valley of the Motagua. Truck traffic is especially heavy, since this is the route to Guatemala's main port, Santo Tomás de Castilla. Be prepared for buses trying to pass each other on curves. There are plenty of gas stations along the way, most with acceptable diners attached.

GUATEMALA CITY TO COBAN

Heading out of Guatemala City on the Atlantic Highway, the traveller passes through one of the few visually dreary parts of Guatemala. After an area of factories and food-processing plants on the outskirts of the capital, the road winds through increasingly dry hills, through gorges bare except for an occasional sloping patch of corn, and finally down into the arid valley of the Motagua River. It's a surprising landscape for those who know the rest of Guatemala: dry scrub vegetation dotted with cactus, cattle grazing here and there in the brush, whitewashed houses baking in the sun, occasional green spots where the waters of the Motagua have been diverted to irrigate fields. To the north of the valley is the great ridge of the Sierra de las Minas, which blocks off the rains that keep Alta Verapaz green throughout the year. Off to the south is the lower ridge of mountains running along the borders with El Salvador and Honduras.

EL RANCHO
Kilometer 84

Junction for the highway to Cobán. Many small stands sell food, including *quesadillas*, a cheese-bread specialty of the region. The railroad station is a couple of kilometers away in town.

From El Rancho, the highway climbs up through dry hills, then enters a heavily forested area near the summit at Santa Elena.

SANTA ELENA (LA CUMBRE)
Kilometer 132

A cold and windy road junction. There's a toll booth here, at which you'll stop if heading down to Salamá on the branch road to the west. The valley of Salamá is a California-like area in its long, flat expanses of irrigated fields hemmed in by mountains. Easily viewed from the highway as it skirts along the ridge toward the north, the valley was hard-hit in the 1976 earthquake. If you drop down into the valley, you'll find these towns:

SAN JERONIMO
Population 1903; Altitude 999 meters; Fiesta: September 30; Kilometer 142

Reached after winding down the steep grades from the Cobán highway, San Jerónimo was formerly a grape and wine-producing center. Sugar cane is now grown on a large scale.

SALAMA
Population 6941; Altitude 940 meters; Fiesta: September 17-21; "River of boards"; Kilometer 150

Capital of the department of Baja Verapaz, Salamá is a pleasant town with a bit of colonial atmosphere. An old bridge survives from the period of Spanish rule, and is now used only by pedestrians. There's also a large colonial church on the square.

RABINAL
Population 5343 (township 22,733; 82% indigenous); Altitude 973 meters; Languages: Spanish and Quiché; Fiesta: January 23; Market Day: Sunday; "Flying"

Rabinal is known today mainly for its fine oranges (in season in November and December) and for its ceramics. At the time of the Conquest, some of the inhabitants of the area, coaxed by their chieftain, Don Miguel, peacefully accepted the Christianity offered to them by Friar Bartolomé de las Casas. Others who chose to fight the Spanish were dispersed to San Lucas Sacatepéquez and elsewhere.

The archaeological site west of town is similar to other highland defensive cities that were occupied when the Spanish arrived. There was a one-room temple atop one of the mounds, with a triple entrance like the one at Zaculeu. Stairways divided into parallel sections, and tripod ceramic plate holders with human and animal figures, indicate the penetration of Mexican stylistic influence to this area. The site is unrestored.

Rabinal is most easily reached by a branch road from Salamá. A shorter route to Guatemala City via a dirt road is best traveled by jeep. An unpaved road continues from Rabinal, by way of Cubulco, to the large dams on the Chixoy River, 30 kilometers away, where much of Guatemala's electricity is generated.

From La Cumbre, the main road winds across the crest of mountains into an area that receives rainfall all year. Some of the land is unsuitable for farming, and so parts of the dense tropical fain forest remain in a virtually untouched state.

BIOTOPO DEL QUETZAL
Kilometer 161

The Biotopo del Quetzal, or Quetzal Reserve, was set aside to protect the flora and fauna of the high rain forest. The trunks of dead trees provide nesting sites for the quetzal, which can sometimes be sighted here. Even if you don't see the elusive national bird, a walk along any of the three nature trails will take you through an enchanted, fairy-tale environment, where bromeliads, orchids, bromeliads, mosses and ferns mask the branches of trees, and vines and plants with gigantic leaves penetrate into all levels. Roots of trees and plants as well as lowly worms consume and recycle decaying material, whether it lies on the ground or in the crook of a tree.

The nature paths vary in length from 500 meters to three kilometers, and are well marked. The ground is usually moist, more squishy than muddy. Watch your step as you walk. The reserve honors Mario Dary Rivera, the late rector of the University of San Carlos who promoted its creation.

Transportation and Accommodations: To reach the reserve, drive or take a Cobán bus to kilometer 161. At kilometer 156.5 is Posada Montaña del Quetzal, an attractive lodging compound with 18 motel rooms and bungalows, restaurant and pool. The rate is about $6 per person. Phone 314181 in Guatemala City to reserve. If you don't have a car, flag down a bus along the highway to take you from the reserve to the Posada.

Beyond the reserve, the highway enters a long, narrow valley, a green Alpine landscape of grazing land walled in by mountain ridges.

COBAN
Population 14,152 (township 42,575; 81% indigenous); Altitude 1317 meters; Languages: Kekchî and Spanish; Fiesta: August 4; Market: Every day; "Cloudy place"; Kilometer 212

For more than a decade after the Spaniards had subjugated the Indians of the western highlands, the inhabitants of the lands to the north of Rabinal repulsed every effort to conquer them. The area of resistance came to be called Tesulutlán—Land of War—and attempts to impose Spanish rule had pretty much been laid aside when Friar Bartolomé de las Casas proposed the peaceful conversion of the inhabitants. A written contract with the colonial authorities provided that Spaniards were to be kept out of the area for five years, while Las Casas and his collaborators went about their work.

Las Casas did an excellent job of salesmanship. He and three other Dominican friars composed evangelical verses in the Kekchí language, set them to music, and taught them to a few traders who regularly penetrated the Land of War. The traders were given metal knives, mirrors, and other strange European items to distribute as they sang. Before long, Juan Matalbatz, lord of Chamelco, asked for more information, and found that the authors of the verses were a new breed of Spaniards, unarmed, with strange haircuts and robes, and not much interest in getting their hands on gold. A visit from Las Casas brought the Indian chieftain into the fold, and, despite opposition from native priests, the Christian conquest proceeded more or less peacefully. Cobán was founded by Las Casas in 1538, and the conversion of the area that came to be called Verapaz—True Peace—was completed in another ten years.

It makes for a nice story. But the Indians of Verapaz who were conquered by the meek Dominicans fared no better than those in other parts of the country who went through the more usual bloodbath.

Cobán received the title of Imperial City from Emperor Charles V of Spain, and until fairly recently remained the capital of an area pretty much apart from the rest of Guatemala. Even in the days of poor transportation, Verapaz was especially remote, with only a few rough trails heading into the area from the capital, and much of the land lying idle.

Late in the nineteenth century, there was a new takeover of sorts, this time by German immigrants who were granted unused land by President Barrios for the planting of coffee. The Germans came to dominate not only the coffee business in Alta Verapaz, but much of the town commerce and small industry as well. Coffee and other products of the region moved by road, rail and water down the valley of the Polochic River to the Caribbean for export, and it was said only partly in jest that the Germans sent their laundry to Hamburg, since access to the fatherland was so much easier than to the capital across the mountains.

Except for some *Cobaneros* with German surnames, and an occasional fair-haired person, evidence of Nordic influence is now hard to find. The Germans of Alta Verapaz were a tight-knit group. Many men sent home for wives, the German language was retained, and those born in Guatemala of German parents opted for German citizenship. In the late thirties, some were given to ending conversations with "Heil Hitler!" and their social clubs were bedecked with swastikas. When Guatemala entered World War II on the side of the Allies, those who had retained their German citizenship were given the boot, and their fincas were taken over by the government. These *fincas nacionales* still account for a large portion of national coffee production.

Alta Verapaz is a green, green land where the rainy season never really comes to an end, but lightens somewhat in January and February. In the highlands around Cobán, the rains can drizzle down for days on end in what the natives call the *chipi chipi*. The terrain is hilly and broken. Many canyons have no natural outlets, and the water is dammed up in numerous lakes, some permanent, some appearing and disappearing with the rains.

The highlands of Alta Verapaz have been compared to the Garden of Eden, a land of such wealth that only a minimum of labor will bring an abundant harvest. The department is the home of the white nun *(monja blanca)*, the national flower, one of dozens of species of orchids found in the forests; the area where the quetzal, the bird that is a symbol of liberty, still roams; a place where rivers flow along the surface, disappear into the ground, and rise again many kilometers distant. From the hot lowlands around Panzós to the cool mountain valley of Tactic, Alta Verapaz produces a variety of crops ranging from sugar to cardamom to allspice to all-important coffee. Lead and zinc are mined, and in the north, at Rubelsanto near the border of the Petén, Guatemala's first commercial oil wells have been developed.

Like the western highlands, Alta Verapaz is Indian country. But the Indians here differ. Their languages are Kekchí and Pokomchí, unintelligible to Indians from other areas. Their clothing is distinctive: women wear lace-like short huipiles that hang freely, and which are decorated with embroidered flowers. Skirts are pleated, not simply wrapped around the waist, and hang only to the calf. Those women who can afford it wear silver jewelry, one of the handicraft specialties of the area.

Modern Cobán is somewhat less than imperial. The isolation of Alta Verapaz from the rest of the country was finally remedied, an improved road to Guatemala City having opened in 1958. But even before then, some of the richer families of the city had begun to spend more of their time in the national capital. Much of the agricultural output of Alta Verapaz now moves directly to Guatemala City, without a stop in Cobán, leaving the departmental capital to turn into a backwater. Old mansions are

238

slowly deteriorating, and unpaved streets kick up dust when it hasn't rained for a few days and run with mud at other times. The sense of Cobán is of a lost magnificence.

The central park of Cobán is a triangle with a massive colonial cathedral at the base, surrounded by the municipal building, an arcaded palace of the departmental government with a rusting roof, and the local army headquarters. In the park is a rather incongruous Martian-appearing bandshell constructed of superimposed concrete discs (or flying saucers).

Around the square and in the surrounding streets, Cobán sometimes seems *triste* (sad) in the sense that rural Guatemalans use that word—without much activity, dull and faded and routine. One of the few times of the year when the city becomes lively is during the annual departmental fiesta at the beginning of August. In recent years, the fiesta has turned into an internationally attended display of the folklore not only of Alta Verapaz, but of all Indian Guatemala.

At other times of the year, the visitor can sniff out the faded glory of the old days. And the scenery of Alta Verapaz and the charming small towns nearby will repay any visitor who doesn't find much in Cobán itself.

Orientation

Cobán's central area is divided into four quadrants. From the Cathedral, Zone 1 is the section to the northwest, Zone 2 is to the southwest, Zone 3 is to the southeast, and Zone 4 is to the northeast. 1 Calle is the main east-west street leading into town, and runs by the Cathedral.

HOTELS

La Posada, adjoining the central park. Tel. 511495. 14 rooms. $8 single/$12 double.
Even if you had no interest in Cobán, you might want to stay at La Posada and experience the graciousness and tradition of the old days of travel in Guatemala. Comfortable whitewashed rooms, with beamed ceilings, wrought-iron decoration and heavy wardrobes, are off a colonnaded passageway paved with great terra cotta blocks. The flowered courtyard is lovely. Meals are served at regular hours, and are quite good. Reserve by all means.

Oxib Peck, 1 Calle at 13 Avenida, Zone 2, tel. 511039. 11 rooms. $4 per person.
A rather pleasant, homey place. Good value.

Hotel Cobán Imperial, 6 Ave. 1-12, Zone 1. Tel. 766552. 7 rooms. $7/$10.
Recent vintage, comfortable.

Hotel Santo Domingo, two kilometers from the center of town on the road from Guatemala City. 13 rooms, $4 per person.
Clean, modest, best if you have a car.

Hotel La Colonia, 2 Calle 10-88, Zone 4. 12 rooms, $4 per person.
Decent and well-kept, but also a bit far out.

Pensión del Norte, 3 Calle 4-51, Zone 4. 27 rooms. $2 per person.
Frequented by traveling salesmen, a good sign. Rooms are small but clean. Hot showers for a small additional fee.

Other budget lodging places, charging about $3 per person, include: Hotel La Paz, 6 Avenida 2-19, Zone 1, airy and clean; La Providencia, on the square, basic; Hospedaje Maya, 1 Calle 2-33, Zone 4, a pleasant old galleried building; and the Hotel Central, alongside the Cathedral, which accurately advertises its pension-type accommodations and prices.

RESTAURANTS

Aside from snack joints, there's hardly a restaurant worthy of mention in Cobán. You're best-off to take your meals at La Posada, whether you're staying there or not, and enjoy the good service and old-time ambience of the dining room. Breakfast starts at 7 a.m., lunch at 1 p.m., dinner at 7 p.m. Less than $3 for a meal. On the main square, the Restaurant Refugio is somebody's take-off on a steak house. A dozen waiters loiter in a large, dark, near-empty room, ready to pounce on anyone who enters. Char-broiled steaks for $4, sandwiches for less. For hamburgers, ham sandwiches, coffee and pastries, go to the cafeteria of the Hotel Central, alongside the church. The back room is warm and cozy on a rainy afternoon. Livelier is the Café

240

Centro in the arcade on the same street. Tico's Pancakes, 1 Calle 4-40, Zone 3, is open 24 hours for pancakes and light meals. $2 or so. Aside from these places, there's the usual assortment of cheap eateries around the market.

Around Cobán

I can't recommend that you spend too much time wandering around the city. You'll probably be hopping buses or driving out to some of the nearby towns. I like to search out the big, crumbling old houses in Cobán, but you may find that boring. For a nice view, follow 7 Avenida north from 1 Calle, Zone 2, and climb the 131 steps to the Calvario church. The back balcony of the departmental government building on the central park also offers some pleasant sights.

For shopping, the market is low-key. The things to look at are lace-like huipiles and palm-fiber mats. You'll find silverwork in a couple of small stores in Cobán and in nearby San Pedro Carchá. If you're buying silver, note that many of the pieces are silver plated. The silver-braid items are interesting, and you may run across some gold braid. Silver is mined in the northern part of Alta Verapaz.

The office of Guatel, the telephone company, is on the main square. Change travelers checks at the Banco de Guatemala at the corner of 1 Calle and 6 Avenida, Zone 2. The post office is at 2 Calle and 2 Avenida, near the market in Zone 3.

Buses

From Guatemala City: Escobar-Monja Blanca (8 Avenida 15-16, Zone 1) about every hour from 6 a.m. to 4 p.m. Some buses are first-class. From Coban (2 Calle 3-77, Zone 4) about every hour from 4 a.m. to 4 p.m.

Buses for other destinations leave from the terminal lot on 2 Avenida in Zone 4, north of and down the hill from the center of town. Verify schedules there the day before you travel to Lanquín, El Estor or Sebol. There is an early-morning bus to Cunén for connections to Nebaj and Huehuetenango the next day.

NEARBY TOWNS

SAN CRISTOBAL VERAPAZ
Population 7115 (township 25,900; 77% indigenous); Altitude
1393 meters; Languages: Pokomchí and Spanish; Fiesta: July 25;
Market Days: Thursday and Sunday

A lovely and picturesque little town surrounded by fields of
coffee and sugar cane. Three blocks down from the colonial
church is a large lake, nice for jumping in on a hot day. You'll
have to wade out to beyond the reeds to get some clear swimming
space. San Cristóbal is surrounded by pine-covered hills, on one
of which is the Calvario church, a pleasant place to walk to for
views of the valley. The main employer in town is the large
Cobán shoe factory.

When the Spanish arrived, San Cristóbal was known as Cacoj.
The inhabitants sided with the Spanish for a while against rival
tribes. The Pokomchí-speaking people, unlike others in
Guatemala, have no legends about migrations to the area. They
claim that they lived in Guatemala before the arrivals of such
latecomers as the Quichés, and that they speak the unmodified
language of their ancestors.

Buses for San Cristóbal leave from Cobán every hour.

TACTIC
Population 3398 (township 11,351; 84% indigenous); Altitude
1450 meters; Languages: Pokomchí and Spanish; Fiesta: August
15; Market Days: Thursday and Sunday; "White peach";
Kilometer 184

Located to the side of the paved highway from Guatemala City,
Tactic is in a long and narrow valley given over to cattle grazing.
Cream and cheese are produced in town. The cool air, pastures
and piney ridges around Tactic give its setting a Swiss touch. The
most interesting sight in town is the baroque colonial church.
With some searching, you might find a silver workshop.

On the outskirts of town is the *Pozo Vivo* —Living Well—which is
a bit of an overrated attraction, though not to the degree of
roadside hokum in the States. At least, nobody has tried to charge
admission and set up a souvenir shop. To reach it, head for the

242

Esso station along the highway at the entrance to Tactic on the Cobán side. Take the dirt road leading through the pastures and corn fields from opposite the gas station. At the end of the road, cross the barbed-wire fence (there are posts with footholds in them), follow the path across the stream and down to the second fence, and step over into the pasture with the help of some conveniently placed rocks. There are some cows around, but if you're nice to them, they will be nice to you.

As for the Living Well . . . It's a pool fed by an underground spring, with the water rising from the ground in such a way that the mud and sand and rocks and waterlogged wood and tin cans in it swirl and dance about. It makes for a strange effect, more or less like a bubbling cauldron of witch's brew. The locals claim that the well becomes active only when a person approaches it. However, after some squinting from afar, I am unable to confirm or deny the allegation. It may be that the dancing waters are not clearly visible to the observer from a distance, which would make the claim a logical fallacy. But a local man says he has climbed to a facing mountainside pasture and, with the aid of powerful binoculars, looked down to the Living Well at perfect rest.

Buses heading from Cobán to Guatemala City and El Estor pass through Tactic.

Lodging and inexpensive meals are available at the Pensión Central on the main street of Tactic. Rooms are also available at Hospedaje Pocompchí. Both are on the main street.

SAN PEDRO CARCHA
Population 5211 (township 53,759; 95% indigenous); Altitude 1250 meters; Languages: Kekchí and Spanish; Fiesta: June 29; Market: Every Day; Carchá, "gray fish"; Kilometer 217

At the end of the paved highway from Guatemala City, in a coffee and cattle area, San Pedro Carchá is a busy trading center for a large township. The Popol Vuh and the Annals of the Cakchiquels mention a place called Carchá, so there's some opinion that the nations of the western highlands passed through this area during their wanderings. The present city was founded by the Dominicans after the establishment of nearby Cobán, and some of the flavor of the old town is preserved in the colonial bridge over the Cobán River, and in the massive old church. Other than those two items, there's not much to catch the eye except the colonnaded city hall on the central park.

A small regional museum (Museo Regional de la Verapaz) is open weekends from 9 a.m. to noon and 3 to 5 p.m. You can also visit during the week if you knock hard. On display are Mayan ceramics, examples of local textiles, paintings of regional scenes, and photos. Look for the Radio Imperial sign. The museum is across the street.

Aside from the processing of hides and coffee, there's some mask carving in Carchá, and silverwork. The silver shops are located on the edge of town on the road toward Cobán.

Buses run from Cobán to Carchá about every hour. It's also a pleasant walk of about an hour, if you've got the time.

Lodging and meals are available at Hospedaje Central, 7 Avenida 4-17, Zone 1, and Hotel Shangai, Diagonal 1 3-41, Zone 2, both about $3 per person.

LANQUIN
Population 642 (township 8223; 96% indigenous); Altitude 352 meters; Languages: Kekchí and Spanish; Fiesta: August 26; "Place of straw"; Kilometer 275

In the hot country of Alta Verapaz, near the Cahabón River, is Lanquín, a small and picturesque town of wooden and adobe houses and a colonial church, surrounded by mountains. Nearby are some of the natural wonders of Alta Verapaz.

The Lanquín Caves (Grutas de Lanquín), within walking distance of town, stretch for a couple of kilometers underground. Though not extensive by the standards of speleologists, the caves are fabled in Guatemala. Electric lights near the entrance will be turned on by the attendant for a fee. (Inquire first at the municipalidad—they might have to rouse the attendant.) To go in beyond the lights, you'll need your own flashlight and spare batteries. The blue Lanquín River resurges from the caves, and provides some good swimming. You can camp at the cave entrance.

About nine kilometers from Lanquín, is Semuc Champey, a natural limestone bridge in the gorge of the Cahabón River. Atop

244

the 300-meter-long bridge are natural swimming pools, delightful places for a dip. Watch out for sharp rims. Get an early start if you venture out this way, or take camping equipment. To reach Semuc, take the road from Lanquín, and cross the bridge on the Cahabón River, then follow a trail off to the right for about 1500 meters. There's a shorter but more difficult up-and-down trail from another point on the road. Inquire locally.

A narrow, unpaved, rutted road descends through beautiful rain-forest country to Lanquín, 63 kilometers from Cobán. Attempt to drive the route only in a vehicle with high clearance, and watch out for the surprisingly heavy traffic of trucks, which service the oil fields at Rubelsanto. A bus leaves Cobán at about 5 a.m. and gets to Lanquín at 1 p.m. Two rather basic pensions provide rooms and meals for a couple of dollars each. The bus back to Cobán passes through town at about 8 a.m., or you can go on to Cahabón, from where buses operate to El Estor when the road is dry.

SEBOL
Population 758; Altitude 140 meters; "Place of mounds"

For most visitors, there's no reason to pass through Sebol, a small settlement in the north of Alta Verapaz, where the terrain slopes downward toward the jungles of the Petén. But if you've got a taste for adventure and the unexpected, and a lot of patience, Sebol is the starting point for some interesting trips.

With a four-wheel drive vehicle, you might want to take one of the back routes to the Petén. One rutted track through the jungle ends up at San Luis, at the midpoint of the road from Flores to the Río Dulce crossing. This is a difficult route, especially after a few days of rain, and you should approach it with some trepidation, and also a few spare tires.

In better condition is the road that follows a more easterly heading from Sebol, to Modesto Méndez on the Petén highway. This route was improved in connection with the development of the petroleum industry.

An extension of the same road goes westward, across northern Alta Verapaz, toward the departments of Quiché and Huehuetenango. For now, the road goes as far as Playa Grande, on the Chixoy River. A branch road runs to Sayaxché.

An interesting river trip is also possible. Sebol is on a fast-flowing tributary of the Río de la Pasión, which eventually empties into the Usumacinta, the border river between Guatemala and Mexico. Cargo canoes ply the river to Sayaxché, in the Petén, and it's sometimes possible to ship aboard one. You may have to wait for a few days in Sebol until a boat for the Petén shows up. Many of these go only about halfway to a small river settlement called El Pato, where there's nothing more than a small store and school. At El Pato, you may wait a week or more until a boat for Sayaxché appears, and unless you're a bird watcher, you'll be supremely bored. Also, since there's no other way to get out of El Pato than by boat, you could find yourself paying a ransom for onward transportation.

Expect to pay a couple of dollars from Sebol to El Pato, and whatever you can negotiate to continue from there. Bring your own food and cooking equipment, mosquito netting, insect repellent, medical supplies, and a few good books to read. It's none too comfortable sitting atop the sacks of corn and other merchandise.

Buses for Sebol leave Cobán daily at about 5 a.m. There's a small pension in town. Bus service is available to Sayaxché and San Luis in the Petén on an irregular basis. There's also a bus at about 2 a.m. from the terminal in Guatemala City for Sebol via Modesto Méndez on the Petén road, continuing to Playa Grande on the new east-west road across Guatemala. Inquire at the terminal about new services.

DOWN THE POLOCHIC

The Polochic River valley was for many years Cobán's opening to the outside world. Until better roads were built in the last few decades, goods and people would move by road to Papaljá, board the trains of the Verapaz Railroad for Panzós, and continue by boat across Lake Izabal and down the Río Dulce to Lívingston and Puerto Barrios. The journey took a couple of days, and required an overnight stay in malaria-infested Panzós.

A road now leads all the way to lake Izabal, ending at El Estor, which is no paradise, but which is where you'll have to spend the night before catching the ferry to Mariscos on the south shore. If you're driving, you will probably have to retrace your route, since

246

the ferry doesn't carry cars, and the branch road to Cahabón isn't always passable. You might want to go only as far as the lowlands around La Tinta in order to appreciate the changing scenery as the road descends to near sea level, and then turn around.

The valley of the Polochic, except for El Estor, where a nickel mine opened and closed in the seventies, is pretty much a backwater area, passed by as transportation routes changed. Hardly an outsider comes through these days to take a look at what's going on. But the valley is an area of great natural beauty, from the narrow highland canyon, where the steep slopes that hem in the rushing river are covered with coffee plantations, to the great lowland plain, where the full river lazes through rice paddies and steaming pastures dotted with corozo palms.

Buses: Getting to El Estor from Cobán by bus is a seven-hour trip. All along the way, Indians going to market or work in valley towns get on and off. It's a measure of the isolation of this area that the driver speaks to them in their own languages, since few can speak more than a few words of Spanish. Buses leave from the terminal lot in Cobán twice a day for El Estor (recently at 8 a.m. and noon). If the trip seems long, you can take a bus to Tamahú or Tucurú (preferably on a market day) and wander around for a while until the bus for El Estor comes along, or else wait for a return bus to Cobán or Tactic. If you're up to hiking, the highland part of the valley is a beautiful area for walking and bird watching. Walk along the road from Tamahú or Tucurú for a while, or along the river, then flag down a bus. Buses usually stop in La Tinta or Telemán long enough for passengers to catch a meal (the Indian passengers usually remain on board and wait patiently while the driver eats), but the food isn't very good in any of the small diners. You'd do better to pack some snacks.

SAN JULIAN
Kilometer 181

Gas station and restaurant, junction for the unpaved road to El Estor.

From San Julián, the road descends on a mild grade along the river, through an area of tributary streams rushing down and emptying in waterfalls. There's the legendary evidence of fertility here: the fence posts even sprout. But then, some of the posts are merely young trees that have been trimmed, their roots left intact.

TAMAHU
Population 620 (township 6042; 95% indigenous); Altitude 1049 meters; Languages: Pokomchí and Spanish; Fiesta: January 25; Kilometer 191

A small town in a rain-forest valley planted in coffee and bananas. There's some rope manufacturing here, and the inhabitants used to make *suyacales*, rain capes fashioned from palm leaves. But the widespread use of cheap sheets of plastic now provides a less picturesque solution to the rain problem.

TUCURU
Population 732 (township 12,849; 94% indigenous); Altitude 950 meters; Languages: Pokomchí and Spanish; Fiesta: May 8; Market Days: Tuesday and Saturday; "Place of the owls"; Kilometer 206

A town of thatched mud-and-stick houses among palm and orange trees, waterfalls, and forests thick with vines and orchids.

From Tucurú, the road and river drop more quickly, and the canyon gradually expands into a wide valley. The small towns along the way take on a different character. At first they are agglomerations of wooden shacks with rusting tin roofs. Once in the hot, undulating plain, many of the structures are fragile pavilions loosely closed in with bamboo or boards, and covered over with roofs of palm thatch. Traditional Indian modesty lessens a bit in this steaming area. Children run around stark naked in their family compounds, though adults always keep covered, even when taking a bath in a stream.

The road passes through La Tinta (population 4804; altitude 170 meters; kilometer 236) and Telemán (population 2783). Both are languid trading centers, little more than wide spots in the road. From just west of Telemán, a road climbs north into the mountains to Senahú (population 1404; altitude 950 meters; fiesta

248

June 13; kilometer 265), a village in an area of coffee production and spectacularly beautiful rain forest and falls. A small pension provides overnight accommodations.

PANZOS
Population 1995 (township 33,564; 93% indigenous); Altitude 18 meters; Languages: Kekchí and Spanish; Fiesta: August 30; "Place of the green waters"; Kilometer 258

Located on the edge of the swamps near the mouth of the Polochic River, Panzós is an area of beef, citronella and palm oil production. The town used to be the terminus for boats from Lívingston and Puerto Barrios, and the starting point for the Verapaz Railroad, but now it is just another of the valley trading centers. Panzós takes its name from the green waters of the nearby swamp, an area thick with vines and ceiba and palm trees, and inhabited mainly by alligators, monkeys, macaws, parrots and butterflies.

Peasants on their way to a meeting at the town hall in Panzós in 1978 were attacked by the army, an incident that provoked widespread protest.

EL ESTOR
Population 5175 (township 23,513; 80% indigenous); Altitude 2 meters; Languages: Kekchí and Spanish; Fiesta: June 29; Kilometer 312

After a trip down the peaceful valley of the Polochic, the approach to El Estor is a bit of a shock. On the western edge of town, the green-covered mountains have been chopped up and torn apart. Substantial blocks of air-conditioned, look-alike concrete houses stand empty. Tennis courts are fenced-in and unused. Something large has been and gone.

These are the remnants of the Exmibal project, once the largest foreign investment that Guatemala had ever seen. Exmibal had its beginning in a manner reminiscent of the California gold rush, when a plantation owner sent a sample of dirt from his lands to be analyzed. The dirt contained a high concentration of nickel. After a long period of negotiations, the International Nickel Company of Canada began to develop a mine, in the late 1970s.

249

Falling international prices and financial troubles led to a mothballing of the mine after only a short period of operation, and with it, Guatemala's hopes of becoming a major nickel exporter.

Father up the road, along the shore of Lake Izabal, is the old part of El Estor, a settlement of concrete and rotting wooden houses. A sign at the docks reports an average temperature of 39 degrees Centigrade (102 Fahrenheit), which, with a high humidity, might be enough to discourage you from planning to stick around.

El Estor was once a small trading outpost of the United Fruit Company. The locals mispronounced "store" into "estor" and the name stuck. It's a drab and dusty place, and the most highly recommended activity is to go to bed and wait for the morning boat to take you across Lake Izabal to Mariscos.

Accommodations: Hotel Vista Al Lago, a well-kept wooden building with rooms for $4 per person, all with fans. There are several lesser establishments with cheap rooms near the docks, and a couple of simple eateries.

Buses for Cobán leave from El Estor at about 6 and 11 a.m. There may be bus service to Cahabón when the road is passable.

Boats for Mariscos leave daily at 5:30 a.m. The trip takes about two hours. At Mariscos, buses wait to take passengers to Quiriguá or to La Trinchera junction on the Atlantic Highway at kilometer 218, where buses can be picked up for Puerto Barrios or Guatemala City.

MARISCOS
Population 653

A small settlement on the south shore of Lake Izabal. Despite the town's name ("shellfish"), you won't find any seafood.

The main justifications for Mariscos are as a place to launch boats, as a ferry terminal, and as a freight depot for the on-again off-again Exmibal mining project.

If you're heading across the lake to El Estor and Cobán, you can start from Puerto Barrios or elsewhere in the Caribbean area, take any bus along the Atlantic Highway to La Trinchera junction at kilometer 218, and catch another bus for Mariscos. The boat for El Estor leaves at 1 p.m.

EL RANCHO TO THE RUINS OF COPAN AND ESQUIPULAS

Back to the Atlantic Highway, in the dry country beyond the junction for Cobán.

SAN AGUSTIN ACASAGUASTLAN

Population 3787 (township 19,657); Altitude 290 meters; Fiesta: August 28; Acasaguastlán, "place of herons and thrushes"; Junction kilometer 88, 3 kilometers to town.

Located in an area that produces sugar cane, cacao and vanilla in irrigated fields, San Agustín is noted for its ceramics and the manufacture of musical instruments.

The subsoil around San Agustín bears jadeite, the more precious of the two minerals commonly called jade. The jade of the Maya was mined in this area, and the industry has recently been revived. Rockhounds can find a number of interesting mineral specimens by scouting along the roadsides. An idea of what there is can be gleaned from the exhibits in the Estanzuela museum, mentioned below.

Near town is an archaeological site, consisting of tombs with slab roofs covered over with mounds of stone. There was some use of the Mayan corbeled arch here, and a few stelae have been discovered, which leads to speculation that the city communicated with Quiriguá, where the greatest Mayan stelae are found. Some of the tombs have been looted, and no reconstruction work has been carried out.

Kilometer 126.

Toll booth. Stop to have your toll receipt canceled.

Accommodations: Several highway hotels in this area make acceptable stopping points if you're travelling by car. The Motel Longarone, just ahead of the toll booth (tel. 410314) is fairly basic, but has a nice swimming pool. Rooms cost about $15 single, $20 double. Nearby is the new El Atlántico, with similar prices and also with a pool. Across the road is the Motel Nuevo Pasabien, where rooms are $6 single, $10 double. Farther on, at the turn for Zacapa and Copán, is the Motel Río, $4 per person. All of these hotels have restaurants attached, with stocks of

251

ice-cold sodas and juices for parched travellers.

RIO HONDO JUNCTION
Kilometer 135

The branch road south leads to Zacapa, Chiquimula and Esquipulas, and to Copán, Honduras. The towns mentioned below are along this road.

ESTANZUELA
Population 4289; Altitude 180 meters; Fiesta: November 22; Kilometer 140

A dry, whitewashed town amid pastures, Estanzuela is the home of the Museo de Paleontología Bryan Patterson, located about a kilometer up the road from the highway junction. It may seem strange to find a paleontology museum in a country noted for its archaeology, but the arid valley of the Motagua is rich in fossil remains. On display is a mastodon skeleton found in the area, and there's also a large megathere skeleton which was unearthed in a canyon north of Guatemala City. These were reconstructed by the museum's director, Robert Woolfolk Saravia, who's sometimes around to explain the exhibits and chat with visitors.

In addition to such lesser fossils as a giant armadillo shell and a mastodon tusk, the museum has some displays of pottery from archaeological sites in the vicinity. A Chortí tomb from a site near El Rancho has been reconstructed in the middle of the exhibition floor, which, appropriately enough, sits atop an old cemetery. There's also a set of local mineral specimens.

The museum is named for an American scientist who carried out investigations in the Motagua valley. Murals depicting aspects of Guatemala's native heritage cover the interior walls of the building. Hours are 8 a.m. to 6 p.m., Tuesday through Sunday.

If you're heading for Copán by bus, you can take one of the early Esquipulas buses out of Guatemala City, spend a couple of hours at Estanzuela, and continue onward to Chiquimula to catch a bus for the Honduran border.

252

ZACAPA
Population 12,482; Altitude 230 meters; Fiesta: December 8;
"Grassy place"; Kilometer 148

Capital of the department of Zacapa, a relatively infertile
region due to deforestation and the lack of rain. The area around
the city of Zacapa is used mainly for cattle grazing, and for crops
where irrigation water can be drawn from the Motagua River.
Cheese and cigars are made in the city. Pleasant hot baths are
located about three kilometers from town.

This part of Guatemala is known as the *Oriente* —the East—and
the people who inhabit Zacapa, Chiquimula and the nearby towns
have a reputation for being a lot more hot-tempered than most
Guatemalans.

Buses for Esquipulas stop at the terminal in Zacapa, which is a
couple of kilometers off the highway.

Hotels: Hotel Wong, 6 Calle 12-53, best in town, $4 per person;
Hotel del Ferrocarril, at the railroad station, an old place reeking
with faded glory, $3 per person.

CHIQUIMULA
Population 18,965 (township 42,571; 15% indigenous); Altitude
370 meters; Languages: Spanish and Chortí; Fiesta: August 15;
"Place of the linnet" (a bird); Kilometer 167

Capital of the department of Chiquimula, an area with many
mineral deposits and important in the production of tobacco. On
the outskirts of the city, near the highway, are the ruins of a
colonial church.

Buses for Chiquimula leave about every hour from 19 Calle 8-18,
Zone 1, Guatemala City. First bus 5 a.m. Chiquimula is most
important as a transfer point for visitors going to Copán. Direct
buses for the border leave at 6, 9, 10 and 11:30 a.m. and 1 p.m.
More details in the coverage of Copán, below.

Hotels: Hotel Chiquimuljá, on the square, $6 single, $10 double;
Pensión Hernández, 3 Calle 7-41 (on the street into town), $3 per
person; Hotel Dario, 8 Avenida 4-40, $3 per person.

VADO HONDO
Kilometer 177

Junction for the dirt road to the Honduran border at El Florido, and onward to Copán. The towns listed below are along this road.

The road to Copán winds, climbs and descends through the mountain range along the border with Honduras, from one little valley to another, gradually entering a less arid and greener area.

JOCOTAN
Population 2506 (township 21,506; 91% indigenous); Altitude 457 meters; Languages: Chortí and Spanish; Fiesta: Three days ending on Palm Sunday; "Place of the jocote" (a fruit); Kilometer 199

A trading center for an area inhabited by Chortí-speaking Indians who, in the isolation of mountain settlements, have preserved their language and culture, despite the general acculturation of Indians in this part of Guatemala. Indian men of the area dress entirely in white, in a manner that is reminiscent of parts of Mexico. The more traditional women wear a lacy huipil and blue skirt, though most now use cheap dresses of store-bought material. Buildings in town and in most of the surrounding countryside are of mud thrown onto a framework of sticks, with a thatched roof. A church survives from the colonial period.

If you're coming back from Copán and looking for a ride onward, after the last bus, talk to the Guardia de la Hacienda, the treasury guard men in dark green uniforms. They can sometimes point out a pickup truck that's about to leave.

CAMOTAN
Population 810 (township 19,550; 40% indigenous); Altitude 540 meters; Languages: Chortí and Spanish; Fiesta: December 8; "Place of the sweet potatoes"

Sister town of Jocotán, a few kilometers past it on the road to the border. Pickup trucks for the border can be found in the area outside the market, after the last bus has left.

The road onward from Camotán to the border was recently graded and is quite passable. Which is not to say that it will be so when you go this way, especially if it has been raining. In that case, watch out for ruts and rocks. The road fords several streams. If you're driving, take it easy, especially after splashing through water. Your wheels and brakes will be wet, and you may not be able to stop suddenly.

EL FLORIDO
Kilometer 225

A small town a couple of kilometers from the Honduran border. To continue to Copán, take the road beyond El Florido to the Guatemalan and Honduran immigration posts. If you don't have a visa, you can buy a Honduran tourist card or a permit to visit Copán at the border. Either costs about $5. If you already have a visa, you'll pay at a reduced rate. *Important:* If you're planning to travel onward into Honduras from Copán, make sure that you obtain a visa or tourist card, and not a pass for Copán only.

Another 11 kilometers from the border, through increasingly lush countryside, and you arrive at the town of Copán Ruinas. The road being what it is, the trip takes a half-hour by bus. If driving your own car, take the ruts slowly.

COPAN RUINAS, HONDURAS
Population 4300; Altitude 600 meters

The small Honduran town a kilometer from the Mayan ruins of Copán bears the name Copán Ruinas—literally and appropriately, Copán Ruins. It's a small and pleasant place, with an immaculately clean grassy central park surrounded by neat whitewashed buildings with tile roofs. The fertile valley in which the town sits is one of the main tobacco-growing areas of Honduras, producing a fine leaf used in the manufacture of cigars.

Travel Strategy for Copán

By bus, it's easier to get to Copán than to return. From Guatemala City, take Rutas Orientales from 19 Calle 8-18, Zone 1, as far as Chiquimula. Buses leave Chiquimula for the Honduran border at El Florido at 6, 9, 10 and 11:30 a.m., and 1 p.m. Leave Guatemala City three hours before these departure times to make your connection. Minibuses provide onward service to Copán Ruinas from the border. Pack some food for the trip, since you probably won't have time for a meal along the way. With an early start, on the 5 or 5:30 a.m. bus, you can stop at the paleontology museum in Estanzuela on the way. You won't arrive in time to see the ruins the same day, but you can spend some time in the museum in town, and head out for the ruins the next morning.

Buses leave the border at El Florido for Chiquimula at 5, 6, 8 and 10 a.m., and 12:30 p.m. Minibuses leave Copán Ruinas for the border every hour from 7 a.m. You have to leave by noon to connect with the last bus from the border. After that hour, you might be able to arrange a ride in a pickup truck to Jocotán.

The drive to Copán from Guatemala City takes four to six hours via the dirt road from Vado Hondo.

Since bus connections require a two-night stay, consider taking a guided tour to Copán. A one-day tour out of Guatemala City costs about $60 per person. Some tours include Quiriguá, with an overnight stop at Copán. You can also travel by car or bus to Chiquimula and hire a taxi there for the run to Copán and back, an expense of at least $30.

HOTELS AND RESTAURANTS

The currency in Honduras is the lempira, but dollars and quetzales can be passed off with equal facility in Copán.

The Hotel Maya Copantl, on the square, is a pleasant place with gardens in the courtyard. Rates are $8 single, $12 double. A large breakfast costs $2, lunch or dinner about $4. The Hotel Marina, also on the square, is, like the Maya Internacional, gracious and old-fashioned, with tropical birds in the courtyard and a screened-in dining area. Rates for lodging and meals are virtually identical to those at the Maya Copantl. More spartan rooms without private bath are available in the Marina's annex up the street for $3 per person, a good buy.

The Mini-Hotel Paty, a couple of blocks from the square on the road to the ruins, has a few rooms for $3 per person, no bath. The Paty serves set meals for less than $2, including a tiny piece of meat, beans, rice, fried bananas, coffee and tortillas. There's a long list of a la carte items, most of which are usually unavailable. Up the street from the Paty, the Hotel Brisas de Copán also has budget rooms, some with private bath. For cheap food and snacks, try the market behind the museum. Camping is permitted at the ruins, outside the fenced area.

Around Copán Ruinas

Copán Ruinas is a small town where not much is happening. For evening entertainment, there are movies at the Cine Reforma near the market. Sitting on the square is also pleasant. The electricity goes on at 6 p.m.

After climbing around the ruins, you might take a walk down the road past the archaeological site. Although this is a lush tropical valley, it's located more than 600 meters above sea level, so that the temperature isn't oppressive. Along the way you'll see tall buildings of adobe and of wood, used for drying tobacco.

The rainy season usually lasts into November around Copán, but there are few heavy downpours.

THE RUINS OF COPAN

The ruins are located about a kilometer from town along a dirt road. If you walk out, follow the trail parallel to the road, past several mounds and stelae. Admission costs about $2. The site is open from 8 a.m. to 4 p.m.

On sale at the reception center is an excellent stela-by-stela guidebook in English by Jesús Nuñez Chinchilla. The gift shop offers such Honduran specialties as hardwood carvings and cigars at high prices. Snacks and meals are available in the cafeteria next door.

The archaeological site is located across the airstrip from the reception center, beyond a pleasant citrus grove provided with picnic tables. After signing the register of visitors, you'll pass through a fence on which a few macaws are usually found sitting, and down a long avenue lined with tall guanacaste trees, broad ceibas, and acacias with their hanging seed pods.

257

Copán, southernmost of the great Mayan centers, is where Mayan art reached its greatest heights in the intricate, almost oriental designs covering the stelae, temples and stairways. Tikal, Palenque and the Toltec-Maya cities of the Yucatán were greater in extent, and their structures were larger. But nowhere else in the Mayan world, and perhaps in all of pre-Columbian America, was there a flourishing of decorative art as at Copán.

The ancestors of the builders of the ceremonial center probably came to the valley of Copán some thousands of years before the birth of Christ. Here were found the raw materials with which the great structures of a Mayan city could be erected: the chicozapote tree, which yields chicle, and whose wood supplied iron-hard temple lintels; and volcanic rock, easily formed into blocks, and sculptured by scraping away at the surface with the most rudimentary tools of obsidian or harder rock (the Maya had no iron tools). Here also were clay and wood and other materials from which household implements and ceremonial objects could be fashioned. The valley was rich in game, and had a fertile soil able to support the stable and bountiful corn agriculture that was the basis of all civilization in Mesoamerica.

It took centuries for Copán to reach its Classic flourishing, centuries during which cultural currents drifted back and forth between the different Mayan groups and from without the Mayan area, resulting in the standard building techniques common to all Mayan centers, and in the artistic achievements peculiar to Copán.

The recorded history of Copán lasted only from 465 A.D. to 800 A.D., according to interpretations of glyphs on the stelae and altars. It was during this Classic Era that the ceremonial city underwent its most intensive construction and reconstruction. The inhabitants perfected their astronomy and calendar, which were closely connected to their glyphic art forms. And then, suddenly, the erection of dated monuments stopped, for reasons that may never be known.

Civilization at Copán faded. The temples were overgrown with trees and vines, and remained lost in the jungles for hundreds of years. Sustained interest in the area was awakened only in the nineteenth century, when an official of the government of the Central American Federation published articles about the ruins in American and European newspapers. In 1839, the American explorer and diplomat John Lloyd Stephens appeared and, amazed by the lost city, promptly bought the site from a landowner for fifty dollars. A description of the ruins, with illustrations by Frederick Catherwood, appeared in Stephens' classic book, *Incidents of Travel in Central America, Chiapas and Yucatan.*

Scientific investigation of Copán was begun by the English archaeologist Alfred P. Maudslay in 1881. The Carnegie Institution of Washington later supervised the restoration of the ruins. Since 1952. the site has been under the care of the National Institute of Anthropology and History of Honduras.

The ceremonial center of Copán extends over 30 hectares (75 acres, more or less), but burial mounds have been found up and down the valley of the Copán River, throughout the area where the common people lived. The river, a tributary of the Motagua, might have been used as a trade route to carry the obsidian and cacao of the region to the coast of Honduras, and as a connection to Quiriguá, which might have been colonized from Copán. There were probably also overland roads, which over the centuries disappeared into the jungle. The main areas of the ceremonial center of Copán, as named by archaeologists, are these:

The **Ceremonial Court (Great Plaza)** is the grassy area at the northern end of the ruins (toward the airstrip), surrounded by long, low stairways on three sides, and dotted with eight stelae measuring three to four meters in height. These stelae, some of the most beautiful produced by the Maya, were found lying on the ground and broken, near the hollow, cross-shaped offertory chambers which were their original supports. With the aid of concrete and reinforcing rods, the stelae have been patched up and re-erected in their original positions.

The figures represented on the stelae are not ideal human beings, as were those depicted in Greek and Roman art, but combinations of animals and human elements representing the attributes of the Mayan gods and culture-heroes. In this sense, and in the intertwinings and complexity of design, they have something in common with the art of the Orient. Mayan art often leans toward the grotesque, showing fearsome figures representing the forces that dominate the world.

The basic figure in most of the stelae is a short man, probably representing a high official or priest. He stands erect, his feet pressed firmly together to fit within the confines of the stone block. Stubby arms are placed across the chest, and hands often grasp a bar symbolic of lordship. The head is crowned with an

259

elaborate headdress taking up at least the top third of the block. But these are only the basics. In the sandals, loin cloth and anklets of the portrayed figures are rich details and designs, and in every nook and cranny are lesser figures of birds, warriors, snakes and gods. The sides and backs are decorated with glyphs, but only those corresponding to dates can be read.

A brief review of some of the stelae and other monuments in the Ceremonial Court:

Stela A, the southmost monument in the plaza, on the west side, has its supporting vault left open. Such chambers contained offerings of jade beads, pottery, and sometimes animal bones. The inscriptions of the stela include the Mayan glyph symbols for Tikal and Palenque, indicating contact with those cities. Stela 4, to the north, is considered one of the finest of the stelae at Copán. It shows the tendency toward more natural-appearing figures in the last years of the occupation of the city. Stela B, to the north of Stela 4, is famous for two designs at the top which for years were thought to be the trunks of elephants, but which have recently been interpreted to be beaks of macaws. Stela C, slightly out of line from the previously mentioned monuments, is unusual in having human figures carved on both sides. It bears traces of the red paint that once covered all of the stelae.

Stela D, on the north side of the plaza, next to the steps, is noted for having two columns of glyphs on its back. The cement used to repair the monument has come loose, revealing a section of steel mesh underneath. The altar in front shows figures representing Chac, the rain god.

Stela F, northernmost of the row on the east side of the plaza, is unusual in its unity, the robes of the figure on the front extending around to frame the glyphs carved on the back. Altar G, next in line, is a two-headed serpent, and bears a date equivalent to 800 A.D., the latest date inscribed at Copán. Stela H, last in line, is unique in that it depicts a female (to judge by the skirt). Two fragments of a gold statue were found in the vault underneath. Analysis showed that the gold came from Colombia or Panama. Stela I is set in a niche in the eastern stairway, and shows a person with his face covered by a mask.

Stela J, at the eastern end of the adjoining area called the Central Court, shows no human figure at all, but is completely covered with glyphs. The only similar Mayan stela known is at Quiriguá.

The **Ball Court,** south of the Ceremonial Court, is a narrow playing area closed on three sides by slanting platforms faced with stones. The distinguishing marks of the Copán complex are the sculptures along the upper parts of the platforms, representing the heads of macaws, and glyph inscriptions, which date the court at 775 A.D. Two earlier ball courts were found during excavations under the reconstructed one. It is thought that the game was played with a large rubber ball, the object being to strike markers along the upper rim of the slanting platforms. A different version of the ball game, played in central Mexico and the Yucatán, used stone rings as goals, and ended in the sacrifice of the losers.

The **Hieroglyphic Stairway,** south of the ball court, is one of the most spectacular structures in the Mayan world: a set of 63 stone steps containing about 2500 blocks carved with glyphs. The stairway is especially impressive when the sun strikes at an angle that shows the details of the carving. Placed at regular intervals down the center of the steps were five male figures, possibly of gods, one of which has been looted. The stone blocks that compose the stairway were found scattered at the foot of the temple mound, and were replaced in an order that has nothing to do with their original locations. Only a few blocks bearing date inscriptions have been deciphered. The dates range from 544 A.D. to 744 A.D. in the western calendar.

On the south side of the stairway plaza is Stela N, one of the finer of the stelae at Copán, with human figures on each face, and columns of glyphs along the edges. In this relatively late work (761 A.D.), the designs of the faces creep around the edges. It appears that the sculptor or sculptors were attempting to efface the obvious physical attributes of the stone block. One can speculate that if the erection of monuments at Copán had not come to a sudden end, the relief of the stelae might have developed into a form of free-standing statues. Elsewhere in the ruins, three-dimensional sculptures indicate that the artisans of Copán were liberating themselves from the contours of stone blocks.

On the west side of the stairway plaza is Altar O, a block with a depression that might have been a seat of honor. Nearby is Altar 41, with faces carved at either end of the front side, one a jaguar (on the north) and the other a serpent. These figures might have represented the struggle between the dry season and the rainy season. These blocks are called altars for lack of a better term, since their functions are not known.

The **Acropolis** is the group of structures to the south of the Hieroglyphic Stairway. It was named at a time when archaeologists compared Copán and other Mayan centers with Greece and Rome.

The **Western Court** of the Acropolis is bordered on the north by Temple 11, which also adjoins the stairway plaza. The stairways on the south side of the structure are known as the **Reviewing Stand,** since they offer a view of whatever might have been going on in the plaza below. The stairs are decorated with sculptures of giant snails and of some ugly gods, and lead up to the **Temple of the Inscriptions,** named for its panels of glyphs. By coincidence or design, a sculpture at the top known as El Viejo (The Old Man) looks directly at a stela on a distant mountain.

In the middle of the eastern side of the Western Court is Altar Q, a rectangular block with four human figures on each side. Some archaeologists used to take this altar as a depiction of a meeting of Mayan astronomers at Copán in 680 A.D. Recently, however, some beginnings have been made in interpreting the glyphs on the altar, and there don't seem to be any references to the other Mayan cities from which the astronomers would have come. Until relatively recently, most stories giving details about daily life or specific events in the history of the Maya were speculation.

On the west side of the **Eastern Court** of the Acropolis, adjoining the area described above, is the Jaguar Stairway, named for the sculptures flanking its steps. The holes in the jaguars were once filled with polished obsidian.

On the north side of the court is Temple 22. Sculptures bordering the doorway of the structure at the top form the jaws of a monster. At the corners of the structure are figures of Chac, the long-nosed rain god. Because of its many sculptures and its fine proportions, Temple 22 is considered one of the architectural gems of the Mayan world.

On the east side of the court are the remains of a temple platform sitting at the edge of a precipice that drops to the old bed of the Copán River. The river, shifting from its course in the Classic Era, had washed away Temple 20, revealing a cross section of superimposed structures. To prevent further damage, the river was shifted to a new channel in 1935.

A piece of roofing metal along the base of Temple 20 covers the entrance to a tomb. Nearby is the arched opening of an old drain, which still serves to carry rain water from the plaza.

The Archaeology Museum

The Regional Museum of Archaeology, on the square in the town of Copán Ruinas, houses many of the artifacts excavated at Copán, as well as altars and sculptures removed from the ceremonial center and outlying area. Hours are from 8 a.m. to 4 p.m. every day. All exhibits are well labeled in both English and Spanish. There is a small admission charge.

There's a variety of bone, shell and jade jewelry, and a skull reveals that the Maya used jade to fill tooth cavities. Polychrome vases on display show dance and ceremonial scenes. A few of the pottery pieces show similarities in style to ceramics unearthed at Teotihuacán, evidencing some sort of cultural influence reaching down this way from Mexico. Some of the stone sculptures are expressive enough to have been given names, e.g., "the melancholy woman," and there are smaller busts executed in clay. A complete panel of glyphs from Temple 11 is embedded in the northern wall, and above it is a human-bat sculpture from Temple 22. Another bat sculpture, large and obviously male, is in the courtyard. The bat is presumed to have been the emblem of Copán.

Now, back to Guatemala. If you leave Copán via Jocotán and turn south at the paved highway, you'll end up in Esquipulas.

ESQUIPULAS
Population 7226; Altitude 950 meters; Fiesta: July 25; Pilgrimages: January 15 and Holy Week; Kilometer 223

The Basilica of Esquipulas is the home of the Black Christ, goal of Catholic pilgrims from all over Central America, and famed among the devoted for miraculous cures of ailments.

As with many other aspects of Catholicism in Guatemala, the veneration of the Black Christ may have its roots in pre-Conquest religious practices. It's known that the pantheon of Guatemala's Indian nations included several black deities, and to this day, Indians have a special devotion to the Black Christ that is missing from their attitude toward other Church figures.

Reliable historical details are lacking, but it appears that in about 1595, an Indian had a vision of Christ on the spot where the

263

basilica now stands. Natives hired the sculptor Quirio Cataño to execute a statue of Christ as the Indian had seen him, and so a figure was carved in dark brown wood. According to another version, Spanish authorities ordered the creation of the figure in order to appease the Indians, who had become restive after their temples had been burned and the worship of their traditional gods prohibited. If this was the case, the Spanish may have reasoned that a dark Christ would be more readily accepted as a substitute for the old gods.

A small chapel was built to house the Black Christ, which over the years gained a local fame for curing illnesses and removing curses. The church recognized the powers of the statue in 1737, when archbishop Pedro Pardo de Figueroa came before it and was cured of a contagious disease. The archbishop ordered the construction of a large church for the Black Christ, which was moved to the new basilica in 1758. Pardo is buried at the foot of the main altar of the basilica's sanctuary.

The Esquipulas of today has two contrary faces. On one side of the main street is the basilica, a massive, squat colonial structure designed to resist earthquakes, which it has done admirably over the years. It is particularly impressive when bathed in floodlights at night, especially if one sees it when approaching town via the road winding out of the mountains.

Inside, some pilgrims line up for a chance to kiss the statue, while others make the long approach down the nave entirely on their knees. Many people slowly back down the aisle when leaving, facing the statue all the time. The smoke of incense and candles drifts into the air, and attendants scurry about scraping wax from the floors.

Elsewhere, some pilgrims bathe in the hot springs near the church in search of recovery, while others buy packets of the white kaolin dug from the surrounding mountains, calling it holy earth, and believing that it will have a curative effect when eaten or taken in water.

The other side of Esquipulas is the frankly commercial aspect. The sidewalks opposite the church are crowded with vendors selling straw hats with fake flowers, the emblem of those who have made a pilgrimage to the Black Christ. Cheap straw bags, baskets and candies are piled high, to be peddled to eager buyers. While some visitors go about their devotions in the church, others drink late into the night in the noisy bars and restaurants across the street. Esquipulas is a serious religious center. But it's also

264

a place to have a high and good time, not only for Guatemalans, but for Hondurans and Salvadorans who cross over the nearby borders.

The busiest time of the year at Esquipulas is January 15, when thousands of pilgrims pour in from all over Central America on chartered buses. But there are few times when the town isn't teeming with visitors.

HOTELS

Most rooms in Esquipulas are claustrophobically small. All hotels are along or near the street running in front of the church.

Hotel Payaquí, 2 Avenida 11-56, tel. 431143. $15 single/$28 double. Best in town, with pool, protected parking, shops.

Hotel Los Angeles, 2 Avenida 11-94, tel. 431254. $8 per person.

Other fair hotels are the Montecristo (3 Avenida 9-12, $6 per person with bath), and the Hotelito Lemus 2 (2 Avenida 10-30, $4 per person). There are fully two dozen other lodging places, with small rooms without bath for as little as $1.50.

Food is relatively expensive in Esquipulas. Expect to pay about $4 in any hotel for an indifferent meal. The Hotel Payaquí has two restaurants, one serving native-style food.

Buses: Rutas Orientales, 19 Calle 8-18, Zone 1, Guatemala City. 15 departures daily from 5 a.m. to 6:30 p.m., from Guatemala City to Esquipulas and vice-versa. There are buses about every hour to Puerto Barrios, to the nearby Honduran border at Agua Caliente, and to the border of El Salvador at Anguiatú.

THE CARIBBEAN

Back on the Atlantic Highway, you'll continue down the dry valley of the Motagua River. Past kilometer 175, the countryside suddenly turns to a green land of rich pastures, banana plants, and palms. Houses are not the thick-walled adobe and block buildings of the dry lands, but wooden and bamboo huts with thatched roofs. To the north, the ridge of the Sierra de las Minas takes a sudden plunge, permitting the passage of abundant rainfall.

As recently as a hundred years ago, Caribbean Guatemala was a sparsely inhabited sea of jungle and swamp. Some goods moved up from the coast by boat along the Motagua River as far as Gualán, at the edge of the dry country, where they would be taken by road and trail onward to Guatemala City. But mostly, no use was found for this area whose mosquitoes and malaria made it deadly for human habitation.

President Barrios made a start in developing the Caribbean in the 1880s, when he ordered that railroad tracks be laid down the Motagua valley. The tracks didn't get far until the 1890s, when the line was taken over and completed by the International Railways of Central America. The commercial twin of the railway was the United Fruit Company, which obtained land concessions as well as the right to import much of its equipment free of duty. The result was the clearing of the jungle and the establishment of an American banana empire in Guatemala.

For a time, just about everything that went on in the area was under the control of United Fruit and the railway. Foreign executives, living in compounds of screened-in airy houses, supervised the planting, cutting and shipping of bananas. The railroad gave preference to bananas and charged high rates for other goods. Since it had a monopoly on transportation to the Caribbean, the railroad could act as it pleased.

A hybrid culture developed in the banana lands. There were mixtures of West Indian laborers, Indians from the highlands, Ladinos from eastern Guatemala, and North Americans and Europeans brought in by *La Frutera* to supervise operations. Small settlements along the railway bore such American-sounding names as Oneida, Huron and Virginia. Workers bought their food in company stores, obtained treatment for malaria and hookworm at company clinics, and passed many a month living hand to mouth when bananas weren't being cut.

Gradually, company dominance over the area came to an end. An epidemic of Panama disease forced the abandonment of much of the Caribbean banana land in the thirties, and new plantations were started in the Pacific lowlands. A highway was completed from Guatemala City to Puerto Barrios in the fifties, ending the railroad's transportation monopoly. Cattle grazing, sugar cane, cacao and rice were introduced, and the staple crops of corn and beans began to be cultivated more widely, ending the seasonal pattern of wage labor. Eventually, the railroad was sold to the government of Guatemala, and United Fruit sold its banana lands, though bananas are still one of the more important crops of the region.

QUIRIGUA
Population 1297; Altitude 50 meters; Fiesta: First Thursday to Sunday of June; Kilometer 203

Quiriguá is notable mainly for the ruins located three kilometers away. The town itself is a banana shipment center, and consists of little more than a bunch of ramshackle structures grouped around the railroad station. The big United Fruit Company hospital, formerly a leading center for the treatment of tropical diseases, has been converted to a school and other uses, and there are still a few screened company houses set above the ground on stilts.

Trains for Puerto Barrios leave from Guatemala City several times a week at about 7 a.m. and reach Quiriguá at 4 p.m. Trains from Puerto Barrios stop at Quiriguá at about 10:30 a.m.

Buses
From Guatemala City, buy a ticket for Quiriguá on the Litegua line (15 Calle 10-30, Zone 1), which serves Puerto Barrios. The ride takes about three hours. To continue from Quiriguá to Puerto Barrios, Guatemala City or Esquipulas, catch a bus out on the highway.
A bus for Mariscos passes on the highway at about 11 a.m., getting you there in time for the afternoon ferry to El Estor on the north shore of Lake Izabal.

Hotel Royal. Pleasant and airy wooden building, an oasis in this hot town. Clean rooms are about $4 per person. Parking, shops. The food is good and inexpensive: $2 for breakfast, $3 for lunch or dinner.

Posada Doña María, kilometer 181 on the Atlantic Highway. $4 per person. A simple, shady compound, up the road a piece.

267

QUIRIGUA RUINS

To get to the ruins, take the Atlantic Highway to the junction at kilometer 205, just past the Texaco station. This is where to get off the bus if you're not planning to stay in town. Follow the dirt road about three kilometers to the entrance to the site. Motorscooters provide a sort of taxi service along the road. If you arrive in the town of Quiriguá by train, walk along the branch line of tracks that leads out to the east from the main line. The tracks run directly to the ruins, about two kilometers from town. It's a sweaty walk on a hot day, and most days are hot around Quiriguá.

The ruins are open from about 6 a.m. to 6 p.m. There's a simple diner at the entrance, but you might want to bring a snack, since the selection of food is limited.

Quiriguá is most noted for its sculpture, for the deep carving and rounded forms that appear on its altars and stelae. Because of the similarity in styles between sculpture at Copán and Quiriguá, and the relative nearness of the two sites, which could have communicated with each other by river, it's thought that Quiriguá was a satellite of Copán.

As is the case with other sites, nobody can tell exactly when Quiriguá was settled, though the oldest pottery found at the site was made between 200 B.C. and 200 A.D. in the Late Pre-Classic Era, to judge by its style. Monuments with glyph inscriptions date from as early as 478 A.D., but the stelae and zoomorphs (animal gods) in the main plaza bear dates ranging from 692 A.D. to 810 A.D., using the Western calendar. The buildings of the Acropolis were also constructed and reconstructed during this period in the Late Classic Era, when Quiriguá flourished.

The great blocks of easily worked sandstone used to build temples and to carve into stelae were brought from the mountains north of the area by some unknown means. The Maya did not use the wheel or beasts of burden, so it must have taken hundreds of men to drag the materials. Judging by the size of the ceremonial center, there was a large population in the area when the city flourished. But there are no remains of house mounds as at Tikal. The houses at Quiriguá might have been of a light material, perhaps not too different from the thatched huts seen today.

Quiriguá first came to the attention of the Western world in the nineteenth century, after it was visited by John Lloyd Stephens.

Stephens tried to buy the site, but he had less luck at Quiriguá than he was to have at Copán. The United Fruit Company later maintained the site while the Carnegie Institution of Washington carried out excavations. The ruins are now a national park. New excavations are being carried out by the University of Pennsylvania.

The site of Quiriguá consists of a great grassy plaza dotted with stelae, the complex of buildings known as the Acropolis, and some lesser, outlying groups of monuments.

The nine stelae in the plaza of Quiriguá are the tallest in the Mayan world, rising in one case (Stela E) to more than eight meters (26 feet). The style is similar to that of Copán, though the carving is more shallow and geometric, and the headdresses are less florid. Compared to the stelae at Copán and Quiriguá, with their full-face views and busy decorations covering every space, those at Tikal and other centers in the Petén appear positively flat and primitive. As at Copán, the stelae at Quiriguá usually have a basic figure portrayed on one side of the slab, with glyphs covering the sides and back. The Quiriguá personages hold small, human-like forms in their hands, rather than the simple bars characteristic of Copán stelae. Stela H is unusual in having a diamond pattern on the back. On another stela are unusual full-figure glyphs representing numbers, in place of the more generally used dots and bars.

Partial decipherings of the inscriptions on the stelae give a fragmentary history of Quiriguá. In 724 A.D., a ruler, known to present-day archaeologists as Cauac Sky, ascended to power, and it was during the next fifty years that many of the monuments of Quiriguá were carved. In 737, it appears that some upheaval or revolution took place; after that date, the ruler of Copán is no longer mentioned.

Aside from the stelae, Quiriguá is known for its zoomorphs, six blocks of stone carved into fantastic figures. One of these, Zoomorph G, can be identified as a jaguar. The others are monsters of species not currently seen walking the earth. All of the zoomorphs—which are often referred to as altars—are covered with richly complex decorations and finely detailed glyphs.

While the plaza monuments of Quiriguá have been known for many years, it was only in the late 1970s that the Acropolis was excavated intensively and restoration started. On the west side of the complex, a large sandstone sculpture of Kinich Ahau, the crosseyed sun god, was found in one of the levels of construction. In the last, outer layer, marble was the major building material. Many tools of obsidian (volcanic glass) were found, but otherwise, Quiriguá is relatively lacking in artifacts, with few burials and caches, despite its location astride the trade routes for jade from the upper Motagua River valley.

LA TRINCHERA
Kilometer 218

Junction for the road to Mariscos, from which a ferry leaves at 1 p.m. for El Estor (starting point for the trip up the Polochic valley). For more details, see the Cobán section in the previous pages.

BANANERA
Population 2944

MORALES
Population 2193; Altitude 29 meters; Junction kilometer 243

These are twin towns of ramshackle wooden buildings with railroad tracks running down the main street. They're reached by a horribly rutted side road running off the Atlantic Highway. If you're driving, there's absolutely no reason to drop in. But buses for the Petén stop in Bananera for an hour or more, as do some of the buses for Puerto Barrios.

Bananera, built as headquarters for the United Fruit Company, features such incongruities as old shop signs in English meant to catch the attention of foreign employees, and an airstrip with an adjoining one-hole golf course in the middle of the busiest section of town.

LA RUIDOSA
Kilometer 245

Junction for the dirt road leading to the Río Dulce and on to the Petén. There is microbus service about every hour to the Río Dulce, where lodging is available, but service onward to the Petén is poor. The last bus for Flores passes at about noon. After that time, you can try to buy your way aboard a truck heading north.

PUERTO BARRIOS
Population 24,235; Altitude 1 meter; Fiesta: July 19; Kilometer 297

Puerto Barrios is a relatively new town, established at the end of the nineteenth century as the terminus of the railroad from Guatemala City. Capital of the department of Izabal and named for President Justo Rufino Barrios, the city is a teeming, steamy tropical port of wooden houses, and a lot of railroad tracks. Bananas still move out from the docks at Barrios, arriving in freight cars insulated with banana leaves. But most ocean-going ships put in at the modern container facilities of nearby Santo Tomás de Castilla.

Run-down for many years, Barrios has been cleaning up. Many streets have been paved, and some of the girlie shows have left. There's still plenty of action, though, and a good measure of low life. The city comes alive after dark, when the heat of the day has dissipated. Sailors, prostitutes, and assorted characters from around the world hang out in the bars, and the streets are filled until dawn with music and people milling about. If such scenes don't thrill you, then your only excuse for being in town is to catch a boat for Livingston and the Río Dulce.

Streets in Puerto Barrios are poorly marked. As a reference, the road into town merges into 8 Avenida. The street running alongside the market is 8 Calle.

HOTELS

Hotel del Norte, at the end of 7 Calle on the waterfront. Tel. 480087. $10 single/$16 double. The older section is an atmospheric, traditional Caribbean building, of wood construction, with screened verandas. Expect Greenstreet to tap you on the shoulder. There's also a newer concrete section with air-conditioned rooms. Best location, away from the hubbub, with a view to the harbor and the bay of Amatique.

Hotel Puerto Libre, out of town at the junction for Santo Tomás de Castilla, kilometer 292. Tel. 480447. $10 to $18/$14 to $24. Nice air-conditioned rooms, swimming pool, satellite t.v., good food. Best if you have a car.

271

Hotel Español, 13 Calle between 5 and 6 avenidas. Tel. 480738. $5/$6 with fan, $8/$12 with air conditioning. All rooms are airy and pleasant, and the cheaper ones are the best buy in town.

Hotel Europa, 8 Avenida between 8 and 9 calles, tel. 480127. $5 per person with private bath. Clean, central, parking.

Hotel Internacional, 7 Avenida between 16 and 17 calles. $3 per person, or $7/$10 with air conditioning. Newish, with a pool of sorts stuck in a corner of the parking area.

Hotel Reformador, 16 Calle at 7 Avenida. $4 per person. Modern building, pleasant, fans only. Good buy.

Hotel Caribeña, 4 Avenida between 10 and 11 calles. $2 per person, or $4 with private bath. Block building, parking, restaurant. Good value.

Hotel Canada, 6 Calle between 6 and 7 Avenidas. $4 per person with private bath. Parking, fans, central location.

Hotel Miami, 3 Avenida off 12 Calle. $5 single or double. Newish brick building, convenient to the Lívingston boat for a quick escape.

Hotel Xelaju, 9 Calle at 7 Avenida, across from the market. Less than $2 per person. Can be noisy, but the location is central, and there's inside parking in the courtyard if you need it.

RESTAURANTS

For tranquil eating, your best bets are the Hotel del Norte and the Hotel Puerto Libre. Meals are $4 and up at either. The restaurant of the Caribeña Hotel serves Carib-style cooking. The shellfish soup is good. About $3.

Away from the hotels, none of the eateries is especially attractive. El Timón, 7 Avenida between 8 and 9 calles, serves seafood and beef. Lisama, at 9 Calle and 5 Avenue, is your basic Formica eatery with a couple of flies buzzing about. Open 24 hours for $2 meals. Similar is Cafesama, at the corner of 6 Avenida and 8 Calle, also open 24 hours. Bric Brac, 8 Calle between 6 and 7 avenidas, serves Chinese as well as Guatemalan food. All of these places are near the market.

Buses: Guatemala City to Puerto Barrios: Litegua (15 Calle 10-30, zone 1). 19 daily departures from 5:30 a.m. to 5 p.m. Tickets may be bought in advance. Slower buses leave from 18 Calle and 9 Avenue, Zone 1, throughout the day. Puerto Barrios to Guatemala City: Litegua buses leave from 6 Avenida between 9 and 10 calles, near the market. First bus 1 a.m., last bus 4 p.m.

There is also hourly service from the market area to Esquipulas; a daily bus for San Salvador; and a daily bus to El Florido (for connections to Copán, Honduras).

Boats for Lívingston leave from the foot of 12 Calle every day at 10:30 a.m. (10 a.m. on Sundays) and 5 p.m. and fill up fast. Be there at least 30 minutes before departure. Departures from Lívingston at 5 a.m. and 2 p.m. The voyage takes an hour and a half, and even if you don't plan to stay in Lívingston, the round trip is a pleasant excursion. Park your car in a protected area (such as at a hotel) before catching the boat.

A boat for Punta Gorda in Belize leaves Tuesdays and Fridays at 7:30 a.m. Inquire at Agencias Marítimas, 9 Calle near the dock. Make sure you stop in at the Migración office on the same street before you get on the boat.

On weekends, there are excursions to Punta Manabique, at the tip of the peninsula that borders the Bay of Amatique. Inquire at the Lívingston dock for schedules.

Trains for Guatemala City and intermediate points leave at 7 a.m. on Tuesday, Thursday and Saturday. From Guatemala City (10 Avenida and 18 Calle, Zone 1) at about 7 a.m. on the same days. The trip takes all day. Verify schedules the day before you travel.

Banks: Several, including Bancafe and Banco de los Trabajadores, are located in the financial district of Puerto Barrios, on 7 Calle between 6 and 7 avenidas. Also Lloyds Bank, 7 Calle and 2 Avenida.

Post and Telegraph Office: 6 Calle and 6 Avenida. Look for the radio tower.

273

Guatel, for telephone calls, is at the corner of 8 Avenida and 10 Calle, a block from the market. Look for the microwave tower.

Around Barrios

Girlie shows and low-down bars are the scene in Barrios. The joints are on 9 Calle toward the docks.

Unlike other Guatemalan towns, Puerto Barrios, which grew during a period of American commercial domination, is spread out in a sort of suburban sprawl. Most houses are set back from the street, and buildings are well separated. The distances you'll walk are greater than what you will have become used to. And in the local heat, you'll stop at a corner store for a cold soda or juice on the way from anywhere to anywhere. Open drainage canals line the streets. Watch your step and don't fall in.

What do you do in Barrios? Watch the hubbub around the market. Cool off with a beverage at any time of day or night in an eatery or bar. Look out to sea from the little park next to the Hotel del Norte. Observe the loading of bananas. The depot of Bandegua, the banana company (now owned by Del Monte) is the most notable building in town, with its open galleries and rusting tin roof. If for some reason you're not going to Lívingston, take a weekend boat to the beach at Punta Manabique. There's no savory place to swim in town.

SANTO TOMAS DE CASTILLA (MATIAS DE GALVEZ)
Population 4974; Altitude 3 meters

Located just around the curve of Amatique Bay from Puerto Barrios, Santo Tomás de Castilla is what Barrios isn't, a planned city with up-to-date port facilities, pleasant parks, wide paved streets, and modern housing and shipping offices. Santo Tomás was settled by Belgians in the nineteenth century, but the colony was abandoned after a few years. The town's name was officially changed to Matías de Gálvez in 1958, but the old name continues in use.

Deep-water docking facilities make Santo Tomás the busiest port in the country. Much of El Salvador's trade also moves through the port.Local buses run frequently between Puerto Barrios and Santo Tomás.

ALONG THE RIO DULCE

LIVINGSTON

Population: 3184; Altitude 10 meters; Languages: Carib (Garifuna), Spanish and English; Fiestas: Christmas week and May 15

On a hill above the Caribbean where the waters of the Río Dulce laze into the sea sits Lívingston, a town of brightly painted wooden houses, fishing boats and coconut palms. Named for Edward Livingston, the jurist whose codification of the laws of Louisiana was adopted in Guatemala for a short time in the nineteenth century, Lívingston for a while was the capital of the department of Izabal, until Puerto Barrios outstripped it as the most important town in the region.

Lívingston is the home of the Carib people, and the Caribs are a bit of lost history. Early in the conquest of the Americas, the Red Caribs on the island of St. Vincent gave shelter to and intermarried with escaped and shipwrecked slaves. In 1795 they rebelled against British rule, were defeated, and were deported to Roatan, off Honduras. From Roatan, they traded and settled along the coast of Central America, mainly in southern Belize, around Lívingston, and in mainland Honduras. The Black Caribs, or Garifuna, as they call themselves, are basically African in racial makeup, but they speak a South American language, and their customs are a mixture of old African rites, remnants of the Red Carib culture, and the Catholicism adopted along the way by their ancestors.

Legends about the Caribs abound. Some say that they have a secret royalty and practice voodoo and cannibalism. If any of this is true, the anthropologists who periodically spy on the culture haven't dug up any supporting evidence. But even without the legends, the Caribs are a fascinating people.

Many of them are true linguists. In addition to their own African-accented language, they speak the Spanish of lowland Guatemala. Many know the soft-toned English of the West Indies, having picked it up from relatives in Belize, and it's said that in the days when German merchants moved through Lívingston on the way to Cobán, they spoke to the locals in German.

When a Carib dies, nine days of chanting follow the burial, in an attempt to raise the soul of the deceased from purgatory to

275

heaven. When the chanting ends, the presumed success of the effort is celebrated by a dance in which the feet hardly move, though the body does a lot of shaking and writhing. At Christmas, a similar dance called the Yankunú is performed to the accompaniment of a rhythm pounded out on a two-toned log drum, and the festivities are often joined by Indians from the Polochic valley, who perform the Dance of the Moors. At the fiesta of San Isidro Labrador, attended by Caribs from neighboring Belize, the Punta and the Yankunú are performed. On the main day of the festival, May 15, there is a re-enactment of the arrival of the Caribs to Guatemala.

The religious customs of Lívingston are part of a puritanical form of folk Catholicism peculiar to the Caribs. On Sundays, no music is played and hardly a shop is open. But as in other parts of Guatemala, the Protestant evangelism brought by missionaries is making inroads on local practices.

HOTELS

Hotel Tucan Dugu. On the hill above the boat landing. Entrance off the main street. Tel. 315213 in Guatemala City. 39 rooms. $69 single/$79 double. A dramatic, modern Caribbean structure, two-storied and gleaming white, with a high thatched roof, extensive use of hardwoods, tiled walkways. Large pool, and beach. Altogether pleasant, though most of the time the hotel is nearly empty.

Casa Rosada, on the bay, reached by taking the path to the left as you get off the boat from Puerto Barrios. Walk about 800 meters (or pull up to the hotel's dock in your own boat). A secluded place, with small, comfortable thatched cottages going for $6 single, $10 double. A large, English-style breakfast is available, as well as simpler fare. Boat storage facilities. Children not accommodated. Reserve by telegram.

Hotel Flamingo. $10 double, or $15 with private bath. Along the Caribbean side of town. Turn left off the main street at the Happy Corner store, then turn right at the Catholic church. Simple, attractive rooms, and one cute bamboo cottage. The high walls of the compound can make it uncomfortably hot at times.

The Hotel Caribe, just to the left of the ferry, and the Hotel Río Dulce, on the main street, are basic, at $3 per person. There are also some nice rooms under the African Place restaurant, at $5 to $10. Small houses are also available for rent by week or month. They often lack such amenities as flush toilets, but rents are low.

FOOD

The cuisine of Lívingston has a Creole flavor. Coconut bread and a plantain stew are local specialties, and if you're around at the right time, you can gorge yourself on shrimp, though much of the catch of the Lívingston fleet goes directly to Puerto Barrios for shipment to Guatemala City. Breadfruit is sometimes eaten, as is cassava root, which requires laborious preparation to remove its harmful acids. Most of the food specialties are eaten only at home, so unless you stay for a while and get to know a few locals, you'll miss out.

At the small diners on the main street, you'll get home-style Guatemalan cooking with a bit of Carib flavor. At the Comedor Malecón, near the dock, your strip of beef will be smothered with onions, and you might get potatoes on the side, or rice mixed with coconut. Quite good. Next door, at Restaurant Raymundo, the fare is similar. At Margoth (turn left at the Happy Corner store), the flavor is more genuinely Carib, with fish dishes and shellfish soup. At all of these places you can get a meal with a beverage for $3. For a classier atmosphere, there's the dining room of the Hotel Tucán Dugu. Breakfast $4, lunch or dinner about $8.

In a class by itself stands the African Place. Wow! Take a look! It's a Moorish palace, reduced in size and transported from southern Spain, complete with crenelated ramparts, whitewashed walls, and a walkway over a dry moat. Inside, the restaurant is airy, with cross breezes and cool blue tiles. Ogive arches and wrought-iron decorations take you to Andalusia. The owner, who comes from Spain, spent seven years creating the environment, adapting genuine elements to local conditions and his own way of thinking. He'll explain everything. As for the food . . . The pescado a la nigeriana, fish cooked in a curry sauce with rice and onions, is superb, as is the shellfish soup. You'll also find a good Spanish omelette, shrimp, and fried fish. Lunch or dinner will cost $4 or less. Breakfast is served as well. To reach the African Place, turn left at Refresquería Happy Corner, just after the Koo Wong general store.

In the early afternoon, look for the children who sell coconut bread from baskets carried on their heads. The bakery on the main street makes good bread and cookies, and sometimes has yogurt.

Boats

Unless you land in a small plane at Lívingston's airstrip, the only way to get to town is by boat.

Boats leave from the foot of 12 Calle in Puerto Barrios at 10:30 a.m. (10 a.m. on Sundays) and 5 p.m., sometimes at 3 p.m. as well. Return trips from Lívingston at 5 a.m. and 2 p.m. There may be an extra boat at 7 a.m. The fare is less than a dollar for a cruise of an hour and a half. Not a bad buy. Get to the dock at least 30 minutes early to be sure of getting a seat. The boat pulls out of the Bay of Amatique and keeps a prudent distance from the shallows near shore, but you can still see scattered thatched houses and an occasional vacation home at the edge of the water.

A boat usually leaves on Tuesday and Friday at 7:30 a.m. from Puerto Barrios for Punta Gorda in Belize, with a stop in Lívingston at about 9 a.m. There may be other departures during the week. If you're planning to leave Guatemala by this route, check in first at the Migración office in Puerto Barrios. You can also take this boat only from Puerto Barrios to Lívingston.

The canoe for El Relleno (where the Petén road crosses the Río Dulce) usually leaves on Tuesdays and Fridays at 11 a.m., and will take on passengers for about $6 per person. You can also charter a canoe for the trip, for about $50. The canoe operators are like taxi drivers. Don't count on their tender mercies when you negotiate a fare. A better bet is the excursion to the most scenic part of the river in a motorized *cayuco* (native dugout) to take in the gorge of the Río Dulce, the Golfete and some side rivers. You can stop at some hot springs, at a spring-fed pool, and at the Chocón Machacas manatee reserve. Good for bird watching and orchid hunting. The cost is about $30 for up to four people. Inquire about cayuco trips at the Casa Rosada, or along the main street. You can also rent a small cayuco to paddle. Handling a cayuco is a bit tricky, and the current of the seemingly sluggish river can pull you downstream surprisingly quickly.

Facilities: There's no bank in Lívingston. Telephone service is available at the Guatel office on the main street, near the entrance to the Hotel Tucán Dugu.

Around Lívingston

In addition to the Carib community, you'll notice Ladinos, Chinese, Lebanese and East Indians among the population. The different ethnic communities have their separate quarters of the town, but there doesn't seem to be any communal friction in affable Lívingston.

While the Caribs maintain strict standards of behavior, there's no hostility directed toward visitors who go around in abbreviated outfits, as there is sometimes in highland Guatemala.

While you're on the main street, take note of the Monumento a la Madre next to the entrance to the Tucán Dugu. This statue of a pale-skinned woman with her hair pinned up looks like no native mother ever seen in Lívingston.

For evening entertainment, there's an occasional movie at the Cine Koo. Or, you can take in a movie being shown in the open along one of the streets.

The waters around Lívingston are shallow for a long way out from shore, and, except for a patch of sand brought in to the Hotel Tucan Dugu, there isn't any beach right in town. For swimming, you can walk north along the coast to some unspoiled beaches. You have to go a couple of kilometers. The huddled houses of Lívingston extend quite a ways along the water. The dock at the Casa Rosada extends out far enough for diving.

There's good bird watching at the mouth of the Río Blanco, a clear stream that enters the bay across the mouth of the Río Dulce. You can paddle across to it in a cayuco.

About six kilometers north of Livingston are the *Siete Altares* (Seven Altars), a series of small pools and waterfalls where a river empties into the sea. It's an idyllic and deserted place for picnicking and bathing, reached by walking up the beach and wading through a river along the way. The water's sometimes low in the pools when it hasn't rained for a while.

Above Lívingston, the Río Dulce plunges through a great gorge between green cliffs. Trees laden with vines and bromeliads grow right down to the water, and mangroves clog the shallows. Tropical and sea birds flutter about and soar above the tangled vegetation. There are a few Kekchí villages, clusters of peaked, thatched houses, and patches of corn with palms overhead, but most of the land along the lower part of the river remains in its

279

natural state. If you take one of the regular cayucos, you might stop at a settlement to pick up a passenger or bring supplies to a boatbuilder. A fisherman paddles by now and then in a dugout, but mostly there is solitude.

Beyond the gorge is the Golfete, a lake-like stretch of water. On its north shore is the Chocón Machacas Reserve (Biotopo), established to protect the fresh-water manatee, or sea cow, a mammal weighing up to a ton, which inhabits the swamps at the mouth of the Polochic River and along the Río Dulce. Manatee-hunting is now prohibited. Even if you don't see any manatees, you can follow the trails of the reserve, listen to the songs of birds, and appreciate a nearly undisturbed tropical forest. The only way to reach the reserve is by boat.

Past the Golfete, the river is sluggish, and dotted with a few islands. There is more settlement in the steaming hills of this area, and much of the natural growth has been shaved away, and the land planted in corn. Near the bridge at El Relleno are many vacation houses, several hotels, and a marina.

EL RELLENO–RIO DULCE CROSSING
Population: 226; Kilometer 275

A bridge spans the Río Dulce at this point. Traffic for the Petén used to cross the river on a ferry, around which the little settlement of El Relleno grew up. El Relleno is the starting point for visiting Castillo San Felipe upriver, and for taking a boat to any of several hotels downstream. A few stands offer fried river fish and other snacks. If you're driving, stop to pay a small toll.

HOTELS AND MARINAS

Turicentro Marimonte. A hotel-resort complex fronting on the south shore of the river and the road from the Atlantic Highway. Rates are about $15 per person. There's a pool, and a launching ramp in case you're trailing your own boat and want to head out on the river. Reservations and information in Guatemala City, telephone 314437.

Hotel Marilú. Basic accommodations on the north bank of the river, where there is a noisy, 24-hour settlement. About $2 per person.

Pensión Don Humberto, at Castillo San Felipe (see below). Pleasant.

Hotel Del Río, six kilometers downriver. $15 per person. Telephone 310016 in Guatemala City for information.

Hotel Catamarán, on an island two kilometers downriver from El Relleno. A luxury hotel with marina and swimming pool, and boats available for trips along the Río Dulce. Rates start at $20 single, $30 double. To arrange transportation, telephone 324829 in Guatemala City.

Mañana Marina, opposite the Catamarán. Docking facilities, and a chandlery with a limited range of supplies. They'll also take care of renewals of boat permits. Ask for Clyde.

Buses

The only direct buses from Guatemala City to the Río Dulce are those of the Fuente del Norte line heading for the Petén. Since these often stop for a while in Bananera, you'll do better to take a Puerto Barrios bus as far as La Ruidosa junction at kilometer 245. Catch a microbus onward to El Relleno. There's service about every hour. The last bus for the Petén usually passes at about 1 p.m.

Cayucos (boats) to Lívingston Tuesday and Friday at 7 a.m., from the north shore. Fare about $6. Look for the canoe of Edgar Campbell, who might be persuaded to stop at the Chocón Machacas reserve and some hot springs along the way. Or you can charter a boat for the trip, for about $50. If you're driving, you can park safely at the gas station.

CASTILLO SAN FELIPE

At the entrance to the Río Dulce is the fortress of San Felipe, a relic of the days when pirates roamed the Caribbean and sought to get their hands on indigo, cacao, gold and other loot of the Spanish colonies. Sir Francis Drake and other privateer captains became bold to the point of sailing up the Río Dulce to Lake Izabal in order to stock up on food and harass overland mule trains. After many futile attempts to engage the pirates in battle, the Spanish erected the fortress of San Felipe de Lara. It was completed in 1652, and a chain was stretched across the river to keep pirates out of the lake.

It turned out that the fortress was never a very effective defense. It was burned by the pirate Sharp in 1686, and later rebuilt. Since the fortress was 20 nautical miles from the sea, pirates could still sail part of the way upriver unmolested. Political changes in Europe finally brought an end to piracy, and the fortress was used as a prison until independence.

The restored fortress can be visited by boat from El Relleno. You can sleep out near the fortress, or stay in the nearby Hotel Don Humberto, which charges about $5 per person.

LAKE IZABAL

Largest of Guatemala's lakes, Izabal is a gentle expanse of water hemmed in by the Sierra de las Minas to the south and the Santa Cruz range to the north. It covers 590 square kilometers (228 square miles) and its surface is less than a meter above sea level. The lake measures about 45 by 20 kilometers, and has a maximum depth of 18 meters.

The waters of the lake are rich in perch, tarpon and other game fish. Herons, alligators and lizards abound in the shore areas, and there are a few manatees.

Boats for fishing or cruising on the lake can be secured at El Relleno, the Río Dulce hotels and Livingston, and sometimes at Mariscos and El Estor.

The Petén

Guatemala's new frontier is the Petén, the vast and sparsely settled department covering the northern third of the country. Thousands of years ago, the Maya settled the area. They burned away jungle to plant patches of corn, traded by way of rivers and laboriously constructed roads, and built great ceremonial cities that endured for centuries. They abandoned the Petén for unknown reasons, though a later group of Toltec-Maya immigrants from the Yucatán settled near Lake Petén Itzá and remained unconquered by the Spanish until 1697. After the Petén was nominally brought under Spanish control, only a few scattered settlements were established in the wilderness.

The Petén is an area of dense hardwood forests and dry jungle, of grassy savannas and small hills and valleys, dotted with lakes and seasonal swamps, cut here and there by rivers draining into the Gulf of Mexico and the Caribbean. In the southeast part of the department, the Maya Mountains rise to 500 meters, but most of the land is much lower. Thick layers of underlying sedimentary rock give evidence that much of the Petén was covered by the sea 200 million years ago, then slowly emerged and eroded into its present form.

Until relatively recently, about the only product that came out of the Petén was chicle, the raw material for chewing gum, bled from chicozapote trees in the forests of the north by a rough-and-tumble breed of workers, and shipped out by plane. There were no roads running into the area from the rest of Guatemala, and so the forests remained unspoiled refuges for birds, wild boars and dogs, jaguars, and other animals that had disappeared long ago from the settled parts of the country.

Today, the face of the Petén has changed. Thousands of people from the crowded and overworked lands of the south have moved to the virgin lands of the north. Forests are cut and burned off to

283

create new farmland, simple pole-and-thatch houses are quickly erected, and whole communities spring up where maps still show empty land. A flight over the Petén will reveal that most of the land remains untouched. But a few wide swaths run across the landscape wherever a road has been built, and the land cleared for farming a few kilometers to either side. The Petén already produces a large surplus of corn, and mahogany and other hardwoods are shipped out. Potential riches, including petroleum deposits, remain to be developed. The opening of the Petén is administered by FYDEP, a government corporation in charge of building roads, bringing in settlers and exploiting forest and mineral resources.

Travel Strategy for the Petén

Scattered around the Petén are the old ceremonial centers of the Maya, some of them cleared of jungle growth, but many still remaining to be explored. Flores, capital of the Petén, is easily reached from Guatemala City by air, and makes a good base for visiting Tikal, the greatest of the Mayan centers, and some of the other archaeological sites. Air service to other parts of the Petén has disappeared with the demise of the chicle industry.

Distances in the Petén are not great by North American standards. Flores is 515 kilometers (320 miles) from Guatemala City by road, and 270 kilometers (168 miles) distant by air. In a country the size of Guatemala, however, these are long runs, made longer by the unpaved roads.

Buses from Guatemala City to Flores can take forever, and sometimes longer. The run is scheduled for 12 hours, but muddy roads, breakdowns and rest stops often extend the trip into an ordeal of up to 20 hours. The buses are usually crowded, and the trip in most parts isn't as visually interesting as one might expect, since much of the land along the road has been cleared, and slash-and-burn agriculture soon becomes boring.

To take your overland travel in shorter doses, you can visit the Caribbean and then pick up a bus for the Petén at La Ruidosa junction on the Atlantic Highway or at the Río Dulce bridge. If you miss the last bus through La Ruidosa (usually at about 1 p.m.), you can try to buy your way north on a truck, though the trip may be even less comfortable than on a bus. If your funds are limited and it's a matter of going by bus or not at all, then by all means go. The wonders of Tikal are well worth even a grueling trip.

Despite the rigors of bus travel, driving to the Petén isn't too difficult—if you're prepared. The road is paved to Puerto Modesto Méndez (kilometer 335), about one-third of the way from the Atlantic Highway to Flores, and the rest of the route will be asphalted within the next five years. For now, beyond Modesto Méndez, the road is unpaved, rutted, and often muddy during the rainy season (which can last into December or January in the Petén). Heavy trucks kick up dust and obstruct passage. However, there are few narrow stretches, curves and grades. A low-slung American passenger car might have difficulty, but a pickup truck or van will do fine. Make sure your vehicle is in top condition, since service is non-existent. And carry a couple of spare tires or tubes, food, and water for you and the radiator. Gasoline is available only in the scattered towns along the way, so fill up whenever possible. You can expect to make the run from Guatemala City to Flores in a minimum of nine hours. But a more restful plan is to stop at Quiriguá or the Río Dulce, and then get an early start on the long stretch of unpaved road.

If you're driving a rented car, leave it in Guatemala City and fly to the Petén. Jeeps can be rented in Flores.

The easiest way to get to the Petén and back is by plane. There are direct flights every day from Guatemala City to Flores (see below).

TO FLORES

The road to Flores starts at La Ruidosa junction, kilometer 245 on the Atlantic Highway, and cuts through an area where the green hills have been cleared and re-cleared for cattle pasture and patches of corn. Beyond the hills, the road continues through a flat section to the Río Dulce bridge at El Relleno (kilometer 275, see page 280).

PUERTO MODESTO MENDEZ
Population: 148; Kilometer 335

A town of stilt houses amid low swampy lands along the Sarstún River, where the departments of the Petén and Izabal meet. Belize is just downriver. From this point, roadside markers give the distance from Flores, 172 kilometers away.

This is the hilliest part of the Petén, and from Modesto Méndez to beyond Poptún there are a few curves and narrow stretches where the road dips down into river valleys. This is the most difficult part of the route for driving. Usually only in these valleys will you see any natural forest or jungle. After a morning rain, the jungle is full of mist and glistens in the sun. But most of the time, it's dry and dusty.

Here and there along the road are small settlements with general stores and simple eateries. And everywhere are the pastures and corn fields of newly opened farmland.

Compared to the neat and carefully tended fields of the highlands, the farms of the Petén have a decidedly sloppy appearance. Agriculture here is relatively extensive. Natural growth is so abundant that fields can hardly be kept cleared of weeds. A corn crop developing toward maturity will be entangled with encroaching undergrowth. When the next crop is ready to go into the ground, the field will be burned off again, and the stumps of trees charred down a bit more. Eventually, the nutrients in the soil will be used up, and the land will have to be returned to jungle.

SAN LUIS
Population 2445; Altitude 450 meters; Kilometer 118 from Flores.

A dirt road from Sebol in Alta Verapaz joins the road to Flores at this point. Occasional buses take this route to Sebol from Poptún. The road is recommended only for four-wheel drive vehicles.

POPTUN
Population 6362; Altitude 510 meters; Kilometer 100 from Flores.

Located to the west of the road in any area of pines, Poptún is one of the fastest-growing towns in the Petén. Nearby are the only attractive accommodations between the Río Dulce and Flores.

Accommodations
Finca Ixobel, an American-owned farm off the highway near kilometer 101, has three acres of pine forest set aside for

camping, with shelters and treehouses, spring water, and showers. Meals are served in the main house: breakfast and sandwiches, and a family-style dinner for a couple of dollars. The eggs and vegetables come right from the farm, and the bread is homemade. Swim in the pond, bird watch, take a nature walk, explore the caves of the vicinity, play baseball or soccer. You could easily stay a few days in this idyllic place. The fee for camping is about $1, and there are also rooms in a guest house for about $3. From Poptún, the farm is a fifteen-minute walk away, cutting across the airstrip. Mainly drop-in. If there's more than a few of you, reserve by letter or telegram to Mike DeVine, Finca Ixobel, Poptún, Petén.

In the center of Poptún, rooms are available at several basic pensions on the main street for about $2. These can get foul, as the water in town goes on and off, and in any case, late-night cantina noise makes sleep difficult.

There's one interesting eating place in Poptún. Comedor Ixobel, on the main street, offers the usual small-town fare, and, of all things, Tex-Mex burritos and chimichangas, as well as pizzas. $2 for a light meal, and not bad. Open until all hours.

Facilities in Poptún include an office of Guatel, for long-distance calls, and a gas station, where buses for Guatemala City and Flores stop. Inquire there for schedules. The last bus south leaves at about 2 p.m. In addition to buses from Guatemala City, there are three daily buses to Flores. And there is occasional service to Sebol, Alta Verapaz.

The hills to the west of Poptún are combed with caves. The cave at Naj Tunich ("Stone House") was apparently used by the Maya during the Classic period for religious ceremonies and, to judge by the unusual erotic themes of its cave drawings, for orgies. Also depicted are games and musicians. Inscriptions on the walls bear dates ranging from 733 to 762 A.D., the time when Tikal, 100 kilometers to the north, was at its height.

Trips to Naj Tunich with a guide can be arranged at Finca Ixobel. The cave is about a day's walk from the farm. Visitors stay over for two nights with an Indian family. The cost is about $15, plus food, with a minimum of three persons. Trips to caves closer in, and to a subterranean river, are also available, at moderate cost. Guests at the finca can also pick up a map and explore the area on their own.

DOLORES
Population 1734; Altitude 370 meters; Junction kilometer 78 from Flores.

One of the oldest towns in the Petén, founded about 1708, with a fine colonial church.

FLORES
Population 1324; Altitude 127 meters; Fiesta January 15; 515 kilometers from Guatemala City

SANTA ELENA
Population 4816; Altitude 115 meters

SAN BENITO
Population 7903; Altitude 115 meters

The island city of Flores, founded in 1700, is the successor to the last stronghold of the Maya. Centuries after Tikal and other cities of the Petén had been abandoned, some of the inhabitants of Chichén-Itzá in the Yucatán migrated southward and founded Tayasal on an island in Lake Petén Itzá. The Spaniards were aware of the existence of Tayasal. Cortés spent three days there in 1525 while on a march from Mexico to Honduras, and a statue of one of Cortés' wounded horses became one of the principal idols of the town. But for almost 200 years, the Spaniards were occupied with conquering and administering a continent, and paid little attention to the city in the jungle. Some friars visited Tayasal in about 1618, but they only managed to earn the hatred of the people by destroying their equine idol. A military expedition led by Martín de Ursúa finally managed to subjugate Tayasal in 1697.

By the time the Spaniards moved into the area, the old Mayan causeways had long been covered with jungle growth. Though the building of a road through the Petén to Belize remained a dream for many years, nothing was done about it, and Flores and the towns of the area remained isolated outposts, subsisting on corn-and-bean agriculture, and sending workers out to bleed chicle trees in the jungle.

With the opening of the Petén, first by airplane and later by highway, the area around Flores has boomed. Most of the growth has been in Santa Elena and San Benito, opposite Flores on the mainland. Flores itself sits on a small island, with no room for expansion. It remains a charming and quiet old place, with only a bit of dust kicked up now and then by vehicles traveling the road around its rim.

HOTELS

In Santa Elena:

Hotel Tziquinaha. Tel. 811216 (20258 in Guatemala City). $18 single/$21 double. Near the airport. Air conditioning, pool, cable t.v., restaurant. Food not great.

Hotel Monja Blanca, tel. 811285. 25 rooms. $3 per person. A jungly compound, along the first road to the right as you come in from the airport. Basic rooms.

Jaguar Inn, to open in 1988 near the airport, under the same management as the Jaguar Inn in Tikal.

The hotels above are within easy walking distance of the air terminal in Santa Elena (if you don't have much luggage) and are a couple of kilometers from the center of Flores. There's no noise problem, since only a few planes land during the day.

Hotel Maya Internacional, tel. 811208 (61920 in Guatemala City). 16 thatched cottages. $15 single/$20 double. Near the causeway to Flores. The units are currently reached by rickety walkways over the watery grounds. Jeep tours arranged.

Hotel Don Quijote, tel. 811252. 20 rooms. $3 per person with shared bath. Simple rooms in a modern building, a half-block from the causeway to Flores. Inexpensive restaurant. The area is often dusty because of heavy traffic (or muddy if it's been raining).

Hotel San Juan. On the main street of Santa Elena. $3 per person. Bare rooms with shared bath. So-so, but a good travel base, as buses for Tikal leave from the hotel.

In Flores:

Hotels on the west side of the island, with a view to San Benito and some open water, are preferable to those on the south side, where you'll only see the causeway, and traffic kicking up dust in Santa Elena.

Hotel Yum Kax, west side, tel. 811386. $7 single/$12 double. Newish, well-kept building. Plain, comfortable rooms with overhead fans. The restaurant has a varied menu, including game.

Hotel Itzá, tel. 811368. 13 rooms. $4 per person. South side, modern building.

Hotel Petén, tel. 811392. 22 rooms. $5 single/$8 to $10 double. West side, modern building. Rooms are crowded in tiers, but the lake views are good.

Hotel Santana, 15 rooms. $5 per person, shared bath. West side.

In San Benito:

San Benito, the red-light district of metropolitan Flores, is a hodgepodge of buildings strewn around a market. It's not the most pleasant place in which to stay, but there are a couple of dreary hotels with rooms for about $3 per person.

In El Remate: The Camino Real Hotel, under the same management as the Camino Real in Guatemala City, will open in 1988 or 1989. El Remate is about 31 kilometers from Flores on the Tikal road.

Camping

The excellent Gringo Perdido campground has good swimming, fishing, boating, a mini-zoo, meals, and low rates. There are a couple of bungalows as well. Phone 370674. Turn left off the Tikal road at kilometer 33. A sign points the way.

RESTAURANTS

Elegant cooking is nearly unknown in the Petén, which is still largely a frontier area. Chicken is invariably rubbery, and your filet mignon will be something tough and unrecognizable. Don't let yourself in for disappointment by ordering something that local hands aren't up to preparing.

On the other hand, the Petén is now settled enough to have its own *moyenne cuisine,* based largely on such native game as tepezcuintle (cavy), wild boar and turkey, and brocket deer. I wouldn't pass up the chance to try these. At the Mesa de los Mayas in Flores, you can enjoy a meal with local game, that is not elegant, but wholesome, well-cooked, and reasonably priced at about $4. You're also safe with fish, beef on skewers, and Guatemalan-style steak in onions and tomatoes. This is an unpretentious place, with reed mats decorating the walls. There are similar menus and prices at the Restaurant Gran Jaguar and La Jungla, both nearby in the center of Flores.

Almost all of the hotels, as well as these restaurants serve reasonably priced breakfasts. The cafeteria at the Hotel San Juan, the base for buses to Tikal, is open at 6 a.m.

Buses

For recent schedules and information about new routes, inquire at the Hotel San Juan on the main street in Santa Elena. The terminal for the Flores area is in Santa Elena, a couple of blocks south and east of the causeway.

Guatemala City to Flores: Fuente del Norte, 17 Calle 8-46, Zone 1, has several departures for Flores (or Santa Elena, to be exact about it) from 2 to 7 a.m., and a 9 a.m. departure for Poptún. The trip to Flores takes at least twelve hours. Book your seat the day before you travel. Flores to Guatemala City: There are two late-night departures for Guatemala City from the terminal in Santa Elena, and others at 5 a.m. and 10:30 a.m.

Buses to Poptún leave Santa Elena at 6 a.m., noon and 4 p.m. For buses to Tikal, and remote border areas, look a few paragraphs ahead ("Flores as a base . . . "). Service is also available to other Petén towns (see town listings, below).

Air Service

Daily flights to Flores are operated by Aerovías, Avenida Hincapié and 13 Calle, Zone 13, tel. 316935 (tel. 811513 at the airport in Flores); and Tapsa, Avenida Hincapié, hangar 14, tel. 314860. Both companies have departures at about 7 a.m. from their hangars on the east side of the airport (not from the main terminal on the west side). Bus 20 from downtown serves these companies, but you'll probably take a taxi to make your flight. Return flights leave at 4 p.m. Fare is about $40 each way, less for locals. Aerovías has a downtown office, 8 Avenida 16-11, Zone 1, tel. 81463. You can stop by, or reserve with either airline by phone (personnel speak some English).

Aviateca has two afternoon flights a week to Flores, returning the same day. These depart from the main terminal of Aurora airport. Fare is about $40 each way.

The airport for the Flores area is located about two kilometers east of the center of Santa Elena. Taxis run to town, or you can walk to one of the nearby hotels, or continue directly to Tikal (see below).

Facilities:

A post office and a branch of the Banco de Guatemala are located in the center of Flores. The tourist office is at the airport in Santa Elena. Guatel, the telephone company, is on the mainland in Santa Elena, about three blocks west of the causeway. Look for the microwave tower.

The Hotel San Juan in Santa Elena is a good place to get recent travel information. Several bus lines are headquartered there, and air tickets are sold.

Jeeps are rented by Koka Rentauto, Calzada Rodríguez Macal at 1 Avenida B (tel. 811233); and at the airport (tel. 811526).

Around Flores

Even if there were no spectacular ruins accessible from the town, Flores would be a pleasant place in which to spend a vacation. The cayucos (dugouts with sides built up of planks) plying the surface of Lake Petén Itzá, the thickly forested surrounding hills, the tropical bird life, and a sense of remoteness all give the place a unique atmosphere.

Flores is located at a bend in the southwest corner of Lake Petén-Itzá, which covers 99 square kilometers (38 square miles) and is dotted with a number of smaller islands. The lake is a large depression filled with ground water, fed by a few small streams and emptied by underground seepage. The name Petén was applied by the Itzá Maya to the island where Tayasal was located. It was later used as a name for the lake and finally for the whole region.

Until the causeway connecting Flores with Santa Elena was built, the only way to get to the island was in small cayucos. A commuter service of motorized cayucos still operates between Flores and San Benito. The fare is a few cents. The owners will also hire their boats out for trips around the lake. You might want to take one to the shore of the peninsula north of Flores, where a walk through the forest will take you to an unexcavated and rarely visited pyramid. Also to the north, on an island about a 20-minute boat ride away, is Petencito, an outdoor zoo. All the animals—ocelots, pumas, jaguars, monkeys, tepezcuintles and alligators—are native to the Petén. For swimming, you can jump in the lake anywhere, though the water around Flores is encrusted with vegetation and is not too appetizing. Head for a spot away from the settled area, either on foot or in a canoe.

For the best views from Flores, walk up to the town square (in this case a circle) at the crest of the island. You'll be able to look down on the western end of the lake, and over to the low surrounding hills.

For spelunking, ask for the way to the cave at Actun Kan, on the outskirts of Santa Elena. There are also caves at Jobitzinaj. Take the street leading off the Flores causeway through Santa Elena, turn right at the end, then take the first street left, and continue to the caves, about three kilometers away. Take a flashlight and spare batteries, or candles.

I recently went looking in Flores for several hotels that I used to know, and found that their lower floors had disappeared below the rising waters of Lake Petén Itzá. Sic transit. In fact, between breakneck growth and changes in water level, the Flores area is the most altered of all the places I have revisited. But who knows? The level of the lake is said to be falling again. Some hotels could re-open, and the Hotel Maya Internacional might even recover its beautifully landscaped grounds and swimming pool.

Around the lake from Flores is the Biotopo Cerro Cahuí, a reserve established to protect the Petén turkey and other wildlife of the region. The biotopo is still in development. You'll see a sign pointing the way along the Tikal road, about 28 kilometers from Flores, at El Remate.

FLORES AS A BASE FOR VISITING TIKAL AND OTHER RUINS

As accommodations at Tikal are limited, you might want to spend your nights in Flores, and take buses or tours to Tikal during the day.

Daily tours to Tikal are offered by the Yum Kax, Petén, Maya Internacional, and other hotels in Flores. Or you can arrange your tour in Guatemala City, or simply fly in and pick up a tour at the airport.

Buses usually leave the terminal in Santa Elena at 6 a.m. and noon, make many stops, and take at least 90 minutes to reach Tikal. Buses depart Tikal promptly at 6 a.m. and 1 p.m. Fare is about $1. To give yourself more time at the ruins, take the express microbus that leaves from the Hotel San Juan in Santa Elena at 6:30 a.m. This gets you to Tikal in an hour, and departs again at 3 p.m., or whenever the passengers can be rounded up. Fare is about $5. Sign up at the Hotel San Juan the day before you travel, and you'll be picked up at your hotel. A bus operated by the Jungle Lodge in Tikal meets flights at the airport and takes passengers to Tikal for about $5 each way, or more if there are not many people aboard.

If you're going to camp out at Tikal for a night or two, and plan to do your own cooking, stock up on food in Flores. Oranges, grapefruits and other fruits make good snacks in the ruins. Leave what you can at your hotel in Flores, since there's no safe place to stow belongings at the Tikal campsite.

Aside from Tikal, it's difficult to get to many of the Mayan sites in the Petén by public transportation. Uaxactún can be reached in a day on foot from Tikal. Sayaxché, reached by bus, is the starting point for river trips to El Ceibal and a few sites near Lake Petexbatún. El Ceibal can also be reached by a jeep road from Sayaxché. Yaxjá and Nakum, east of Tikal, are accessible by jeep during the dry season. Piedras Negras, Altar de los Sacrificios and other sites along the Usumacinta River are reached by motorized canoe from Sayaxché. Yaxchilán, on the Mexican side of the Usumacinta River, can also be reached by chartered plane from Guatemala City or by road to a point on the river opposite the ruins. One of the greatest Mayan sites, El

Mirador, near the Mexican border in the north of the Petén, is reached by a two-day hike from Carmelita, a settlement that is accessible by bus from Flores. Tours to the more remote sites, as well as river and fishing trips, are offered by the Panamundo travel agency in Guatemala City.

Onward from Flores

Bus service is available to some remote border regions with few facilities for the conventional traveller. Take the daily Calzada Mopán bus, and you can continue overland into the jungle of Campeche. I don't guarantee that you'll get there quickly. Or take the daily bus to Naranjo, northwest of Flores, catch a boat on the San Pedro River, and continue by boat the next day to La Palma, on the border (there's an immigration post, so it's all legal), and Tenosique in the Mexican state of Chiapas, on the rail line to Merida. There is a surer chance of getting through on this route.

TIKAL
Altitude 254 meters; Kilometer 64 from Flores

Tikal, greatest of all Classic Mayan cities, lies to the northeast of Flores, towering above a dense jungle. In this remote area, one of the greatest civilizations of its time established a city that endured for centuries. Restoration efforts started in the 1960s, but only in the last ten years or so has it been possible for visitors to reach the site with relative ease.

Tikal is a place for wondering, not only at the engineering accomplishments of the Maya, but at the jungle splendors of the Petén. The site of Tikal is a national park, one of the few accessible areas of the Petén that has not been taken over by agriculture, and where the native flora and fauna still flourish relatively undisturbed. The park is dense with mahogany, chicozapote, cedar, ceiba and palm trees, and intertwining vines. Howler and spider monkeys roam among the treetops, and snakes prowl the ground. The hundreds of bird species include toucans and macaws, easily visible for their size and bright colors.

GETTING TO TIKAL

Air Service: Tikal has an airstrip, but there is no direct service unless you charter a small plane in Guatemala City. Scheduled flights operate to Flores, 60 kilometers away by road (see page 292). A bus from the Jungle Lodge meets all planes and charges about $5 per person for the trip to Tikal, or more if there are few passengers. Return buses leave Tikal in time for departures to the capital. You can also take a taxi for about $25, rent a car at the airport, or take local buses from Flores.

Buses: There are daily buses and express microbuses from Flores to Tikal (page 294). Buses leave Tikal for Flores promptly at 6 a.m. and 1 p.m. The microbus leaves at about 3 p.m., and you're assured of a seat only if you've booked from Flores. To travel to Belize, take the Flores bus from Tikal as far as El Cruce, and wait there for a bus to Melchor de Mencos on the Belize boundary.

Driving: See notes at the beginning of the Petén chapter. From Flores, follow the road east to El Cruce (kilometer 29), then turn north for Tikal. Most rental-car companies would prefer that you not take their vehicles overland to Tikal. Jeeps can be rented in Flores.

The ruins of Tikal are extensive, and you should allow two days to see them, if you have the time. You can fly to Flores one morning, take the bus up, and fly back to Guatemala City the next afternoon; or you can go back to Flores for the night, since overnight facilities at Tikal are limited.

An admission fee of less than $1 is collected when you arrive at the Tikal national park.

Staying at Tikal
Don't expect much from the hotels at Tikal. Or from the food. Supplies have to be trucked in from some distance. There has been talk for years about closing down the hotels at Tikal, and accommodating visitors at a new center. Just in case this comes to pass, go and stay at Tikal now! Despite less-than-luxorious conditions, spending a night at Tikal, listening to jungle noises and waking to the squawking of parrots and monkeys, can be a memorable experience.

Hotels, restaurants, the museum and campground are all grouped around the airstrip, which is about a twenty-minute walk from the ruins.

HOTELS

The best hotel in Tikal is the **Jaguar Inn.** The charge is about $20 double. Unfortunately, there are only two double rooms, so you should write well in advance if you'd like to stay. Send a deposit and your phone number. They'll meet your plane in Flores. The **Posada de la Selva (Jungle Lodge)** offers cottages for $20 double, and rooms in the hotel section for $6 per person. Reserve in Guatemala City by phoning 760294. The **Tikal Inn** charges $5 per person for a bare room, or $10 per person in a screened bungalow. There is a pool, but I have never seen water in it.

Camping
There's an ample grassy campsite right at the entrance to the

visitors' reception area, with running water, shower and toilets, open thatched shelters, and plenty of room for vehicle parking. Best of all, there's no charge to use the site. The diners nearby rent hammocks and mosquito nets for a couple of dollars a night, with a deposit required. A blanket will be useful in the dry season (December through May) since it can get surprisingly cold at night. Mosquito repellent will come in handy in the rainy season. There are fireplaces for cooking, and plenty of firewood is available for gathering. Campers should note that dogs are not allowed into the national park. Try to choose your spot as soon as you arrive. Conditions at the campsite are a great improvement over those just a few years ago, when you had the fetch water from a crocodile-infested pond. The crocodiles are gone now, but so, unfortunately, are a couple of workers.

Restaurants

At the Jaguar Inn, on the north side of airstrip, meals are served in a pleasant and cool thatch-roofed pavilion. The food is as good as you'll find in Tikal. Breakfast costs about $3, lunch or dinner $4, and there are sandwiches, vegetarian dishes, and an a la carte menu more varied than you'd expect way out here. They'll also pack a picnic. The Jungle Lodge serves plain meals, as do a couple of inexpensive diners south of the airstrip.

Other facilities at the Tikal reception area include a post office and a jungle nature trail. That's all. The nature trail, or camino interpretativo, which starts by the Jaguar Inn, is still being developed. It passes through a chicle-gatherers' camp. This is a chapter of the Petén's history that has just recently closed, with the substitution of other ingredients in the manufacture of chewing gum. Take a walk of an hour or two, depending on your interest and condition.

The Museum

The Tikal Museum, located just north of the airstrip, contains a collection of some of the artifacts discovered during excavations at the ruins. Most interesting is a reconstructed tomb complete with skeleton and offerings of jadeite jewelry and pottery. A number of rubbings on rice paper show the designs of stelae more clearly than does a direct glance at the sculpture. Other items include stone tools and grinding stones, pieces of jewelry formed of mosaics of jadeite and shell, flint tools, and the remains of

Stela 29, one of the oldest pieces of Mayan carved stone yet discovered, dating from about 292 A.D. Photographs show the process of excavating and restoring the ruins. The museum is open from 9 a.m. to 5 p.m., weekends to 4 p.m. Another building at the entrance to the reception area houses some of the Tikal stelae.

THE RUINS OF TIKAL

Wear light cotton clothing and a hat when you go out to the ruins. The sun is usually strong, though you can escape it for a while by ducking under a tree or into a temple. Carry some fruit or a canteen of water, or both. Bottled sodas are sold at various sites in the ruins, but no food. The Jaguar Inn will pack a box lunch if you've come without a hamper. Wear shoes with non-slip soles for climbing temples. Getting up the long flights of steps is no problem, but if you've got a fear of heights, getting down can be hairy. A flashlight will be useful for looking into temples and underground chambers.

On foot, follow the road from the airstrip. (Vehicular traffic is prohibited.) It's twenty minutes to the main plaza. The site is open from 6 a.m. to 6 p.m., though the guards start to clear visitors out at 5 p.m. You can get into the ruins during the full moon if you request permission at the inspectoría, a little building beside the trail from the airstrip.

As is the case with all Mayan sites, the origins of Tikal are only barely discernible. Findings of pottery dating from a few hundred years before Christ give evidence that the site of Tikal was inhabited at that time, perhaps by people who were attracted by its height above surrounding swamps, and by deposits of flint, useful for making tools. No intact buildings have been found from the earliest periods of Tikal settlement, since the Maya were in the habit of destroying old structures in order to use the materials for new buildings.

By the time of Christ, the Great Plaza had already taken its basic form, with platforms and stairways constructed on the north side. Over the next few hundred years, the city grew in extent and height, as old buildings were razed and covered over with new ones, and tombs set into the plaza floor. The corbeled arch came into use, as did new-style pottery vessels painted in three or more colors. Similarities in artistic styles, tools and materials suggest that the pre-Classic Maya of Tikal were in contact with other peoples of Mesoamerica.

The Classic era of the flourishing of Tikal lasted from about 300 to 900 A.D., more or less the time when Copán and Palenque were also at their heights. In addition to raising their temples to ever greater heights, the Maya of Tikal worked changes on the landscape. Ravines were dammed to form reservoirs for seasonal rains. Causeways were built to connect different parts of the city, and to provide trade routes to other Mayan centers. Trade developed with far-away peoples who could provide jadeite, obsidian and other useful raw materials.

Some sort of residential city grew around Tikal, though its nature is a matter of debate. The great buildings in the center are assumed to have been temples and palaces for religious purposes, though they might also have been residences for the noble classes. Scattered for more than four kilometers in every direction from the center of Tikal are thousands of platforms that might have been the foundations of houses of stone and wood. As many as 50,000 people lived in Tikal and its hinterland, perhaps many, many more. Estimates of the population depend on interpretations of how many people would have lived in one house, whether all houses were occupied at one time, and, perhaps most importantly, on how much food could have been produced in the surrounding area.

The most visible evidence of a large population, a bountiful agriculture, and a highly developed social organization, is, of course, the very magnitude of Tikal. Many laborers had to work over long years to carry the rock and rubble needed to fill the bases of temples. While the fill was being set in place, masons had to build retaining walls, and later to face structures with carefully cut blocks. Meanwhile, lime mortar had to be made by burning limestone, a process that required the cutting of immense quantities of wood. All this had to be done with brute human labor, for the Maya did not know the use of the wheel, nor of iron, nor did they have beasts of burden.

While all this hard labor was going on, artisans were at work scraping away at limestone to form the low-relief sculptures of stelae, and incising designs into beams of chicozapote. This wood, carved when fresh and soft, would take on an iron hardness when exposed to air. The original temple lintels of Tikal, the finest examples of Mayan wood carving, have endured the jungle climate for centuries.

Additional workers had to patch up fallen bits of plaster, replace missing blocks of limestone, keep the temples painted, plaster over plaza floors worn with use, and maintain the reservoirs. Artisans created jewelry and beautiful pottery vessels with painted scenes of daily life, and jadeite jewelry and mosaics of shells and stones for personal decoration and as funerary offerings. Priests had to preside over human sacrifices, the victims of which might have been secured in raids on neighboring peoples (if one is to believe recent interpretations of scenes depicted on some Classic Mayan pottery vessels). Other priests and officials had to supervise matters ranging from ball games to the administration of justice to the calculation of the calendar.

All the people who were tending to the organized activities of civilization in Tikal could hardly have devoted much time to growing food. So in addition to the workers and nobility of the town, there must have existed a large class of farmers. The Maya of Tikal took seemingly dreadful jungle swamps, with their store of water, and reworked them into resources that supported large population centers. Drainage canals were dug, and dirt piled up to create raised planting beds. Cassava, yams and corn and ramon nuts could have provided a complete and varied diet, along with wild game.

Today, one can sit atop a pyramid, gaze at the Great Plaza and roof combs rising up from the sea of jungle, and imagine the times more than a thousand years ago when the plaza was alive with activity and the city was surrounded by cultivated fields dotted with houses. But one can do little more than imagine. There is no coherent history of Tikal and there may never be one. Bits and pieces of information are picked up from drawings on pottery and bone, finds of tools, similarities in artistic styles between Tikal and other Mayan and non-Mayan centers, and the few glyphs that have been deciphered up to now.

Written dates on stelae at Tikal range form the fourth century A.D. to 869 A.D., which is thought to have been the period during which civilization in the city reached its greatest development. Some short time after the last stela was erected, Tikal entered a period of rapid decline. Buildings were left unfinished, and population decreased dramatically. A number of possible explanations have been proposed: exhaustion of the land, drought, disease, revolution, invasion, perhaps the coming of a prophet who led his people back into the jungle. It's all a matter of

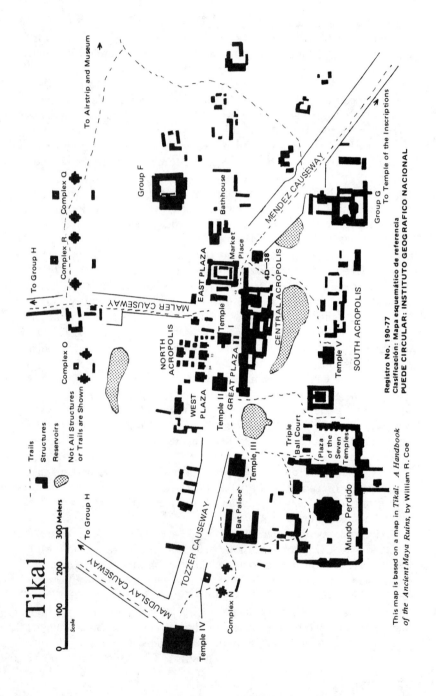

Tikal

Scale

| 0 | 100 | 200 | 300 Meters |

Trails ---

Structures ▪

Reservoirs ⬭

Not All Structures
or Trails are Shown

To Group H

MAUDSLAY CAUSEWAY

TOZZER CAUSEWAY

To Group H

Complex O

NORTH ACROPOLIS

WEST PLAZA

Temple II

GREAT PLAZA

Temple III

Bat Palace

Triple Ball Court

Plaza of the Seven Temples

Mundo Perdido

Temple IV

Complex N

Complex Q

Complex R

MALER CAUSEWAY

EAST PLAZA

Market Place

Temple I

CENTRAL ACROPOLIS

4D—38

SOUTH ACROPOLIS

Temple V

Group F

Bathhouse

MENDEZ CAUSEWAY

Group G

To Temple of the Inscriptions

To Airstrip and Museum

Registro No. 190-77
Clasificación: Mapa esquemático de referencia
PUEDE CIRCULAR: INSTITUTO GEOGRAFICO NACIONAL

This map is based on a map in *Tikal: A Handbook
of the Ancient Maya Ruins*, by William R. Coe

speculation. Whatever happened at Tikal might have occurred at Copán and Palenque as well, for those cities began to decline at the same time.

After the fall of civilization at Tikal, the city was inhabited intermittently, but there was never the kind of highly organized social system that characterized Tikal at its height. Tombs were occasionally looted, monuments were moved, and buildings were left to decay. Trees took root among the temples, their roots holding the stone and plaster together, and the stelae were covered over with moss.

The first systematic exploration of Tikal was carried out by Modesto Méndez and Ambrosio Tut, officials of the government of the Petén, in 1848. The report of Méndez awakened European interest in Tikal. A Swiss scientist showed up and carried off some of the temple lintels, and Alfred Maudslay arrived from England in 1881 to start clearing and photographing the ruins. Over the next fifty years, exploration was carried out by archaeologists sponsored by the Peabody Museum of Harvard University and the Carnegie Institution of Washington. From 1956 to 1969, the University Museum of the University of Pennsylvania undertook a massive excavation and reconstruction project in cooperation with the government of Guatemala. Work at the site is now supervised by the Institute of Anthropology and History of Guatemala.

Tikal consists of thousands of constructions ranging from temples on pyramid bases to palaces to ball courts to tombs and burial chambers to stelae. Many of the structures remain in the form of mounds into which they collapsed during centuries of abandonment of the site, and many others lie buried under later buildings. Most of the restored and partially restored structures date from the Late Classic Period, which lasted from about 550 A.D. to 900 A.D. The major monuments are in clusters, some in the vicinity of the Great Plaza, others in outlying areas reached by following causeways built by the Maya.

The **Great Plaza,** dominated by Temples I and II, sits on an artificially leveled tongue of land between two ravines, at the center of Tikal. The grassy plaza was originally covered over with lime mortar, which was renewed every few centuries.

Temple I, also called the Temple of the Giant Jaguar, rises 44.2 meters (145 feet) over the east side of the plaza. The base is formed of nine terraces with sloping sides, supporting a platform on which sits a three-room temple building. (Note that the standard descriptive terms are somewhat confusing. The word "temple" refers both to the entire construction, including the great rubble-filled base, and to the relatively small superstructure.) The crowning roof comb appears to have been mainly decorative. Roof combs were hollowed out to lighten their weight, and faced with carved limestone blocks. The eroded figure of a seated person can barely be made out on the comb of Temple I. The stairway now visible was used during construction. It was once covered over by a more formal set of steps.

The Maya built temples by creating mountains and placing molehills on top. At the base of Temple I (and under most of the other temples) is a great burial vault, a reconstruction of which may be seen in the Tikal Museum. The body of a noble was placed on a masonry bench in the chamber, along with offerings of ceramics and pieces of jewelry. Inscriptions indicate that the noble was called Ah Cacau (Lord Cacao), and that he ascended to power in 682 A.D. and ruled for almost fifty years. A corbeled arch was built above his chamber and capped with wooden beams, after which began the laborious process of building retaining walls, filling the spaces with rubble to form the first layer of the pyramid base, then building successive layers to the desired height. After the artificial mountain had been raised, a temple building was constructed at the top. The corbeled arch used by the Maya to create interior space in temples consisted of layers of stone successively protruding inward, until they could be capped by a single block. This arch could span only a narrow width, so massive Mayan structures contain claustrophobically small amounts of interior space.

Inside Temple I, some of the original carved wooden beams are still in place. Lintels at the entrances to temples were left undecorated. A secondary burial, dating from after the completion of Temple I, was found beneath the floor of the rear room.

Temple II, known as the Temple of the Masks for the decorations on its stairway, reaches a height of 38.1 meters (125 feet) over the west side of the plaza. With its roof comb intact, it might have stood almost as high as Temple I. The walls of the inside rooms are scribbled with ancient graffiti. No tomb has yet been found under the base, but the temple is thought by some to honor the wife of the ruler buried in Temple I. It may be her portrait that decorates an interior wooden lintel.

Both Temple I and Temple II date from relatively late in the life of Tikal, about 700 A.D.

Placed around the plaza are stelae and associated altars, some plain, others carved in low relief. Many appear to have been moved after the fall of Classic civilization at Tikal. Later stelae (the date glyphs can be read) were larger and sculptured more skillfully out of harder rock than the limestone of the earlier stelae, on which many of the inscriptions have worn away. The portraits on the stelae might have represented nobles to whom they were dedicated. Faces on some of the stelae appear to have been smashed intentionally, perhaps when the portrayed figure died or was succeeded in office.

The **North Acropolis,** fronting on the north side of the Great Plaza, is one of the most heavily constructed areas of Tikal. Hidden under the visible structures are many superimposed earlier buildings.

Excavations in Structure 5D-34 revealed a tomb cut into the bedrock deep below, containing the skeletons of a noble and his retainers, along with turtles, a crocodile, and pottery. In Structure 5D-33, facing the plaza, a number of layers of construction are visible. Here, the outer layer has been removed on the left side, revealing a great mask decorating one of the earlier buildings. On the right side, a matching mask may be seen by entering an excavation in the intact outer structure. Still another temple base covered the outer structure seen today, but was so badly eroded that most of it was stripped away during the reconstruction of the North Acropolis. Stela 31, now in the Tikal museum, was found buried in the second-layer building. One of the most beautiful of the early stelae at Tikal, it was defaced prior to the building of the now-destroyed outermost temple. Paradoxically, burial in rubble preserved it from further damage. Pictured on it is a ruling noble whose name glyph has been read as Stormy Sky. This may be the person whose mutilated skeleton was found in a tomb under the structure. Some archaeologists now believe that the Sky family were hereditary rulers of Tikal. Glyphs on another tomb in the North Acropolis identify an earlier ruler of Tikal called Curl Nose, who might have come from Kaminaljuyú.

South of Temple I is a small ball court. Scenes painted on pottery suggest that players hit the ball with padded knees and hips. South of Temple II, another pyramid contains no ruins on top, suggesting that it might have been capped with a perishable thatched structure. Excavations in the plaza floor southeast of the stairway of Temple II have revealed *chultuns*, chambers carved in bedrock and filled with what appears to be trash. Many of these chambers have been found, though their original use remains unknown.

Adjoining the south side of the Great Plaza is the complex of buildings known as the **Central Acropolis.** The buildings here are called palaces, not because they were royal residences—nobody knows what they were used for—but to distinguish them from the temples and pyramids elsewhere around the Great Plaza. The palaces are relatively long, low buildings surrounding small plazas, or courts, on different levels. Many are unrestored.

The palaces were constructed at different times, sometimes on top of older buildings. Alterations went on after construction was completed, with the addition of doorways, second stories and outside stairways. The interior rooms have benches, which might have been used for seating or as sleeping platforms. The palaces are multi-story structures only in a primitive sense, since the upper floors are set back and supported mainly by a layer of rubble fill behind the rooms of the lower floors. Only one of the palaces, fronting on Court 6, has an interior staircase. Many of the palace facades were decorated with low-relief friezes, only a few of which survive intact.

The **Palace Reservoir,** just south of the Central Acropolis, was created by damming a ravine and sealing the porous limestone with clay. Nearby terraces were sloped so that water would drain into the reservoir.

Along the eastern end of the northern base of the Central Acropolis is the Late Classic Structure 5D-43, a platform supporting a two-room building. The rectangular molding on the base, and the sections jutting out above and below the molding, are similar to architectural features at Teotihuacán in Central Mexico, indicating a possible flow of architectural influence from that site, or from Kaminaljuyú, a Teotihuacán outpost in present-day Guatemala City.

North of Structure 5D-43 is the open area known as the **East Plaza.** On its east side is a ball court, beside which is a quadrangle of buildings called the **Market Place.** Farther to the east is a large, rubble-filled platform which might be the foundation of a temple left uncompleted. On the east rim of the platform is a building believed to have been a steam bath, with a low doorway and an inside firepit. Temple 4D-38, to the southeast of the plaza at the entrance to the Méndez Causeway, is notable for the cache of human skulls discovered under the base of a stairway, which suggests that human sacrifice was practiced at Tikal.

The **West Plaza,** to the northwest of Temple II, includes a large palace on the north side, an unfinished temple covering a tomb on the west side, and a number of stelae, which might have been moved from their original positions after the fall of Classic civilization at Tikal.

Leading west from the West Plaza is the **Tozzer Causeway.** The causeways at Tikal were wide, raised roads paved with mortar. Most are now named for archaeologists. A foot trail winds among the buildings to the south of the Tozzer Causeway.

Temple III, 54.9 meters (180 feet) high, is also known as the Temple of the Jaguar priest, after the figure on an interior lintel of a fat man in a jaguar skin. A stela at the base of the stairway contains a date glyph equivalent to 810 A.D., indicating that Temple III was probably built in Late Classic times. Near Temple III is the **Bat Palace,** or **Window Palace** (so called for the unusual window openings on one side), another Late Classic structure, the second story of which fell down long ago.

Beyond Temple III is **Twin-Pyramid Complex N,** a set of structures of a kind peculiar to Tikal and Yaxjá. Two identical flat-topped pyramids with stairways on each side face each other across a plaza. A row of uncarved stelae and altars stands in front of the east pyramid. Off to the side is an enclosure containing a stela and altar. In the case of Complex N, these are among the finest examples of stone sculpture at Tikal. Complex N is dated 711 A.D. Dates on stelae in similar complexes elsewhere in Tikal indicate that such complexes were erected every twenty years.

Temple IV, at the end of the Tozzer Causeway, is the tallest known structure in the Mayan world, with a height of 64.6 meters (212 feet). It may also have been the tallest structure in pre-Columbian America, depending on whether one takes into account the base platform. The top is reached by a difficult trail (the stairway is gone), and affords spectacular views of the other temples. The three-room temple at the top contained two exquisite lintels, which were carried off to Switzerland. Impressions of the carvings on the top sides of the beams may be seen in the interior doorways. Glyphs on the lintels date Temple

IV at 741 A.D.

From Temple IV, a trail follows the **Maudslay Causeway** through the jungle to the northeast, ending at **Group H,** which includes two twin-pyramid complexes. The first, Complex M, was partially destroyed, possibly when the causeway was built. Complex P includes some relatively large rooms, the walls of which are covered with ancient Mayan graffiti.

The **Maler Causeway,** with a footpath down its center, runs from Group H back to the East Plaza. Midway is a set of twin-pyramid complexes. Complex Q, the easternmost of the group, is the only twin-pyramid complex to have been partially restored.

Back to the center of Tikal. From the East Plaza, the **Méndez Causeway** runs to the southeast, passing **Group G,** a complex of palace-type buildings, the walls of which are scribbled with graffiti. At the end of the causeway, about a twenty-minute walk from the East Plaza, is the **Temple of the Inscriptions,** named for the many glyphs on the roof comb and on the temple trim.

South of the Central Acropolis lies the **Plaza of the Seven Temples,** reached most easily by a trail running south from Temple III. This group is named for a series of temples in a north-south row. The central one features decorations of crossed bones and a skull. On the north side of the plaza is the **Triple Ball Court,** an unusual series of parallel playing areas.

To the west of the Plaza of the Seven Temples is the area recently re-christened **Mundo Perdido (Lost World),** which is only now being explored intensively by archaeologists. The **Great Pyramid** (structure 5C-54) rises 32 meters (105 feet) above the Lower Plaza. It consists of five superimposed pyramids constructed between 700 B.C. and 250 A.D., the last at the end of the pre-Classic period. Stairways ascend on each side of the outermost, visible layer. Two mascarones ("masks," or head sculptures), of the original 16, survive on the western side of the pyramid, and are sheltered by thatched roofs.

Beyond the Plaza of the Seven Temples to the east is **Temple V,** last of the great pyramid temples of Tikal, 57.9 meters (190 feet) high. Unusual features include a stairway finished with moldings along the edges, rounded corners on the base and superstructure, and an interior room small even for a Mayan structure.

After a look at Temple V, you can continue with explorations of the outskirts of Tikal, if you wish. From the southwest corner of the Mundo Perdido complex, follow a trail down steps and over a stick bridge, then follow a jungle trail 300 meters to a recent excavation site. You can enter a thatch-covered trench to inspect several large stone sculptures of faces. The trail continues back to Group G. If you search around, you may find other such little-visited areas on the periphery of Tikal where you can see restoration work in progress.

UAXACTUN RUINS

Uaxactún is in many ways a primitive, miniature version of Tikal. Like the larger site, Uaxactún consists of groups of temple and palace structures. But at Uaxactún, the highest temple rises to only a bit over eight meters (27 feet).

Excavations at Uaxactún have given some clues to the evolution of the Classic Mayan temple. Post holes in one of the earlier levels of construction indicate that temple bases might once have been capped with wooden houses. Explorations have also turned up painted murals.

The eight groups of structures at Uaxactún are located on either side of an airstrip. Group E, east of the airstrip, is noted for a set of three temples, oriented so that an observer standing opposite would see the sun rising over the northernmost temple on the day of the summer solstice, and over the southernmost temple on the day of the winter solstice. Two large stucco faces flank the stairway on the facing temple base, which is one of the oldest visible Mayan structures in the Petén.

Uaxactún, about 25 kilometers north of Tikal, was discovered by Sylvanus Morley, who coined its name from the words meaning "eight" and "stone" in the modern Mayan language, after finding a stela bearing a date from the eighth cycle of the Mayan calendar, equivalent to 68 A.D. Other stelae at the site bear dates up to the equivalent of 639 A.D.

A jeep trail, passable in the dry season, leads from Tikal to Uaxactún. On foot, the trip takes about six hours. The village of Uaxactún, with a population of about 400, was originally a chicle shipping center. Beans and tortillas are available, but not much else. If you walk from Tikal, plan on camping out at Uaxactún. The ruins remain almost totally unrestored.

LAKE YAXJA

At kilometer 61 on the road from Flores toward Belize, a branch road leads north for eight kilometers to the twin lakes called Yaxjá and Sacnab. On the north shore of Lake Yaxjá are the Yaxjá ruins, unusual among Mayan sites in that small sections appear to have a grid street pattern. Other ruins, on Topoxte Island near the south shore of the lake, show elements of the Yucatán Maya style, indicating that a migration from the north to this area might have taken place after Classic civilization in the Petén had come to an end.

A jeep trail, passable in the dry season, leads from the end of the branch road to the Yaxjá ruins. Alternatively, you can try to hire a boat at the village at the end of the branch road in order to reach Yaxjá and Topoxte Island. The lake is a pleasant place to stop if you're traveling in a camper.

MELCHOR DE MENCOS
Population 3521; Altitude 106 meters; Fiesta: May 16; 112 kilometers from Flores; 653 kilometers from Guatemala City.

Situated on the boundary with Belize, Melchor de Mencos is appropriately named for a sergeant who once battled English pirates. Traditionally a base for chicle workers, Melchor de Mencos, like other towns in the Petén, is now a storage and shipping point for corn.

Buses for Melchor de Mencos leave from Santa Elena/Flores three times during the morning, the first at 5 a.m. The first bus from Melchor de Mencos for Flores leaves at dawn, the last at about 3 p.m.

Continuing to Belize
The authorities in Belize sometimes turn back travelers who have long hair or who don't carry what they consider to be sufficient amounts of money. No visa is required for nationals of most countries.

Buses are available in Benque Viejo, on the other side of the boundary, for Belmopán and Belize City. From Belize City, you can continue by bus to Mexico, by jet to Miami or New Orleans, or by small plane to the idyllic offshore cayes. Buses usually leave from Benque Viejo in the morning, but at other times, it's possible to buy your way onto a truck.

For more details on travel in Belize, see **Belize Guide,** by the author of this book, published by Passport Press. The independence of Belize is recognized by most nations, but Guatemala is pressing a long-standing claim to the former British colony.

RIO AZUL

This isolated site, 80 kilometers northeast of Tikal, includes a 47-meter-high (155-foot) pyramid temple. The Maya reworked the landscape extensively around Río Azul, constructing dams, canals, and fortifications. An intact burial chamber from about 400 A.D. was discovered here by archaeologist R. E. W. Adams, amid dozens of other tombs that had been looted. Also unusual is a pot with a screw-top lid. Río Azul is still inaccessible to visitors.

Southwest of Flores:

LA LIBERTAD
Population 1815; Altitude 180 meters; Fiesta: December 12; Kilometer 29 from Flores

Founded in about 1795 by immigrants from the Yucatán, La Libertad lies in an area of savannas. For a number of years in the nineteenth century it was the capital of the Petén.

SAYAXCHE
Population 2136; Altitude 125 meters; Fiesta: June 13; "At the ceiba tree"; Kilometer 68 from Flores

Sayaxché is a jungle port of stilt houses and huts, not far from a number of archaeological sites. The town was founded late in the nineteenth century by monks from Antigua, who set up missions in order to assert Guatemalan sovereignty in lands claimed by Mexico. The area around Sayaxché is rich in mahogany, cedar, rubber and balsam, which are exploited mainly along the rivers. The town sits on the south bank of the Río de la Pasión, a tributary of the Usumacinta that borders Chiapas. Some of the corn grown in the township is shipped by canoe upriver to Sebol, far to the south in Alta Verapaz.

Buses leave Santa Elena (near Flores) for Sayaxché twice daily (recent schedule: departures at 6 a.m. and 1 p.m.). The trip takes two hours. The bus drops you on the north bank of the river, where you can catch a cayuco or the car ferry to the other side, for a small fare.

Airstrip: West of town. No scheduled service.

Hotel: The Guayacán, to the left of the ferry landing as you cross over, is a well-kept building. Rooms are less than $5 per person, and meals are available, sometimes including wild game. Several small diners in town serve meals. There is also a fishing lodge on Lake Petexbatún (see below).

Beyond Sayaxché

Several archaeological sites are accessible from Sayaxché by water. The Tamarindito ruins sit on a north-facing rock outcrop about four kilometers west of Lake Petexbatún, which lies south of Sayaxché. Aguateca is above a creek that runs into the south side of the lake. Dos Pilas is about 12 kilometers west of the river flowing out of Lake Petexbatún to the Río de la Pasión. There are also some sulfur springs along the shore of the lake.

Don't attempt to reach the ruins without a guide. You might also want to consult the detailed maps of the Instituto Geográfico Militar in Guatemala City. The settings are spectacular, as is the jungle scenery. But the sites are relatively small, and are unrestored.

A trip by motorized cayuco can be expensive unless you've got a few people to share expenses. To Lake Petexbatún, Aguateca or Dos Pilas, the cost will be at least $60. The long trip to Yaxchilán, on the Mexican side of the Usumacinta, will cost as much as $300. Negotiate prices with the boat owners. Most cayucos will safely hold up to four people, including the operator.

Large cargo cayucos heading for Sebol, Alta Verapaz, will sometimes take on passengers. Be ready to go immediately, or to wait a week or more until a boat leaves. For more details, see the coverage of Sebol.

Fishing in Lake Petexbatún for snook, peacock bass and smaller species, and for tarpon in July and August, is said to be excellent. A lodge on the lake is available for fishing parties, and as a base for groups visiting archaeological sites. Inquire at Panamundo Guatemala Travel Service in Guatemala City to arrange accommodations at this unusual facility.

EL CEIBAL

The ruins of El Ceibal, up the Río de la Pasión from Sayaxché, can be reached by jeep (tours from hotels in Flores are available) as well as by boat. Features of the site include a stairway decorated with many glyphs, and numerous stelae. The later ones show Mexican clothing, faces, and design motifs, suggesting that the decline of the Classic Maya, at least at El Ceibal, was associated with domination by peoples from the north. Structures at El Ceibal are relatively short and, strangely, most do not use the corbeled arch typical of the Maya. The finely carved stelae, depicting priests, ballplayers and other personages, are well preserved. The last inscribed date at the site is equivalent to 889 A.D.

ALTAR DE LOS SACRIFICIOS

The ruins of Altar de los Sacrificios are downriver from Sayaxché, at the point where the Río de la Pasión joins the Chixoy River to form the Usumacinta. The site was discovered in 1895 by Teobert Maler, who named it for its great stone altars. Altar de los Sacrificios is unusual among Classic Mayan sites in that its structures were built without arches.

YAXCHILAN

Farther north, Yaxchilán stretches for several kilometers on the Mexican side of the Usumacinta, at a sharp bend. Considerable clearing has been carried out among the structures, which follow the contours of the land instead of being set on artificial platforms, as at other Mayan sites. Figures are carved on stelae and elsewhere in unusually deep relief. Interpreters of Mayan glyphs believe that Yaxchilán was ruled by the Jaguar dynasty. Dated structures were erected at the site until the equivalent of

840 A.D.
Yaxchilán and several other sites on the Usumacinta are threatened by plans for hydroelectric development.

PIEDRAS NEGRAS

Downriver from Piedras Negras on the Guatemalan bank is Piedras Negras, named for rocks of blackish limestone in the river sand. The site is thought to have flourished in Early Classic times, and is known for the carved stone lintels in its structures, and for its rather numerous stelae. Many of the important structures at the site were roofed with straw or some other perishable material. Most of the stelae, which were erected every five years, have been removed to museums, leaving the site relatively bare. The large number of stelae with obviously interrelated inscriptions enabled modern-day cryptographers to interpret Mayan glyphs indicating dynasties and city names.

The Usumacinta was an ancient trade route of the Maya, who are thought to have used it for commerce with coastal regions along the Gulf of Mexico. But strangely, few artifacts from the coast or from the Guatemalan highlands have been found at Piedras Negras.

The site is reached by boat or by chartered plane.

Travel Information

GETTING TO GUATEMALA

Airlines

From the United States, Guatemala City is served directly by: Aviateca, the Guatemalan airline, from Miami and New Orleans; Eastern, from various cities, connecting in Miami; Pan American, connecting in Houston, Miami and Los Angeles; Mexicana and TACA, from Los Angeles; and LACSA, from New York. Various airlines provide through service via Mexico City as well, and a route is projected from Cancun to Guatemala City via Belize and Flores.

The cost of flying to Guatemala is not inconsiderable. A regular economy round-trip ticket from New York currently costs about $700. From Miami, the round-trip fare is $425 (less on Aviateca). Excursion fares on direct flights and on interline routings cut these prices by about 25%. With a $50 ground package—which need only consist of lodging at budget hotels for part of your stay—the price will drop further.

You can sometimes negotiate discount fares with high-volume travel agencies. For example, I recently flew on Eastern for about a third less than the lowest price the airline would quote me directly. Shop around.

To get the latest posted fares, call the airlines: Aviateca (800-327-9832), LACSA (800-225-2272), Pan American (800-221-1111), Eastern (800-327-8376), and Mexicana (800-531-7921). Most of these numbers work from both the U.S. and Canada.

All other things being equal, choose the airline and routing that get you me to Guatemala City at the earliest time of day, especially if you're travelling without hotel reservations.

315

From Europe, Iberia, Sabena and KLM operate weekly or twice-weekly flights to Guatemala City, with stops along the way. Connections are also available through New York, Miami or Mexico City.

Onward service is available from Guatemala City to most Central American capitals, to San Andrés island in the Caribbean, and to several South American points. A stop in Guatemala can be arranged on a routing to Costa Rica and other points for little or no extra cost.

Whenever possible, buy a round-trip ticket. Tickets purchased in Guatemala are subject to local sales taxes. The Guatemalan departure tax, about $10, is not included in your ticket price.

Private Planes

Private planes may enter Guatemala if the pilot and passengers obtain visas or tourist cards in advance. Pilots must call Guatemala radio (126.9) before entering the country. Radio frequency and navigation information for Guatemala City (TGE) can be obtained from aviation maps.

The standard visual navigation system for the approach from the Mexican border is to count seven volcanoes and then turn left to Aurora Airport. Pilots who have tried this system in cloudy weather have been known to end up in El Salvador, or even worse.

Private Boats

Send a notice of arrival by wire to the captain of the port where you plan to enter Guatemala. All passengers should obtain tourist cards or visas in advance. The captain should present a list of passengers in triplicate, preferably notarized by the Guatemalan consul at the port of departure, as well as ownership documents. Boat owners who stay for a while (this will generally be at the marinas on the Río Dulce) will have to renew their boat papers periodically, in the same manner as owners of cars.

Bus

The disadvantages of bus travel all the way to Guatemala are obvious—long hours in a sitting position, inconvenient connections, border delays, and much else. You can, however, see the sights along the way, and the price is right. Total fare through Mexico to Guatemala can be as low as $50.

316

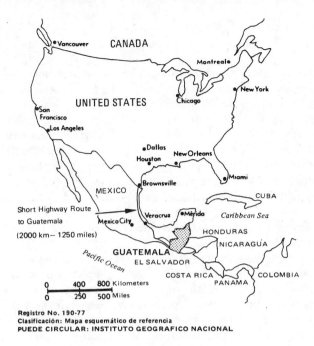

First-class buses, similar to Greyhound units, operate from all U.S. border points to Mexico City, a trip of from 10 hours to two days, depending on where you cross the border. Buses of the Cristóbal Colón line, connecting with Guatemalan buses, depart Mexico City at least twice daily for the border points of Talismán and Ciudad Cuauhtémoc, each about sixteen hours away. From eastern Texas, the trip can be shortened by taking buses along the Gulf coast to Veracruz, avoiding Mexico City.

Note that Mexican officials may require you to show a Guatemalan visa and buy a transit visa if you mention that your final destination is Guatemala. Keep your mouth closed. A tourist card or visa for Guatemala can be picked up at the Guatemalan consulate in Mexico City or Tapachula.

First-class buses operate through Central America to Panama. In case you're interested, total fare from Brownsville, Texas, is about $125. Costs can be reduced by using less comfortable, slower, second-class local buses.

Driving

If your time is limited, don't even think about driving to Guatemala, with the possibility of breakdowns, difficult mountain roads, and unfamiliar conditions. But if you're going south for the winter, or are planning extensive travel in Mexico or elsewhere in

317

Central America, if you're camping, or if your vehicle is simply indispensable, driving may be indicated. Rest assured that getting to Guatemala is eminently possible.

The shortest highway distance from Brownsville, Texas, to the Guatemalan border at Talismán is less than 2000 kilometers (1250 miles), following the Gulf coast to Acayucan, cutting south across the isthmus of Tehuantepec, then following the Pacific coast to Guatemala. On the last leg, you can also drive into the mountains by way of Comitán, in order to enter Guatemala in the highlands, at La Mesilla. Even from California, the going is easier and not much longer by following this route and avoiding mountain driving in central Mexico.

Your major requirement is a vehicle in good shape. Have it checked out, tuned up and greased before you leave home. Replace cracked or withering belts and hoses, bald tires, and rusting brake lines. If you're planning extensive travel off the main roads, consider taking a couple of spare tires, a gasoline can, water for you and the radiator, points, plugs, electrical tape, belts, wire, and basic tools. Otherwise, there's no reason to prepare for a safari, and the family sedan will serve you well. Consult your auto club for advice about dealing with the lack of unleaded gasoline.

If you stick to the main roads, driving should be only a bit more strenuous than at home. Most Mexican highways are two lanes wide, and gasoline stations are located only in major towns. Fill up when you can, with the highest grade of gasoline, and watch out for potholes, animals, people, and vehicles parked in the road.

Mexican officials may demand transit fees if you mention that your final destination is Guatemala. Visas or tourist cards for Guatemala can be obtained in Mexico City or at the Guatemalan consulate in Tapachula.

U.S. state driving licenses, Canadian provincial licenses and international licenses are all legal in Mexico and Guatemala. You will also need your vehicle registration card. The Sanborn insurance agencies in U.S. border towns usually have accurate information on road conditions in Mexico. Consult your own agent about coverage for damage to your vehicle. Only liability coverage is available in Guatemala.

Vehicle permits for Guatemala are issued at the border and are generally valid for 30 days and can be renewed. For more information, see "Getting Around," a few pages ahead.

ENTERING GUATEMALA

Tourists entering Guatemala must have visas or tourist cards, with a few exceptions. Visitors entering by land may be asked to show sufficient money to cover their expenses. No vaccination certificate is required for travellers from most countries.

Tourist Cards, valid for up to six months, are available to citizens of the United States and Canada. They cost $1 and must be used within 90 days of issue. Tourist cards can be obtained from Guatemalan consulates or from airlines, upon presentation of a passport, birth certificate, or other proof of citizenship. Currently, tourist cards are issued at Aurora airport and at border entry points as well. Children under 12 may be included on the cards of their parents. Tourist cards must be stamped by the immigration department (address below) if the visitor stays longer than 90 days (or less in some cases). A tourist card can be used for multiple entries if it retains 30 days of validity. Holders of tourist cards should also carry a passport, which is the preferred identification for cashing travellers checks.

Passports and Visas

Visas are issued by Guatemalan consulates. U.S. and Canadian citizens may obtain visas, though a tourist card may allow a longer initial stay. Tourists may apply for a visa by mail. Businessmen must appear in person. Visas are not required of citizens of: Austria, Belgium, Denmark, Finland, France, Holland, Italy, Israel, Japan, Luxembourg, Liechtenstein, Norway, Spain, Sweden, Switzerland and West Germany.

If you travel on a passport (whether or not you need a visa), and plan to stay more than 30 days, have your passport stamped by the immigration department (Migración), 8 Avenida at 12 Calle, Zone 1, Guatemala City. You'll have to apply again for permission to stay longer than 90 days. Ask at the information window for the form for a prórroga (extension), which may take a few days to process. You'll need an exit visa, unless you're a U.S. citizen, if you stay in Guatemala for more than 90 days.

Minors traveling alone should have a letter of permission from both parents, notarized by a Guatemalan consul.

319

Customs

Tourists are allowed an exemption of $100 in customs duty. No more than three liters of liquor, two cartons of cigarettes, a still and a movie camera, and six rolls of film may be included in the goods on which duty is waived. Customs officers generally won't bother you if you bring some extra film or cigarettes. The exemption is in addition to clothing and personal items that a visitor would normally need. Firearms are permitted into Guatemala only with a permit issued by the Ministry of Defense.

Border Hours and Fees

Land borders are open from 8 a.m. to noon and 2 p.m. to 6 p.m., Monday through Friday; and from 8 a.m. to noon on Saturdays. Bus and car passengers may enter outside these hours, at an extra charge of about 50 cents per person. A fee of a couple of dollars is charged all cars entering Guatemala. Vehicles entering or leaving outside regular hours pay an extra $5. A small toll is imposed at bridges on the Mexican border. The exit tax is $1.50 for all persons leaving Guatemala by land, and about $10 for those leaving by air.

Pets

Dogs should be accompanied by a certificate of vaccination, stamped at a Guatemalan consulate.

Guatemalan Consulates

U.S.A.
2220 R Street NW, Washington, DC, tel. 202-745-4952 (embassy).
548 S. Spring, Los Angeles, CA 90013, tel. 213-489-1891
870 Market Street, San Francisco, CA 94102, tel. 415-781-0118.
25 Southeast 2nd Avenue, Miami, FL 33131, tel. 305-377-3190
333 N. Michigan Ave., Chicago, IL 60601, tel. 312-332-1587.
Int. Trade Mart 1601, New Orleans, LA 70130, tel. 504-525-0013.
57 Park Avenue, New York, NY 10016, tel. 212-686-3837.
9700 Richmond Ave., Houston, TX 77042, tel. 713-953-9531.

Honorary Consulates (for visas and tourist cards only)
3109 East Warren Avenue, Denver, CO 80210, tel. 303-756-2010.
4772 East Conway Drive NW, Atlanta, GA, tel. 404-255-7019.

5803 Loch Raven Blvd., Baltimore, MD tel. 301-435-6223.
508 E. Elizabeth Street, Brownsville, TX, tel. 512-542-3506.
3010 Potomac, Dallas, TX 75205, tel. 214-363-9070.
2121 Constantinople St., Laredo, TX 78042, tel. 512-723-4343.
2001 6th Avenue, Seattle, WA 98121, tel. 206-624-5920.

Canada: 1130 De Maisonneuve W., Montreal, Quebec H3A 1M8, tel. 514-288-7327.
294 Albert St., Ottawa, Ontario K1P 6E6, tel. 613-237-3941 (embassy).

Belize: Belize City and Benque Viejo (may not operate)

El Salvador: 15 Avenida Norte 135, San Salvador, tel. 216097.

France: 73, rue de Courcelles, 75008 Paris, tel. 2277863.

Honduras: Villa Don Clemente, Col. Los Angeles, Comayaguela, tel. 335702; 4 Avenida Noroeste 28, San Pedro Sula

Mexico: 1 Calle Sur Poniente No. 42, Comitán, Chiapas;
1 Calle Central Oriente No. 10, Ciudad Hidalgo, Chiapas;
Paseo de Montejo 495, Mérida, Yucatán (honorary);
Vallarta 1, Colonia San Rafael, Mexico 4, D.F., tel. 5464876;
3 Avenida Norte No. 1, Tapachula, Chiapas.

GETTING AROUND

Driving

Driving in your own or a rented car is one of the best ways to see Guatemala. Distances between most places of interest to visitors are short, so you can take it easy and enjoy the breathtaking scenery.

Entry permits for visitors' cars (and motorcycles and bicycles and boats) are initially granted for from 30 to 90 days upon presentation of registration and license at point of entry. Extensions may be requested at the customs office (Aduana), 10 Calle between 14 and 13 avenidas, Zone 1, Guatemala City. For a small fee, one of the customs men will write out your request for an extension on legal paper.

Insurance is not required, but it will save you possible detention if you're involved in an accident. Inexpensive short-term liability policies are available at the Granai y Townson agencies in Huehuetenango and Quezaltenango, and at many agencies in Guatemala City. Coverage for damage to your own vehicle is not available, so talk to your insurance agent before you leave home.

Road Conditions: 3023 kilometers (1889 miles) of paved highways run from Guatemala City to all of the large cities and to the borders of Mexico and El Salvador. Paved roads reach all major points of interest, with the notable exception of Tikal. Surfaces on major roads are generally well maintained, but the many curves and grades in the highlands could take some getting used to.

Unpaved roads vary from good to barely passable. Some details of current conditions are mentioned in the text. Always inquire locally, preferably at a service station (gasolinera), when heading out on an unpaved road. Dry season travel is usually no problem, except for dust. The rainy season can turn dusty roads into mud. Sturdy vehicles with high clearances, such as vans, pickup trucks and jeeps, are recommended. Gasoline stations are sparse along unpaved roads, so fill up your tank before leaving a paved highway, and whenever you find a gas station thereafter. In the more remote areas, basic tools, tape and extra gasoline and water should be carried. You should also check with your embassy about possible security concerns.

Roadside kilometer posts give distances, usually from Guatemala City, but sometimes from smaller towns or junctions.

The best road map is the general map of Guatemala sold by the Instituto Geográfico Militar in Guatemala City. The Guatemala Tourist Commission map is also adequate, and your auto club can provide you with a map of Central America.

Warning signs using easily understood symbols are posted along the Pan American Highway and most major roads. On secondary roads, signs may be hand painted. Unless you know Spanish, you may think they're signs for somebody's store. The most frequent warnings and instructions are: *viraje obligado* (required turn in the direction of the arrow); *pendiente peligrosa* (dangerous grade); *frene con motor* (brake with motor); *derrumbes* (landslide zone); *túmulos* (bumps in the road surface—slow down!).

Many side roads are not posted with hazard warnings. Take it easy if you're driving a road for the first time.

322

Some local hazards and practices:

A branch on the road indicates a disabled vehicle ahead. Exercise caution. There's often no shoulder on which a vehicle in difficulty can pull off. If you break down, follow local practice and place a branch on the road to warn approaching traffic.

Beep your horn when approaching a curve. Others might not do so, so be prepared to veer suddenly.

The biggest hazard, aside from drunken drivers, is drunken pedestrians, especially on weekends and at fiesta times.

The driver going up a hill has the right of way.

Always carry your automobile documents with you. They may be checked at police posts.

Unattended automobiles should be locked and, if possible, parked in a protected area. Remove all valuables. Never leave a broken-down vehicle unattended.

Repairs: Parts for many different makes are imported to Guatemala, and are readily available in Guatemala City. If you need major service, have it done in the capital.

Car Rental: Automobiles can be rented in Guatemala City at prices higher than those in most U.S. and Canadian cities. You will be substantially liable for any damage to a rented vehicle, so confirm before leaving home that your own policy will protect you. See page 75 for listings of car-rental companies.

Camping and Trailer Parks: There are only a few trailer parks in Guatemala, located at Amatitlán south of Guatemala City, and near Flores and Tikal. Elsewhere, arrangements can be made to use hotel parking areas, or gasoline stations. It's generally unwise to pull off to the side of the highway for the night.

Towing a trailer is not a problem on most major highways. However, take a careful look at the highway notes in this book to discover a few tight spots, such as the approaches to Panajachel on Lake Atitlán.

White gasoline for Coleman stoves is difficult to obtain. LP gas tanks can be filled at plants in Guatemala City, but in few other places. Consider buying a small kerosene stove and lamp in Mexico, where such appliances are cheap. Kerosene is available everywhere.

Buses

First-class buses comparable to those operated in North America run between Guatemala City and all major cities and border points. Fares are reasonable. It costs $10 or less to go from the capital to the Mexican border, San Salvador, or Puerto Barrios. Many first-class lines will reserve seats.

Ordinary second-class buses *(camionetas)* operating to all points in the country are another story. These are similar to American school buses (some of them actually are used American school buses), with stiff seats and up to seven passengers crowded into each row. Stops are frequent at small towns and junctions, where peasants will climb aboard, place their machetes next to the driver, argue about the fare (usually unsuccessfully), and get off a few kilometers down the road. Women may clutch a recently acquired chicken or nurse their children, and somehow, a lot of people manage to doze off despite the bumping and shaking and cramped quarters. Except for small parcels, all baggage rides atop the bus. Fares on second-class buses are very cheap, less than two cents per kilometer.

Buses can be caught at their terminals or anywhere along the route simply by flagging them down. To get off, call out "aquí no más" or "baja." You have the right to request to see the fare card (tarifa) if you think the conductor is ripping you off. Retain your fare receipt ("ticket") until you leave the bus, when you hand it to the driver.

Be aware that even though drivers of ordinary buses make every effort to accommodate just one more passenger, sometimes you will not be taken aboard at mid-route. If time is important to you, not to mention comfort, rely on buses mainly to travel between major towns. If you're hopping from place to place by bus, plan to finish your travel well before nightfall. There is hardly any bus service after dark.

If traveling by bus, you'll often have to get an early start to make the best connections. A travel alarm clock will be useful. Also, tell the manager of your hotel that you'll be leaving early, and just in case, find out who has the key to the front door and where he sleeps. Hotel entrances are often chained shut for the night, and on a number of occasions I've had to make daring escapes from second-story windows (breaking and exiting) in order to catch an early bus. You can achieve some comfort by trying to ride in the front, where there's less bouncing, and if you've got long legs, you might try to get the seat behind the driver, or else

324

sit next to the aisle. Make sure that you go to the bathroom before you get on a bus (nobody else will tell you this), and don't drink too much coffee before you set out.

Unless you reserve a seat on a first-class bus, get to the terminal early. Buses often fill up long before departure time.

Current schedules for many destinations are given in this book. To go to a place for which no schedule is listed, ask for information at the tourist office in Guatemala City, or at the bus terminal in a nearby large town. Bus companies are listed in the telephone directory under "Transportes de Pasajeros Extraurbanos."

Taxis

If you're with a few other people, it's economical and convenient to go by first-class bus to a large town, and then hire a taxi for excursions to nearby small towns, to which bus service may be inconvenient or uncomfortable. Even intercity taxi runs are a practical alternative to cramped buses or tours. From Guatemala City to Panajachel on Lake Atitlán, a trip of 145 kilometers (90 miles), you might expect to pay about $75. Always get guidance about fares from the local tourist office before you engage a taxi.

Tours

Tour buses operate from Guatemala City to all major areas of interest, except Tikal, which you can reach by a combination of plane and tour bus. Most excursions are for one day and take you back to the capital, although staying in the countryside is much to be preferred. Some of the available tours are mentioned in the Guatemala City chapter. From time to time, tours are available from Antigua, Panajachel and Quezaltenango as well.

Packages of hotel, meal and tour arrangements that you book when you buy your airplane ticket vary from a few nights in a hotel in the capital to complete arrangements for a week of travel around the country. The low-price packages allow you to take advantage of cheaper air fares. The more complete packages, of course, spare you much planning and attention to details.

Air Service

Domestic service is limited to flights from Guatemala City to Flores, which serves as a gateway to Tikal and the Petén. Service is provided by Aviateca, the national airline, and a couple of smaller companies. There are numerous airstrips around the country, and direct flights in small planes and helicopters to towns and archaeological sites can be arranged through companies at the airport in Guatemala City, or through travel agents.

Boats

There is scheduled boat service across Lake Atitlán from Panajachel, from Mariscos to El Estor on Lake Izabal, and from Puerto Barrios to Lívingston. Small boats can be hired for cruising on Lake Atitlán, Lake Izabal, and the Río Dulce.

Trains

Service from Guatemala City to the Pacific lowlands and to Puerto Barrios is provided by Guatemala's rickety, low-priced trains. See page 84.

Directory of Practical Information

Business Hours

Hours mentioned in the Guatemala City section apply generally throughout the country. Note that the midday break is rarely referred to as the "siesta." It doesn't take long to get used to doing your shopping before noon or after 2 p.m.

Children

I've travelled around Guatemala with one of my children. He liked the bus rides more than his mother and father did, loved climbing Mayan temples and palaces, and enjoyed swimming. But he didn't appreciate being told not to touch this and not to eat that. Personally, I think it would be hard to take small children from place to unfamiliar place by bus and car for more than a short period, and this is the kind of travel that suits Guatemala. On the other hand, if you're settling in for a few months in one or a couple of places, Guatemala could be a great place for the kids. In any case, you know your own children.

In general, take the same precautions for children as for adults (see Staying Healthy, below). Speak to your pediatrician or consult your community health department before you travel. If you're going to spend time in the sun—and it's practically unavoidable, even if you don't go to a beach—make sure that your child gets plenty to drink, and stays covered up at first. And of course, watch what your child puts in his mouth, and what other people give him.

Pack clothing items similar to those for adults. As well, take a few books and toys (the latter are expensive locally), including a pail and shovel for the beach. Take baby wipes for quick clean-ups. Children need their own identification for immigration purposes, even if they're included on your tourist card.

For babies, take changing supplies and bottle-feeding equipment, if needed. Disposable diapers are available in many towns, but not always in all sizes. The price is higher than in the States, so you might want to take some along.

Gerber baby foods (instant cereals and strained vegetables and meats) are available in supermarkets in large towns, and sometimes in pharmacies in rural areas. Other readily available food items for babies include canned condensed milk, refrigerated pasteurized milk in some areas, canned fruit juice, cheeses, fruits, and powdered formulas.

With kids in tow, you'll spend considerable time in your hotel room. Be more selective than you might otherwise be. A television in the room and a swimming pool are attractive amenities for the kids, even if you don't need them for yourself.

Hotels in Guatemala rarely charge for children up to three years old. Older children will pay a small extra-bed charge.

If you decide to rent a house or stay in a hotel for an extended length of time, you'll find that you can hire a mother's helper for very little money. Or you can engage a short-term baby sitter through many hotels. A laundress can usually be found to wash and boil cloth diapers.

Private nursery schools and elementary schools in large towns will generally accept visitors' children for short-term enrollment. There are bilingual schools in Guatemala City and Antigua. Most schools are closed in December and part of January for summer vacation.

Cost of Living

If you take a look at the prices mentioned throughout this book, you'll see that the cost of living in Guatemala is rather low. In almost any town, a good meal can be obtained for $3 or less, and comfortable lodging is available for $5 or less. Second-class bus transportation is available for less than 2 cents per kilometer, and first-class travel for slightly more. It's still possible for two people to travel in Guatemala at a basic level and keep expenses for food and lodging to the proverbial five dollars per day. Even in the best resort hotels, a room rarely costs more than $60 double.

Nevertheless, some things are expensive in Guatemala. Imported items are subject to high customs duties. Film, tape recorders, cameras and radios all cost about double, in dollars, what they do in the United States. Good western-style clothing usually costs a bit more than in the States, though blue jeans are exported and it's inexpensive to have clothing made to order. Gasoline costs slightly more than in the States, and automobile ownership and maintenance are expensive.

Canned and packaged foods can be expensive, especially if they're imported from outside Central America. A can of evaporated milk, for example, will sell for about a dollar, while fresh pasteurized milk goes for 40 cents a quart in Guatemala City. Beef is somewhat cheaper than in the United States, and is one of Guatemala's major exports. Local rum and drinkable vermouth can be found for as little as $2 a bottle. A six-pack of beer costs $3 or more. A cheap French wine is at least $5 per bottle. Baby food costs about 50 percent more than in the States.

Fresh produce varies in price considerably from season to season. In the town where I lived for a number of years, for example, tomatoes cost about eight cents per pound during the dry season, but more than 50 cents during the rainy season. Price variations tend to be less in Guatemala City. If you buy what's in season and what's produced locally, your food costs will be very low.

Cigarettes range upward in price from about 50 cents per pack for local brands to about a dollar for American and British brands manufactured in Guatemala. Good cigars and pipe tobacco are expensive.

Housing varies considerably in cost. In small towns, comfortable houses, when available, may be rented for from $150 per month, exclusive of appliances that might normally be included in North America. Rents are higher in resort and vacation areas, such as Lake Atitlán and Antigua, and much higher in Guatemala City. With low wages for household workers, fewer electrical appliances, minimal real-estate taxes, and no need for heating, total housing costs are quite low.

In general, persons who are not too attached to mechanical gadgets and pre-packaged, processed foods can maintain a comfortable standard of living for less than in the United States.

Climate and Weather

Despite the "eternal spring" label often applied to Guatemala, weather conditions vary considerably from region to region and season to season.

The difference between rainy season and dry season is most clearly defined in the highlands and along the Pacific coast. The dry season lasts from late October or early November through late April or early May. It's called *verano,* or summer, even though Guatemala is in the northern hemisphere. In the highlands, days are warm and sunny, except for a very rare rainstorm. Nights are clear, ideal for stargazing when the moon's not out. With the absence of clouds, the day's heat dissipates quickly. Nights can be positively chilling at the higher altitudes, and winds add to the effect. A heavy sweater is a necessity if you're out late or getting up early. Temperatures sometimes drop below freezing above 2150 meters (7000 feet).

April is the warmest month in the highlands. Days are longer, and there are few breezes. Temperatures rise to about 85 degrees Fahrenheit (30 Centigrade) for a few hours in the afternoon. During the rest of the year, the high will be from 75° to 80° F (25° to 27° C), with much variation according to altitude.

The rainy season, or "winter," starts at the end of April or sometimes as late as the middle of May. Mornings are clear, but the sky is usually overcast for at least a few hours in the afternoon. Nights are warmer in the highlands during the rainy season, as the clouds hold in the heat of the day.

It's a rare day in the rainy season when there isn't at least some sun. The general pattern is for clear skies in the morning to be followed by the approach of dark clouds and then a downpour. The dark clouds usually give you enough warning to head for shelter. The rains may last for an hour or continue into the night. Usually, the skies clear up for a while in the afternoon. Rainfall is much heavier along the coast than in the highlands. June and September are the months when it rains most.

For rainy season travel, take along a raincoat or umbrella. There are enough sunny hours for swimming, walking and sightseeing.

To the north and northeast of Guatemala City, the rainy season isn't as well defined as in the southern part of the country. The Petén receives some rainfall throughout the year, though it's generally light from February to April. In Alta Verapaz and along the Caribbean, rainfall is lightest in December and from February to April, when there are only a few days of precipitation. As in the south, temperature ranges depend on altitude, though Alta Verapaz lacks the cold extremes of some of the higher elevations to the west of Guatemala City. Near the Caribbean, the high temperature may approach 100° F (37° C) in May and June, while in January it's usually about 86° F (30° C). It's always cooler along the beaches.

Courtesy

Most Guatemalans are pleasantly formal. You'll fit into the local scene better if you observe local courtesies.

In small towns in the highlands, it's normal to say "buenos días" (good morning) or "buenas tardes" (good afternoon) to anybody you pass on the street. Elsewhere, and in big cities, it's better to keep your mouth closed.

Likewise, it's proper to give a general greeting when you get on a bus or enter a small eatery, and to say "gracias" when you get off or leave. Always use the formal "buenos días," "buenas tardes," or "buenas noches" (good evening). "Hola" (hi) is a distressingly familiar form.

Shake hands when you're introduced to somebody. A light handshake rather than a bonecrusher is appropriate.

Try not to be outlandish in your dress. Take a look around and see what's the norm. In the highlands, for example, it's considered gross to go around in shorts or abbreviated outfits, and to show too much thigh or chest or bouncing breast. Bathing suits are considered proper for the beach only. In the lowlands, attitudes are more relaxed.

Locals are becoming accustomed to seeing tourists in Indian clothing, with men wearing women's huipiles and women in men's shirts. Try to sort out the gender of your clothing, and don't go overboard in dressing as a native.

Guatemalans, who are soft-spoken, sometimes find foreigners terribly loud. Use a moderate tone of voice, even if you're arguing with somebody.

Try to be unobtrusive when taking photos of people. If you've blown your cover, ask for permission to take the picture (which may cost a few cents). A telehoto lens will help you to get close-ups with a minimum of hassle. Avoid photographing religious rituals, unless they're of a public nature (such as fiesta processions).

Earthquakes

Earthquakes are frequent in Guatemala. Most are minor tremors, and if you're not used to them, you may mistake the rumblings of the earth for the vibrations caused by a passing truck. Major earthquakes, such as that of February 4, 1976, have occurred about every 50 years or so.

In the unlikely event that you're caught in a major quake, in Guatemala or elsewhere, stand in a doorway, or get outside if possible. The greatest danger is in collapsing roofs. The pretty tile roofs of houses in the highlands did much damage in the 1976 quake. In many cases they were supported by nothing more than rotting wooden beams.

Electricity

Electricity in Guatemala City and in most of the country is supplied at 110 volts alternating current. In a few smaller towns, service is at 220 volts. When you're outside of any large city, check the local voltage before you plug anything in. Sockets take standard American plugs without grounding prongs. Some isolated towns have their own generators, which may be turned on only at night.

Fishing

Guatemala's lakes aren't especially known for their sport fishing. Mountain lakes such as Atitlán and Amatitlán are rich in mojarras, pepescas, pupos and butes, which will be familiar to some visitors as the cichlids, banded tetras, mollies and toothcarps that they keep in their aquaria at home. Such tropical fish are sometimes caught and eaten by locals, but they're not much sport. Lake Atitlán also has eels, black bass and crappies, though few hotels provide fishing equipment. Natives use spears to get the black bass. In Lake Petexbatún, in the Petén, snook and peacock bass are found, as well as tarpon at the height of the rainy season, in July and August.

In the lowlands, Lake Izabal offers snook (róbalo), tarpon (sábalo), and mullet (lisa) for sport fishing and eating, as well as sawfish. Out in Caribbean waters are snook, snappers (pargo), tarpon, mullet and crevalle jacks. There are also also oysters, crabs and shrimp, and, along the reefs, turtles and mussels. Tarpon in large numbers enter the rivers, especially the Río Dulce, from March to June. In the flats near the Belizean border bonefish and permit are plentiful. Fishing boats and equipment are available at hotels along the Río Dulce. On the Pacific side, there are yellow and black tuna, snappers, bonito, crevalle jacks, roosterfish, and plentiful dorado from about three miles out. Sailfish, also quite large, are farther out, and in deep waters, twenty miles offshore, are marlin. Except for some shrimping, not much fishing is done from Guatemala's Pacific ports, though the sports potential is great.

Serious sport fishermen should bring their own equipment.

Flora and Fauna

There's not much interesting or exotic animal life in the southern, heavily populated part of Guatemala. This is because the land has been used for settled agriculture for many centuries, and wild animals have been hunted and killed, not for their food value, but to prevent them from doing damage to crops. In the countryside, one will see such small forest creatures as squirrels, skunks and an occasional snake or fox. But the deer and other large animals that figure in the designs of traditional highland weaving are now rare. The northern jungles of the Petén are quite another story. There, on a visit to Tikal, one has a good chance of running across spider monkeys and howler monkeys, armadillos, deer and tepezcuintles (spotted cavies). Off the beaten track are jaguars, pumas, and wild boars. The rush to settle the Petén has seen little provision for protection of jungle animals, and some could become extinct in the not-too-distant future.

Birds are too vast a subject for more than passing mention here. Guatemala's symbol of national liberty is the quetzal, a rare species of trogon reputedly unable to live in captivity. The quetzal has been sighted in the forests of Alta Verapaz and high on the slopes of some volcanoes. A stuffed quetzal forms part of Guatemala's coat of arms in the reception hall of the national palace in Guatemala City. Bird watchers know, of course, of Guatemala's enviable reputation as a home or stopover for hundreds of species, and will review and bring along their bird books, as well as check out the variety of stuffed native birds on display at the Museum of Natural History in Aurora Park in Guatemala City. For an extensive Guatemala bird list, send $2 to Russ's Natural History Books, Box 1089, Lake Helen, Florida 32744-1089.

Flora constitute a subject even more overwhelming and intimidating than birds, given the variety of climates in Guatemala. Most notable are the orchids that flourish in highland forests, including the national flower, the *monja blanca* (white nun). The national tree is the *ceiba* (kapok, or silk cotton), which shades the main square of many a lowland town with its long-reaching, leafy branches. To give you an idea of the variety of flora in Guatemala, here are some examples of the wild and cultivated trees and plants found at different altitudes:

Sea level to 600 meters: palms (coconut palm, African oil palm, American oil palm, etc.), logwood, mangrove, sapodilla (chewing-gum tree, or *chicozapote),* mahogany, cedar, lignum-vitae, macawood *(hormigo),* laurel, quinine, banana, rubber, walnut, guanacaste earpod, silk cotton *(ceiba),* cotton, cacao, sugar cane, rice, bamboo.

600 to 1800 meters: coffee, corn, beans, cardamom, citronella, ramie, agave (century plant), pasture grass, liquidambar, wild fig *(amate),* orchids and bromeliads, citrus, avocado, mango, cactus, pomegranate, papaya.

1800 meters and higher: pine, fir trees (silvertree, etc.), cypress, alder, madrone, oak, elder, willow, wheat, oats, barley, peach, apple.

Visitors interested in Guatemala's plant life should stop in at the botanical garden in Guatemala City, where a wide range of species is represented.

Food and Drink

Unless the visitor makes an effort, he will probably encounter few distinctively Guatemalan dishes. Many restaurants serve what is locally known as international cuisine, which is a combination of standard North American and European food. Most items on the menu will be familiar to visitors: *bistec* (beef), *pollo* (chicken), *mixtos* (ham and cheese sandwiches), *hamburguesas* (hamburgers) and *chuletas* (pork chops). Some of this nomenclature can be deceiving in the native environment, however. For example, except at a McDonald's or similar franchise, your hamburguesa will consist of a speck of meat in a bath of mayonnaise and wilted lettuce. Be tolerant at modest eateries, or ask in detail about what you'll be getting.

Genuinely Guatemalan dishes are usually eaten at home, in the more inexpensive restaurants, at eateries in markets, and in a rare better restaurant advertising its *comida típica* (native food). In such places, the bistec is likely to be a strip of beef, grilled over coals and served with *chirmol,* a sauce of fresh tomatoes, onions

334

and spices. The hot sauce— *salsa picante* or *salsa de chile* —is usually placed in a separate dish for the diner to add as he chooses. Those who want a tender piece of meat ask for *carne guisada* stewed beef served in a tasty sauce. Most beef in Guatemala is on the tough side, since it's fed on grass and isn't aged or chemicaly tenderized. But the better restaurants manage to soften it, sometimes by pounding a steak into a large wafer.

Vegetables on the side may include *guisquil*, or vegetable pear, a vine vegetable cooked in much the same way as potatoes, and there might also be some *guacamole*, mashed avocados served with onions and tomatoes. Instead of bread, a native-style meal is served with tortillas, flat cakes made from corn soaked in lime water (which softens the outer layer of the kernel) and then ground. Tortillas are used to scoop up bits of food and to make little fold-over sandwiches. Ideally, the meal should be taken in a small eatery, with a charcoal or smoky wood fire in the corner, and the food washed down with beer or steaming cups of coffee to fight the chill of the evening air.

A standard breakfast in a small town will probably include oatmeal *(mosh)* flavored with sticks of cinnamon, or corn flakes served with hot milk, eggs, black beans with white, crumbly cheese, tortillas, and steaming cups of weak coffee. The ideal setting is the same.

Other local specialties include *plátanos fritos*, fried plantains (green bananas); *chiles rellenos*, stuffed peppers; breaded and fried native vegetables, such as *pacaya*, which has long, finger-like appendages and a slightly bitter taste; and *chuchitos* corn dough stuffed with spicy meat and wrapped in a corn husk. An occasional appearance will be made by the Mexican enchilada, a tortilla rolled around a chicken or cheese filling. These items are often sold as snack food by roadside vendors who stand at highway junctions and scurry aboard buses that stop for a few minutes. You'll also have a good chance of finding native food at a place that advertises itself as a *comedor* (diner), rather than at a *restaurante*.

A few items appear only on holidays. *Tamales*, the big brothers of chuchitos, may have a spicy turkey filling in the corn dough, and are wrapped in banana leaves. *Fiambre* is a sort of salad prepared from vegetables and bits of meat and fish. *Pepián* is a dish of meat served in a dark, spicy sauce that includes squash seeds.

Coffee is one of the disappointments in many a smaller

Guatemalan restaurant. Guatemala produces some of the finest mild coffee in the world. But most of the good stuff goes for export. Cheaper restaurants will usually serve a weak brew made from second-rate beans, often with the sugar already added. You'll get used to it, maybe, as a part of standard native cuisine. When the coffee's good, however, it's superb. In better restaurants, coffee is served either black, or half and half with hot milk. You'll sometimes be brought small pots of hot coffee and milk to mix in the proportions that please you. The concept of coffee with cream is understood only in hotels and restaurants that have a foreign clientele.

Variety in food is provided by restaurants serving foreign cuisines, usually Spanish, German or Chinese. Most of these are in Guatemala City, but there are Chinese restaurants in many large towns, and Chinese dishes may be served in any eatery. These days, chow mein (or *chao mein*, as it's known locally) is as Guatemalan as a good *hamburguesa*.

Quality of service in restaurants varies considerably. In general, things will be a bit slower than what you're used to, and you'll have to call the waiter when you want the bill (*la cuenta*). There's no need to tip in small, family-run eateries, though it's a nice gesture. In larger restaurants, ten percent of the bill is usually an adequate tip.

For reassurance about whether the food's safe to eat, see "Stay Healthy," below.

Guatemala produces excellent beer. Popular brands include Gallo (Rooster) and Cabro (Goat). Higher-priced brands are Medalla de Oro and Marzen. Moza is a good dark beer. Most beers come in the bottle, though draft beer is available in Guatemala City and some of the larger towns. Beer has a relatively light alcoholic content, but if you are not used to the altitude, it will wallop you.

The most popular local liquors are rum *(ron)* and *aguardiente*, which, like rum, is distilled from sugar cane. Most rums are quite good. Decent vodka is also distilled locally. Guatemala produces whiskey, anisette and a variety of other spirits. Like rum and aguardiente, they're low-priced, but quality is not high.

Liquor is sold in bottles ranging from an *octavo* (an eighth of a liter, or about four ounces) to a *botella* (three-quarters of a liter, or about a fifth). Imported liquor is quite expensive.

Local wines are made from grape concentrates, oranges, and

cashew fruit. They're not award winners, though some of the local grape wines, such as Santa Vittoria, can be tolerated by the unfussy. Local vermouths are a better bet. The cheaper wines are quite sweet, and are best mixed with soda water or avoided. Look for a wine made from *mosto de uva* or *pasas,* rather than an orange or cashew-fruit wine.

The cheapest places for drinking are ordinary bars without licenses to serve mixed drinks. At these places, you can order a small bottle of liquor for about the price you would pay in a grocery store, along with some juice or bottled sodas, and mix your own drinks at your table. Cheap bars are best frequented in small towns. Bars serving mixed drinks are more expensive. You can often bring your own bottle to better restaurants, but you may have to pay a bottle fee, called the *descorche.* Most bars serve snacks *(boquitas)* with drinks.

All supermarkets in Guatemala City have large selections of liquor, wine and beer. In smaller towns, you can purchase liquor by the bottle at bars and small grocery stores *(tiendas)*, though the selection may not be large. The deposit on a beer or soda bottle may be higher than the cost of the contents.

Geographical Notes

Mountains: The major mountains of Guatemala are part of the Sierra Madre-Andes chain. The main branch crosses southern Guatemala from west to east. In the western highlands, the peaks of the Sierra Madre rise to more than 3000 meters. The mountains east of Guatemala City are lower. The Cuchumatanes, a branch of the Sierra Madre in the department of Huehuetenango, include the highest non-volcanic peaks in the country, reaching up to 3800 meters above sea level. The Chamá mountains in Alta Verapaz are a lower continuation of the Cuchumatanes, separated from the main range by the Chixoy River. Their eastern continuation is the Santa Cruz range on the northern side of Lake Izabal. Other mountain ranges are the Sierra de Chuacús in the southern part of the departments of El Quiché and Baja Verapaz, and their continuation to the Caribbean, the Sierra de las Minas, which forms the northern part of the valley of the Motagua River; the Mico range bordering the Caribbean lowlands to the north; and the Copán range along the border with Honduras.

Volcanoes: There about thirty named volcanoes in Guatemala, most running in a chain between the Pacific lowlands and the main branch of the Sierra Madre mountains. The actual volcano count is a matter of some confusion. A couple of peaks in the Quezaltenango region, Zunil (3542 meters) and Santo Tomás (3505 meters), and Santa Clara (2450 meters), near Lake Atitlán, used to be included, until the National Geographic Institute decided that these were the eroded peaks of run-of-the-mill mountains. There are also mini-volcanoes and secondary craters. Cerro de Oro (1892 meters), dwarfed by its neighbor the Tolimán volcano, is not counted, perhaps because it rises only 300 meters above the surface of nearby Lake Atitlán. In any case, a book about Guatemala is supposed to include a list of volcanoes, so here are the ones with altitudes of more than 2000 meters, and the towns near which they're located:

Tajumulco	4220 meters	Tajumulco, San Marcos
Tacaná	4093	Sibinal, San Marcos
Acatenango	3975	Alotenango, Sacatepéquez
Santa María	3772	Zunil, Quezaltenango
Agua	3766	Santa María de Jesús, Sac.
Fuego	3763	Alotenango, Sacatepéquez
Atitlán	3537	San Lucas Tolimán, Sololá
Siete Orejas	3370	San Martín Sacatepéquez, Quez.
Tolimán	3158	San Lucas Tolimán, Sololá
Cerro Quemado	3027	Quezaltenango, Quezaltenango
San Pedro	3020	San Pedro La Laguna, Sololá
Chicabal	2900	San Martín Sacatepéquez, Quez.
San Antonio	2750	San Antonio Sac., San Marcos
Lacandón	2747	Ostuncalco, Quezaltenango
Cuxliquel	2610	Totonicapán, Totonicapán
Pacaya	2552	San Vicente Pacaya, Escuintla
Jumay	2176	Jalapa, Jalapa
Alzatate	2045	San Carlos Alzatate, Jalapa
Suchitán	2042	Santa Catarina Mita, Jutiapa

For the Guatemalan who lives nearby, a volcano is a useful bit of real estate for growing corn or some other crop, and something to watch out for in case an eruption should spew ashes onto his crop or send a boulder flying through the roof of his house. Over the longer term, eruptions have their benefits. Weathered volcanic soil is rich in organic matter, phosphates and nitrates,

338

and retains water. Volcanic products useful to the ancient Maya included obsidian (volcanic glass), out of which tools were made, clay (weathered ash) and hematite, or iron-oxide pigment.

For the visitor who doesn't see a volcano every day, and who perhaps has read a novel by Malcolm Lowry, a volcano is of great psychic and magical value, signifying the life-forces of the universe grumbling just under the surface of the earth. When one is this close, it's tempting to hasten up to the crater of a handy volcano, as evidenced by the people who climb Agua and Atitlán, sometimes by the dozen, and camp out at the top on the night of a full moon. The magnificent views are more than sufficient reward for most who make it all the way up and back.

There are, however, some possible drawbacks. For the visitor who is not in excellent physical shape, a successful ascent and descent will be followed by days of soreness, which could make the remainder of a vacation miserable. And an attempt to go up alone, or in the rainy season, or without camping equipment or food or warm clothing, or in ignorance of where the trails are supposed to go, could be fatal. The ascent of most of the volcanoes in Guatemala is an arduous task, not an easy daytime outing.

Rivers: Guatemala's rivers are divided into three groups. Those that flow down to the Pacific are relatively short, and include, among others, the Suchiate, Tilapa, Naranjo, Madre Vieja, Michatoya, Los Esclavos and Paz. The longer rivers rise in the highlands and flow toward the Caribbean or the Gulf of Mexico. The major river of the first group, the Motagua, rises not far from Chichicastenango, runs eastward, and then turns to the northeast for its long trip down a dry valley to the Caribbean. The Polochic and its tributaries drain much of Alta Verapaz, empty into lake Izabal, and then into the Caribbean as the Río Dulce. To the north, the Usumacinta runs along the border with Mexico, picking up the waters of the Pasión and other rivers that drain the Petén, and carries as well the waters of the Río Chixoy, or Negro, along which a large hydroelectric project is sited. In the department of Huehuetenango, the westward-flowing Cuilco and Selegua are tributaries of the Grijalva River, which crosses southern Mexico and empties into the Gulf of Mexico, as does the Usumacinta.

Lakes: The largest lake in Guatemala is Izabal, near the Caribbean, but the most beautiful is Atitlán, in the western

339

highlands. Others are Amatitlán, south of Guatemala City; Guija, on the border of El Salvador; Ipala, in the crater of the volcano of the same name in the department of Chiquimula; and Petén Itzá, Petexbatún and many others in the Petén.

How to Get into Trouble

Laws and customs, and the way they're enforced, may differ in Guatemala from what you are used to. In order to avoid problems, you should be aware of local practices. Some pointers:

Possession of any illegal drug, including marijuana, can lead to a prison sentence of from three to five years, as well as heavy fines and civil penalties. Be discreet. Even if you eventually beat a drug rap, you could languish in jail for months while a judge intermittently investigates the case. Your embassy will probably be of little use.

Carry your passport or tourist card at all times. You may be asked for identification and searched by police or the army at checkpoints and roadblocks. Treat the authorities with appropriate deference.

Guns, of course, should not be carried, but pocket and hunting knives can also be considered illegal weapons. And, at times, customs, military and police officials have been known to regard fancy radios, electronics equipment and other unfamiliar items as suspicious. Avoid trouble by leaving the gizmos at home.

Though its tempting to try to extend your stay by working in Guatemala, even at low wages, without a work permit you'll have no protection against employer abuses.

Although you're on vacation, exercise normal precautions. Women especially should not go around unaccompanied at night, especially on weekends and at fiesta times, when liquor flows. Keep valuables in a safe place. Pickpockets lurk at fiestas and in crowded markets.

If you have a problem with the police, be polite and try to understand what the difficulty is. For minor offenses, such as drunkenness or creating a disturbance, it's probably best to submit to a small fine. For major offenses, remember that you have the right to get in touch with your embassy, though it may not be very helpful.

Money and Banking

Guatemala's currency is the quetzal, named after the national bird. The quetzal is divided into 100 centavos.

Guatemalan paper currency comes in 50-centavo, one-quetzal, and larger-denomination notes. All banknotes bear an illustration of the quetzal, as well as both Arabic and Mayan numerals. The 25-centavo coin has a portrait of a woman of Santiago Atitlán; the ten-centavo coin a stela from Quiriguá; the five-centavo coin the ceiba, the national tree; and the one-centavo coin a portrait of Friar Bartolomé de las Casas, protector of Indians in colonial times.

For decades the quetzal was worth exactly one U.S. dollar. But foreign debt, low prices for Guatemala's principal exports, and loss of confidence in the economy and government led to a collapse in the value of the quetzal in the mid-1980s. At this time, it is worth approximately 40 cents American.

At present, banks pay a free-market rate for U.S. dollars slightly above the official rate, and street money changers—who cluster around the main post office in Guatemala City—pay slightly more. There is some danger, of course, in changing your money with street characters who could abscond with your travelers checks. Try one of the stores near the post office, or ask a resident foreigner to steer you to an honest black marketer. If such dealings make you nervous, then by all means change your money at a bank, where the rate is only slightly lower and still gives you a lot of buying power.

Banks will accept U.S.-dollar travelers checks for exchange into quetzales, but some will not take U.S. cash. Canadian cash and other currencies are useless in Guatemala.

Spend or exchange your quetzales before leaving Guatemala. Exchange offices abroad pay unfavorable rates.

Travelers Checks can be cashed at most commercial banks in Guatemala City, when you present your passport. Outside the capital, cash travelers checks at branches of the Banco de Guatemala located in the major town of each department. Hours are 8:30 a.m. to 2 p.m. on Mondays through Thursdays, to 2:30 p.m. on Fridays. In villages where there are no banks, and on weekends, travelers checks may be useless. Make sure you have local cash for the weekend and before setting off to small towns.

The quickest way to get money from home is to have a bank order a telegraphic or Telex transfer through one of the large banks in Guatemala City. For reasons I have never understood, banks at home often send the money to a different bank from the one you specify. A more reliable but slower alternative is to have an international money order sent to you by registered mail. Regular money orders and personal checks are difficult to cash.

Credit Cards—American Express, Diners Club, Master Card and Visa—are accepted by airlines, by most hotels that charge $10 or more for a single room, and by many restaurants and stores in Guatemala City. Master Card cash advances can be obtained from some banks, and from Credomatic de Guatemala, 7 Avenida 6-26, Zone 9, Guatemala City, with a five percent kickback subtracted from the proceeds. Your rate of exchange when using a credit card may be less favorable than what you get for exchanging cash or travellers checks.

Post Office
The main post office in Guatemala City is open weekdays from 8 a.m. until 6 p.m., until noon on Saturdays. Elsewhere, weekday hours are 8 a.m. to 4:30 p.m., though there may be some local variation.

Among causes for delayed or disappearing mail are illegible foreign writing, failure to mark letters "air mail" *(correo aéreo)*, letters from abroad marked "Guatemala, Mexico" or with similar nonsense, insufficient postage, and enclosure of valuables. If you have any doubt about the proper postage, weigh your letter at the post office, and tell your friends at home to do the same. And never, never, ever send anything of the slightest value except by registered mail, and never send cash.

Postal rates are quite cheap by world standards. It costs less than the equivalent of 10 cents U.S. to send a five-gram letter (one sheet of air mail paper in an air envelope) to North America, for example.

Parcels should be wrapped securely in cardboard boxes (which are sold in most small stores), covered with brown paper, and tied with cord. The clerk may want to inspect the contents, so be prepared to unwrap. Insurance on new items is available to most countries for a small fee. Payment of postage is by the even kilo. Packages take about two weeks to reach the U.S. by air, up to six weeks by surface, longer to other countries. The rate for air parcels to the U.S. is under $1 per kilogram. Rates to Canada are slightly higher, and are much higher to Europe.

Postal regulations are subject to local whim. In small towns, clerks may accept parcels only early in the morning, or may impose lower weight limits than the official ones (ten kilos to most countries). You could face a wait of hours when several tourists with parcels descend on a lone postal clerk in some un-metropolitan locale. Avoid hassles by mailing your parcels in Guatemala City, when possible. There are also agencies, such as the Pink Box in Antigua and Panajachel, which will take care of mailing.

To receive general delivery mail, have it addressed to your name at Lista de Correos in the town and department where you'll pick it up. For example:

Harry Matamibas
Lista de Correos
Antigua Guatemala, Sacatepéquez
Guatemala, Central America

A small fee is charged for each general delivery letter picked up. Mail is held for a month, sometimes longer.

Avoid having items sent to you in Guatemala. Though books, newspapers, magazines and tape recordings will get through without any problem, almost all other merchandise must be picked up in Guatemala City after payment of a heavy customs duty. Tell the folks at home to send a money order instead (by registered mail).

Retirement in Guatemala

Under a law enacted in 1973, retired persons with a stable income of $350 per month may establish residence in Guatemala and enjoy a number of benefits not usually granted to foreigners or Guatemalans.

Among these benefits are: an exemption of $7000 in customs duties on household furnishings; permission to import an automobile free of duty every four years; and exemption from taxes on income from abroad. Other advantages for retirees are: a mild climate and beautiful surroundings; a genuinely friendly attitude toward foreigners; and a generally low cost of living, especially for household help, fresh food and local liquor.

Among possible disadvantages: the complexity of proving amount and stability of income; difficulty in communicating in

343

Spanish; availability of housing suitable for retirees in only a few communities; periodic instability; the high cost of trips back home, and of certain goods; and concentration of services, ranging from medical specialists to repair of exotic automobiles, in Guatemala City.

Obviously, retirement in Guatemala is quite different from visiting as a tourist, and requires careful consideration. An English translation of the retirement law, and applications for retirement residence, are available from Guatemalan consulates and from the tourist office in Guatemala City.

Shopping and Bargaining

More than in most countries, one of the main activities of visitors in Guatemala is shopping. Hand-woven clothing and Indian textiles, heavy woolen blankets, jewelry, antiques, and such utilitarian items as hammocks, kitchen utensils and pottery, are all available at reasonable and sometimes ridiculously low prices.

One of the biggest choices is whether to buy in a store or in markets. Stores usually offer fixed prices, though in some cases you can get the price down. The larger handicraft stores in Guatemala City and in a few other towns frequented by visitors, such as Antigua and Panajachel, often have a more varied selection of higher quality items than you'll find in a market. The prices are usually higher than those you'll be able to obtain by going directly to Indian artisans. But unless you're planning to buy large quantities of one item or will be going to many of the smaller towns, you can do fairly well by shopping in stores.

In markets, you'll be doing a lot of bargaining. Some of the key phrases in striking a deal are: ¿Cuánto vale? (How much is it?); ¿Cuánto menos? (For how much less will you sell it?); ¿Cuánto lo menos? (What's your lowest price?) The vendor will say to you at various times in the bargaining process: Hay trato, puede ofrecer (You can bargain, you can make an offer); ¿Cuánto mas? (How much more will you pay?).

Most likely, you'll have no idea of what is a fair price for any piece of merchandise. Test out the prices by negotiating with a few sellers. But remember that once you settle on a price, you have to buy. In any case, if an item is unique and you really want it, you're at the seller's mercy.

Don't hesitate to walk away when the seller reaches his "lowest" price. Prices drop when you start to leave. Prices will often come down to half the first figure. But there are many variations from item to item and market to market.

Hard bargaining is the mark of the intelligent buyer, but it can be at times a tedious and nerve-wracking process. Take plenty of breaks.

One of the problems in looking at textiles is to distinguish cloth woven by hand on a backstrap loom from cloth made on a foot loom. Take a close look at the material. In cloth woven on a backstrap loom, the warp strands are much more visible than the cross-woven woof strands; the woof strands form "ridges"; a number of imperfections may be detected; and the ends need not be sewn across to prevent unravelling. Garments made from cloth woven on a backstrap loom consist of small sections sewn together, since the small loom limits the dimensions of the cloth produced. Foot-loomed cloth is more uniform, is used in larger pieces, and is often sewn across the ends to prevent unraveling. Both horizontal and vertical threads are easily visible.

Always look closely at what you're buying. With blankets, examine the ends to see if cotton warping is used or if the item is pure wool. Prices will vary according to the size of the blanket, quality of wool, thickness, and how much the blanket has been combed.

Some blouses and shirts are sold used, or are sewn partly from sections of used material. Examine such garments carefully for holes. If a section of used material is suspiciously bright, it has probably been run over with dye, and will run in the first wash.

Fabrics are woven in threads of varying qualities. The finest thread is lustrina, which defines the pattern much more sharply than the thread in lower-quality material.

If the sewing and loose fit of some items of native clothing don't particularly suit you, you can have them altered by a local tailor, usually at a reasonable price, before you take them home.

To preserve the colors of most native fabrics, it's best to wash them in cold water with some salt and vinegar added. Be warned, however, that even with the best care, only the heaviest fabrics hold their shape and still look good after several washings.

Stay Healthy

A trip to Central America doesn't necessarily mean stomach cramps, mad dashes to find a toilet, and general malaise as unknown microbes attack your insides. With caution and some changes in your eating habits, you should be as healthy in

Guatemala as you are at home.

Some pointers:

Keep up on your tetanus, polio and other general vaccinations. If you're planning to be in Guatemala for more than a few weeks and to go to out-of-the-way places, you should get a typhoid booster and a gamma globulin shot. For travel in the hot lowlands, take a malaria-preventive pill, such as Aralen, which is available locally without prescription. The usual dosage is two tablets per week starting two weeks before travel to a malarious area. Insect repellent will also come in handy.

Water in Guatemala City is chemically treated. In many towns the water is untreated. Stick to coffee or bottled drinks. If you must drink tap water, make sure that it's been boiled or filtered, or else treat it with laundry bleach (two drops per liter, let stand a half-hour) or a tablet such as Halazone.

All fresh meat should be cooked thoroughly. If your hamburger is pink in the middle, send it back to the kitchen. Fruits that grow on trees are generally safe to eat. Strawberries, lettuce, cabbage and other fruits and vegetables that might have been irrigated with contaminated water should be cooked or treated in a bath of a few drops of iodine in a gallon of water. If you have any doubts about whether such items have been treated, as you might in some of the more rustic eateries, leave them on your plate.

Generally, it's not in the cities that you have to worry about food preparation, or in the really remote villages where few visitors go, but in between. Be especially cautious of eateries frequented by travelers in small towns. Local sanitation methods may not be up to handling the constant influx of new germs. When you're ill, try not to eat out and spread your germs.

If you pick up dysentery (characterized by intermittent cramps and diarrhea) or some other intestinal ailment, you'll find many medicines available without prescription. Avoid overkill and try a mild preparation, such as Kaopectate or Pepto Bismol, along with fruit juice with honey and a pinch of salt, to replace lost body fluid. Some readily available medicines for diarrhea, such as Entero-sediv and Enterovioform, contain ingredients that some doctors consider dangerous. If you've picked up worms from partially cooked fresh meat (symptoms are loss of energy and abdominal pain), try one of the milder preparations, such as Bryrel, first.

Take it easy on liquor until you are used to the altitude, and lay off it if you're sick. Liquor destroys the effectiveness of some medicines.

Stay away from fleabag hotels. Fleas are not only bothersome in themselves, but can carry disease. If you discover these or other crawlies, try Dermax, a locally available treatment for skin parasites.

None of the above should be taken as professional medical advice. If you become more than mildly ill, consult a doctor. Doctors' fees in Guatemala are usually quite reasonable. Relying on the advice of pharmacists, who may be poorly trained, is chancy.

Study Programs

A number of Spanish-language study programs are offered in Guatemala. A typical four-week course includes classroom sessions, and several hours of individual instruction daily. The emphasis is on conversation. At $450, including room and board with a Guatemalan family, these programs are a bargain. Some schools are flexible in the duration and intensity of their programs, and offer even lower rates.

Among the schools offering language instruction are: Proyecto Lingüístico Francisco Marroquín, Apartado 237, Antigua Guatemala; International School of Spanish, Apartado 265, Quezaltenango; Tecún Umán Linguistic School, 6 Calle Poniente No. 34, Antigua Guatemala; and Centro Internacional de Español, 4 Avenida Norte esquina 2 Calle Oriente, Antigua Guatemala.

Write to the schools for information. Because there are so many language schools, especially in Antigua, there's no need to send a deposit or reserve a place unless your schedule is tight.

Taxes

Most goods and services in Guatemala are subject to a 7 percent value-added tax ("I.V.A."). Goods bought in markets are exempt. Hotel rates are subject to an additional tax of 10 percent, bringing the total to 17 percent. At the airport, the exit tax is about $10. There are small taxes and fees when you cross into Guatemala at land borders.

Telegrams

International telegrams are handled by Guatel, the telephone and communications company. Telegrams to the United States cost 45 cents per word or more, depending on the destination city,

347

with a seven-word minimum. Rates are higher to most other countries. Address and signature are included in the word count. Where there is no Guatel office, the post office or the adjacent Telégrafos office will accept international telegrams, at higher rates.

Telegrams within Guatemala are handled by the post office or the adjacent Telégrafos office. The rate is just a few centavos per word, double for foreign-language messages and on Sundays and holidays. Use telegrams to reserve hotel rooms and otherwise communicate when your spoken Spanish may not be understood on the phone.

Telephones

Telephone calls can be made to any place in the world from Guatel (telephone company) offices, from hotels, and from pay phones. In some small towns, long-distance calls are handled by the telegraph office. Guatel hours are generally from 7 a.m. to 10 p.m., with some local variation. Personnel rely on wristwatches to time calls, not always accurately. A three-minute call to the United States costs $6 or more, depending on the region called. To Canada, the minimum is about $8. Calls to outside the hemisphere cost $18 or more. Collect calls can be placed to the United States, Canada, Spain, Italy, Japan and Sweden.

To reach a telephone outside the capital, dial 0 plus the six digits of the local number (061 plus four digits for Quezaltenango). To reach Guatemala City from elsewhere in the country, dial 02 plus the number. It's generally easier to call from a pay phone than through a hotel or Guatel operator. Just place a couple of 25-centavo coins on the rack before you dial. It's quite inexpensive to phone ahead, so take advantage of the phones to make your hotel reservations.

To reach a number in Guatemala from abroad, follow directions in your phone book.

Coin telephones are available, to a greater or lesser extent, in Guatemala City and some large towns. You'll generally find them outside the Guatel office, next to the city hall (municipalidad), on the main square, and, sometimes, in hotel lobbies.

Time

Guatemala is on Central Standard Time, equivalent to Greenwich Mean Time less six hours.

348

Tipping

In restaurants, a ten-percent tip is appropriate. Tipping is optional in small, family-run restaurants. In hotels, give the porter a quetzal if you need his help to carry your bags. If you stay a few days, you may want to leave a couple of quetzales for the maid or some other member of the staff. Guides extract generous commissions from stores and even from market vendors, so there's no need to tip them except for special favors. Don't tip a taxi driver once you have negotiated a fare. When in doubt about whether or how much to tip, remember that a tip is a reward for good service. Poor service means no tip.

Toilets

In many toilets in Guatemala, you'll notice a basket. It's for used toilet paper, in cases where the water pressure won't handle the job. In your travels, you might want to carry a roll of toilet paper, since that amenity is sometimes lacking in the toilets of lesser hotels and restaurants.

Weights and Measures

Weights and measures in Guatemala are a hodgepodge of the metric system, the English system, and old Spanish measures.

Highway distances are measured in kilometers. Eight kilometers are equivalent to five miles. To convert kilometers to miles, multiply by 5/8, or .62. Distance along the railroad are measured in miles. And Indians will often speak of a certain town as being so-and-so many leguas distant. A legua is about four miles, or 6.7 kilometers, and informally refers to the distance a person will walk in an hour.

Meters and yards are both in use for measuring shorter distances, though yards, feet and inches are more common. A meter is equivalent to 39.37 inches, or a yard plus another ten percent. Native fabrics are often sold by the vara, a Spanish measure equal to .836 meters or about 33 inches. A standard corte, or length of skirt material, which you'll often find in the market, is usually six varas long.

Land measurement follows Spanish usage. The smallest unit is the square vara, or vara cuadrada. A cuerda is usually a square of land 32 varas on a side (equivalent to 716 square meters or 7701 square feet), though it may also be 40 varas on a side. A manzana is equivalent to about seven-tenths of a hectare, or 1.727 acres, and a caballería is equivalent to about 45 hectares, or 111.5 acres.

Weight is usually measured in pounds and ounces. 25 pounds make an arroba and 100 pounds a quintal (abbreviated qq.). At the post office, however, grams and kilograms are used. It takes about 29 grams to make an ounce and 454 grams to make a pound. A kilo is 2.2 pounds.

Gasoline is sold by the U.S. gallon, equivalent to 3.8 liters. For other liquid measures, liters are usually used. Many products, including liquor, are sold by the botella, equivalent to three-quarters of a liter, or 25.4 ounces.

Is all this clear?

What to Take and Wear

When packing for your visit to Guatemala, remember that the climate is mild. For Guatemala City and the highlands, take what you would wear during the spring at home. A light sweater or jacket may be required during the evening. In the dry season, especially from December to March, make it a heavy sweater. Since you'll be spending time outdoors, and highland temperatures vary from cool in the morning to hot at midday, it's wise to dress in layers, perhaps a sweater over a shirt and tee shirt. A shoulder bag is handy for carrying the layers you take off, as well as for hauling camera equipment. Comfortable walking shoes are a must.

In the rainy season, you'll want to take along a raincoat or folding umbrella, though you may also need these at other times of year in the north of the country or the Caribbean.

For visiting archaeological sites, beaches, and the lowlands, you'll want light-colored, lightweight, all-cotton clothing. Sunglasses, and a hat to keep the sun off, are essential. Take at least one long-sleeved top in case you overexpose yourself to sun. Cheap straw hats may be purchased in any market, but the fit is often tight on gringos. Take shoes with non-slip soles. Don't forget your bathing suit for the lakes and beaches, and a sunscreen lotion.

In general, informal clothing is suitable. If you're used to dining in a jacket and tie, or in a snazzy dress, then by all means take those items. But even in the best hotels you may dine in slacks and a sports shirt or blouse. Jeans and sandals are fine for the countryside and smaller towns, but look out of place in the cities. Shorts are not worn in Guatemala City and the highlands. Very low cut blouses and patched clothing are considered outrageous in certain quarters. A neat appearance is preferable. (I hate to lecture about this kind of thing, but the locals do have their attitudes.)

Bring a moderate amount of reading material. Books in English are readily available in Guatemala City at reasonable prices. Film is expensive, so bring more than you think you'll need. Bring your own cigars or pipe tobacco. Pick up a few bottles of duty-free liquor on the way down, if you have a favorite brand. For nights in the lowlands in cheap hotels, and for camping out, take insect repellent. Take sufficient deodorant, shave cream, etc. These are high-priced, especially in aerosol form, as are Tampax, and local versions of American-brand perfumes. Toothpaste is cheap, if you run out. Sportsmen will want to take all the equipment they anticipate needing for fishing or camping. You just can't get it locally. Take your own medicines, and spare glasses or a copy of your prescription. Sunglasses are helpful.

In general, remember that although the cost of living in Guatemala is low, just about anything smacking of mechanics or technology is likely to be more expensive. So if your tape recorder or radio or some other gadget is indispensable to you, take it along.

More Information

For maps and brochures, write to the Guatemala Tourist Commission, P.O. Box 144351, Coral Gables, FL 33114-4351. From outside the United States and Canada, write to the Guatemala Tourist Commission, 7 Avenida 1-17, Zona 4, Ciudad de Guatemala, Guatemala, Central America.

Use the toll-free numbers given in this book to get as much information as you can on current hotel rates, automobile rentals, etc., and write to the addresses I've mentioned for language schools, bird lists and the like.

One large Guatemalan travel agency, Clark Tours, has a representative at 114 East 32 St. no. 1104, New York, NY 10016, tel. 212-477-5081. They'll deal with you or your travel agent. (If you're reading this in Europe, try Marion Stephan Representations, Hans Messnerstr 18b, 6384 Schmitten 3, West Germany, tel. 06082-17-16.)

This Week in Central America, a respected newsletter that covers events in all the Central American countries, is published in Guatemala City and is available by subscription. Write to Apartado 1156, Guatemala City.

FUNDESA, a Guatemalan businessmen's organization, publishes Guatemala Watch, a monthly newsletter, and Viva Guatemala, a semiannual magazine. The first covers events in Guatemala, the second includes feature stories of interest to prospective visitors and to businessmen. For sample copies, write to FUNDESA, Apartado 865-A, Guatemala City.

If all else fails, write to me in care of Passport Press, and I'll see if I can find information for you in my files.

Calendars

Browse through this section to check up on market days, town fiestas and national holidays for the days when you'll be in Guatemala.

MARKET DAYS

Whenever possible, visit an Indian town on a market day, when people come in from outlying districts to meet and deal with their neighbors as well as with itinerant merchants. On other days, the town center is likely to be nearly deserted, as the vast majority of men tend to the fields while women do household chores.

Market days are listed here for towns mentioned in this book. Indian towns may have more than one market day during the week, or hold a market every day. If one of the days is especially busy, that fact is noted in parentheses in the "every day" category. Some Indian towns, and most Ladino and lowland towns, have no special market day.

Every Day
Antigua Guatemala (especially Monday, Thursday and Saturday)
Chimaltenango (especially Monday and Thursday)
Cobán
Guatemala City
Huehuetenango (especially Thursday and Sunday)
Quezaltenango
San Juan Sacatepéquez (especially Friday and Sunday)
San Pedro Carchá
Santa Cruz del Quiché (especially Thursday and Sunday)
Santiago Atitlán (especially Friday)

Sunday

Aguacatán	Huehuetenango	Ostuncalco
Cantel	Joyabaj	Panajachel
Chiantla	Momostenango	Parramos
Chichicastenango	Nebaj	Patzún
Cuilco	Nahualá	Rabinal

353

Sunday (contd.)
Sacapulas
San Cristóbal Totonicapán
San Cristóbal Verapaz
San Juan Sacatepéquez
San Lucas Tolimán
San Mateo Ixtatán
San Pedro Sac., San Marcos
San Raimundo
Santa Eulalia
Santa Cruz del Quiché
Santa Lucía Utatlán
Santiago Atitlán
Tactic
Tecpán Guatemala
Tacaná
Uspantán
Zacualpa
Zunil

Monday
Antigua Guatemala
Chimaltenango

Tuesday
Comalapa
Olintepeque
Patzún
San Andrés Semetabaj
San Lucas Tolimán
San Marcos
Santa Clara La Laguna
Sololá
Sumpango
Totonicapán
Tucurú

Wednesday
Almolonga
Momostenango
Palín
Patzicía

Thursday
Aguacatán
Antigua Guatemala
Chichicastenango
Chimaltenango
Huehuetenango
Nebaj
Ostuncalco
Patzún
Sacapulas
San Cristóbal Verapaz
San Mateo Ixtatán
San Pedro Sac., San Marcos
Santa Cruz del Quiché
Tactic
Tecpán Guatemala
Uspantán
Zacualpa

Friday
Comalapa
Palín
San Francisco El Alto
San Juan Sacatepéquez
San Lucas Tolimán
San Marcos
San Martín Sacatepéquez
San Pedro Sacatepéquez
Santiago Atitlán
Sololá

Saturday
Almolonga
Antigua Guatemala
Patzicía
Santa Clara La Laguna
Santiago Sacatepéquez
Sumpango
Todos Santos Cuchumatán
Totonicapán
Tucurú

FIESTAS

Fiestas are the times of year when a whole town celebrates, usually in honor of its patron saint. In Indian towns, the cofradías carry their statues of saints in noisy processions, accompanied by the melody of the chirimía—a flute with the sweet sound of the oboe—and the beat of the tun—a drum made from a hollowed-out log, cut so as to sound two notes. Every few yards, the procession comes to a halt, and rocket bombs are fired as a symbolic form of communication with the gods. Enormous sums of money—by local standards—are spent for the liquor, fireworks, food and costumes that are all part of the cofradía ritual. Traditional fiesta dances are performed, though they often deteriorate into drunken endurance contests. Itinerant photographers and food vendors may set up shop on the square, and along with the mechanical soccer games and games of chance, they give a town a carnival atmosphere for up to a couple of weeks before the main fiesta day.

In the less traditional Indian towns, and in Ladino towns, fiestas may include beauty contests, sporting events and social dances. The common denominator everywhere is liquor, plenty of liquor. Fiestas are times to let loose and forget about the everyday worries of work and survival.

Not everything about a fiesta is a delight. The fun of clumsy Indian ritual dancing and mass drunkenness is sometimes lost on outsiders. Fireworks are often set off with no safety precautions, and accidents can and do result. The amplified blaring of marimba orchestras for hours or even days on end may send you screaming and fleeing from town in search of peace and quiet. Buses going to a place where a fiesta is being celebrated are likely to be jam-packed, and hotel space may be unavailable. Guatemalans are used to such goings-on and inconveniences, but the foreign visitor, with different sensibilities, may react negatively. If you do plan to visit a town at fiesta time, make sure that you have hotel reservations, especially if you're traveling by bus.

In the listings below, I've given the fiesta dates only for places of possible interest to visitors, namely towns in the western highlands, near Guatemala City, in Alta Verapaz and in the Petén; and a few of the larger towns in the lowland areas. Of these, the most interesting fiestas are in large Indian towns, such as Chichicastenango, Santiago Atitlán and Todos Santos Cuchumatán.

Only the main day of the fiesta is given. In the larger towns, the festivities may start a week before the principal day. In smaller towns, fiestas are one-day affairs. A number of places have no special attractions and are not mentioned elsewhere in this book, but can be interesting at fiesta times. To help you find towns on maps, the departments in which they are located are indicated. Religious holidays which are celebrated generally are also listed. In the larger Indian towns, there are a number of lesser fiesta days in addition to the one mentioned.

January 2: Santa María de Jesús, Sacatepéquez. 6: Epiphany (Day of the Three Kings)*: San Gaspar Ixchil, Huehuetenango. 15*: Chinique, El Quiché; Flores, El Petén; La Libertad, Huehuetenango; Santa Catarina Barahona, Sacatepéquez; Santa María Chiquimula, Totonicapán; Sibilia, Quezaltenango. 17: San Antonio Ilotenango, El Quiché; San Antonio Sacatepéquez, San Marcos. 18: San Sebastián Huehuetenango. 20: El Tejar, Chimaltenango; San Antonio Aguas Calientes, Sacatepéquez; San Sebastián Coatán, Huehuetenango. 21: San Raimundo, Guatemala; Santa Lucía La Reforma, Totonicapán; 22: San Vicente Pacaya, Escuintla. 23: Rabinal, Baja Verapaz. 25: Patulul, Suchitepéquez; San Pablo La Laguna, Sololá; Tamahú, Alta Verapaz. Moveable: Last Sunday: Mixco, Guatemala.

*Epiphany (January 6) is celebrated throughout Guatemala. January 15: Principal pilgrimage to Esquipulas.

February 2: Chiantla, Huehuetenango; Cunén, El Quiché; Flores Costa Cuca, Quezaltenango; Ostuncalco, Quezaltenango. 8: Patzité, El Quiché. 9: Santa Apolonia, Chimaltenango. 12: Santa Eulalia, Huehuetenango.

Moveable: First Friday of Lent: Antigua Guatemala; Palestina de los Altos, Quezaltenango; San Pedro Ayampuc, Guatemala. Carnival (Mardi Gras): Mazatenango, Suchitepéquez.

March 10: Villa Canales, Guatemala. 15: Coatepeque, Quezaltenango. 19: San José, El Petén; San José Ojetenán, San Marcos; San José Poaquil, Chimaltenango.

Moveable: Second Friday of Lent: Chajul, El Quiché; La Democracia, Huehuetenango. Fourth Friday of Lent: Cabricán,

Quezaltenango. Fifth Friday of Lent: San Pedro Necta, Huehuetenango. Palm Sunday: Jocotán, Chiquimula. Easter Tuesday: San José Chacayá, Sololá

Holy Week (Easter Week) is celebrated throughout Guatemala. Processions are especially vivid in Antigua Guatemala.

April 24: San Jorge La Laguna, Sololá. 25: San Marcos, San Marcos; San Marcos La Laguna, Sololá.

Moveable: 40 days after Holy Week: Aguacatán, Huehuetenango; Zacualpa, El Quiché.

May 1: Poptún, El Petén. 3: Amatitlán, Guatemala; Barillas, Huehuetenango; Cajolá, Quezaltenango; La Esperanza, Quezaltenango; San Benito, El Petén; Santa Cruz Balanyá, Chimaltenango; Santa Cruz Verapaz, Alta Verapaz. 8: Tucurú, Alta Verapaz; Uspantán, El Quiché. 10: Santa Cruz La Laguna, Sololá. 14: Melchor de Mencos, El Petén. 15: Livingston, Izabal. 20:Patzún, Chimaltenango. 28: Dolores, El Petén.

June 11: Acatenango, Chimaltenango. 13: Purulhá, Baja Verapaz; San Antonio Huista, Huehuetenango; San Antonio Aguas Calientes, Sacatepéquez; San Antonio Palopó, Sololá; Sayaxché, El Petén; Senahú, Alta Verapaz. 24: Comalapa, Chimaltenango; Olintepeque, Quezaltenango; Alotenango, Sacatepéquez; San Juan Atitán, Huehuetenango; San Juan Chamelco, Alta Verapaz; San Juan Cotzal, El Quiché; San Juan Ixcoy, Huehuetenango; San Juan La Laguna, Sololá; San Juan Sacatepéquez, Guatemala. 29: Almolonga, Quezaltenango; Chisec, Alta Verapaz; Chuarrancho, Guatemala; San Pedro Carchá, Alta Verapaz; San Pedro Jocopilas, El Quiché; San Pedro La Laguna, Sololá; San Pedro Sacatepéquez, Guatemala; San Pedro Sacatepéquez, San Marcos; Soloma, Huehuetenango; Yepocapa, Chimaltenango.

Moveable: Corpus Christi*: Patzún, Chimaltenango. First Thursday to First Sunday: Quiriguá, Izabal.

*Corpus Christi is celebrated throughout Guatemala. Processions are especially vivid in Patzún.

July 2: Santa María Visitacíon, Sololá. 3: Tajumulco, San Marcos. 12-18: Huehuetenango (dates may vary). 19: Puerto Barrios, Izabal. 21: Tectitán, Huehuetenango. 22: Magdalena Milpas Altas, Sacatepéquez. 25: Antigua Guatemala, Sacatepéquez; Cubulco, Baja Verapaz; Esquipulas, Chiquimula; Momostenango, Totonicapán; Patzicía, Chimaltenango; Jocotán, Chiquimula; San Cristóbal Cucho, San Marcos; San Cristóbal Totonicapán, Totonicapán; San Cristóbal Verapaz, Alta Verapaz; Santiago Atitlán, Sololá; Santiago Chimaltenango, Huehuetenango; Santiago Sacatepéquez, Sacatepéquez; Tejutla, San Marcos. 26: Chimaltenango, Chimaltenango; Malacatancito, Huehuetenango; Santa Ana Huista, Huehuetenango. 30: Ixchiguán, San Marcos; Palín, Escuintla;

Moveable: Holy Trinity: Río Blanco, San Marcos.

August 4: Cobán, Alta Verapaz; Mixco, Guatemala; Sacapulas, El Quiché; Santo Domingo Xenacoj, Sacatepéquez. 10: San Lorenzo, San Marcos. 12: Santa Clara La Laguna, Sololá. 15: Cantel, Quezaltenango; Colotenango, Huehuetenango; Chiquimula, Chiquimula; Guatemala City; Joyabaj, El Quiché; Jocotenango, Sacatepéquez; Nebaj, El Quiché; Sololá, Sololá; Tacaná, San Marcos; Tactic, Alta Verapaz. 18: Santa Cruz del Quiché, El Quiché. 24: San Bartolo, Totonicapán; San Bartolomé Jocotenango, El Quiché; San Bartolomé Milpas Altas, Sacatepéquez; Sipacapa, San Marcos. 25: San Luis, El Petén; Salcajá, Quezaltenango. 26: Lanquín, Alta Verapaz. 28: Chahal, Alta Verapaz; Sumpango, Sacatepéquez. 29: Sibinal, San Marcos. 30: Panzós, Alta Verapaz.

September 6: Cahabón, Alta Verapaz. 15: Quezaltenango, Quezaltenango. 20: Salamá, Baja Verapaz. 21: San Mateo, Quezaltenango; San Mateo Ixtatán, Huehuetenango. 29: Pochuta, Chimaltenango; San Miguel Acatán, Huehuetenango; San Miguel Chicaj, Baja Verapaz; San Miguel Dueñas, Sacatepéquez; San Miguel Ixtahuacán, San Marcos; San Miguel Siguilá, Quezaltenango; Totonicapán, Totonicapán. 30: San Jerónimo, Baja Verapaz.

October 4: Panajachel, Sololá; San Francisco, El Petén; San Francisco El Alto, Totonicapán; Tecpán Guatemala, Chimaltenango. 9: Pastores, Sacatepéquez. 12: Zaragoza, Chimaltenango. 18: San Lucas Tolimán, Solola; San Lucas

Sacatepéquez, Sacatepéquez. 24: San Rafael La Independencia, Huehuetenango; San Rafael Petzal, Huehuetenango.

November 1 (All Saints' Day)*: Todos Santos Cuchumatán, Huehuetenango. 11: San Martín Jilotepeque, Chimaltenango; San Martín Sacatepéquez, Quezaltenango. 18: Malacatancito, Huehuetenango. 22: Estanzuela, Zacapa. 25: Nahualá, Sololá; Santa Catarina Ixtahuacán, Sololá; Santa Catarina Palopó, Sololá; Zunil, Quezaltenango. 28: Cuilco, Huehuetenango; San Andrés Sajcabajá, El Quiché; 30: San Andrés, El Petén; San Andrés Itzapa, Chimaltenango; San Andrés Semetabaj, Sololá; San Andrés Xecul, Totonicapan.

*All Saints' Day is marked by festivities in the cemeteries of all Guatemalan towns, and by the flying of huge kites in Santiago Sacatepéquez.

December 4: Santa Bárbara, Huehuetenango; Chinautla, Guatemala. 7: Burning of the Devil.* 8: Camotán, Chiquimula; Ciudad Vieja, Sacatepéquez; Concepción, Huehuetenango; Concepción, Sololá; Concepción Chiquirichapa, Quezaltenango; Escuintla, Escuintla; Retalhuleu, Retalhuleu; Zacapa, Zacapa. 12: La Libertad, El Petén. 13: Santa Lucía Milpas Altas, Sacatepéquez; Santa Lucía Utatlán, Sololá. 15: San Carlos Sija, Quezaltenango. 19: Chicacao, Suchitepéquez. 21: Chichicastenango, El Quiché. 24: Huitán, Quezaltenango. 25 (Christmas*): Santa Lucía Cotzumalguapa, Escuintla. 28: Chiché, El Quiché; Lívingston, Izabal; Parramos, Chimaltenango. 31: La Democracia, Escuintla.

From Advent until December 7, men dressed as devils chase children through the streets of highland towns. The custom is celebrated with particular zest in San Cristóbal Totonicapán. The Burning of the Devil (La Quema del Diablo), December 7, is celebrated with the burning of trash in the streets of Guatemala City and highland towns. Christmas is preceded by nine days of posadas, house visits which re-enact the search of Joseph and Mary for shelter.

NATIONAL HOLIDAYS

Businesses are closed on the days indicated below, as well as on local fiesta days.

Holidays falling on weekends are celebrated on either Friday or Monday.

January 1	New Year's Day
	Holy Thursday
	Good Friday
May 1	Labor Day
June 30	Army Day, and Anniversary of 1871 Revolution
August 15	Guatemala City fiesta. Businesses closed in Guatemala City only.
August 29	Postal Workers Day. Post offices closed.
September 15	Independence Day
October 20	Anniversary of 1944 revolution
November 1	All Saints' Day
December 24	Christmas Eve (afternoon only)
December 25	Christmas
December 31	New Year's Eve (afternoon only)

Guatemalan Spanish

For a general overview of Spanish, consult any good dictionary or phrase book. Here's a brief rundown of the language as used in Guatemala, along with a few points to keep in mind about Spanish in general.

The Spanish spoken in most parts of Guatemala uses old forms, terms of politeness and honor, and Indian words. It's spoken relatively slowly, and is considered by people from other Spanish-speaking countries to be quaint and archaic.

The word **don** is usually added before a man's name, and **doña** before a woman's. It's Señor Humberto Urruaquín, but Don Humberto. **Don** means "sir," more or less, and was originally a Spanish noble title, but is now used generally as a term of respect.

A pronoun used in Guatemala and a few other parts of Latin America is the familiar **vos. Vos** takes the place of **tú** ("you"), and corresponds somewhat to the "you all" used in the southern United States in tone, though it is singular. The conjugation is as follows: **vos sabés** instead of **tú sabes, tenés** instead of **tienes** (the accent is shifted to the last syllable, and the regular verb stem is used, even with irregular verbs).

Many words of Indian origin contain an **x**, which is pronounced **sh**. The **j** in Guatemala is quite breathy, and is pronounced even at the end of a word. Pronunciation of other letters follows standard Latin American usage.

Indians sometimes use their own very logical forms, ignoring the exceptions to the rules of Spanish grammar. An Indian might say that a building is **verdo** instead of **verde**, or **yo sabo** instead of **yo sé** (I know). Be careful whose Spanish you imitate.

Remember that most people have two last names, the first of which is used when talking to or about them. Humberto Urruaquín Ixcán is Señor Urruaquín. However, María Majún de Urruaquín is the wife of Señor Urruaquín, and is referred to as Señora de Urruaquín (Mrs. Urruaquín).

In general, to be best understood when speaking Spanish, or when using an occasional Spanish word, pronounce each syllable slowly and clearly. There is no slurring as in English. The name of the country is "Guah-teh-mal-lah," not "Guaduhmaluh." Follow written accents for emphasis. When no accent is written, the emphasis is on the last syllable; or on the next-to-last syllable if the ending is a vowel, n or s.

Here's an odd assortment of non-standard words used in Guatemala, standard Spanish words as they are used locally, and English words which have passed into the local language, or which are used in strange ways.

aguas	bottled soft drinks
banano	banana; only a plantain (for cooking) is a **plátano**
bistec	a cut of beef, often nondescript
caites	native-style sandals
camioneta	intercity bus
canasta	basket
canche	light-skinned, fair-haired person
capixay(o)	woolen tunic used by some Indian men
carterita	book of matches
cash	cash
chapín	Guatemalan; **guatemalteco**
chucho	dog; also, a snack food of corn dough stuffed with meat, and wrapped in a corn husk; also **chuchito**
chulo	cute; **chula:** cutie (as a cute girl)
chupar	to drink liquor
colocho	curly
comedor	a simple diner, as opposed to a more formal **restaurante**
corte	a length of skirt material
en ocho días	in eight days; in a week
fijarse (en)	take note (of); get this
finca	farm or plantation
goodbye	hello; **goodbye my love:** hi there, sweetie
gringo	any foreigner, but especially a North American or Northern European; the word is not necessarily pejorative
guaro	liquor
horita	right now; in a little while; a little while ago;
huipil	an Indian woman's blouse (from the Nahuatl word for a covering); also spelled **guipil**
indígena	Indian; used in preference to **indio;** also **natural**
invierno	the rainy season, "winter"

jaspe	cloth woven from strands of tie-dyed thread
len	**centavo,** or cent
milpa	corn field
monte	brush; uncultivated area or forest
morral	shoulder bag; also **bolsa**
mosh	oatmeal
panela	a loaf of brown sugar
parque	any park, but usually the **parque central,** the main square
patojo	boy, child; **patoja:** girl
perraje	shawl
petate	a woven mat, often made from reeds
pila	outdoor sink
pisto	money
poncho	blanket
psst	a sound used for getting your attention, often accompanied by a limp-wristed motion indicating "come here"
pues	a word often tagged onto short expressions, as in "sí pues"; sometimes used for emphasis
pullman	first-class bus
¿qué horas tiene?	
	what time do you have? (I've always suspected that people ask the time to see if you understand Spanish.)
rancho	a simple house
refajo	skirt
regalar	make a gift of; used as a polite form of "give me," as in "regáleme un fósforo" ("give me a match")
regatear	to bargain, to haggle; also, **hacer trato**
seño	short form of **señora** or **señorita**
shilet	razor blade (from Gillette)
tícket	bus ticket
típico	native style, as **comida típica,** native food
traje	the distinctive costume of an Indian town
typical	see **típico;** a **typical store** is not a run-of-the-mill store, but a store that sells handicrafts
tzut	an Indian man or woman's head covering or all-purpose cloth
va	a muttered syllable used to express agreement
verano	the dry season, "summer"

Index

365

366

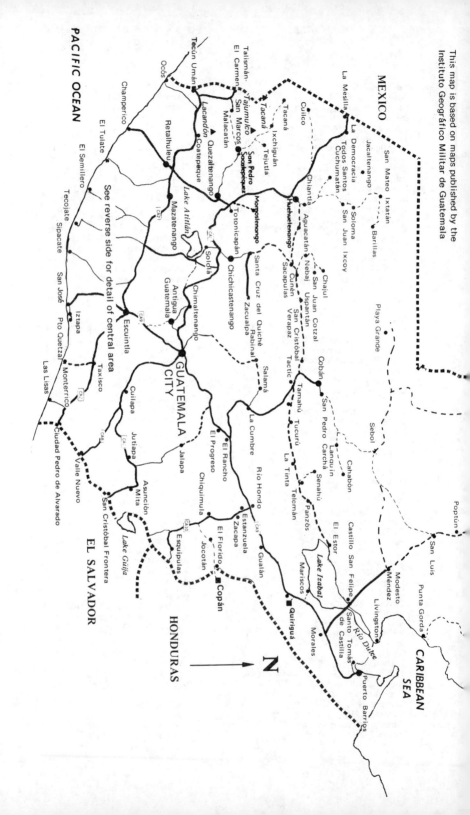

GUATEMALA
Towns and Highways

Legend:

- Cities and Towns
- ▲ Volcanoes
- ■ Archaeological Sites
- [G10] Highway Numbers

Major	Secondary
———	-----
Paved Highways	Unpaved Roads

0   25   50   50 Miles
0   50   100 Kms

MEXICO

Piedras Negras
Yaxchilán
Altar de los Sacrificios
La Libertad
Sayaxché
Carmelita
San Benito
El Ceibal
Flores
El Cruce
Lake Petén Itzá
Lake Petexbatún
El Mirador
Tikal
Uaxactún
Nakum
Yaxjá
Dolores
Melchor de Mencos
Belmopan
Corozal
Orange Walk
Belize
Stann Creek

Passport Press publishes comprehensive guides to Guatemala, Costa Rica and Belize, and other travel-related books. For a current book list, write to Passport Press, Box 1346 Champlain, NY 12919.

Passport Press guides are also available at these travel bookstores:

Easy Going, 1400 Shattuck Ave., Berkeley, CA 94709
Quo Vadis, 427 Grand Ave., Carlsbad, CA 92008
Map and Globe Store, 1120 E. Colonial Drive, Orlando, FL 32803
Pacific Travellers Supply, 529 State, Santa Barbara, CA 93101
Word Journeys, 971-C Lomas Santa Fe, Solana Beach, CA 92075
Lloyd Books, 3145 Dumbarton Ave NW, Washington, D.C. 20007
The Savvy Traveller, 50 E. Washington, Chicago, IL 60602
Globe Corner Bookstore, 3 School St., Boston, MA 02108
Traveller's Bookstore, 22 West 52 St., New York, NY 10019
Powell's Travel Store, 701 SW 6th Ave., Portland, OR 97204
Wide World Books and Maps, 401 NE 45 St., Seattle, WA 98105
Ulysses Bookstore, 1208 St-Denis, Montreal, Quebec H2X 3J5
Librairie Artou, 8 rue de Rive, 1204 Geneva, Switzerland
Journey Latin America, 16 Devonshire Rd, London W4 2HD U.K.